# Celebrity Writing in America

## A Thematic Reader for Composition

## William Vesterman

Rutgers University

D1341181

Longman

New York   San Francisco   Boston
London  Toronto  Sydney  Tokyo  Singapore  Madrid
Mexico City  Munich  Paris  Cape Town  Hong Kong  Montreal

Acquisitions Editor: Brandon Hight
Development Editor: Anne Brunell Ehrenworth
Senior Supplements Editor: Donna Campion
Media Supplements Editor: Jenna Egan
Senior Marketing Manager: Alexandra Rivas-Smith
Managing Editor: Bob Ginsberg
Project Coordination, Text Design, and Electronic Page Makeup:
    Electronic Publishing Services Inc., NYC
Cover Design Manager and Designer: John Callahan
Cover Image: Courtesy of Getty Images, Inc.
Visual Researcher: Rona Tuccillo
Manufacturing Manager: Mary Fischer
Printer and Binder: RR Donnelley & Sons Company
Cover Printer: Phoenix Color Corporation

**Library of Congress Cataloging-in-Publication Data**
Vesterman, William, [date]-
  Celebrity writing in America : a thematic reader for composition /
William Vesterman.
      p. cm.
  Includes bibliographical references and index.
  ISBN 0-321-32890-6
  1.  College readers. 2.  English language—Rhetoric—Problems, exer-
cises, etc. 3.  Celebrities—United States—Problems, exercises, etc.
  4.  Report writing—Problems, exercises, etc.  I. Title.
  PE1417.V465 2005
  808'.0427—dc22

                                        2005030752

Visit our website at www.ablongman.com

ISBN 0-321-32890-6

12345678910—DOH—08070605

# ANNOTATED CONTENTS

## PART I    Constructing and Representing a Private Self     1

## 1    Origins and Turning Points     3

## 2  Becoming and Overcoming          43

# 5 Self-Presentation                                                           171

# Rhetorical Contents

The following categorizations are intended to make the organization of a course more convenient. The list in any category does not include all the essays that employ a given rhetorical mode at some point, nor are any of the essays in a given category limited to the exercise of its defining mode.

## Classification

## Analogy and Metaphor

## Comparison and Contrast

## *Humor*

# PREFACE

In Gerald Graff's latest book, *Clueless in Academe: How School-ing Obscures the Life of the Mind* (Yale University Press, 2003), this long-time observer and critic of English studies takes on Composition. His basic explanation for the chronic discontent within introductory writing courses is a familiar one—students and teachers do not connect. But in a review of Graff's book for *Academe* (Jan.–Feb., 2004), Shirley Brice Heath, Professor Emerita at Brown, points out that, while Graff pleads for course content to move closer to student interests in general and popular culture in particular, many of his suggested remedies for the supposed genera-tion gap in the classroom assume that students watch CNN, read about world affairs, and think about what they learn in school in relation to contemporary issues. Heath comments:

> Sadly, many college instructors find little evidence of such seri-ous engagement. Were intellectual curiosity and civic engage-ment the norm, students would be far more likely to come to classrooms prepared to argue, muster evidence, and take up a search for information to build knowledge.

Unsurprisingly, many beginning students are not so prepared (though, according to many experienced teachers, one of the most noble functions within the multitasking of Composition is precisely so to prepare them.) On the other hand, it is equally evident that almost all students are already "engaged" with America's democ-ratic mass culture and its cult of celebrity, if not in "serious," surely in enthusiastic, well informed, and often very articulate ways that obviously give them great pleasure to express outside of class, where they sometimes do their unassigned reading in preference to that assigned—believe it or not.

One publication may fairly represent that reading. Some thirty years ago *People* magazine launched from a single page in *Time* to become one of the most rapidly successful magazines in history, with 3.6 million copies of each issue circulated today. Even after the explosion of celebrity media in the past decade, providing many rivals in many forms, *People* magazine continues its national and multigenerational popularity. The overwhelming majority of names that appear in its pages can be recognized not only by most undergraduate students of Composition in contemporary America, but by their mostly young instructors as well. Few if any head notes are needed by either group for the people in *People*—a claim to name recognition in a table of contents that surely no current textbook can make.

The claim I can and do make here is that the cultural failures Graff and Heath point to and the cultural successes that *People* magazine represents may both combine to suggest not so much a problem as an educational opportunity. In any event, I propose to test this hypothesis by means of the book in your hands.

I imagine (perhaps wrongly) the most immediate objections to this book would be that the project trivializes not only authorship but the discipline of writing, the topics of writing appropriate to higher education, and the modes of writing traditionally taught. In Daniel Boorstin's phrase, celebrities are merely those "well known for being well known." That may be true about some celebrity authors, though not of those included here. But it is also true that all the stars of American mass culture are like students, citizens in a democracy with the right to their own opinions on any issue of concern to the rest of us. Given current political and cultural demographics, the opinions of many stars may be mocked from the Right of the student body politic for their lack of expertise ("What do the Dixie Chicks know about foreign policy?") but only in the same way Ronald Reagan's political views were mocked from the Left as those of a mere actor, and just as Charleton Heston's views on gun control still are. But what's new about controversial essays or essays that leave you feeling as if you understand its subject better than the author does? Since when has student expertise been required to write about important issues? It is also true that the methods of reasoning and techniques of expression in a few (*very* few) of the essays of this book might be judged inferior in skills to those of a first-year student. But so much the better for the morale of that student! May not he or she thereby gain confidence by demonstrating, in an important area, a personal competence superior to that found in some of the rich and famous? On the other hand—and despite their exalted status—the stars of American mass culture may be seen here to write on the same private and public subjects and in the same rhetorical forms of discourse as those exemplified by more respectable authors in countless anthologies intended for English Composition.

The head notes of those anthologies—representing eager efforts to mark social diversity in authors who are for the most part unknown to their student reader—are surely less necessary in this book. For one thing, my readers will probably assume a much more complete sense of where a given author is coming from personally and socially than any head note could provide. For another, fame is an equal opportunity employer—diversity of race, class, gender, and sexual orientation naturally comes with the territory. It may be evident that from the perspective of personal experience—the issues that begin the book—celebrities and students begin automatically on an equal basis of expertise. Tom Cruise's essay on his dyslexia is touching, clearly written, and informative. Whoopi Goldberg's recollections of Christmas in New York City are supported by a prose style as tender as the styles of Spike Lee and Donald Trump are tough when they deal with business matters. Further, the models of exposition and argumentation offered here are in line with those of other writing anthologies. If some of the celebrity authors have been aided and supported by ghost writers to varying degrees, surely the help they receive is analogous to that provided to students throughout the writing process by teachers and by peer review.

All the other elements of the book's design are intended to ask a serious question about methods of higher education in a democratic society pervaded by mass culture: whether the goals of composition courses might be supported and advanced with the help of readings students like to read by figures they feel they know something about. The hope is that using such readings—ones that make cultural curiosities and engagements preliminarily prior to intellectual and civic ones—students would be far more likely to come to classrooms prepared to argue, muster evidence, and take up a search for information to build knowledge. In sum, given that we all live within a mass culture, why pretend it doesn't exist on campus? Why avoid the celebrities that students talk about outside class, as if those figures could only be the embarrassing poor relatives of more respectable authors? Why not see what celebrities have to say and what students have to say about them?

The organization of the book is flexible enough to accommodate the organization and theoretical bases of most writing courses. The subjects of the 63 mostly brief essays and 5 visual arguments move in general from the personal to the public, while the modes of writing move in general from the expositional to the argumentative. The section on business addresses a topic generally neglected (except in some cross-curricular anthologies), but of interest to many undergraduates, whether or not they are business majors. The book provides the critical apparatus for individual essays and for chapters. That apparatus is designed to be neither exhaustive nor exhausting and includes thematic and stylistic questions along with writing assignments. Finally, the book's rhetorical contents will show that the variety of writing modes offered is a balanced one, thereby allowing the book to be used easily in courses that organize themselves by these modes.

I wish to thank the instructors who reviewed this manuscript at various stages of development and who provided invaluable feedback: James Allen, College of DuPage; Cathryn Amdal, Harrisburg Area Community College; Tim Catalano, Marietta College; F. Brett Cox, Norwich University; Geraldine A. Draper, Fort Peck Community College; Ruth A. Gerik, University of Texas at Arlington; Crystal R. Gorham, University at Buffalo; Keith Gumery, Temple University; Betty L. Hart, The University of Southern Indiana; Jeff Johnson, Brevard Community College; Alexis Khoury, Reedley College; Deborah Kirkman, University of Kentucky; Liz Kleinfeld, Red Rocks Community College; Patricia A. Kramer, Rock Valley College; Laurel Lacroix, Houston Community College—Southwest; Jennifer Lane, Glendale Community College; J. L. McClure, Kirkwood Community College; Sarah Kretz McDowell, Augustana College; Rebecca Mills, Hillsborough Community College—Brandon Campus; Lyle Morgan, Pittsburg State University; Chandra Tyler Mountain, Dillard University; Jeffrey L. Newberry, Abraham Baldwin Agricultural College; Christine Norris, University of Nevada—Reno; Kimme Nuckles, Baker College of Auburn Hills; Lisa Louise Rhodes, Temple University; Will Weaver, Bemidji State University; Patricia Webb, Arizona State University; Steven J. Zani, Lamar University

WILLIAM VESTERMAN

# To the Student

For all of us, the celebrities of mass culture are both remote and familiar. You might have seen them in person only as distant figures on a concert stage or in a ballpark, but at the same time you probably know more about some of them—about details of their lives and about their views—than you do about some of your relatives and neighbors. You may know, for example, that Tom Cruise suffers from dyslexia; but did you also know that he has written a very interesting essay on his condition and how it affected his education? It appears in this book.

Many, many celebrities have written for publication, but it seems that the money to be gained is for them only a secondary motive at best, given the enormously greater profits to be gained from sticking with their day jobs. The fact is, they write because they want to express themselves, to tell other people what it is like be who they are and what they think about things. In their desire to communicate, they are like most people. Unlike you, however, they are not required to learn how to write better in order to pass a course—they want to do so, as you have no doubt been told all your life that you should want to do. And if improvements in their writing have been assisted by their personal assistants and editorial staffs, you yourself have the valuable assistance of your teachers and your classmates.

You may never become a celebrity writer yourself, but in any field that you do enter you will need to learn to write. Even in something as apparently remote from English composition as engineering design, for example, you may get by for a while without having to write much. But the moment you advance beyond the entry level and start to manage other people, you will be charged with both telling them what you want done and telling your superiors what has been achieved. If you can't do either of these things in clear memoranda, your whole career will be slowed or stopped. Ask anyone who has been there. Nationwide, writing courses are the last of the college-wide required courses. They remain so as testimony to the fact that writing courses are the most important courses you can take in college.

This book is designed to support your instruction and to help you improve your writing by offering examples of writing done by some of the stars of our mass culture. A more complete rationale for the plan of the book may be found in the preface, but the basic idea is to ask you to respond to writing by people you already know something about—and may even care something about. In most collections of essays for writing courses, the focus is primarily on the topics of the essays alone. Head notes are included to identify these otherwise anonymous experts to some degree. But—though very brief head notes are included here too—you will already know something about most of the authors in this book. And for the most part, the celebrity authors are no more expert on the topics they address than you are. Most of these topics involve issues on which everyone can have a valid opinion. Furthermore, it is as true in writing as it is in conversation that you can understand someone you know something about much more clearly than you can understand a stranger, because knowing where someone is coming from provides an important context for the meaning of any form of communication.

Your own course may not be arranged strictly along the organizational lines of this book, because Composition is taught in many different ways, yet the contents of this book are flexible enough to support many different forms of instruction. Very simply, in whatever way your course might be organized, the celebrities represented here have already done what you will have to do. They have chosen topics and expressed themselves in written English. By doing so, each composed a 'self' for self-expression, a self that views the world and is viewed by the world through language. Their experiences and their words along with your own experiences and your own words will make up the material you work with in your course—and of course none of the material by either party needs to be boring. Finally, the essays here may also provide models—and sometimes antimodels—of skills to imitate and pitfalls to avoid.

As you will see, the table of contents here is organized around a movement outward into the world—from a focus on a private self to the presentation of that self in public actions. Each rough stage of the process is represented by selections that focus on a wide range of celebrities and on a wide range of topics. You may be given different writing assignments, but the assignments in this book ask you to begin by writing about what you know best— you own life. Those assignments then move into the public sphere to examine the problems involved in finding a voice for yourself by addressing some public issues. The discussion questions that accompany all the selections focus on reading and writing, both in terms of theme and in terms of technique. They are designed to provide you with material for your own writing and to help in crafting that material.

In general, you will find that the celebrity writers represented here have faced the same problems of expression that you will face as a writer. As mentioned earlier, for example, you will find that Tom Cruise has probably had more problems with his own reading and writing than you will ever have. You will also find that he therefore values what he has achieved all the more for the difficulty of its attainment.

The American philosopher John Dewey said that when it came right down to it, education was no more than a teacher on one end of a log and a student on the other. For all the computer aids and Web sites and smart classrooms available to education today, his insight still holds. This book is intended to be the log in the formula—to provide solid material to support the discussions between you and your instructor on many topics, including the topic of writing.

# Constructing and Representing a Private Self

# CHAPTER 1

# ORIGINS AND TURNING POINTS

You have probably already learned that "Where are you from?" is the question most often asked by students meeting one another for the first time. The reason for the frequency of the question is plain: Who you are as a private person is inevitably constructed in important ways by yourself and by others out of the public meanings that cluster around your place of origin with all its associations and significances. It is these associations and significances, as well as your own attitudes toward them, that can provide you with material for forming and representing your own identity and can provide other people with passages of the text wherein they read who you represent yourself to be.

The public meanings and private associations of your origins can help you in getting started as a college level writer by providing you with subjects for composition, subjects on which you are already something of an expert. "Write about what you know" is a classic bit of advice often given to authors of fiction and nonfiction alike, and you certainly know where you came from. You also know better than anyone else the turning points that have changed the direction of your travels through life. In fact, you know as much about your own origins and turning points as the celebrities represented here do, and you can therefore start off as a writer and reader on approximately equal footing with them. Like you, their task is to find a language to express in writing something about what it is like to have grown up and faced crises.

You can learn how to write by analyzing how they have written on similar topics. Reading their accounts will both stimulate your memory and provide you with models for talking about your own past.

The celebrities featured in this chapter know how important their experiences have been to them—for better, and sometimes for worse—but the ways they use language to express themselves vary greatly. For example, we see from the manner of her writing how much Whoopi Goldberg relishes and cherishes her memory of childhood Christmases in New York City, where she was born and raised. The unembarrassed tenderness of her style avoids sentimentalizing her past but still provides vivid concrete images of what it is like to grow up in a warm and loving family.

In the next selection we see that Sissy Spacek feels she was virtually made at home, as her title suggests. What it was like to grow up in a world worlds away from New York City and yet to come there herself as a young adult gives her essay built-in drama. She arrived at the mecca of actors and actresses with a homemade background completely different from that of Whoopi Goldberg, a native New Yorker. And yet, Spacek shows how her origins strongly affected this major turning point in her life and career.

Joe Piscopo is more brash than tender about his origins—on the surface at least. But like many high-spirited and witty people, he manages to create a style that allows him to suggest his private feelings about the public space he grew up in, while simultaneously addressing and defying the stereotypical readings by others of his New Jersey origins. As a comic, he knows how to make fun of himself and to be serious at the same time.

Unlike Joe Piscopo, Margaret Cho was too oppressed as a child by the malicious ways others read her identity in her Korean-given name to be very defiant, but she gets her own back to some degree now, in her unself-pitying account of her early persecution. It is possible to see how some of the strengths of her style as a take-no-prisoners stand-up comic might have been forged in the crucible of childhood bullying. She recounts her sad story with an objectivity that is itself an expression of her current self-confidence.

Though the local color of one's childhood can provide material for the construction of a personal identity, major turning points at any period in one's life provide occasions for even more complicated aspects of the self to be expressed. Tom Cruise, for example, tells us how he suffered through a long and secret struggle with a serious learning disability. Even while he was becoming more and more publicly successful as an actor, his well-concealed private failings kept haunting him. Cruise did overcome his handicap, as he explains, and he now supports foundations sponsoring research into the problems he found he shared with a great number of people.

When Joan Rivers' husband killed himself after a long struggle with depression, she began her own struggle to come to terms with his suicide. In the course of her mourning, she came to understand that her initial, apparently irrational response of denial was in fact the most common reaction experienced by all victims of disaster—the inability to believe that what happened really happened. She explains that facing a major problem is the necessary first step in overcoming it.

The chapter closes with an account by Sting that is not so much a clarification as it is a deepening of mystery. The major turning point that began the process of forming Sting's identity as a world-famous musician began in his childhood with powerful musical impressions he did not even begin to understand. He tells us in an essay first delivered as a college graduation speech how music often works like religion in mysterious ways its wonders to perform.

# Whoopi Goldberg

## Christmas in New York                                    (1997)

*Born Caryn Elaine Johnson in the Chelsea neighborhood of Man-*
*hattan, Whoopi Goldberg started out as an improvisational*
*comic before gaining prominence for her supporting role in* The
Color Purple *and her one-woman HBO special on Moms Mabley.*
*The following sketch is taken from her autobiography,* Book.

1    Christmas was it around our house. The high point, the focal
point, the main point.

2    We had the drill down. My mom would come home with
the tree. Nothing special, just a tree, and she'd put the tree in
that little tree holder thing and tighten it up so it stood straight.
She'd leave it up for a few days, maybe a week or so, and it'd
just be standing there, all bare and good-smelling, and I'd come
home from school and hang up my jacket and look around to
see if there were any presents underneath it, or if anything had
magically materialized around it during the day. But there was
never anything under the tree. It was just bare, and waiting.

3    Still, I'd look, and breathe in that wonderful real Christmas-
tree smell, and try to imagine what was coming. That smell
always got me. Even today, I have to have that sweet pine
mixed with the juicy aroma of our slow-cooking turkey, which
my mother used to put in about nine o'clock on Christmas Eve.
Give me that smell on Christmas, honey, and I'm set.

4    Finally, one night pretty close to Christmas, we'd start in
with the lights and circle the tree. It was just me and my mom
and my brother. Sometimes there was my cousin, but usually
it was just the three of us, which was how it was the rest of the
time anyway, so, you know, that was cool. Our Christmas-tree

lights were red and green and orange and yellow, and they'd flick on and off. We used the same lights every year. We couldn't go buying new stuff. We had our lights and we were set. We also had the string with the liquid bubbling up inside the lights, and we'd circle the tree with that too, and then we'd rip open a new package of tinsel, and run and tear and toss the tinsel. The tinsel you couldn't keep from one year to the next; you had to buy new stuff. We did our Isadora Duncan moves, and we got it up on the tree in all kinds of configurations. Next came the peppermint candy canes, then the liquid snow they used in department-store windows. We'd spray the snow on the windows at an angle, so it looked like it had built up from being blown against the panes by the wind.

5       Sometimes we'd write "Merry Christmas" on the windows with a stencil and a rag dipped in pink window cleaner, or do up a picture of a reindeer. You'd dot the rag around and, just like that, you had a reindeer on your window.

6       This all happened in one night. From bare tree to a done-up department-store window took just a couple hours. We'd have the Christmas music going, or if the decorating ran into Christmas Eve, maybe we'd have the television tuned to the yule log broadcast on Channel 11, for the background music. We'd never actually sit and *watch* the yule log, because even we knew that was kinda cheesy, but we'd listen and put all the stuff on the tree and laugh and laugh and laugh. It was the most delicious time. There were still no presents under the tree, but we knew Mom was just waiting for us to go to sleep.

7       Finally, when the decorations were through, we'd watch *A Christmas Carol,* the British version, the one with Alastair Sim, which for my money is the only one to watch. We'd all gather in front of our black-and-white television set for the last piece of the routine. After the movie, we'd go to bed. I still watch that sucker every Christmas Eve, and I still go to bed right after. I need Alastair Sim and the smell of the tree and the turkey, else Christmas ain't really happening for me, you know.

8       In the middle of the night, my brother used to wake me up with a tap on the shoulder and take me into the living room. He was all, "Shhhhhh, Caryn, shhhhhh," until I was all the way awake, then I was the one shushing him. It was a small

apartment, just two rooms. It was tough to move about without attracting attention. Mom sometimes slept in the living room, but on some nights she doubled up with me, so we never really knew if we'd be found out on our midnight run. I'm sure she knew. She had to know. We were giggling too much for her not to know. But she never stirred. We were about as quiet as two kids could be, banging into things but she never stirred.

9      I remember coming down our darkened hallway, and turning the corner into the living room, and seeing the reflection of the lights on the walls. On and off, and on and off. Man, it was an enchanted sight. The apartment lights were all out, but the Christmas tree was lit up like Vegas. It was the main strip, right there; it was like the room had been dipped in all the colors of the rainbow. On and off, and on and off.

10      And then—there it was. My brother, Clyde, and me, we never tired of the game. We never knew how Mom got all those presents underneath the tree in that small apartment without our noticing. We could never figure out where her hiding places were, or when, exactly, she jumped into action. It was one of the wonderments of our growing up, but there'd always be these great presents, like a bicycle, or skates, or whatever we were into that year. All the things a kid could possibly want for Christmas were laid out under our tree, all beautifully wrapped and waiting for our greedy little paws to tear them open. It'd just knock us out. I never had any idea how she even afforded it, forget the logistical problem of getting the stuff wrapped and under the tree undetected. But we had to hurry back into bed before Mom caught us. We couldn't open the presents until morning, and even then we couldn't open them until after breakfast. We'd be jumping up and down, shouting "Merry Christmas!" over and over, but we'd have to polish off our Maypo before we could do anything about it.

11      We'd bring out our little gifts for each other. I was big into these little perfumes for my mom, or some scarves. Basically anything I could get at the five-and-ten for not a whole lot of money that was kinda nice. I'd collect the Hoffman soda bottles and trade them in for nickels, and I'd usually have some

money left over from my birthday, which was back in November. I'd buy my brother some socks, or a book, and that was about as far as my money went, but that was enough.

12    If there was snow, we'd head out to play. We'd get on Clyde's Flexible Flyer and sled down Tenth Avenue. Remember those serious snowstorms? We don't get them much anymore, but back then, the city would just shut down and Tenth Avenue became the Alps. My brother would push me from behind. He'd run and run and run and push and push and push and then finally hop on. He'd be yelling in my ear, "Hold on, Caryn. Hold on." Or he'd be tellin' me to lean this way or that way. Now, there wasn't much of a pitch to Tenth Avenue, but if the snow was packed just right and you got a good run going, you could slide forever. He'd make like I was a bad driver, and that I was gonna hit a parking sign or something, and he'd holler and laugh. Whenever we came to a stop I'd look up from my laughing and say, "Do it again." That was the line, "Do it again." And Clyde would grab the rope he had tied to the front of the sled and pull me back up the street for another ride.

13    Christmas was one of the best times of all in our house, with the tree and the turkey and the three of us. Just the best. And not because we were celebrating the birth of Christ. That wasn't what it was about for me. It was a seasonal thing, a ritual, something to look forward to. It was the ticking off of another year. It was looking outside and finding a fresh snowfall to surpass the one we'd sprayed on the window the night before, which happened maybe once or twice but somehow has become part of the memory.

## Theme

1. In her account, Goldberg first pays attention to the Christmas tree. Name the other major themes she addresses in her essay.

2. The author mentions several times that "it was just the three of us." What are some other ways in which she stresses the closeness of her family?

## Technique

1. Goldberg begins with her memories of the *smell* of Christmas. Point to examples of other senses than that of smell she uses to retrieve and express her past.

2. In her account of sledding, Goldberg sometimes uses dialogue and sometimes reported speech. In what ways does her dialogue express rituals of affection rather than the communication of information? Explain your view of the effectiveness of this technique.

## Writing

Write an essay that analyzes the ways in which Whoopi Goldberg's writing appeals to the five senses of her reader.

# Sissy Spacek

## Homemade in Texas                                        (2003)

> *Mary Elizabeth (Sissy) Spacek grew up as a tomboy in Quitman,
> Texas. As she recounts at the end of the following reminiscence,
> she came from Texas to New York where (with the help of
> her cousin Rip Torn) she broke into show business, enrolling in
> The Actors Studio and studying at The Lee Strasberg Theater
> Institute. She went on to win an Oscar for her lead role in*
> Coal Miner's Daughter, *the life story of country singer Loretta
> Lynn, and was nominated for a Grammy for her rendition of
> the title song.*

1    I've always had a deep sense of pride about being a Texan,
and I remember thinking as a little kid, "Oh, how lucky I am
to be born in Texas, in this little town, in this house, with these
parents, and with Ed and Robbie as my brothers." Quitman was
a wonderful place to grow up—it was the center of my universe, my brier patch. There wasn't a lot of outside interference—no satellite TV, no Internet. There was a picture show,
but it closed when I was about six.

2    In a little town, everybody's kind of pulling for you; it's hard
to fail in an environment like that. So as a kid, I got to explore
and do a lot of different things and find what I was best at and
what I enjoyed. I feel like the basis of me is tied so closely to
my childhood. It's that little kid that ran around barefoot in
Quitman and just knew no fears, knew no strangers, rode her
bike everywhere, rode her horse everywhere. It was an idyllic
life, where the summers were long and I had enormous freedom and incredible security. We traveled a lot too, all over
Texas, and I got a real good sense of my roots. My mother was

SOURCE: Reprinted by permission from the February 2003 issue of *Texas Monthly.*

from down in the Rio Grande Valley and my father was from Granger, in Central Texas, and everyone there spoke Czech. When we visited, we were the "Spah-chek" family.

3     I started singing at talent shows and church functions in Quitman when I was around five or six. It was something creative that I was pretty good at, and people seemed to want to listen. I can't tell you how many Rotarians I entertained—just me and my guitar, mostly folk music and old standards like "Copper Kettle." I was also starting to write my own songs. You know, I never thought, "I'm going to learn to play guitar so I can get out of here." But then, in 1967, a friend invited me to go along with her to New York, and I flew up for the summer after my junior year. I was lucky—my cousin was Rip Torn and his wife was Geraldine Page, and I stayed with them and saw a side of the city most seventeen-year-olds never dreamed of.

4     It was a great time to be in New York. I think I arrived in a little flowered suit and little patent leather shoes, and of course I had my two guitars. I didn't go anywhere without my guitars. Both Rip and Geraldine were in plays, on Broadway and off, and they took me everywhere with them. They were artists, and I can remember being included in many evenings with their artist and actor friends, and they'd be talking about creative things I knew nothing about but that were just so exciting. By August, when I went back to Texas, I was into moccasins and bell-bottoms and out of the little flowered suit.

5     My parents wanted me to go to the University of Texas, and I was planning on it, but my brother Robbie was very ill with leukemia and he died in September. That changed everything for me. All these plans we had made for college, it was almost like they were made for somebody else. I had changed; what I wanted had changed. So when I was accepted at UT the next year I went for about a week and I actually went through rush, but college just wasn't for me. I wanted a piece of what I had experienced in New York. I've often wondered what would have happened if I had stayed in Austin. There was such an amazing music scene—Janis Joplin, Threadgill's.

I wonder sometimes if I would have stuck with music. Or would I have been a baton-twirling teacher? I'll never know.

6    That winter I moved to New York and started playing at clubs in Greenwich Village in my moccasins and bell-bottoms. I also jammed with my musician friends in Washington Square Park, hanging out and waiting for a glimpse of Bob Dylan. I fell in with a bunch of young musicians at the Brill Building and started doing background vocals and studio work. I sang on the soundtrack for one of Andy Warhol's films, which I never saw, called Lonesome Cowboys and was an extra in his Andy Warhol's Trash, but I think my scene was cut. I also met these guys who ran Roulette Records and recorded two songs for them. They had a gimmick and a song and they needed a girl. They even had a name: Rainbo. The song was "John, You Went Too Far This Time," a commentary on John Lennon's nude album cover. I can't tell you how long it took to live that one down. There was a lot of stuff happening in New York, and in some ways I was more a witness than a participant. I just didn't seem quite as weird as everyone else. I was pretty normal. I mean, I loved my parents.

7    Around 1970 I met a guy who eventually became my manager. He suggested that I study acting and start auditioning for things, so I started classes at the Strasberg Institute. I remember feeling like an impostor because everyone else in class seemed very dramatic and really into it. I was a little self-conscious about the acting exercises, thinking I was too well-adjusted. I just didn't know how to be a teacup. Someone even told me that if I didn't lose the Texas accent I might as well take the next plane back home.

8    The funny thing is, my Texanness is what got me noticed. I met a young director named Terrence Malick, who's from Waco, and we just clicked. He cast me in his movie *Badlands,* and that was when things really began, when I was actually working with artists. And not just Terry. I also met Jack Fisk, who was the film's art director. Suddenly I was part of a group of artists, and acting felt like what I had experienced making music. It wasn't about being a star; it was about being a part of this thing, this living thing that was happening. It was a true collaboration.

## Theme

1. Sissy Spacek says she felt secure growing up in her home-town. In your own words, list some of the ways in which she expresses her sense of security.

2. In this brief account of her early life, the author mentions several major turning points. Point to each one and explain any differences between the person who came to the turn-ing point and the person who moved beyond it.

## Technique

1. Sissy Spacek started out in Texas but ended up in New York and Hollywood. Explain how nevertheless her title still may be said to accurately introduce all the phases of her life.

2. Spacek often tells us what she was wearing on a given occa-sion. Explain how she uses each outfit to express the social identity she maintained at the time.

## Writing

The author claims to be "pretty normal" both before and after her fame. Write an essay that analyzes how she expresses a sense of normality in her writing to her reader.

# Joe Piscopo

## It's a Jersey Thing                                      (2003)

*Joe Piscopo was born in (where else?) New Jersey and with Eddie Murphy became a star in the second generation of* Saturday Night Live. *With his friend and neighbor Murphy he produced a short film for SNL about living in the Jersey "burbs" where he may still be found today.*

1    "Y̶ou from Jersey? What exit?"

2    Yeah, I wrote that. A long time ago. Ya gotta have a sense of humor. But let me tell you how I really feel about my home state.

3    If you've got an attitude, if you show one ounce of insincerity or pretentiousness, don't even think about it. You won't mean a thing to citizens of the Garden State. We are not easily impressed. But if you're the real deal—a sincere person, whether you're New Jersey-born or you just moved down the Parkway—you are one of us, and we will die for you.

4    It's true when they say that if you want to find some terrorist punk in a far-off land, send two guys from Jersey in a Buick. Be over in two days.

5    It's also true that when a real Jersey Boy dies, his gravestone reads, "Whatta you lookin' at?"

6    As a matter of fact, if you're really lucky when you die, we'll put your name on a rest stop.

7    Vince Lombardi, Thomas Edison, Walt Whitman, Joyce Kilmer—they've all got rest stops. Someday, long after the Nets beat the Spurs in five games for the franchise's first NBA championship, the team will rest in peace knowing a piece of the New Jersey Turnpike lives on in their memory.

SOURCE: By permission of Joe Piscopo.

8     But I'll stop the big talk there because in Jersey, talk is cheap, and respect is everything. We respect our opponent, whether it's the Spurs or the Mighty Ducks. Not to say we won't kick their asses, but this isn't Boston or Philly. We'll treat them with respect when they come to . . . I was going to say town, but is East Rutherford anybody's town? I don't think anybody even lives there. Man, we've got to move the Nets and Devils to Newark.

9     Here in Jersey, we've always been second-class citizens; we're the Rodney Dangerfield of states. Maybe I've contributed to that by writing all those Jersey jokes, but if you're from here—and only if you're from here—you can joke about it. It's part of who we are. And it's a big part of why this incredible season for our teams means so much.

10     But you know what counts for even more? That the Nets and Devils, from the ownership on down to the players, are real. We're talking about some outstanding people. I spend a lot of my time working with kids, and that's how I came to serve on the board of the Nets/Devils Foundation. You wouldn't believe how involved in the community guys like Raymond Chambers, Lewis Katz, Lou Lamoriello, Rod Thorn, Byron Scott, Jason Kidd, Kenyon Martin, Marty Brodeur and many others truly are. They also get Jersey. Even George, as in Steinbrenner, gets Jersey. After all, the corporation is called YankeeNets.

11     The truth is I get basketball better than I get hockey. When I was growing up in Bloomfield, all the rich kids across the avenue played hockey. I was all baseball and basketball. We were all diehard Yankees fans—still are—and we rooted for the Knicks and the Rangers. But then we got the Nets and eventually the Devils, and things changed. We had our own teams. New York couldn't neglect us anymore.

12     After I got my big break with *Saturday Night Live,* I'd do promotional events for the Nets. I even sang the national anthem at one of their games. I got to know all the players and really got hooked. I've been teased by some teams I thought would win big, but of course they never did. Until now.

13     I can't see the Nets losing in The Finals. This is the best team in the NBA. You can't fully appreciate these guys until you

watch them play live. I've never seen a player of Kidd's caliber. And what a strategist Scott has become! I used to work out with him at Arnold Schwarzenegger's gym back in L.A. The guys would bust my chops because every time I would take my shirt off, Arnold would look at me and say, "*Joe,* please. Put your shirt back on."

14    Well, I'm back home, where I belong. And there's nothing to be embarrassed about—especially not our sports teams. You from Jersey? Yeah, me too. And proud of it.

## Theme

1. List the "Jersey jokes" that the author makes in the course of the essay. Explain in each case what the joke is on. Who or what is being laughed at and why?

2. What is the author proud of about his native state? Again, make a list with explanations.

## Technique

1. Piscopo uses both *ya* and *you* second-person pronouns in paragraph two. Explain the difference in effect created by the difference in spelling.

2. In paragraph ten Piscopo uses "real" to describe both the ownership of sports teams and players on those teams. Explain how Piscopo goes on to define what he means by "real" through implication and example in his essay.

## Writing

In paragraph nine Piscopo writes: "...but if you're from here— and only if you're from here—you can joke about it." Write an essay in which you explain how the values and assumptions behind this statement are representative of the values and assumptions behind the essay as a whole. Use examples.

# Margaret Cho

## Friendless in Frisco                                        (2001)

> *Margaret Cho was born and raised in San Francisco where she dropped out of high school to pursue a career as a stand-up comic. By the age of 23 she had her own television series and in 1999 her one-woman show* I'm the One That I Want *was named Great Performance of the Year by* Entertainment Weekly.

1    My family went to church every Sunday, at first to the one by Stonestown, where my grandfather led the services, and later to the big Korean Methodist Church on Powell Street that was in the middle of Chinatown. Sometimes big Chinese funeral processions would lurch slowly down the street. There would be a brass band made up of men dressed like they were in the military, playing solemnly as they marched by. Then there'd be a black convertible, with an enormous black-and-white photo of the deceased, bordered with black bands to signify the departure into the afterlife, attached to the windshield. The hearse would follow, its windows crammed with flowers behind a white curtain, hiding the mysterious gleaming casket. I wanted to hold my breath as it went by. I thought if I got too close and looked into the hearse, a bony hand would emerge from it and drag me inside. Carloads of mourners trailed behind, and they all moved so slowly, it seemed like it would take forever to get where they were going. But it hardly mattered. There is lots of time when you are dead. These processions made me dread and look forward to Sunday at the same time.

2    The church services were held in Korean, so a massive Sunday school system existed to accommodate all the exclusively

English-speaking kids. It was broken down into two groups, the baby classes with Jesus coloring books and the Methodist Youth Foundation, which was for the teenagers who cut class and went into Chinatown to smoke cigarettes and talk about what they'd done Saturday night. When they did go to class, it was like a cool "rap" session, involving young pastors getting out their acoustic guitars and talking about the "downer" of premarital sex.

3    They *hated* me there. Everyone. From the babies all the way to the teenagers. Maybe the teachers and the young pastor didn't, because they'd spend time trying to protect me and involve me in some activities, the same ones the other kids would try to exclude me from. I don't think anyone could have been more hated. School was bad enough, but now it seemed like the whole world was a hostile place.

4    This was the '80s and I was twelve, a preteen with a Dorothy Hamill haircut and braces. Hated. Hated. Hated. I tried to ignore it, spending summers away with cousins who lived in magical Glendale, where I would sit by their swimming pool reading a waterlogged copy of *Seventeen*. Lori Laughlin set the beauty standard, and as I looked at her, my troubles would melt away. "Someday I will be seventeen . . ." But the thing that I couldn't admit to myself was that I was really wishing "Someday . . . I will be *white*."

5    Whenever I read those magazines and tried to plug into the teenage fantasy they were selling, I couldn't see myself at all. I studied those pictures and the TV and movies like *Little Darlings* over and over. Then in the mirror I would be confronted with the awful reality that I was *not that*. It was almost too much to bear.

6    My Koreanness, my "otherness," embarrassed me. When I had school projects that required the use of glue, a product my family had little need or money for, my mother would substitute leftover rice. My face would get all red and I would shake and stammer, "Why can't we have American glue!! I hate you, Mommy!!!!" Then I would stamp my feet up the stairs and throw my hot face down on my canopy bed.

7    Since I didn't really have friends who I was not related to, and the kids that were cruelest to me were other Koreans, my

entire world was an exercise in not belonging. The answer seemed to lie in being white, so in my fantasy life, I chose to be Lori Laughlin. In my mind, I got ready for dances, wearing only a neat white towel wrapped under my arms, spraying myself with Love's Baby Soft, wiping a cotton ball soaked in 10-0-6 lotion over my troublesome T-zone, lining my big, big eyes with Aziza by Prince Matchabelli, putting on a long, ruffled denim skirt with a petticoat underneath and then a puffy-sleeved blouse with a big ruffle forming a V on my ample but not slutty chest. Then finally, I'd let my naturally curly chestnut hair fall across my narrow shoulders, pulling it up close to my head with red oval barrettes. The only time the fantasy would change would be if I decided to be Charlene Tilton instead of Lori Laughlin, but this occurred less frequently because I read in *Teen Beat* that Charlene took forty-five minutes to blow-dry her hair, which even then I found unreasonable.

8    I usually never got to the dance, because my fantasies were all about getting ready, looking a certain way, about not being me. How sad to use such a rich and vibrant imagination to dream about *grooming,* and not only that, but *grooming someone else.*

9    Sometimes, I would get so caught up in the fantasy that I would actually go to the dance, but since I'd never been to one yet, that image was rather muddled. I'd end up slow-dancing to Air Supply with the cutest guy in my grade, Steve Goldberg, a hot Jewish kid with blonde hair and a huge ass. Steve was relentlessly mean to me, perhaps because he knew I had a crush on him, but he was also in his own pain because of his big behind. Once, on a field trip, he made all the kids in the class say "Hi Margaret" to a big golden retriever as they walked by. "Hey everybody, say hi to Margaret. She's a dog! Get it?!" I wasn't offended. I always thought dogs were beautiful. It hurt me only because it was *meant* to, but it was nothing compared to the treatment I got at church.

10    It started with my name. I was born Moran Cho. Moran is a Korean name, meaning peony flower, a plant that blooms even in the harshest winter. My father gave me this thoughtful, unusual name without the knowledge that someday the kids I

grew up with would use it against me. It started when I was around twelve, not at school, but at church.

11    "MORON!! YOU ARE NOTHIN' BUT A MORON!!!" They said my name every chance they got.

12    "Excuse me, but MORON didn't pass the basket this way."

13    "Hey! I have my hand up. You can't see me past MORON'S fat head."

14    "May I be moved? I don't want to sit next to MORON!"

15    "Jesus loves everyone, even MORON."

16    It was stupid, but it hurt my feelings so much. Especially since the main instigators had once been close friends of mine.

## Theme

1. In paragraph six Cho writes: "Since I didn't really have any friends who I was not related to, and the kids that were cruelest to me were other Koreans, my entire world was an exercise in not belonging. The answer seemed to lie in being white, so in my fantasy life, I chose to be Lori Laughlin." Her reasoning here may not make logical sense, but does it make psychological sense in your view? If you think so, explain how. If you think not, explain the nature of the muddle.

2. In paragraph seven Cho writes: "How sad to use such a rich and vibrant imagination to dream about *grooming,* and not only that, but *grooming someone else*." Cho says her actions seem "sad" here. In your opinion, does sadness generally characterize her present view of her past unhappiness? If you think so, explain how she creates that sense through her writing about another moment in her past. If you think not, explain the attitude you feel she does take toward her past and how that attitude is created through her writing.

## Technique

1. This excerpt from her autobiography *I'm The One That I Want* begins and ends with Cho's Korean church. Does this

technique effectively frame the fantasies that take up the middle of the essay in your view? Explain why or why not.

2. Cho often introduces quoted dialogue into her narration. Rewrite a scene eliminating the dialogue while remaining true to the events described. Then explain how in your view the dialogue does or does not contribute to the effectiveness of the scene.

## Writing

Write an essay in which you analyze how as a child Margaret Cho tried to overcome her loneliness and alienation through fantasy.

# Sammy Sosa

## Growing Up Poor in Consuelo                    (2000)

*Sammy Sosa is the fifth of seven children whose father died when Sammy was only seven years old. After breaking Roger Maris's home run record in 1998, he became in 1999 the only player in history to hit 60 home runs in two different major league seasons.*

1    What I remember most about those days was working—we all worked. I started going out with my brothers, shining shoes. We would also take a bucket of water and some soap and wash whatever cars we could.

2    My mother cooked for people, she sold lottery tickets, and she worked day and night. Because of what had happened, the only thing we could do was to unite as a family. My mother always told us we had to stick together, so all us kids became very close. We would share everything. We shared our food, we shared our clothing. If one of us didn't have any shoes to wear, we would borrow from each other. My brother Luis became my hero. I saw how hard he worked for us, and he always watched out for me; he let me go with him wherever he went.

3    For the next three years we stayed in Consuelo, but things were very hard. I was getting up early in the morning to shine shoes. Then I would go to school until the late afternoon. Then I would work with my brothers washing cars until really late at night. Whenever I could, I would play baseball in the park, but the truth is I didn't have much time for the game. The other thing I did a lot was fight. I was always fighting with the neighborhood kids. I loved to fight and would never back down from any challenge. I wasn't afraid of anyone.

SOURCE: From *Growing Up Poor in Consuelo* by Sammy Sosa. Copyright © 2000 by Sammy Sosa. By permission of Warner Books.

4    But things were getting worse and worse at home. There just weren't any opportunities in Consuelo. When my father was alive, we always ate three solid meals a day. There was always food in the house. But now, even with my mother working nonstop and us helping her, we started to go hungry. Sometimes we only had two meals a day, sometimes only one. We ate a lot of rice and beans, fried plantains and Yucca.

5    But if my mother was ever scared or worried, she never showed it. We all depended on her, and she never wavered. People ask me now why I blow a kiss to my mother after all my home runs. I always say there are many reasons for that, and they go all the way back to our days in Consuelo.

6    I remember one conversation in particular. My mother came up to me—I was probably eight or nine—and said, "*Mijo* (my son), your mother doesn't have money for food tomorrow. Do you think you could go out and work and bring some money home?"

7    I said, "*Si,* Mommy. Don't worry. I'll bring home some money." That day I went out and worked really, really hard shining shoes. And I brought back money for my mother, money she used to buy food. I would do anything for her because I knew she would do anything for me.

8    Above all, she instilled in us a deep sense of honesty. She always said that whatever money or things we brought into our house had to come from the sweat of our brows. Where we lived there were lots of kids who were poor like us but who carried a lot of money sometimes. Or you would see them with a nice piece of clothing. They would tell their parents that they had found it or something—or that someone had given them a gift.

8    Most times their parents would look the other way, say they believed them when they really didn't. But my mother would have never permitted that. If we had ever brought something home that she knew we hadn't earned, she would have gone with us to take it back.

9    Despite her honesty, things just kept getting worse and worse financially. My brothers and I would be staying out really late at night, working. Sometimes we wouldn't get home until midnight or one in the morning.

10    What we would do is go to the nice part of town, see a car parked in the street, and wash it. Then we'd have to sit there and wait until the owner came out so we could ask him if he would give us any money for washing his car. Sometimes that would take hours. My brothers and I would have to stand there, waiting and waiting.

11    We'd laugh and joke with each other, but those hours spent waiting, trapped in a way because we couldn't afford to leave, made a big impression on me. When you don't have any control over your economic situation, when your stomach is empty, when you see your mother working so hard and you have to stand around for hours, waiting for someone, it leaves a mark on you.

12    That experience made me realize how hard it is to earn money, and it burned inside me that I didn't want to live this way for the rest of my life. Sometimes we wouldn't even get paid—all those hours wasted!

13    But, as in so many other facets of my life, those moments taught me once again how much my mother loved us. As tired as she was from working, she just couldn't lay herself down to sleep for the night unless all her children were home. So we'd be out, waiting to collect money for washing cars, and she'd be home, looking out the window for us. Sometimes she couldn't bear to wait, and she would come out looking for us.

14    Looking back then, we boys didn't understand completely why our mother would be out at 1:00 A.M. hunting us down. In fact, I remember we'd get embarrassed if our friends made fun of us. She'd find us and we'd explain to her, "Mommy, we can't leave. We washed these cars and we have to wait until the people come out so we can collect some money." Sometimes we'd all go home together. We were poor and we weren't building much of a bank account, but as a family we were building something a lot more important.

## Theme

1. The dust jacket of Sammy Sosa's autobiography speaks of his childhood as one of "crushing poverty." Does that phrase

seem to you to characterize fairly his description of the
period in the excerpt you have read? Explain why you do or
do not think so.

2. Sosa says that as children he and his brothers were sometimes
   embarrassed by his mother's coming to look for them. In your
   view, what is the emotion that now characterizes his feelings
   about his mother's concern? Explain why you answer as you
   do by pointing to and explaining evidence from the text.

## Technique

1. Sosa describes his early poverty without ever citing mone-
   tary figures. Point to some of the ways he does create
   a sense of his standard of living at the time without
   using numbers.

2. The excerpt combines a sense of economic poverty and rich
   family life. Point to some of the ways in which Sosa
   expresses a sense of the richness of that family life.

## Writing

At the end of the passage Sosa writes: "We were poor and we
weren't building much of a bank account, but as a family we
were building something a lot more important." Write an essay
in which you describe what it was his family was building and
the means they employed to build it.

# Tom Cruise

## My Struggle to Read                                        (2003)

*Born Tom Cruise Mapother IV to nomadic parents, the future
movie star graduated from high school in Glen Ridge, New Jersey*—salve magna parens. *Giving up plans to become a priest, he
started his acting career with a small part that gained large
notice in* Endless Love.

1   **O**ne of my dreams, as a child, was to be able to fly
an airplane.

2   My whole life we moved around a lot. As a young child,
everywhere we went, these are the things that traveled with
me: a stuffed animal for the first few years and pictures of
planes—a Spitfire and a P-51. When I was 22, when I was making *Top Gun,* I got the chance to make my dream come true—
to become a pilot. I thought, "This is the time to do it," so I had
a couple of lessons. But then I just blew it off.

3   When people asked what happened, I told them I was too
busy preparing for the film, just didn't have time. The truth is,
I couldn't learn how to do it. When I was about 7 years old, I
had been labeled dyslexic. I'd try to concentrate on what I was
reading, then I'd get to the end of the page and have very little memory of anything I'd read. I would go blank, feel anx-
ious, nervous, bored, frustrated, dumb. I would get angry. My
legs would actually hurt when I was studying. My head ached.
All through school and well into my career, I felt like I had a
secret. When I'd go to a new school, I wouldn't want the other
kids to know about my learning disability, but then I'd be sent
off to remedial reading.

4   I made new friends in each new school, but I was always
closest to my three sisters and my mom. As a kid I used to do

ad-lib skits and imitations for my family. I always enjoyed making them laugh. My mom kept saying. "You've got so much potential. Don't give up." She worked three jobs and took care of my sisters and me, but with everything she had on her plate, she would also work with me. If I had to write an assignment for school, I would dictate it to her first, then she would write it down, and I would copy it very carefully. I went to three different high schools, so I was always given the benefit of the doubt for being the new kid. And I had different techniques for getting by in class. I raised my hand a lot. I knew that if I participated, I'd get extra points and could pass. If I had a test in the afternoon, I'd find kids at lunchtime who'd taken the test that morning and find out what it was like.

5   I went out for athletics—baseball, wrestling, soccer, football, hockey, you name it—and really blew off a lot of steam there. My senior year in New Jersey, I got the part of Nathan Detroit in the school's production of *Guys and Dolls.*

6   I graduated high school in 1980 but didn't even go to my graduation. I was a functional illiterate. I loved learning, I wanted to learn, but I knew I had failed in the system. Like a lot of people, though, I had figured out how to get through it. I did the same thing when I moved to New York City, and then Los Angeles, to become an actor. When I auditioned for parts and was given a script to read cold, I'd get the director and producer to talk about the characters and the film. I'd glean information from them and I'd use that. I got pretty good at ad-libbing. In 1981 the door cracked open for me with *Taps. Risky Business* came out in 1983 and my career took off. I wanted to produce movies. I wanted to know more about my craft. I wanted to work with writers. I had stories I wanted to tell. But when I backed out of the flying lessons while making *Top Gun,* I thought to myself, "What the hell am I going to do now?"

7   I'd gotten to where I was operating on the force of sheer will.

8   But I knew I was flying by the seat of my pants. I knew that if I didn't solve this problem, the trapdoor was going to open up and that would be it.

9   In 1986, the year *Top Gun* came out, I became a Scientologist. A friend gave me a picture book on Scientology, and through this I was introduced to the writings of L. Ron Hub-

bard, who had founded the religion. Mr. Hubbard was also an educator who had been researching the field for decades. He had found that literacy and comprehension levels were declining worldwide, so in the 1960s he had developed "Study Technology." It pinpoints three barriers to learning: Lack of mass (you can't learn to fly a plane by just reading about it—you have to sit in the cockpit or at least have a picture of a plane); skipped gradients (trying to master skills or information without mastering or understanding that which comes before them); and misunderstood words (the most important one and a cause for stupidity).

10    Once I started focusing on those problems, everything fell into place. I had a lot of catching up to do, but that was it. I had run the gamut, hiring specialists for myself privately, bringing in tutors and hearing why I would just have to "learn to deal" with being dyslexic. Many people had tried to teach me, but no one had taught me how to learn or how to study; I had been told I had all the symptoms of dyslexia, but no one had given me a solution.

11    I realized I could absolutely learn anything that I wanted to learn. In 1989 I learned to race cars while preparing for *Days of Thunder*. And about 10 years ago I learned to fly. When I was studying for my pilot's license, I kept a model airplane nearby as reference and pictures of a cockpit in front of me so I could study the instruments. I would often go over to a shop where mechanics were working on planes. Finally I took off on my own from the Santa Monica Airport. After the flight I called my mom, and she started crying. My family is very close and they were so happy for me.

12    I'm now a founding board member of the Hollywood Education and Literacy Project (H.E.L.P.), which opened its doors in 1997.

13    H.E.L.P. is a nonprofit program that uses the Study Technology in a totally secular setting to provide free tutoring in communities all over the world. Before this, I was supporting Applied Scholastics, H.E.L.P.'s parent organization, which was started by teachers to make Study Technology available broadly.

14    When you consider that schoolteachers are sometimes dealing with four or five different levels of literacy in one classroom, you can see what they have to contend with. I had so

many different teachers and I really feel for them. I see how they struggled with me. They were rooting for me and cared about me and wanted to see me do well, but they didn't have the tools to really help me.

15    I don't want people to go through what I went through. I want kids to have the ability to read, to write, to understand what people are saying to them, to be able to solve life's problems.

16    If you're flying a plane, and you are using all you know, and yet barely keeping it in the air, you're not truly flying that plane.

17    When the fuel gauge gets down to "E" and you haven't paid attention, your engine is going to stop. When you know how to fly, you're watching the instruments. You can properly prepare for landing. You can keep your view outside. That's the view of life people should be able to have.

## Theme

1. Point to some of the ways in which Tom Cruise dramatizes the nature of his affliction and what it was like to live with it.

2. Point to some of the ways in which Cruise tried to cope with his problem before he found a more successful method.

## Technique

1. Explain some of the ways in which what might be called "the airplane theme" helps to organize and structure Cruise's essay.

2. Cruise ends his essay with an extended analogy involving an airplane. Do you find this an effective technique? Explain why you do or do not think so.

## Writing

Write an essay that analyzes and demonstrates the ways in which Cruise uses concrete examples in describing what it was like to be burdened with dyslexia and what it was like to overcome it.

# Joan Rivers

## Responding to Suicide (1997)

*The comedian and talk show host was born Joan Alexandra Molinsky and graduated from Barnard College of Columbia University. She was married to Edgar Rosenberg for twenty-two years before the tragedy she recounts in the following excerpt from her autobiography.*

1  "MOMMY, DADDY KILLED HIMSELF."

2  I sat in stunned silence as Melissa broke the news to me: My husband—dead? Had committed suicide?

3  Suicide? Edgar? Surely it had to be some kind of mistake. Edgar and I had spoken many times about suicide, and he had always believed it to be a permanent solution to temporary problems. Could this man who had once loved life and adored his daughter have taken that life and left Melissa fatherless?

4  Like many people who hear bad news unexpectedly, I was in a state of disbelief. Maybe they meant another Edgar Rosenberg. Maybe this was someone's idea of a very sick joke.

5  How was it possible that Edgar had sunk so deep into depression that he saw no way out other than taking his own life? I wondered. How had we tumbled so very far, so very fast?

6  The year 1986 had begun on a high note, with the launching of *The Late Show With Joan Rivers* on the new Fox-TV network. Edgar and I were both ecstatic. The show was our reward for twenty-five years of hard work. It was the payoff for my long years in tiny comedy clubs; the endless one-nighters, alone in hotel rooms away from my family for weeks at a time; and then my slow, steady climb to stardom. It was the return on all the planning and wisdom and love Edgar had poured into my career.

7    My husband and I had always worked wonderfully together, I on stage and Edgar behind the scenes. And so, when Fox offered me my own late-night talk show, he and I assumed that our partnership would continue to be as fine as ever. However, Edgar and Barry Diller, the chairman and CEO of Fox, disliked and distrusted each other from the start. When the show didn't quickly live up to the network's expectations, Diller and his colleagues graciously blamed Edgar.

8    A proud man's pride had been shattered, in spite of my efforts to protect both Edgar and the show. In June, Fox canceled *The Late Show With Joan Rivers* and issued press releases that were a family two-cushion shot: They vilified Edgar and humiliated me.

9    In the months that followed, Edgar suffered greatly and changed from a secure man into a self-doubting, bitter, and depressed one. The doctors didn't realize it at the time, but the medication he had been taking since his heart attack in 1984 was creating a chemical imbalance that led to deep depression. That condition, combined with the stress and humiliation he had faced at Fox, broke Edgar's spirit. He was angry all the time and frequently turned his anger on me. His black moods lasted longer and longer, until they were no longer moods but an endless despondency.

10    It was so painful for me to see Edgar in such misery—painful and frightening. What had happened to the man I had known and loved for so many years? What was going to happen to him if he didn't get help immediately? All that summer I tried desperately to convince him to get psychiatric care, something beyond his occasional talks with a psychologist, but he ignored my pleas. On August 10 I returned home from a trip to New York and called Edgar to tell him I had landed safely in Los Angeles. During that phone call I again mentioned psychiatric care. And again he refused.

11    Finally I had to accept the fact that Edgar was a drowning man, and that he was taking me down with him, to the bottom of a sea of despair where I could be no good to him, to myself, or to our daughter. I was so weary of fighting him, so tired of trying to help someone who refused my outstretched hand and my support, that I simply did not know how I could continue.

12    "Edgar," I heard myself say, "if you won't agree to get psychiatric help, I'm not coming home to you."

13    And I didn't. I went straight to the Century Plaza hotel, where, exhausted and tearful, I fell asleep in my clothes. The next day Edgar flew to Philadelphia to see his best friend and business adviser, Tom Pileggi. Phoning from there, Edgar told me that he had done a lot of thinking; and he promised that, when he returned to Beverly Hills, he would at last get treatment for his clinical depression. He was lying, of course.

14    Later that night he spoke to Melissa on the phone, said he was feeling optimistic for the first time in a long time, and was eager to get home. She was the last person to speak to him. And he was lying to her, too: He had already made plans to take his life.

15    After Edgar's suicide Melissa and I told ourselves, with agonizing guilt, that we shouldn't have believed him when he'd said he was okay. I kept saying that we should have had someone guard him day and night until he came home and admitted himself to a hospital; and Melissa felt guilty that she had not said something on the phone to stop him.

16    However, I have learned, through my work with other suicide survivors, that if someone really wants to kill him- or herself, that person will do it—after convincing everyone he or she is okay.

17    And Edgar *had* convinced us. He had made all of us believe that he was feeling well and optimistic again. Melissa and I had allowed ourselves to be optimistic, too. She had spent time with her friends and had started getting ready for her sophomore year at the University of Pennsylvania; and I had gone into the hospital for some minor cosmetic surgery, thinking that feeling good about my appearance would help me recover from some of the battering my ego had taken since *The Late Show* was canceled. I imagined that when I got home from the hospital and Edgar returned from Philadelphia, we would once again be happy, mutually supportive, and ready to face life's challenges.

18    But the news Melissa brought me that morning shattered all those hopes. Edgar had overdosed on Valium and Librium, and had washed the pills down with a miniature bottle of Scotch

from his hotel room's minibar. I wanted to believe that his overdose was accidental, but Melissa told me her father had left three audio cassettes—one for her, one for me, and one for Tom Pileggi. The police had transcribed the tapes and there was no doubt: Edgar's death had been a suicide.

19     Even with that evidence, I still needed time to believe what I was hearing. And these days, as I travel around the country giving my lectures, I learn over and over again that disbelief is an almost universal initial reaction to bad news:

20     "When I heard the storm warnings before Hurricane Andrew hit," says a woman named Karen, who told her stories at one of my survival lectures, "I took the kids to my sister's place, away from the eye of the storm. I watched the news coverage on TV in Terri's living room and saw the houses on my street wash away. And still I couldn't believe it. I thought somehow my own home would be spared, or that I was just in the middle of a horrible dream."

21     It was only after the storm, when Karen went back to her old neighborhood and saw for herself that her home was gone, that the reality began to sink in.

22     "My home had been destroyed. There was simply nothing salvageable left. And yet I had to go back three times before I really believed it."

## Theme

1. Point to and summarize some differing ways in which Rivers tries to understand the causes of her husband's suicide.

2. Point to and summarize some ways other than a search for a cause in which Rivers responded to her husband's suicide. For example, how may the composition itself be seen as a kind of response?

## Technique

1. Explain how Rivers dramatizes and illustrates her sense of disbelief on hearing of her husband's suicide. Point to

some examples and explain why they are or are not effective for you.

2. Explain how the theme of disbelief organizes and structures the excerpt. Think of some ways in which the same facts might have been differently arranged. Explain the advantages and disadvantages of her methods and yours.

## Writing

Rivers says her husband originally believed that suicide was "a permanent solution to temporary problems." Write an essay in which you analyze and demonstrate how Rivers creates a sense of her husband as a man who had ceased to believe in his earlier credo.

# Sting

## The Mystery and Religion of Music    (1994)

*Born Gordon Matthew Sumner, the son of an English milkman,
Sting got his nickname from a black and gold rugby shirt that
made him look like a bee. His song "Every Breath You Take" is
the most requested song on radio of all time and still earns him
an average of $2000 a day. He gave the following speech to the
graduating seniors of Berklee College of Music in 1994.*

1   My earliest memory is also my earliest musical memory. I
remember sitting at my mother's feet as she played the piano.
She always played tangos for some reason—perhaps it was the
fashion at the time, I don't know. The piano was an upright
with worn brass pedals, and when my mother played one of
her tangos she seemed to become transported to another
world, her feet rocking arhythmically between the loud and
soft pedals, her arms pumping to the odd rhythms of the tango,
her eyes intent upon the sheet music in front of her. For my
mother, playing the piano was the only time that I wasn't the
center of her world, the only time she ignored me, so I knew
that something significant, some important ritual, was being
enacted here. I suppose I was being initiated into something,
initiated into some sort of mystery, the mystery of music.

2   And so I began to aspire to the piano and would spend
hours hammering away at atonal clusters in the delusion that,
if I persisted long enough, my noise would become music. I
still labor under this delusion. My mother cursed me with the
fine ear of a musician but the hands of a plumber.

3   The piano had to be sold to help us out of a financial hole,
and my career as an atonal serialist was mercifully stunted. It
wasn't until an uncle of mine emigrated to Canada, leaving
behind an old Spanish guitar with five rusty strings, that my

SOURCE: Used by permission of Steerpike Limited..

enormous and clumsy fingers found a musical home and I found what was to become my best friend. Where the piano had seemed incomprehensible, I was able to make music on the guitar almost instantaneously—melodies, chords, song structures fell at my fingertips. Somehow I could listen to a song on the radio and then make a passable attempt at playing it. It was a miracle. I spent hour after hour, day after day, month after month just playing, rejoicing in the miracle and probably driving my parents round the bend. But it was their fault in the first place.

4    Music is an addiction, a religion, and disease. There is no cure, no antidote. I was hooked. There was only one radio station in England at that time, the BBC, and you could hear the Beatles and the Rolling Stones side by side with bits of Mozart, Beethoven, Glenn Miller, and even the blues. This was my musical education; its eclecticism, supplemented by my parents' record collection of Rodgers and Hammerstein, Lerner and Loewe, Elvis Presley, Little Richard, and Jerry Lee Lewis. But it wasn't until the Beatles that I realized that perhaps I could make a living out of music. The Beatles came from the same working class background as I did. They were English, and Liverpool wasn't any fancier or more romantic than my own hometown. My guitar went from being the companion of my solitude to the means of my escape.

5    There's a lot that's been written about my life after that time, so that I can't remember what's true and what isn't. I had no formal musical education, but I suppose I became successful by a combination of dumb luck, low cunning, and risk-taking born of curiosity. I still operate in the same way, our curiosity in music is never entirely satisfied. There's always something more to learn.

6    Musicians aren't particularly good role models in society. We really don't have a very good reputation: philanderers, alcoholics, addicts, alimony jumpers, tax evaders. And I'm not just talking about rock musicians: Classical musicians have just as bad a reputation. And jazz musicians—forget it. But when you watch a musician play, when he enters that private musical world, you often see a child at play—innocent and curious, full of wonder at what can only be adequately described as a mystery, a sacred mystery even, something deep, something strange, both joyous and sad, something impossible to explain in words. I mean, what

could possibly keep us playing scales and arpeggios hour after hour, day after day, year after year? Is it some vague promise of glory, money, fame? Or is it something deeper? Our instruments connect us to this mystery, and a musician will maintain this sense of wonder 'til the day he or she dies.

7     I had the privilege of spending some time with the great arranger Gil Evans in the last year of his life. He was still listening, still open to new ideas, still open to the wonder of music, still a curious child.

8     We students of music have mastered the laws of harmony and the rules of counterpoint, the skills of arranging and orchestrating, of developing themes and rhythmic motifs. But do any of us really know what music is? Is it merely physics? Mathematics? The stuff of romance, or of commerce? Why is it so important to us? What is its essence? I can't even pretend to know.

9     I've written hundreds of songs, had them published, had them in the charts, won Grammys, and have enough written proof that I'm a bona fide, successful songwriter. Still, if somebody asks me how I write songs, I have to say I don't really know, I don't know where they come from. A melody is always a gift from somewhere else. You just have to learn to be grateful, and pray that you will be blessed again some other time. It's the same with the lyrics; you can't write a song without a metaphor. You can mechanically construct verses, choruses, bridges, middle eights, but without a central metaphor you ain't got nothing. I often wonder, where do melodies and metaphors come from? If you could buy them in a store, I'd be first in the queue. Believe me, I spend most of my time searching for these mysterious commodities, searching for inspiration.

10    Paradoxically, I'm coming to believe in the importance of silence in music, the power of silence after a phrase of music. For example, the dramatic silence after the first four notes of Beethoven's *Fifth Symphony,* or the space between the notes of a Miles Davis solo. There is something very specific about a rest in music. You take your foot off the pedal and pay attention. I'm wondering whether, as musicians, the most important thing we do is merely to provide a frame for silence. I'm wondering if silence itself is perhaps the mystery at the heart of music. And is silence the most perfect music of all?

11     Songwriting is the only form of meditation that I know, and it is only in silence that the gifts of melody and metaphor are offered. To people in the modern world, true silence is something we rarely experience. It is almost as if we conspire to avoid it. Three minutes of silence seems like a very long time: It forces us to pay attention to ideas and emotions that we rarely make any time for. There are some people who find this awkward, or even frightening. Silence is disturbing. It is disturbing because it is the wavelength of the soul. If we leave no space in our music, and I'm as guilty as anyone else in this regard, then we rob the sounds we make of a defining context. It is often music born from anxiety to create more anxiety. It's as if we're afraid of leaving space. Great music is as much about the space between the notes as it is about the notes themselves. A bar's rest is as important and significant as a bar of demisemiquavers that precedes it.

12     What I'm trying to say here is that if ever I'm asked if I'm religious, I always reply that, yes, I'm a devout musician. Music puts me in touch with something beyond the intellect, something otherworldly, something sacred. How is it that some music can move us to tears? Why is some music indescribably beautiful? I never tire of hearing Samuel Barber's "Adagio For Strings," or Faure's "Pavane," or Otis Redding's "Dock Of The Bay." These pieces speak to me in the only religious language I understand. They induce in me a state of deep meditation, of wonder, they make me silent.

13     It's very hard to talk about music in words. Words are superfluous to the abstract power of music. We can fashion words into poetry so that they are understood the way music is understood, but they only aspire to the condition where music already exists.

14     Music is probably the oldest religious rite. Our ancestors used melody and rhythm to co-opt the spirit world to their purposes, to try to make sense of the universe. The first priests were probably musicians, the first prayers probably songs.

15     What I'm getting round to saying is that as musicians, whether we're successful, playing to thousands of people every night, or not so successful, playing in bars or small clubs, or not successful at all, just playing alone in your apartment to the

cat, we are doing something that can heal souls, that can mend us when our spirits are broken. Whether you make a million dollars or not one cent, music and silence are priceless gifts. May you always possess them. May they always possess you.

## Theme

1. How does the narrative of the essay's first paragraph reflect the essay's title? For example, which images and thoughts reflect "mystery" and which images and thoughts reflect "religion" in his account of his mother's piano playing?

2. Find some examples from the rest of the essay in which the key title terms of "mystery" and "religion" are given expression as aspects of music.

## Technique

1. In paragraph four Sting writes: "Music is an addiction, a religion, and disease." Used as metaphors and linked with religion here, "addiction" and "disease" are words that have generally negative connotations. Yet surely some of the particular connotations of the different terms combine to express further what music means to the author. For example, addictions can mysteriously dominate our relations with the world in spite of the objections of our reasoning faculties, just as religion can. What other metaphoric implications of the apparently negative terms make them seem apt for his purpose?

2. At the end of his essay, how does Sting implicitly define the meaning of the term "successful"? In what ways does he use the word "priceless" to express his view that music transcends success?

## Writing

Write an essay analyzing the ways in which this world-famous performer creates a sense of personal modesty through the language he uses to address an audience of college seniors.

# EXERCISES

## Intertextual Questions

1. Sissy Spacek proudly claims that she is "homemade." Sammy Sosa says he learned great things from his less comfortable upbringing. Discuss the ways these different authors feel about what exactly each has gained from his or her origins. Point to examples from their writing to support your analyses.

2. Wherever you come from, being made fun of is usually part of everyone's life. Compare and contrast the differing ways in which Joe Piscopo and Margaret Cho deal with mockery. What kind of response does the manner of each writer serve as an answer to real or would-be mockers? That is, neither writes in an angry tone of voice, though anger would be an understandable response. Nor does either try to reason with an opponent. Characterize the tones of voice the writers do employ and discuss how their writing styles serve as important means of expression in themselves.

3. Whoopi Goldberg says that the religious meaning of Christmas was not the most important part of that holiday's meaning for her as a child, though clearly her feelings ran very deep. Sting, on the other hand, uses a religious vocabulary to express how important music has been to him, though music is not in any literal sense a religion. Discuss the ways these and other writers in the chapter manage to find vocabularies to express how important and deeply felt the experiences they describe have been. What kinds of words do they depend on? Are their most important words used in literal or figurative senses?

4. Tom Cruise and Joan Rivers both tell us how they moved on from major turning points in their lives, but both writers also make their suffering clear to us. How else do the writers seem similar to you in the way they deal with their subjects? How are they different in their approaches? Discuss some examples from each essay.

5. Which of the writers represented here evoked most strongly for you memories of your own origins or turning points in your

own life? Discuss with examples how and why the brief written account was effective in creating responses in you as a reader.

## Suggestions for Writing

1. Write a short sketch about your own origins. Pick a topic from your past that you feel as strongly about as Whoopi Goldberg does about Christmas. While you might use her essay as a model, you might also find several others useful for nostalgic stimulus and technical examples useful in representing your past through language.

2. Write a short sketch of a major turning point in your own life. Pick something that affected you as strongly as Sting's early experiences of music affected him. Again, you may find the essays from the chapter both stimulating for memory and helpful for the written expression of memory.

3. In your view, which of the writers handles unhappy topics best? Write an essay in which you analyze what you admire about the author both as a person and as a writer. In your writing be sure to give examples of what you admire and to explain how and why the examples work well for you.

4. In your view, which of the writers describes the joys of the past most skillfully? Write an essay defining and defending the reasons for your choice.

5. Which of the essays seemed least successful to you as writing? Write an essay in which you define your terms of critical judgment and demonstrate their appropriateness through the analysis of evidence from the text you chose.

# CHAPTER 2

# BECOMING AND OVERCOMING

The themes of the essays in this chapter build on the themes of Chapter 1, but now the subjects move beyond specific points of origin and specific turning points. The focus here is on self-creation and on overcoming the obstacles to self-creation—finding both a conception of identity and a language to express that conception. Yet several of the essays that follow show many different pressures both inside and outside the self that may oppose the achievement of those goals. The obstacles to be overcome include some unfortunate psychological habits as well as the competing viewpoints of others that inevitably surround any individual.

In the first two essays, Queen Latifah in a serious way and Bill Murray in his characteristically more humorous manner describe exploring and cultivating individual styles of living through performance. "Being a Queen" explains how a self-created regal style can help to overcome self-doubt by forming a persona that implies complete self-confidence, whereas Bill Murray recalls his real-life experiences involving a caddyshack only slightly less off-beat than those in his famous movie of that name. The comic art of his performances both in golf and in acting show how an indirect approach may often turn out to be the shortest path to success.

Cancer makes the very serious subject of the next two essays. Fran Drescher uses her surgeon's words for her title, "Now I'm Concerned." Her physician had just found out that Drescher's uterine cancer was much more advanced than the initial tests had suggested. The author goes on to tell us what her own concern was like at this crucial stage of her life.

Lance Armstrong had already become a success as a world champion cyclist when, at the age of 25, cancer threatened to end not only his career but his life. Fortunately, like Fran Drescher, he was able to overcome his disease, but the elimination of that threat did not end his crisis. Rather, his physical victory led to a serious psychological defeat, one that needed to be overcome before he could go on to reachieve the self he had all but lost.

Toni Morrison addresses other kinds of psychological obstacles in a meditation on a traditional fairytale that she calls "Cinderella's Step-Sisters." Originally presented as a graduation address at Barnard College, the women's division of Columbia University, this essay by a leading African-American novelist analyzes some of the threats to a woman's self-creation that may come from other women.

Arnold Schwarzenegger has led something of a fairytale life himself. Beginning with his success as a bodybuilder, he has followed a career path that has led through many movies to the steps of the California governor's mansion. As he explains in this excerpt from his book on weightlifting, proper training is as much about finding a successful psychological style as it is about building greater physical strength and endurance, and once again we learn how becoming involves overcoming.

If training for effective performance in athletics requires the cultivation of a proper approach to the tasks involved, so does the training involved in performing the social interactions through which we create our relations to other people. Nowadays books of etiquette are often considered merely funny or relics of an older era by young people, but the professional humorist P.J. O'Rourke tells us that as a child he took one such book very seriously. In Emily Post's *Etiquette*, he found an imagined a world of thoughtful consideration, tact, and kindness that seemed completely different from the real world he inhabited at the time—a real world that was not at all a laughing matter.

In the next essay Melissa Etheridge tells us of her struggle to express her own artistic style in the record production world, where the collective nature of the enterprise can sometimes get in the way of the individual artist. Etheridge discovered that self-expression in her music was not fully achieved by the initial recording of her first album, and she also learned that finding the right producers and engineers turned out to be just as important as finding the right songs. Melissa Etheridge finally did take charge of becoming herself in her album, but she needed some prodding from friends before she did so.

Putting off doing what one knows one should do is called pro-crastination, and that word makes the title of the last essay in the chapter by Dr. Joyce Brothers. For decades she has presented psychological advice through many channels of American mass media, but here she confesses that, like millions of students, she herself has a problem, with the p-word. In sharing her own solution to that problem she shows once again how the two processes of becoming and overcoming may be intrinsically linked in the process of forming an individual identity.

# Queen Latifah

## Being a Queen                                    (1999)

> *Born Dana Owens, the future Queen Latifah saw many sides of*
> *life very early. Growing up in New Jersey with two policemen*
> *brothers, she broke into hip-hop at 18 and also attended Rutgers*
> *University. Still known as a singer and rap artist, her career as a*
> *movie star flourished with her role in* Chicago *(2002) and then*
> *in* Bringing Down the House *(2003), where she taught her co-*
> *star Steve Martin (Chapter 4) the necessary hip-hop slang.*

1    When I came out of the water, I was exhilarated. Until I realized that I was trapped. The stairs leading back to the restaurant were on the other side of where I had landed, and the only way to get there was to swim across, climb up the rocks again, and dive from the other side. This time, I was ready to do it. There were a couple of people up there, and we all held hands and jumped together.

2    I had conquered the fear, which was what I had set out to do in the first place.

3    I'm afraid all the time. I'm afraid of being alone. I'm afraid of commitment. I'm afraid of failure. I'm afraid of becoming someone I'm not in the music business. I'm afraid of not having a child before I get too old. But none of these fears rules my life. Fear is a breeding ground for fear. If you don't control it, it will control you. One of the books that has influenced me the most is *Feel the Fear and Do It Anyway* by Dr. Susan Jeffers. She says we have the power to create anything and that there are aspects of our lives we cannot control. But we *can* control how we handle them. If I wake up and it's dark and gloomy outside, do I lie there and complain about how nasty the day is? Or do I say, "Hey, I'm going to go out and have a

SOURCE: pp. 7–12 from *Ladies First* by Queen Latifah and Karen Hunter. Copyright © 1999 by Queen Latifah, Inc. Reprinted by permission of HarperCollins Publishers, Inc. William Morrow.

good time today"? We can control an enormous amount: our attitude, perspective, actions—and we must control them. It may seem like common sense, but think about how often we allow outside influences to dampen our attitude and mess with our perspective.

4    We've all done things we know we shouldn't have, simply because we chose not to think about them or because we ignored an inner voice—perhaps it was *easier* to be passive than to control our actions. I am not afraid to hear the truth and hold myself accountable to that truth. I am never afraid of pushing myself to be my best.

5    But how do fear, pride, and determination make Dana Owens a queen, you ask? And what right does *anyone* have to call herself a queen without sounding like one helluvan arrogant sista? Well, first of all, each of us has a queen inside. She was placed there before we were even formed, in the womb. It's just a matter of bringing her out. Being a woman puts you halfway there. But there's so much more. It starts inside by feeling good about yourself. A queen has high self-esteem. She is proud of who she is, whether she is a corporate executive or a cleaning lady, whether she's an athlete or a housewife.

6    She knows right from wrong and strives to do her best. She doesn't player-hate, or try to put other women down. Women have a tendency to be catty or jealous of what other women are doing or have. They will sleep with another woman's man "just because." They will have a nasty attitude toward another woman and say things like "She thinks she's cute!" Well, that ain't cute. A real queen is so focused on keeping herself tight that she doesn't have time to be worried about the next one. A real queen is so intent on raising herself up that she can be proud of what her sisters are doing, because she's okay with herself and with God.

7    Queenliness is an attitude that starts on the inside and works its way out. The way you hold your head up makes you a queen. It says something about how you feel about yourself. If you walk around with your head down, you have a tendency to feel down. You are telling the world that you lack confidence, and that can signal to people that you are a target, that you will let stuff by you. It's a simple body language that exposes what you truly feel inside. If you're feeling down, you tend to look

down. You'd be amazed at how changing your body language, lifting your head up, can give you a whole new perspective on life. You start to see things much differently, and it will begin to affect how you feel. It has to. You're no longer staring at the ground, at your problems, and not feeling good about yourself.

8    It's harder to feel bad with your head held high.

9    A queen, a woman with self-esteem, handles adversity with grace. Even when her world is crumbling around her, she never lets her crown fall. Life will put you through plenty of tests and throw many obstacles your way, but it's how you pass those tests, how you overcome those obstacles, that distinguishes you as a queen.

10    Think of Jacqueline Kennedy Onassis. Remember those pictures of her at President Kennedy's funeral, holding the little hands of Caroline and John-John? Just days before, she had witnessed the assassination of her children's father, her husband. She could not have felt anything but a pain too immense to put into words. Yet there she was, giving strength to the entire country. She had a pride and a will to represent something higher than herself. She was making a statement for others. She was a champion. And in many ways, she was the closest thing this country has ever had to a queen. She is remembered not for her extreme wealth and jewels, nor for her exquisite taste—although that was very much a part of who she was—but for her grace in the face of adversity, for her generosity and charity. And for always holding her head up high.

11    Another woman who held her head up high for the nation was, of course, Dr. Betty Shabazz. She is also a queen. As the wife of Malcolm X, she stood by a man whom many believed to be a negative force in this country. His was not a popular stance. But she was there for him. She was there when their home was firebombed. And she was in the front row at the Audubon Ballroom in Harlem when he was gunned down. She used her body to shield her four little girls, while pregnant with twins.

12    After her husband's tragic death, she carried on. She got her master's and doctorate and raised six girls alone. She never let anything stop her from becoming the woman she was born to be—a true American inspiration. Even after her death—in a fire set by her grandson in 1997—she remains a figure of dignity, honor, and royalty.

13    A queen never sells out. She will sacrifice quick money and material goods for the greater purpose of keeping her soul. She may take three jobs to take care of her two kids when Daddy's money ain't coming through, and she doesn't complain.

14    That was my mother, Rita Owens. She laid the foundation for me to become a self-proclaimed queen. She made the ground fertile for me to persevere, no matter what the obstacles, and to keep my head up. My mother always told me how smart, beautiful, and talented I was. In her mind, there was nothing I couldn't do. When I wanted to learn the drums and guitar, she paid for lessons. When I entered talent shows, she sat in the front row. When I played basketball, she was there, cheering the loudest. And when I got into trouble and started running the streets, she talked with me, and she prayed for me. She never limited me. My mother believed in me before I even believed in myself. And because of that, no one can shake my confidence now.

15    I know there are many, many young women who don't have a solid picture of what a queen is because there isn't one in their lives. But even if you don't know a strong mother—or a grandmother, a tough aunt, a straight-talking teacher, or an encouraging neighbor who can be your champion—you can still be a queen.

16    It starts with you. You have to want to be a queen. You have to want it for yourself. You have to know yourself.

17    I know who I am. I am confident. I know God. I can take care of myself. I share my life with others, and I love—I am worthy of the title Queen.

18    So are you.

## Theme

1. The essay begins with an account of overcoming fear quickly followed by the statement: "I'm afraid all the time." Summarize the ways in which being a queen helps Queen Latifah to overcome her fears.

2. According to the author, what qualities does a queen possess besides the ability to overcome fear?

## Technique

1. Paragraph four begins with questions. Explain how this technique helps to organize what precedes the questions as well as what follows them.

2. The author mentions other women in the course of her essay. How do they serve to support and further her argument? What would the argument lose if those women were eliminated?

## Writing

Do you think Queen Latifah successfully answers the questions she raises in paragraph four? Write an essay in which you defend your position.

# Bill Murray

## Caddy Shot    (1999)

*Bill Murray was the fifth of nine children, many of whom also worked as caddies. After dropping out of college where he studied pre-med, he got his start in comedy on* The National Lampoon Radio Hour *where he met Dan Akroyd (Chapter 3) and John Belushi, who brought him in to join the cast of* Saturday Night Live *in its second season.*

1    Often, after I've sought out a more pastoral, more private route from tee to green, my communion will be interrupted. That spooky pro partner of mine, Scott Simpson, that big lovable lug—thrifty, brave, clean, and reverent—is also a great tracker. When I ask how he finds me, he smiles and says, "I follow your spoor. Whatcha got, partner?"

2    "It's a caddy shot," I say, and he knows what I mean. Pros don't go to these spots on the course without a fiancée. The shot, if you can call it that, is so ridiculous as to be invented by a cruel challenger. But this is how we passed time in the caddy yard of my youth. I've been here in my mind's eye before and have little doubt I will again.

3    A caddy shot was a golf shot learned in the caddy yard. The yard was outside the caddyshack and hit the recreational trifecta by serving as football field and basketball court, too. And when we were still too young to do so inside the caddyshack, we learned to curse, smoke, and play cards for money in the bushes behind the ninth green. The rest of the time, we made a living.

4    My dough was going toward my education. I caddied to make enough money to pay my tuition to Loyola Academy, a

Jesuit high school. This was a tradition among the hardwork-ing Murray boys—a tradition that did not include Andy and John, who were gifted and lazy and attended public school with the heathens. It was those two who kept caddying from becoming the family business.

5   If you worked all summer, you'd make your tuition, and have a little money left over. That money would be gone by Thanksgiving. You'd then be broke until springtime, but your time was free and the sense that you had spent all summer working your way through school would be a memory.

6   It was quite an achievement to pay your way through school, and it felt great to tell the folks you had. But amassing the sum was slower than watching a cut heal. Three dollars and fifty cents per bag. Seven for doubles. Twenty-five cents if you were rained upon. Tipping was not permitted. I could not wait to get rich and start breaking that rule. Once I hit thirteen, I carried dou-bles. Before that, singles. Before that I was a shag boy.

7   Here's the shag boy premise: Empty a bag of golf balls onto the practice tee, turn, and run for your life. Anxious-to-improve hackers would start their slashing when you were still thirty yards away with your back turned. They were usually new members who couldn't get a game until they reached the level of simply terrible. You tried to make a game of fielding them like a baseball outfielder. But baseball has three outfielders, doesn't it?

8   That stuff I didn't much like.

9   My brothers sort of paved the way. So by the time I got there, Ed (five years older) was already in the pro shop (he always wanted more) and Brian (four years) was the shoe guy.

10   Back then, we'd play matches using odd, old clubs, first pick getting a twenty-year-old niblick, fourth pick a Bobby Jones mashie. Eighteen-hole matches, the course charted by the win-ner of the previous hole. Behind bushes, around trees, over the caddyshack. The creative process, along with appropriate gamesmanship, taught you that you were never out of a hole. You could rally from anywhere, and a stymied shot was never daunting. It was dare-to-be-great golf....

11   Lou Janis was the caddy master. You had to get there by six-thirty to get a good loop. Louie didn't get there until seven, but

if you were there waiting … He drove a Ford Falcon, although I don't think that was the car he saw himself driving. Always immaculately dressed—not in great clothes but very neat—the prince of polyester. He was just trying to beat it somehow, trying to get an edge. Louie was a gambler. He'd bet on anything—whether a member on the putting green would sink one or two of his three three-footer warm-up putts, whether or not a guy would pick up his tee after his opening drive, just about anything.

12    Louie had a scam he moved with the caddies, too. If you didn't go out, you had no money, but you still got hungry, so Louie let you charge against what you might make. He had everyone's charges up on the wall, and you'd pay them off after you got back in. Ed would go out twice but bring home only $12.80 because he bought something to eat. That was okay, but one day Brian came home with only $2.50. So at dinner the whole family grilled him.

13    "I had a hot dog and a Coke—that's eighty-five cents."

14    "And then what?"

15    "And then I had an ice cream sandwich."

16    "That's fifteen cents. You're still missing $4.50 …"

17    He was really sweating. In the end, it became known that Brian was smoking cigarettes, had bought some, and was trying to lie about it. He was about fifteen at the time.

18    B caddies would loop for Louie on Mondays—really so he had someone to take his bag when he wanted to play—so he could point out mistakes you made that were keeping you from seniority. Once you were a made man, you caddied for him when he played with his friends. All the area caddy masters played $5 skins with "umbrellas," a combo game with a point for prox, a point for low ball, and a point for low two-man team total. With birdies, everything doubled. I looped for him a few times—also helped him pick college football teams. Back then he knew me as "New Murray."

19    So these days, when the chips are down and my ball's in trouble and my opponent is tittering, I think back to the caddy yard of my youth. I actually relax when I see a so-difficult shot that requires Shakti visualization. I prefer it. To me, the scariest words in all of golf are, "It's a straight putt."

## Theme

1. The essay begins and ends with "the caddy shot." List the other themes that Bill Murray explores in between.

2. Point to the moments in the essay where the reader's knowledge of golf is taken for granted. What, for example, do you suppose the author means in the first paragraph by a "more private route from tee to green?" If you don't know golf, can you still understand what he means?

## Technique

1. In what ways does "the caddy shot" stand for more in the essay than a way of making a golf stroke? How does it make a representative anecdote for the entire phase of Murray's youth recalled here?

2. Explain how Murray uses details to create a sense of personality in Lou Janis, the Caddy Master. Point to some examples and explain how they work.

## Writing

Pick an oddly acquired skill of your own that stands for something larger in your past. Using Murray's essay as a model, write about this phase of your life.

# Fran Drescher

## "Now I'm Concerned" (2000)

> *Fran Drescher was born in Flushing, Queens, New York where she attended high school with Ray Romano. After her first movie break in* Saturday Night Fever, *she continued to fill minor roles until she came up with and developed the idea for* The Nanny *in which she starred. More recently she has appeared on a new television show of her own.*
>
> *The essay reprinted below comes from* Cancer, Schmancer, *the book she wrote about being a cancer survivor, and tells how she came to her first knowledge of the true seriousness of her disease.*

1   Over the weekend I worked with John writing our MTV pilot. I remember awakening during the night in one of my scared moments of tears and whispers, begging him to finish the script with me. "Who knows what's going to happen? This may be our last chance to complete it." I wanted to see his idea become a teleplay. I hated the idea that I might be leaving this earth with an unfinished piece of work. So with the weight of an uncertain future resting squarely on my shoulders, we pulled out the laptop and attempted to write a comedy. And I'm grateful we did, because it was fun to return to our make-believe world. I thought it romantic, the notion we were creating a place no one else knew about but us. It was an escape from reality I welcomed.

2   I also prepared the guest house for my parents' arrival, and continued to hike as well. When Monday rolled around, John left for work and I geared my day around the barium I was to drink that afternoon in preparation for the colonoscopy on Tuesday. My dad had had one recently and said it was nothing. I thought it strange that everything I was getting, my mom

or dad had also recently gotten. They were able to share their experiences with me, guiding me with firsthand knowledge. It was like I was a child again, a big 140-pound baby—something I hadn't allowed myself to be in a long time.

3      Rachel and her husband, Greg, made plans to come out to the beach and have lunch with me before I had to take the barium drink. After that, I'd only be able to have liquids or Jell-O until I came through the surgery on Wednesday. It was a beautiful day, the sun was glistening on the ocean, and I made a reservation at Geoffrey's, a restaurant on a cliff overlooking the Pacific. I always feel like I'm in Hawaii when I go there, and I thought Rachel and Greg would enjoy dining alfresco by the sea.

4      We talked about poor Nancy Marchand dying of lung cancer. Not too morbid while having a little lunch. How wonderful for her she got to play such a great part on such a landmark television series as *The Sopranos* all the way up to the end. I saw her perform off-Broadway in *The Cocktail Hour*, and always loved her after that.

5      I was glad I'd done *The Nanny*. It made me feel successful in my career goals. What would be my next part? *Would* there be a next part? I ordered the fish, grilled crispy over spinach and whipped potatoes. Usually I like pasta, but this sounded good. Greg and I had wine; Rachel never drinks. We raised our glasses and toasted to it all going well, and all being over on Wednesday.

6      As we all got back in my car and headed home, I called for my messages on the cell phone. The nurse had left a message saying that the surgeon had more information from the most recent biopsy (the one my sister had insisted on) and would like me to stop by her office before going in for my colonoscopy tomorrow. That's as much as I heard before the phone went dead and I was stuck in a cellular void of no reception for the rest of the way home. Now, it couldn't have been more than ten minutes, tops, but I felt my entire piece of salmon get stuck in my chest as I frantically kept trying to get a signal so I could connect with the nurse.

7      When Greg, Rachel, and I arrived at the house, Angelica and Ramon were still there. "Fran, how many minutes can

you record on your video camera?" Ramon asked as I entered the kitchen.

8      "I don't know, forty?" I guessed as I dialed the nurse on my hard line. Ramon and his timing, always with the obtuse questions. It's part of his charm, I guess.

9      Rachel tried to ground the situation with simple logic: "Whatever it is, we'll just deal with it, that's all."

10    I remembered I had to take the barium drink. Greg, otherwise known as "the bartender from hell," prepared it. When I got through to the nurse, she simply repeated the message she'd already left, but I dug in my heels and said, "I'm sorry, but there's no way I will be able to wait until tomorrow to find out what this new information is!" She explained that Doctor #9 was in surgery all day.

11    "I don't care!" I answered, with panic in my voice. "Can't she call me on her way from one operation to the other?" It seemed unfathomable to wait. I mean, how torturous. She said the doctor would be coming out in a few minutes and she'd try to get her to call then.

12    Rachel said, "We'll wait with you."

13    "Are you sure? I mean, I know you probably should be getting back to the kids," I said, feeling like a burdensome pain.

14    "Don't be ridiculous, the kids are fine. We're not leaving," she insisted. Once again, I was learning something valuable: When those around you offer to help carry the load, take it for the life-saver it is and simply say *thank you*. So we all went into my bedroom and played with Chester. That dog was so intelligent and plugged in to me, he sensed right away something was wrong and anxiously awaited the surgeon's call along with the rest of us.

15    Well, just as I was massaging Chester's little old bones (he was now eighteen years old) and listening to Rachel tell a story, the phone rang. We all froze. Rachel stopped talking, Angelica stopped folding laundry, and I grabbed the receiver. It was Doctor #9.

1      I picked up my notepaper and pen from the side of the bed as Rachel and Greg held their breath. There was no small talk, no pussyfooting around, no soft-pedaling. She came right out

and said, "I'm glad we listened to your sister because the second biopsy shows a more advanced cancer than the first."

16    "What do you mean, 'more advanced'?" I said. I looked up
at Rachel, who was hanging on every word.

17    She explained that a more extensive scraping of the uterine
tissue indicated not only cells that were grades of one and two,
but also threes and fours.

18    My head was whirling. Thank God for Nadine. The request
she made for a second biopsy might have seemed like overkill
at the time, but proved to be one of the single greatest pieces
of advice I'd received from a medical professional throughout
this whole unfortunate mess. How could this be happening?
"What does that mean exactly?" I asked, always trying to understand and write down everything she said.

19    "Well, before, it appeared to be what I think of as a baby
cancer, where the cells are just beginning to turn, but to now
find cells that are grades three and four—I gotta be honest with
you, Fran, now I'm concerned."

20    I'll never forget those three words: *now I'm concerned.* A
malignant tumor can have cells in it varying in grades from one
through four (four being the worst). Which grade of cells dom-
inates determines what grade the tumor is. If it's a grade-four
tumor, suffice it to say, you're in pretty bad shape.

21    "I'm going to want to do a radical hysterectomy. That means
you'll have to lose your ovaries and I won't be able to perform
the surgery laparoscopically or vaginally; we'll have to cut into
the abdomen."

22    Rachel held my hand. She knew from the look on my face
I was devastated. I don't know what made me think of this
right then—maybe it had been in the back of my head all
along—but I said, "I want to freeze my ovaries just in case
they're disease-free. Maybe I could harvest the eggs someday."
And then I added, "I'm going to want a plastic surgeon to sew
me up, too."

23    She still thought surgery would essentially cure me, since
uterine cancer is pretty noninvasive and slow growing. In that
respect I was lucky. Even though as a young, thin woman I
was atypical for uterine cancer (it mostly affects post-
menopausal or obese women), out of all the gynecological

cancers I could have gotten, this was the best—"best" meaning least likely to spread if caught early. There I was, *finally* too young and thin for something, and I get it anyway.

24    "But," she explained, "with all cancers, we never know what stage it's at until the surrounding tissue and lymph nodes are removed and biopsied. How deep and how far-reaching the cancer has gone will determine what stage of the disease you have."

25    Meanwhile, I'd read somewhere that uterine cancer was the only gynecological cancer with a mortality rate that was on the rise, in part due to late diagnosis. So there you are.

26    I hung up the phone and wept in Rachel's arms. "I think it's better they take everything anyway," Rachel said. That's what we call being Talmudic about life. "What do you need it for? Get it all out and be done with it, be clean of it."

27    I called my mom again, who was busy getting ready for their flight to L.A. on Tuesday, and told her this unexpected plot twist. She was in full agreement with Rachel. "Get it the hell outta ya," were her exact words. She'd never felt comfortable with the surgeon's doing a partial hysterectomy anyway. The radical seemed more thorough, more efficient. Let's hope so, anyway, because that's what I was getting. Thanks to my sister, we were all better prepared. Not only was the surgeon better able to judge the type of surgery I needed, but I'd now go under the knife knowing exactly what to expect.

28    I reached Elaine on her cell phone at a charity event. "Oh Elaine," I wept. "They got the results back from the biopsy and it's much more advanced than the surgeon thought. I think it's time we tell Peter." Up until this point I really hadn't wanted to worry him. He was so far away, and had gone through so much already, not only with the divorce but with having lost both his parents to cancer years before. I'd been thinking I'd write him a letter after it was all done, but things had changed. The situation seemed graver, and I worried that the news might leak to the press. I didn't want him to find out that way, so I asked Elaine, as one of our oldest friends and faithful manager, to please tell him.

29    From her charity event, in the hotel parking lot in an evening gown, she called Peter on her cell phone. He began to cry immediately, she later told me. All the anger melted

away and what was left, all that was left, was the love. He told
her to tell me that he knew about John and understood, but if
I needed him, he'd jump on the next flight out and be by my
side through it all. When Elaine called me back and relayed his
message, I cried like a baby. It was the sweetest expression of
love we'd shared in years, one of many silver linings to come.

30     When the phone rang again, it was John returning my 911
page for the second time in less than a week. With fear in his
voice he said, "Are you okay? What's the matter?" I told him the
cancer was worse and the surgery would be more radical. He
said he'd leave work immediately. He was never to return to
the job again.

31     As for me, I felt sick to my stomach, and ran to the bathroom. The barium had kicked in....

## Theme

1. In this portion of her story, Fran Drescher finds herself in
the middle of a series of medical tests. Point to some examples in which the tests themselves—rather than their possible results—seem to be her greatest concern.

2. The second biopsy changes the emotional level in her life
and in her writing. Point to some examples that demonstrate
her greater anxiety about the results of the tests she has
undergone.

## Technique

1. The essay makes a chapter in Drescher's book, *Cancer,
Schmancer,* and of course the earlier chapters have already
made clear the identities of many people mentioned here
without explanation. For example, "Peter" is her former husband and "John" is her current partner. Yet even a reader
without that context can often tell who is most important to
Drescher and how. Point to some examples where she
makes implicit distinctions about the relative importance to
her of the people she mentions.

2. Drescher often treats events both seriously and comically at the same time. Pick an example and explain how she creates both narrative attitudes through her writing.

## Writing

Write an essay that analyzes some of the many ways Drescher creates a sense of personal anxiety in her story.

# Lance Armstrong

## Back in the Saddle                                          (2004)

> *At the time of this note's composition, Lance Armstrong was a
> five-time winner of the Tour de France. The fight with cancer
> described in the essay that follows began after an earlier victory
> in 1996 when he was just four months shy of his 25ᵗʰ birthday
> and recently ranked number one cyclist in the world.*

1   I become a happier man each time I suffer.

2   Suffering is as essential to a good life, and as inextricable,
as bliss. The old saying that you should live each day as if it's
your last is a nice sentiment, but it doesn't work. Take it from
me. I tried it once, and here's what I learned: If I pursued only
happiness, and lived just for the moment, I'd be a no-account
with a perpetual three-day growth on my chin. Cancer taught
me that.

3   Before cancer, whatever I imagined happiness to be, pretty
soon I wore it out, took it for granted, or threw it away. A port-
folio, a Porsche, a coffee machine—these things were important to me. So was my hair. Then I lost them, including the hair.
When I was 25, I was diagnosed with advanced testicular cancer, which had metastasized into my lungs and brain. I sold the
car, gave up my career as a world-class cyclist, lost a good deal
of money, and barely hung on to my life.

4   When I went into remission, I thought happiness would
mean being self-indulgent. Not knowing how much time I had
left, I did not intend to ever suffer again. I had suffered months
of fear, chemotherapy so strong it left burn marks under my
skin, and surgery to remove two tumors. Happiness to me then
was waking up.

Source: Reprinted by Permission of *Forbes ASAP* Magazine © 2004 Forbes Inc.

5    I ate Mexican food, played golf, and lay on the couch. The pursuit of happiness meant going to my favorite restaurant and pursuing a plate of enchiladas with tomatillo sauce.

6    But one day my wife, Kristin, put down her fork and said, "You need to decide something: Are you going to be a golf-playing, beer-drinking, Mexican-food-eating slob for the rest of your life? If you are, I'll still love you. But I need to know, because if so, I'll go get a job. I'm not going to sit at home while you play golf."

7    I stared at her.

8    "I'm so bored," she said.

9    Suddenly, I understood that I was bored, too. The idleness was forced; I was purposeless, with nothing to pursue. That conversation changed everything. I realized that responsibility, the routines and habits of shaving in the morning with a purpose, a job to do, a wife to love, and a child to raise—these were the things that tied my days together and gave them a pattern deserving of the term living.

10    Within days I was back on my bicycle. For the first time in my life, I rode with real strength and stamina and purpose. Without cancer, I never would have won a single Tour de France. Cancer taught me a plan for more purposeful living, and that in turn taught me how to train and to win more purposefully. It taught me that pain has a reason, and that sometimes the experience of losing things—whether health or a car or an old sense of self—has its own value in the scheme of life. Pain and loss are great enhancers.

11    People ask me why I ride my bike for six hours a day; what is the pleasure? The answer is that I don't do it for the pleasure. I do it for the pain. In my most painful moments on the bike, I am at my most self-aware and self-defining. There is a point in every race when a rider encounters the real opponent and realizes that it's … himself. You might say pain is my chosen way of exploring the human heart.

12    That pain is temporary. It may last a minute, or an hour, or a day, or a year, but eventually it subsides. And when it does, something else takes its place, and that thing might be called a greater space for happiness. We have unrealized capacities

that only emerge in crisis—capacities for enduring, for living, for hoping, for caring, for enjoying. Each time we overcome pain, I believe that we grow.

13      Cancer was the making of me: Through it I became a more compassionate, complete, and intelligent man, and therefore a more alive one. So that's why I ride, and why I ride hard. Because it makes me hurt, and so it makes me happy.

## Theme

1. Lance Armstrong's story has a beginning, a middle, and an end. In one sentence do your best to summarize that story.

2. Explain how and why boredom paradoxically became an energizing factor in Lance Armstrong's life.

## Technique

1. Armstrong's title has both a literal meaning and a figurative, proverbial meaning. In your own words explain how each meaning of the title ties into the story it introduces.

2. The essay begins and ends with sentences that express paradox. Count the number of paradoxical sentences in the essay as a whole. Do you think Armstrong successfully resolves all his paradoxes? Explain your answer.

## Writing

Paradoxes appear frequently in the text. Write an essay in which you analyze the ways in which paradox organizes and energizes Armstrong's account of his life after cancer.

# Toni Morrison

## Cinderella's Stepsisters                                           (1979)

*Toni Morrison began her career as an editor in the publishing industry, but in 1970 went around to the other side of the desk as an author of the best selling novel,* The Bluest Eye. *She went on to win the National Book Award in 1977 for* Song of Solomon *and the Pulitzer Prize for* Beloved *in 1992. The movie production of that novel is described in Chapter 6 by Oprah Winfrey. The following is a commencement address the author gave at Barnard College of Columbia University in New York City.*

1      $\mathbf{L}$et me begin by taking you back a little. Back before the days at college. To nursery school, probably, to a once-upon-a-time time when you first heard, or read, or, I suspect, even saw "Cinderella." Because it is Cinderella that I want to talk about; because it is Cinderella who causes me a feeling of urgency. What is unsettling about that fairy tale is that it is essentially the story of a household—a world, if you please—of women gathered together and held together in order to abuse another woman. There is, of course, a rather vague absent father and a nick-of-time prince with a foot fetish. But neither has much personality. And there are the surrogate "mothers," of course (god- and step-), who contribute both to Cinderella's grief and to her release and happiness. But it is her stepsisters who interest me. How crippling it must have been for those young girls to grow up with a mother, to watch and imitate that mother, enslaving another girl.

2      I am curious about their fortunes after the story ends. For contrary to recent adaptations, the stepsisters were not ugly, clumsy, stupid girls with outsized feet. The Grimm collection describes them as "beautiful and fair in appearance." When we are introduced to them they are beautiful, elegant, women of status, and

clearly women of power. Having watched and participated in the violent dominion of another woman, will they be any less cruel when it comes their turn to enslave other children, or even when they are required to take care of their own mother?

3   It is not a wholly medieval problem. It is quite a contemporary one: feminine power when directed at other women has historically been wielded in what has been described as a "masculine" manner. Soon you will be in a position to do the very same thing. Whatever your background—rich or poor—whatever the history of education in your family—five generations or one—you have taken advantage of what has been available to you at Barnard and you will therefore have both the economic and social status of the stepsisters *and* you will have their power.

4   I want not to *ask* you but to *tell* you not to participate in the oppression of your sisters. Mothers who abuse their children are women, and another woman, not an agency, has to be willing to stay their hands. Mothers who set fire to school buses are women, and another woman, not an agency, has to tell them to stay their hands. Women who stop the promotion of other women in careers are women, and another woman must come to the victim's aid. Social and welfare workers who humiliate their clients may be women, and other women colleagues have to deflect their anger.

5   I am alarmed by the violence that women do to each other: professional violence, competitive violence, emotional violence. I am alarmed by the willingness of women to enslave other women. I am alarmed by a growing absence of decency on the killing floor of professional women's worlds. You are the women who will take your place in the world where *you* can decide who shall flourish and who shall wither; you will make distinctions between the deserving poor and the undeserving poor; where you can yourself determine which life is expendable and which is indispensable. Since you will have the power to do it, you may also be persuaded that you have the right to do it. As educated women the distinction between the two is first-order business.

6   I am suggesting that we pay as much attention to our nurturing sensibilities as to our ambition. You are moving

in the direction of freedom and the function of freedom is
to free somebody else. You are moving toward self-fulfillment,
and the consequences of that fulfillment should be to discover
that there is something just as important as you are and
that just-as-important thing may be Cinderella—or your
stepsister.

7     In your rainbow journey toward the realization of personal
goals, don't make choices based only on your security and
your safety. Nothing is safe. That is not to say that anything
ever was, or that anything worth achieving ever should be.
Things of value seldom are. It is not safe to have a child. It is
not safe to challenge the status quo. It is not safe to choose
work that has not been done before. Or to do old work in a
new way. There will always be someone there to stop you. But
in pursuing your highest ambitions, don't let your personal
safety diminish the safety of your stepsister. In wielding the
power that is deservedly yours, don't permit it to enslave your
stepsisters. Let your might and your power emanate from that
place in you that is nurturing and caring.

8     Women's rights is not only an abstraction, a cause; it is also
a personal affair. It is not only about "us"; it is also about me
and you. Just the two of us.

## Theme

1. If you had to pick one of Morrison's sentences to represent
   the meaning of her essay as a whole, which would it be?
   Explain how you would defend your choice to someone
   who had picked another.

2. What conflict does Morrison see between the ambitions of
   women and their "nurturing sensibilities?" Do you agree with
   her on this point? Explain why you do or don't.

## Technique

1. This essay was originally delivered as a graduation address at
   Barnard College of Columbia University. Use evidence in the
   text that points to its original oral presentation. Do you think

the evidence of oral presentation should have been changed before publication in a book? Explain your answer.

2. To make her point, Morrison dismisses the men of the original fairytale and some of the women figures. Do you find this a justifiable modification of the story? Explain your reasoning.

## Writing

Morrison uses a fairytale as a symbol of women's potential for good and for ill. Do you agree with her assessment of that potential? Write an essay in which you explain and defend your answer.

# Arnold Schwarzenegger

## Weight Training                                    (1977)

> *From growing up in a small village in Austria to becoming gov-*
> *ernor of California, Arnold Schwarzenegger traveled a path that*
> *included Mr. World titles and movie leads in* Conan the Barbar-
> ian *and* The Terminator. *In the following essay he addresses some*
> *aspects of style in bodybuilding, the sport that made the first step*
> *in his career.*

### Choosing Your Gym

1   You'll be doing at least a one-hour workout in the beginning,
and eventually a two-hour workout, so it's important that you
choose a place where you feel one hundred percent comfortable and where you will be inspired to do hard work.

2      In the last fourteen years I've found some gymnasiums I've
felt incredibly good in—where I immediately got wonderful
vibrations and a sudden flow of energy because of the way
they looked—and other gymnasiums that depressed me as
soon as I walked through the door. I especially don't like the
kind of gym that gives a sense of relaxation.

3      One consideration in evaluating a gym is who works out
there. It helps if a lot of bodybuilders are training for competition. That's the kind of atmosphere you want. You can relate
to these people and let them guide you in attaining the proper
workout spirit. I personally choose the places with heavy
wheels and cables and machines, heavy-duty stuff that looks
like torture equipment. That kind of gym gives me the incentive to do a serious workout. I've found that, generally speaking, home gyms can have a negative effect on concentrated
training. Your kitchen and living room are too close. You find
yourself thinking, "Should I do another set or should I watch
television?" There are too many temptations. But if you make

SOURCE: Reprinted with the permission of Simon & Schuster Adult Publishing Group
from *Arnold: The Definition of a Body Builder* by Arnold Schwarzenegger and Douglas Kent Hall. Copyright © 1977 by Arnold Schwarzenegger and Douglas Kent Hall.

the commitment of traveling to the gym for half an hour, you will most likely decide that you're going to put in some work so you won't have gone there for nothing.

4     The gymnasium you choose should have good ventilation. Next to your mental attitude, plentiful oxygen is actually the most important thing while you're training. Without an adequate oxygen supply you will tire easily and be unable to handle a vigorous one- or two-hour workout.

5     The gym should be cool—if it's too hot you will grow languid and feel your strength has been sapped. Preferably you should get fresh air, not air-conditioned air. That's why I like World's Gym in Santa Monica; it's close to the beach and fresh ocean air, which I think gives you a little bit more energy than regular air. If you have the chance to work outdoors (as I sometimes do when I go to the outdoor weight-lifting platform at Venice Beach) do so. Working out in the sun tightens your skin and gives you a good color. Which in turn adds a great deal to the way you feel about your body.

## Mental Attitude

6     Do not underestimate the part your attitude plays in bodybuilding. Mental strain and worry can drain the body and adversely affect both your workouts and muscular growth. A good positive mental attitude ought to go beyond the gym. It should extend to your eating habits, your sleeping habits, and the way you conduct your life in general.

7     Use the time on the way to the gym to outline some immediate goals for yourself, to decide what you want to accomplish in this particular workout session. Don't just go to the gym and say, "Oh, no, another workout." Your attitude should be: "Okay, this is another training session, and today instead of a 100-pound bench press I'll do 105 pounds. I feel stronger today; I can do it. I can do more chin-ups. I can do more sit-ups."

8     You should set goals for yourself that turn you on and make you eager to go in and do bench presses, or squats, or barbell curls. Have a definite reason for wanting to do bench presses. Not just because you want to look better next year. That is a

long-range goal, which is very important—but you should also be setting little short-range goals all the time. For example, tell yourself that tomorrow morning you want to get a good pump in the pectoral muscles. Or, yesterday you saw a picture of a bodybuilder whose waist was 29 inches, and you would like to have really good abdominals, so today you'll do more repetitions: by next Monday you ought to be half an inch smaller in the waist. These little goals are fantastic. They've helped me a lot. Of course I always said I wanted to be Mr. Universe or Mr. Olympia. But that was long-range thinking. In addition I always had day-to-day goals, which included measurement increases of a quarter of an inch, two or three more repetitions, and five pounds of added weight on the barbell.

## The Warm-up Period

9  Very few people have jobs that require much physical exertion. You sit at a desk. You move a lot without being conscious of your muscles. So when it comes time to exercise, it's important to let your body warm up. You can use that period to tune in mentally as well as physically.

10  Give your body a chance to adjust to the new activity. It's a way of saying to the body, "I'm giving you a warm-up now, take your time, fall into it easily. In a few minutes I'm going to hit you hard!" That should be your attitude toward your muscles. Do a warm-up of push-ups, pull-downs, squats with no weights, circling your arms around and a series of stretching movements.

11  I always warm up the specific body parts I want to train. For example, for the shoulders and arms I take a 30- or 40-pound weight, which is really light, and do 20 or 30 repetitions to get a lot of blood into the area. I do curls with light weights, then some triceps bench presses and behind-the-neck presses to warm up the elbow area and the shoulder joints and loosen up my shoulders and arms. I don't try to build the muscle, I only get the blood flowing. The danger of not warming up and preparing your body for heavier resistance training is that you may tear your muscles and get aches that will discourage you from continuing.

12   When I was training for contests, I'd sometimes be so psyched up mentally I thought I didn't need a warm-up. I'd go directly into a heavy workout. Without fail, I'd pull muscles needlessly and set myself back two or three months.

## Training Partner

13   I have found that the best way to get great workouts is to have an enthusiastic training partner. You'll be amazed at how much harder and faster you can work when you have someone to work out with. A good training partner pushes you to handle more poundage and gives you the incentive to grind out more reps per set with a minimum of rest pauses in between (which is real quality training). Workouts are more fun with a partner as well as more competitive. On those days when you feel lazy, your partner pushes you to keep working hard, and you end up with a good workout instead of an incomplete one.

14   Your partner should be someone you like and respect, someone you want to respect you. You can have little competitions. You say to him, "I feel good, today. I'm going to put 200 pounds in the bar and do ten repetitions instead of eight." And he says, "If you do ten I'll do twelve." You challenge each other and yourselves. You bet a mug of beer or a bottle of wine. All these little gimmicks, as childish as they may sound, make a workout exciting, interesting and much more rewarding.

## The Basic Exercises

15   Let me say a word about the ten exercises in this chapter. They are geared for the major muscle groups—not for little muscle groups. They are basic to the development of the major areas of your body. They will give you the foundation and mass you'll need for later refinement. You must use them in the beginning, and you must continue to use them as you progress. The first exercise, the *bench press*, is absolutely necessary for a big chest. There is no exercise to replace it. I started doing the bench press when I was fifteen and I've been doing it now for fourteen years.

16      These exercises are to be done three times a week, with one day between workouts for mending and setting. Basically, the theory is simple. In the beginning you will be training your whole body in one day. This should be followed by a rest day because it takes forty-eight hours for the muscles to recuperate, to rebuild to their normal size and grow bigger. If you trained a muscle every day it would slowly deteriorate—you would be just tearing it down and not rebuilding it. Also, you need forty-eight hours to let the joints recuperate. Since, in the beginning, you will do basic movements for every muscle at each workout, you need a day of rest between your sessions in the gym.

17      The basic exercises will appear throughout the entire training program. There are no alternatives to these exercises. For example, every bodybuilder has to do squats from the time he starts until he finishes. You can't build your legs without the squat. The detail stuff that gives you more definition is fine, but the basic thigh muscle can only be developed and maintained by doing heavy squats. If you try to get away from them the size of the muscle will go down. Barbell curls, triceps extensions behind the neck, calf raises, sit-ups are the same—you can't get around them. Basic exercises work directly on the muscle. You fall into a groove and don't even have to think about anything except the pump and the form of the exercise. With the complicated exercises, you have to concentrate all your thought on the exercise and not the muscle. I think the reason some bodybuilders use delicate exercises, which I call chicken exercises, is that they don't feel confident with the basic movements or with themselves. The bench press seems so simple, they think they should do something more complicated. But you can't use as much weight when you make the exercise difficult, so it takes away from the meaning of heavy training.

18      It all goes back to mental attitude, back to being confident in your program. You have to believe that sooner or later you will achieve the body you want. You won't waste your time searching for programs, exotic food supplements and "secret" exercises. There are no "secret" exercises in bodybuilding. The secret is not what exercises to do but how to do them.

## Theme

1. Arnold Schwarzenegger begins with psychological rather than physical advice. Only toward the end of the excerpt does he speak (rather casually) about what he thinks are the most important exercises to perform. Do you think he justifies this manner of emphasis? Explain your answer.

2. Schwarzenegger is careful to distinguish between long-term and short-term goals. In your own words, explain the point of his distinction and the difference it makes for him. Does the difference seem justified to you? Explain your answer.

## Technique

1. Throughout the excerpt, Schwarzenegger addresses a "you." How would you characterize the style this technique helps to achieve? Rewrite a passage in a more objective and impersonal style and explain what you think is gained or lost by your revisions.

2. Toward the end of the piece, Schwarzenegger speaks of what he calls "chicken exercises." What does his metaphor allow him to *avoid* in the way of explanation and argument? Suppose for example he had called the exercises "highly specialized" or "goal specific." What issues would you then expect him to address before moving on? Explain your reasoning.

## Writing

Using Schwarzenegger's essay as a model, write an essay of your own called "How to Study Properly."

# P. J. O'Rourke

## On First Looking into
## Emily Post's Etiquette                                    (1984)

> *P. J. O'Rourke talks about growing up in his native Toledo, Ohio,
> in a book review that shows his early interests in the expressive
> possibilities of style and manner. The range of his work as a
> humorist includes a stint at* National Lampoon *as editor-in-chief
> and* Rolling Stone *where he serves (still humorously) as Foreign
> Affairs Editor. The essay that follows comes from his collection*
> Age and Guile Beat Youth, Innocence and a Bad Haircut.

1    I've been paging through the new, totally revised, terribly up-
to-date version of *Emily Post's Etiquette* written by Mrs. Post's
granddaughter-in-law Elizabeth L. Post. It's a big book, thorough, tidy of organization, and legibly printed. I have no doubt
it would be handy if I were planning my wedding or funeral.
And I'm sure it contains all manner of sound advice for con-
ducting a new, totally revised, terribly up-to-date life. However,
all the people I know have been left out.

2    Muriel Manners, Mr. and Mrs. Eminent, Sarah Stranger, and
Mrs. Kindheart are nowhere to be found. The late Mrs. Post
used these friends and acquaintances to illustrate her little dramas of courtesy and faux pas. She sketched her characters with
marvelous economy—never a word about their physical
appearance, inner conflicts, or personal history. Yet they came
alive upon the page. I give this example from my mother's
copy of the eighth edition, published in 1945:

### Names Legally Changed

Whatever may have been the reason for changing the name by
which one has been known, social and business associates should
be notified of the change if embarrassing situations are to be

avoided. The quickest and simplest way of telling them is to send out formal announcements.

MR. AND MRS. JOHN ORIGINAL NAME ANNOUNCE THAT BY PERMISSION OF THE COURT THEY AND THEIR CHILDREN HAVE TAKEN THE FAMILY NAME OF BROWN

3     What subtlety there is in "embarrassing situations," social "associates," and "Whatever may have been the reason." One knows it didn't turn out well for the sad and rather pushing Name family (pronounced Nam-ay). Their import business was expanded with vain optimism and sank beneath a weight of bank debt. Today, John Original, Jr. is some sort of rapscallion Hollywood person and the Name daughter, on her fourth divorce, drinks before noon.

4     There are no such adventures in the new edition. The exotic Names have been replaced by the prosaic Milsokovichs, who are changing their handle to Miller, probably to get something that will fit on a Visa card. And that rapier thrust "may have been" is gone from the opening sentence.

5     In this and every other way Elizabeth L. Post's *Etiquette* is blunt and homely. It contains paragraphs on such subjects as BYOB parties, pregnant brides, illegal drugs, meeting people through personal ads, and unmarried couples who live together. To tell the truth, I already know how unmarried couples live together. I probably need to learn less. Anyway, Emily Post would never have broached the subject. She would have thought it, well, bad manners.

6     Nor would the elder Mrs. Post have held a respectable lady's past up to ridicule. But the new edition of *Etiquette* is decorated with facsimile quotations from the first edition of 1922:

Dishes are *never* passed from hand to hand at dinner, not even at the smallest and most informal one.

There are many places which are unsuitable for young girls to go whether they are chaperoned or not. No well-brought-up young girl should be allowed to go to supper at a cabaret until she is married ...

Do not greet anyone until you are out on the church steps.... "Hello" should not be said on this occasion because it is too "familiar" for the solemnity of church surroundings.

7       Perhaps these weren't inserted for amusement but to show how manners change with time. I found them, though, neither funny nor informative. Instead they filled me with sad longing for the elegance, dignity, and sophistication I knew in my youth.

8       That is, the elegance, dignity, and sophistication I knew *about*. And the way I knew about it was from Emily Post. I was a bookish child brought up in a house with few books. What reading material we had was stuck on some shelves by the front door. One rainy Saturday when I was about eleven, I was sitting on the linoleum examining the spines of a New Testament, a Fannie Farmer Cookbook, *How to Win Friends and Influence People*, a *Reader's Digest* condensation of *Kitty Foyle*, a paperback *Bridge over the River Kwai*, which I'd already read, and a family snapshot album. It was then I noticed a large book on the bottom shelf. The binding was a deep, compelling shade of blue embossed with the single foreign-seeming word *Etiquette* in silver cursive letters. I pulled it out and cracked it open. I think the first thing I saw was a black-and-white photograph of delicate rattan chairs arranged around a low table in a little garden. In the background were brick gateposts with a small fountain visible behind them. The caption read, "AT TEA IN A CITY YARD. The inviting charm of a garden setting—even that of a city yard—is all too often overlooked." Undeniably true of the yards in the factory town where I was growing up. I turned the pages.

> If you carry a stick, it should be of plain Malacca.... Above all—unless you are a dancer on the stage (like Fred Astaire)—avoid an ebony cane with an ivory top.
>
> Boston's older ladies and gentlemen always dance at balls, and the fact that older ladies of distinction dance with dignity has an inevitable effect on younger ones, so that dancing at balls has not degenerated into the vulgarities of wiggling contortions.
>
> Champagne glasses ought to be thin as soap bubbles...a thick glass will lower the temperature at which a really fine champagne should be served and spoil its perfection.

9       I was transported. Here was a world I did not know, had not even hoped, existed. Here was a society where beauty and grace were serious matters. Here were people who made studied efforts not to act like fools. I read on.

The endeavor of a hostess, when seating her table, is to put together those who are likely to be interested in each other. Professor Bugge might bore *you* to tears, but Mrs. Entomoid would probably delight in him, just as Mr. Stocksan Bonds and Mrs. Rich would probably have interests in common.

10     I didn't think I'd be bored to tears by any of them. They all sounded like preferable dinner companions to my two screaming sisters and fat, bullying stepfather. I was only a simple eleven-year-old, but I thought I'd get along all right. After all, Mrs. Post said, "Simplicity is not crudeness or anything like it. On the contrary simplicity of speech and manners means language in its purest form, and manners of such perfection that they do not suggest 'manner' at all." Simplicity I had. As for the other guests, I supposed not even Mrs. Rich would tell me to get the hell out of the house or go soak my head. "The code of a thoroughbred," said Mrs. Post, "is the code of instinctive decency, ethical integrity, self-respect, and loyalty."

11     These people did drink (champagne, at least) but they didn't argue and back over my bicycle in the driveway afterward. And it wasn't just because they were wealthy, for I found my own mother described in *Etiquette*. She was "Mrs. Three-in-one," who had no servants and "must be cook and waitress and apparently unoccupied hostess." Her parties were said to be a delight and invitations to them eagerly sought. Why, my family could live in this world, I thought, if we but willed it. We wouldn't even have to move into the better neighborhood on the other side of Upton Avenue. Mrs. Post said, "A gem of a house may be of no size at all, but its lines are honest and its painting and furnishing in good taste...all of which may very well contribute as unmistakenly to the impression of 'quality' as the luxury of a palace." I resolved never to carry an ebony cane with an ivory ball top to my sixth grade class.

12     The *Etiquette* book had been a wedding present to my mother from exactly the kind of aunt who would give a twenty-eight-year-old woman an etiquette book for a wedding present. I doubt it had been opened before. I appropriated it to my own use and spent hours studying how to address a Duke (call him "Duke," "Your Grace" is for servants and retainers), what color waistcoat to wear with a cutaway (black), and when to use the

"cut direct" (never, and I heartily wished the same were true for a punch in the eye in Toledo, Ohio).

13     But the people were what I liked the best, and they came to populate my fantasies. There was Mrs. Toplofty, very reserved and dignified but awfully decent once you got to know her and she invited you in for Kool-Aid. And Mr. Worldly, who always had something clever to say about the Detroit Tigers. Mr. Clubwin Doe was lots of fun at the YMCA. And the Oncewere family, though they'd fallen on hard times, still had plenty of style at kick-the-can and stoop tag. There were visitors, too, members of European noble families such as Lord Blank, and the vague and haughty Duke of Overthere (none of *us* ever called him "Your Grace"). We always suspected these fellows of having designs on the "better situated" neighborhood debutantes, especially on the spoiled and willful daughter of Mr. and Mrs. Richan Vulgar. No one would actually "cut" the Vulgars, but we were rather cool to them when they wanted to borrow the leaf rake. Actually, certain members of our own set were a bit "fast" themselves. Mr. and Mrs. Uppal Knight, for instance, gave parties that went on until after 11:00 P.M. And the frankly naughty Cigret Colcreme was "separated" and had men friends who drove convertibles.

14     And thus it was that while my boyhood chums were pulling the wings off flies I was discussing ants and grubs with Professor Bugge and Mrs. Entomoid and handling three forks and four different kinds of stemware.

15     Of course, in the real world, I have never quite made my way to that perfect land of kindness, taste, and tact. Though I'd like to think, sometimes, I've been on the path. I hope to get there yet. But I wonder if any bored eleven-year-olds, sitting by bookshelf in trailer or tract house, will be inspired to undertake the same journey by the new edition of *Emily Post's Etiquette*. I fear not.

## Theme

1. In the light of the essay as a whole, why doesn't P. J. O'Rourke find the quotations from the old edition as they

are used in the new edition either funny or informative? Who would find them funny in your view? Explain your reasoning. Who is the "respectable lady" in paragraph six? Would she find them funny? Explain why you do or do not think so.

2. In the last paragraph O'Rourke mentions a "perfect land of kindness, taste, and tact." Point to some of the ways in which his family's manners made for a different kind of environment.

## Technique

1. O'Rourke characterizes the style of the new edition of *Etiquette* as "up-to-date" and "blunt and homely." He does not explicitly characterize the style of the older edition, but gives us a great deal of evidence about that style. On the basis of that evidence, how would you characterize the style of the older edition?

2. O'Rourke invents some characters of his own toward the end of the essay: "Mr. and Mrs. Uppal Knight" and "Cigret Colcreme." How do these characters resemble and how do they differ from the characters in the old edition of *Etiquette*?

## Writing

Write an essay in which you describe one incident in which you were the victim of bad manners and one in which you were pleased by good manners on the part of someone else.

# Melissa Etheridge

## My First Album                                                    (2001)

> *Playing in local bands throughout her teens, Melissa Etheridge*
> *studied at Berklee College of Music (see Sting's Commencement*
> *Address there in Chapter 1). In coming out as a gay person and*
> *in her folk-pop musical style she has famously followed her own*
> *feelings. In this excerpt from her autobiography, she shows how*
> *even the same songs may express different feelings through dif-*
> *ferent artists.*

1    It took a couple of months after I got back to Los Angeles, but, finally, things were all ready for me to go into the studio and record my first album. I flew up to San Francisco with Craig Krampf, a drummer I had worked with the year before, and Kevin McCormick, Craig's bassist friend. I'd known these two for a while—they'd come to see me in the bars—and I felt comfortable with them. When Island asked me who I wanted to record with, they were my first choice.

2    In San Francisco, we met with producer Jim Gaines, who had produced records for Huey Lewis and the News, Journey, and Eddie Money—all performers who were hugely success-ful at the time. I was ready to listen to Jim and take his ideas to heart. I had never made an album before, and I wasn't going to act like I knew more than the experts did. Jim also brought in the keyboard player from Pablo Cruise. Keyboards were very big in those days; everybody had one. But with ten keyboards and the MIDI setup, it would sometimes take us all day just to lay down the keyboard track for one song. It didn't occur to me that layer upon layer of keyboards might not be the best

thing for my music. I didn't really think about it; I was so happy to finally be in the studio. I was working hard, putting my music down on record. Kathleen would come visit. When she'd go home, Jamie would sometimes pop up to say hi.

3      Finally, the album was done. I was a little surprised when I first listened to it. It sounded sorta pop—not how I heard myself at all. Producers want to put their stamp on music albums; Jim's style didn't seem compatible with my sound. Looking back, I realize that I was disconnected from my material. It was like being an artist who gives someone else her paint to use. That person paints a picture with it but then signs the artist's name at the bottom. The album wasn't my picture. It was close, but not me—my vocals, my songs, but certainly not my music. It had been overproduced and had lost its intimate sound. I didn't know there was anything I could do about it, though. I just thought, "Okay, I'm done. Here's the record."

4      I went to meet Chris Blackwell at the Bel Age Hotel in Beverly Hills to get his reaction to the album. He sat down with me and listened to a couple of tracks. Then he snapped off the tape recorder and looked at me. "I don't like it," he said. I was shocked. He didn't like it? What did that *mean?* Is it all over? Do I just pack up and go home? I walked out of the hotel in a daze, not really sure of what to do. I called Craig and Kevin and told them. "He doesn't like it. Oh, my god. What do we do?" They convinced me to ask Chris for another four days in the studio. "Look," they said. "We know what you need. You just need *us* to be behind you. Just the three of us. Just bass, drums, and you. We'll get this engineer we know, Niko Bolas. He'll just record it raw. He knows what you should sound like."

5      So I did. I called Chris and asked him for four days. Four days and we'd re-record the whole album, do it the way it should be done. I promised him it would be that solo girl that he saw and heard in the bars. "That's what I want," he said. "I want the girl in the T-shirt and leather jacket."

6      So we went back to Cherokee Studios, in Hollywood. Chris came to visit us right at the beginning of the session. He laid down a picture on the mixing board. It was a photo of

me standing with clenched fists, wearing jeans, all of my '80s jewelry, a white T-shirt, and a leather jacket, against a red background. That picture would eventually be recreated for the cover of the album. He tapped his finger on it and said, "Make *that* album." I just looked at him, "Okay, Mr. Blackwell." Then Kevin, Craig, Niko, and I got to work. We re-recorded the album. Four long days and four longer nights, but we made *my* first album. It was such a different experience this time. The four of us were just *in* it, all day and all night. I brought in "Bring Me Some Water," which I had just written, and they came up with the whole thing behind it. It was exactly like it should have been. Everything just clicked.

7    I brought the new album to Chris, and he loved it. All except "Like the Way I Do." He thinks I'm sorta hollering on that song. "Don't like that one," he says. Those four days in the studio had really enlightened me about how I wanted to sound on a record. I was much more sure of myself after that experience. "No, Chris," I replied. "That's my favorite song. It stays." Chris just shook his head. "All right, if you have to." To this day, whenever Chris gives me an opinion on what to keep and what to get rid of on an album, he inevitably brings up that he didn't want "Like the Way I Do" on my first album. But the final cut is always up to me. One footnote to the album-cover story. When the photographer was taking the photo of me that was eventually used—a match to the one Chris had held up when he said "Make this album"—I was dancing to "Like the Way I Do."

8    So the album was done and I was on my way, right? Nope. In the music industry, nothing ever works the way you'd like it to. They put off the release date for a few months, and I just had to wait. I went back to playing the bars, back to my old life. Things were going okay with Kathleen, but I wanted to make my mark and all I could do was wait.

9    Luckily, Bill got me a job on a European tour—opening for Martin Stevenson, a folk-rocker from Newcastle, England, who had a huge Jimmy Stewart obsession. It was my first time in Europe and my first real rock-and-roll tour. On the bus

with ten other people; roadies; a new city every day—it was exciting and boring, terrible and wonderful, all at the same time. I'm walking on stage in front of people who have no idea who I am. They don't know me from Adam. Sometimes I win them over. I can see people nodding their heads, smiling, giving me an "Oh, she's *good*" look. And, of course, sometimes I don't win them over, I'm just out there doing my thing and the audience is just biding its time, waiting for Martin.

10     The album wasn't out yet, but the record company in England was trying to garner support for it. I was in the back of a car, being driven crazily through the streets of London to try to make a train when "Similar Features," the first single off the album, came on the radio. It was shocking. "Oh, my god! That's *me*!" I'd never heard myself on the radio before. I broke down in tears, right in the back of the car. Just completely cried when I heard that song. My music pouring out of that tiny radio in the front of the car. And it sounded so good. It sounded great! I was just overwhelmed.

## Theme

1. In paragraph three Melissa Etheridge says that the first version of her first album had been "overproduced." Given your knowledge of the essay as a whole, paraphrase in your own words what she means by this remark.

2. At the very end of the essay Etheridge focuses on the song, "Like The Way I Do." In your own words explain why that song and its title meant so much to her, given what you know about her views from the essay as a whole.

## Technique

1. In paragraph one Melissa Etheridge speaks of "my first album." In paragraph six she speaks of "*my* first album." Explain the difference expressed by this difference of type font.

2. In paragraph four Melissa Etheridge's friends say of the engineer they have in mind, "He'll just record it raw." Literally, "raw" applies to food. In your own words explain the figurative meaning the word is given here.

## Writing

In this essay Melissa Etheridge focuses on her own art, yet also acknowledges help from others and implies the communal nature of the art of record production. Write an essay that analyzes the communal nature of record production.

# Dr. Joyce Brothers

## Procrastination                                                    (1994)

> *For decades Dr. Joyce Brothers has been the most visible psychol-
> ogist in American media, though she is now being given a run
> for her money by Dr. Phil, who appears later in Chapter 5. Dr.
> Brothers appears regularly as a radio personality and newspa-
> per columnist. She has been listed as one of America's "most
> admired women" by a Gallup Poll. In the essay that follows she
> reveals a failing in herself that afflicts many undergraduates as
> well—procrastination—and explains what she has done to kick
> this bad habit.*

1    Unlike perfectionists, procrastinators are incorrigible opti-
mists. They operate under the assumption that if you postpone
things you don't want to do long enough, they eventually go
away. And many of them do. Unfortunately some of the things
the procrastinator did not get around to doing may have been
the opportunities of a lifetime. The procrastinator usually never
knows what might have been. Anne learned the hard way.

2    The boss's secretary called Anne on Saturday morning, leaving a message on the answering machine, asking her to
return the call. She said it was important. Anne got the message, but didn't return the call. Whatever it was, it could wait
until Monday.

3    When she walked into the office on Monday, she discovered that the boss had been taken ill and Cassie had flown to
Dallas on Saturday to take the boss's place at the annual Wid-
get & Sprocket Convention. "We called you first," the secretary
said, "but I guess you were away for the weekend."

4    When Cassie returned, she wrote a detailed report on what had gone on, the people she had met and suggestions for new products, based on what she had learned about their competitors' plans. A few months later, Cassie was made a vice president. The way she had represented the firm in Dallas and her suggestions for new products had put her in the spotlight.

5    Anne was left with a load of "if only" guilt. For months she went around thinking "If only I had returned that call, I might have made vice president. I certainly would have done as well as Cassie." Not every unanswered telephone call is a now-or-never opportunity, but procrastinators may never know when opportunity knocked. They soon become known for what they are. People stop giving them important assignments and asking them to join committees. Procrastinators are tagged as unreliable.

6    Procrastination is easy enough to remedy if you are motivated. If you have had enough of rushing at the last minute or if you realize that people think of you as someone who cannot be relied on to follow through, there are three psychological tools that can help you curb your tendency to postpone—a variation on the Reinforcement List, a Worst-Case Scenario and generous amounts of Positive Reinforcement.

### Getting Started

7    The great thing about most of my psychological tools is that they can be adapted to almost any behavior. In this case, the Reinforcement List is really a Procrastination List. Start by listing everything that you put off till the last minute, including those things that you never did get around to. The list should include all those chores like cleaning the bathroom, sewing on buttons, making out your expense account, calling your mother, writing that thank-you note, picking up the stuff from the cleaner's, planning your daughter's birthday party, typing up your notes on the library board meeting. It will probably seem endless.

8    The next step is to organize your Procrastination List in order of importance. You may run into problems here trying to weigh whether balancing your checkbook should come before paying the dentist. (Balance the checkbook first. You don't want your check to bounce.) If you are unsure of your priorities,

take the time to work out Worst-Case Scenarios. Suppose, for instance, your list included

- paying the rent
- paying the credit-card bill
- calling Joan to see if she and her husband can come to dinner a week from Friday
- making an appointment at the hairdresser's
- signing up for the dog obedience class
- taking the kids' outgrown clothes to the thrift shop

and you can't decide what you should do first. Just think of the worst that could happen if you did not get around to doing each of them. Then base your priorities on this, scheduling the tasks in order of the severity of the penalty for not doing it. For instance, the worst that might happen if you did not pay the rent could be a communication from the landlord's lawyer or even the cancellation of your lease. If you don't pay your charge-card bill, you will be charged more interest, your credit rating may be affected, and your card may be canceled, depending on your record. This is obviously a priority, but the rent has a higher priority. After all, you need a roof over your head.

9      The dinner invitation should probably be next if you want Joan and her husband to come. If you delay asking her, they may have made other plans. As for the hairdresser, the dog obedience class and the thrift shop, fit these in when you have time.

10      Now that you have an idea of the extent of the task that you face, set a goal. A reasonable one might be that every day you will take care of the three top items on your list. You might also set a secondary goal—you will never again postpone doing the items in the first half of your list. If you slip occasionally—and you may—just forgive yourself and keep on working toward your goal.

11      There are little tricks you can use to get started. Circle the days when something should be done on your calendar. Write down the chore and the due date on several index cards and tape them to the refrigerator, the bathroom mirror, next to the telephone, inside the front door, places where you will not be able to miss them, so that you cannot say that you simply for-

got to take the car for an emissions test or to make an appointment with the gynecologist or to return your library books. And then do it.

## My Own To-Do System

12  I have had to fight against my own tendency to procrastinate, and over the years I have devised a system of priorities that works for me. I have three "To Do" baskets in my office and I put things in them depending on their degree of importance.

13  The first basket is for things that absolutely must be done today, the emergencies of my professional and family life, such as letters that must be answered, calls that must be returned, plane reservations that must be made, appointments that must be kept, a lecture that must be prepared, a birthday chat with one of my grandchildren, a television appearance—that sort of thing.

14  I start off every morning by sitting down and deciding what three things I absolutely must do today, the things that will make a difference. And I do them immediately. I can't always complete them. I call someone and he is not in his office. I order a book and it is out of stock. But I have taken a step. Once you have taken the first step you are on your way.

15  I never go to bed without taking care of the contents of the first basket. I am usually able to finish those duties by the middle of the afternoon unless I am out of town. And when I am, the contents of that basket travel with me. I take care of as much as I can from my hotel room wherever I am.

16  When that basket is empty, I get my reward, my Positive Reinforcement, the satisfaction of accomplishment. There is absolutely nothing like it. When I know that I have taken care of the obligations and crises of the first basket, I feel great. I often give myself a double-dip reward. I take time out and go for a walk or a swim in the apartment-house pool, or spend half an hour on the telephone visiting with my daughter. The break energizes me for the rest of the day.

17  The second basket is for after the emergencies have been taken care of—appointments that must be made, paying bills,

writing my columns and books, shopping, reading, the hair-dresser. This basket is always overflowing.

18      Most days I am able to make a start on the second basket. Before I go to bed at night, I review its contents, move some of them into the first basket and leave the rest where they are.

19      The third basket, a large laundry basket, is for everything else. I get to it when I can. At the end of each year, I go through it to check if there is still life in anything there and throw the rest out. Often there are things that I wish I could have done, and I regret that I did not get to them, but it does not matter. What matters is that all year long I do the things that really make a difference today, tomorrow and the next day.

## The Glorious Sense of Accomplishment

20      The Procrastination List is an extremely effective way of estab-lishing the habit of doing things when they should be done. The making of this list is a chore you should not allow your-self to postpone. Once a week, make a list of everything you accomplished on time that week. When you have finished your list, sit back and congratulate yourself. It's a good feeling. But don't leave it at that. Give yourself a little more Positive Rein-forcement—a treat of some sort, a little indulgence—and tell yourself you have earned it.

21      Positive Reinforcement is important. The process of modi-fying a behavior should be as rewarding as possible. I do not mean that you should buy yourself a string of pearls every month you pay the electric bill on time, but do treat yourself to some small delight.

22      One way to get things done and reward yourself at the same time is to do the thing you most dislike first. For each detested task you complete, allow yourself to tackle one you enjoy or that is easy. If you got the newsletter for your local Audubon Society group out on time, reward yourself by doing the least unpleasant chore on your list. Then tackle the next detested job.

23      Your Procrastination List will be a record of your progress from week to week. I suggest keeping it up for eight to ten

weeks. By that time, the habit of doing what has to be done when it should be done should be well established.

24    Do not let yourself think you are a failure if you still procrastinate now and then. No one expects you to be perfect.

## Theme

1. Dr. Joyce Brothers says that her tools are adaptable, though the examples she gives in paragraph seven are largely taken from the world of work and domesticity. Create your own list of examples taken from the world of higher education. Do the different particular examples call for different general advice in your view? Explain and defend your answer.

2. Brothers ends the essay advising you to create a list of accomplishments. In your own words explain the rationale behind this emphasis on something positive and ostensibly different from her announced topic of procrastination.

## Technique

1. Dr. Joyce Brothers chooses a *metaphor* for her subtitle: *"self-sabotage."* What does the metaphor add to the abstract term "procrastination?" Find another metaphor that would be appropriate as a subtitle for the essay and discuss its advantages and disadvantages compared with her choice.

2. Brothers begins the text proper with an anecdote. What internal evidence allows you to see that the story has been made up? Would making the story more realistic by suppressing that evidence have improved her point? Explain the reasoning behind your answer.

## Writing

Using Dr. Joyce Brothers's essay as a model, write an essay of your own called "How to Study Properly."

## EXERCISES

### Intertextual Questions

1. Dr. Joyce Brothers is a longtime professional giver of advice on psychological matters. In your opinion, who else in this chapter also gives good psychological advice? Give examples and explain what you find praiseworthy about them.

2. Bill Murray, Lance Armstrong, and Arnold Schwarzenegger all talk about some kind of sport in their essays. How do their attitudes toward athletic performance differ? How are they similar? What does each writer see as the relation between becoming better at what you do athletically and overcoming the obstacles that stand in your way?

3. Based on what you know from P. J. O'Rourke's essay about the kinds of manners recommended by Emily Post, what do you think Emily Post would have thought about the kind of manners recommended by Queen Latifah? What, in your view, would Emily Post think about the advice Toni Morrison gives? Explain your answers with examples.

4. Melissa Etheridge took charge of a situation that seemed to hinder the artistic expression of the self she wanted to become as a singer and musician. Who else in the chapter finds ways to overcome outside rather than psychological hindrances to self-expression and performance?

5. All the men and women in this chapter express forceful personalities through their writing. Do you find any differences between the men and women in this regard? Pick some examples and discuss the issue by analyzing evidence.

### Suggestions for Writing

1. Some of the authors in this chapter write about the need for self-discipline in becoming who you want to be and overcoming any obstacles that stand in the way of that goal. In your

view, who wrote the best essay on this theme? Write an essay of your own that defines and defends your choice.

2. In differing ways, both Queen Latifah and P. J. O'Rourke address the topic of self-creation through manners. Write an essay in which you compare and contrast the ways each writer understands and expresses the themes of self-image and appropriate behavior.

3. Toni Morrison, P. J. O'Rourke, and Dr. Joyce Brothers are all professional writers. In your view, does their writing differ in quality and effectiveness from that of other authors in this chapter? Discuss this question in an essay that analyzes particular examples from the texts involved.

4. Performance—whether in athletics or the arts—is a major focus in many of the essays in this chapter. Which of the performers seems most to embody the values and assumptions about life that you admire? Write an essay about one figure in which you analyze and express the reasons behind your admiration.

5. The subject described in this chapter covers a wide range of experience. Which of the experiences is most analogous to something comparably important in your own life? Using the essay you chose as a model, write an essay of your own that describes moments of becoming and overcoming in your own life.

# CHAPTER 3

# SIGNIFICANT OTHERS

Both positive and negative judgments about the important people in our lives can serve as ways of defining the values and assumptions we ourselves choose to live by. The essays in this chapter begin to move outside a direct focus on self to explore some of the ways other people can contribute to your identity, either by providing positive role models for admiration and imitation or—less happily—by exerting oppositional forces against which one's own personality needs to be asserted and defined. The celebrities in this chapter all attempt to find a language to express what is important to them by talking about the impact other people have made on the way they have learned to live.

In the first selection one classic star of rock & roll pays tribute to the significance of another master musician in his life. Mick Jagger of the Rolling Stones was always perceived by the public as very different from George Harrison of the Beatles—different as a musician, as a performer, and a personality. But we see in Jagger's tribute to his dead friend that he is perfectly capable of appreciating virtues other than his own and that he recognizes what knowing those virtues in George Harrison meant to him.

Mia Farrow's sketch of her longtime companion and director, Woody Allen, shows some of the couple's difficulties well before the scandal of their breakup. In "With Woody Allen, a House Is Not a Home," Farrow uses living space and landscapes as ways of dramatizing Allen, who in real life seemed to her to persistently play the neurotic character his movies made so famous.

Soul diva Patti LaBelle failed her own sister in that sister's dying days and the failure haunted LaBelle, intensifying her own fear of early death. Acknowledging and overcoming her guilt and her fear make the subject of this essay from her autobiography, *Don't Block the Blessings.*

Professional funnyman, actor, and writer Dan Aykroyd shows us his serious side in "Michael O'Donoghue and *Saturday Night Live.*" Coming from Canada as a rookie to a television show that would revolutionize comedy, Aykroyd found a mentor, a critic, and a role model in a man who seemed to represent New York sophistication to Aykroyd, who considered himself very provincial. Aykroyd composed his tribute shortly after O'Donoghue's death.

LL Cool J projects the image of a street-smart tough guy, and tough guys don't cry. But in "Impotent Demon" he shows us a childhood filled with tears that may have led to his passion for bodybuilding and to the hat fetish for which he is so famous. A man who seemed a savior to the boy's mother turned out to be a relentless devil to the boy himself. We see how, as an adult, LL Cool J has now come to terms with the horrible significance of a man who haunted his early years.

Tito Puente almost single-handedly brought Latin music into the mainstream of American mass culture. In a tribute to his master, Marc Anthony uses a few very heartfelt words to say a great deal about the multifaceted role Tito Puente played in the young performer's life.

The next selection marks the first visual essay in the book. In a combination of words and images, the prizewinning novelist Alice Walker makes a witty and complex statement on the theme of healthy eating in "Do It For Someone You Love." Her public service advertisement reminds us that significant others not only act on you but also need to be acted upon sometimes.

The last essay in the chapter is "Personnel: Up Close and Personal" by Chaka Khan. She shows us how she went a long way around to find the shortest way home by combining her business and personal relationships in people who were important to her. At the end of the selection she speculates on the significance of a man new to her musical career, but who went on to become her husband and partner.

# Mick Jagger

## George Harrison                                         (2002)

> *In the mid-1960s the* Beatles *and the* Rolling Stones *revolutionized the world of rock & roll with Mick Jagger and George Harrison playing major roles in their respective bands. The following tribute was composed almost immediately after learning of George Harrison's death from cancer and shows how friendly musical competition can be.*

1   George deserves recognition. He was always rather overshadowed, there's no other way of putting it, by John and Paul. I mean, to call him "the quiet Beatle," it's like some dopey publicist made that up in 1964. And, of course, he was quite a complicated person. When you say, "Oh, the quiet Beatle," it's like, "Oh, yeah, OK, he sits in the corner." And he wasn't really that. He was very complex, and he was very charming and friendly. I notice that Bob Geldof called him curmudgeonly, which is true, you know, but people are always saying to me—and I don't want to really compare myself to George but they say, "Gosh, you've got lots of faces." And I say, "Well, yeah, but people are complex."

2   So George was very friendly, but he also could be quite quarrelsome at times. He had a side of him, which, if he felt you deserved it, so to speak, would lash out at you. But I'm talking about when he was much, much younger; I never saw that side of him later on in life. But when he was the young man around town, I used to see him a lot. We used to see each other in nightclubs and so on and be drinking buddies. I suppose what I'm trying to say is, he wasn't just a retiring person only, in my mind. He could be funny and charming and also

quite acerbic. He had the sort of quality that normally people would associate with John.

3     And then, later, George developed this other side to him. He very much concentrated on the spiritual side of his life, and it was more than a passing fancy. It looked like it was a sort of faddish thing at the time, but it stayed with him. You got the feeling that most people were dabbling in spirituality, but for George it was perhaps the major part of his life once he discovered it. And it's very easy to ridicule someone who does that, and he was ridiculed, there's no doubt about that, especially in England, for being like that. But he did follow through on the courage of his convictions. He stayed with it and never rejected it. And, of course, he made mistakes—anybody following this who was one of the first people of a generation to do that would make mistakes—but not any glaring ones. You've got to start somewhere.

4     Another thing he did that was groundbreaking was, of course, the idea of rock & roll linked with charity, which was a generous and innovative thing, and was also linked to his generosity of spirit and his spirituality. It was a very innovative thing, even with all the problems that it had. And "While My Guitar Gently Weeps"? It's lovely, plaintive. Only a guitar player could write that; I love that song. And "My Sweet Lord": There's tons of songs with that chord sequence, but that's a very nice one. As a guitar player, he certainly had some nice and memorable licks on those Beatles tunes. Without being a virtuoso, he came up with really nice guitar lines that are integral parts of those tunes. But he had a multifaceted career as a personality. He wasn't just a guitar player. And he did have a sense of humor, and he did take it all with a huge pinch of salt, which is a very English and a very Liverpudlian thing.

5     I'm sorry if this a bit rambly and not assembled, but I just found out about half an hour ago. You know I hadn't seen George for a very long time. He came to a concert that the Stones did in a theater in London called the Brixton Academy in July 1995. And he said to Charlie [in Liverpool accent], "You're very lucky to be in a working band." And it was really nice to see him. We hadn't seen him in a long while at a show. He went through periods of being reclusive, and it was lovely to see him. We would see each other rarely after the Sixties and middle Seventies.

6    Really, whatever I say about my feelings is ridiculous and inadequate. I was very sad, but of course you're very sad, and then you start thinking of the times you spent, you know? And it's very difficult to depersonalize it. It's like part of your life. But, you know, that's probably what most people think. Because the Beatles were a big part of one's life. And when someone like that dies, in a way, a part of your own life is gone.

## Theme

1. Mick Jagger insists that George Harrison was not easily stereotyped and was in fact a very complex person. Make a list of the elements that Jagger mentions as parts of the complexity.

2. Jagger says that, unlike many people, George Harrison was not "dabbling in spirituality." What else does Jagger point to as evidence of the essential sincerity of Harrison's personality?

## Technique

1. In paragraph five, Jagger apologizes for being "a bit rambly and not assembled." Yet the piece does display some organization. Make an outline of the topics covered in the paragraphs. Do you think they might have been better arranged? Analyze one paragraph for its strengths or weaknesses in organization.

2. Most of the paragraphs here begin with transitional words or phrases rather than a simple declaration or assertion. Explain how the transitional remarks add to the flow of the piece. In what different ways do they connect what went before with what comes after?

## Writing

Through his writing here does Mick Jagger seem to display something of the same complexity that he attributes to George Harrison? Write an essay that explains and defends your answer.

# Mia Farrow

## With Woody Allen, a House Is Not a Home (1997)

> *Mia Farrow is the daughter of the director John Farrow and*
> *Maureen O'Sullivan, who played Jane in the early classic Tarzan*
> *movies. After starring in* A Midsummer Night's Sex Comedy,
> *Woody Allen wrote many other parts for her in his films until*
> *their longstanding relationship ended over Allen's widely publi-*
> *cized affair with Farrow's adopted daughter.*

1    I would miss the foghorns' nightly dirges, and the many
bewitching nooks and crannies of Martha's Vineyard—Beetle-
bung Corner, and the wild Squibnocket shore, and Menemsha,
with its tangled heaps of lobster traps and tethered boats nudg-
ing in the harbor, this morning's catch of bluefish, and the
snow on the driftwood, and summertimes with Ruth, Gar,
Thornton, and the Styrons, dear friends through the decades,
and my beloved Wooden House on Lake Tashmoo, as close to
heaven as anywhere on earth.

2    But there is a New England village with white clapboard
houses, circa 1800. It has two churches with steeples, a school,
a library, a general store, a bank, and a post office; there are
cornfields and cows on hills beyond hills, and horses and silos
and tumbledown barns. Nestled on the outskirts of this town
is Frog Hollow.

3    Woodland encircles the white farmhouse and the lake it inti-
mately faces. There is a knobby field at the back, hemmed
carelessly by a colonial stone wall; a mossy creek holds back
the dense woods and winds along the right of the field toward
its upper, northeast corner, where a plain wooden bridge
crosses the stream and leads past a greenish secret pond into
the deep woods.

4    The lake in front of the house is a good five or six acres in size, with an island in the middle big enough for the spruce tree that angles over the water, two sizable rocks you can sit on, a profusion of blueberry and alder bushes, and, in the spring, a goose nest. On the narrow ring of a beach, early in May, a goose couple launches its progeny; it is also where the blue crane wades and watches the beavers ceaselessly trafficking the lake. There are almost no mosquitoes, which seemed a minor miracle after the Vineyard. My school friend Casey has a home nearby, and the Styrons winter here.

5    During the filming of *A Midsummer Night's Sex Comedy* we packed up the encyclopedias, the red canoe, my grandfather's crucifix, and the music box Frank gave me, and we moved everything into the new house. That it was a little run-down didn't matter; but the house had no showers, and since Woody wouldn't touch a bath, I had a fine tile shower built just for him and I hoped he would be comfortable and grow fond of the house and be there as much as possible.

6    There was no doubt in my mind that the gleaming shower would please him; on the evening of his second visit I watched him take a white rubber shower mat (for germs) out of his bag and carry it into the bathroom. But seconds later he emerged with the mat still rolled under his arm. "What happened?" I asked. "What's wrong?"

7    "The drain is in the middle," he said, shaking his head dismissively, as if I should have known. No further explanation ever came.

8    This was an instance when a shower was more than just a shower; it was the reason, he said, that he could not stay at Frog Hollow for longer than a brief overnight visit. So I was determined to get things right. According to his specifications, in another part of the house, I had a whole new bathroom built with a shower that had a drain in the corner. It was called "Woody's bathroom."

9    We were still shooting *A Midsummer Night's Sex Comedy* and settling into Frog Hollow when out of nowhere, *he* began to look for a house. He showed me brochures of fabulous beach houses, but he didn't ask what I thought about them, and when he went to see them, he took Jean, not me. It was as disturbing and mysterious as the drain.

10    In a short time he bought a beach house in the Hamptons for millions of dollars. Through the winter of 1981–82 he and his decorator conferred, and renovated, landscaped, painted, and furnished, and every once in a while Woody was driven out to check the progress. Sometimes he brought seven-year-old Fletcher along. Finally, one windy afternoon in early spring, he took the kids and me out to East Hampton for an overnight visit in the newly completed house.

11    It was impressive, bigger even than I had imagined. A mansion facing the waves, with many cavernous rooms impeccably furnished with pale-pine antiques, all in shades of white except for the Laura Ashley curtains in the bathrooms and a brand-new restaurant-style kitchen. Every appliance, towel, plate, pillow, and billiard ball was in place.

12    While the children flew excitedly in all directions, Woody and I walked down the beach. The sun was setting. It was a lovely evening. But he was troubled, there was something about the house, some indefinable thing he didn't like. He wasn't sure he would even be able to spend the night there. I tried to be positive: the place seemed imposing now but it was only our first visit, it was a big house, it would become familiar, and it would be great to be able to come out on winter weekends, build a fire, and watch storms over the sea. Frog Hollow, I thought to myself, would still be there for summers, when the beaches got hot and crowded. It would all work out. It would be great. And we would get out of the city during the winter months—as things stood we weren't going to Frog Hollow more than once every five or six weeks, because even with the new bathroom he didn't want to go.

13    He paced and worried through the evening. The next morning we left and he sold the house and everything in it.

## Theme

1. Summarize the things that Mia Farrow shows she loves about her new house, Frog Hollow. Point to examples in which she demonstrates her feelings instead of merely naming them.

2. Summarize the attitude that she suggests Woody Allen takes toward his own new house. Point to examples.

## Technique

1. How does the anecdote of the shower become a representative symbol in this brief account of a relationship? What aspects of Woody Allen's personality does the anecdote serve to represent and how does it relate to other examples of his behavior?

2. Mia Farrow describes her own landscape in detail, but in speaking of Woody Allen's house she merely mentions a landscaper. What impressions does this proportional difference in narrative attention create for the reader? Explain your reasoning.

## Writing

In just a few pages Mia Farrow shows that she can write both lyrically and satirically. Write an essay that analyzes examples of her skill in both modes of composition.

# Patti LaBelle

## Don't Block the Blessings

*Patti LaBelle has had one of the longest careers in contemporary music. The soul diva has recorded hits in musical modes that extend from girl-group pop through space-age funk to lush ballads. In the essay that follows, LaBelle tells us something about the other side of her apparently unflappable personality.*

1    This day had been planned for weeks. We were shooting the video for my single, "If You Asked Me To." Everything was in place. We were all set to go and everyone was waiting for me. The camera started rolling, the music began to play—it was time for me to perform. As I moved to my mark, I could feel all eyes following me. I knew what they were thinking. It was written all over their faces: Could I do it? Would I be able to hold it together? Could I make it through?

2    The night before, my husband asked me if I wanted to cancel this shoot. I told him no. I had to do this. It didn't seem, at the time, that I'd ever feel better and I had to find a way to push past the pain. My husband had come in case I needed him. So had my youngest son. But when the shoot began, it was just me—standing all alone in the spotlight dressed in black. It was the first time I would shoot a video solo, without anyone else in the scene, and I had never felt so alone in my life. That was as it should have been because I was alone in my pain and there was no one else to blame for what I was feeling but me.

3    This was my sister's birthday. July 12, 1989. Had she lived to see it, she would have been 44. But she didn't make it. As everyone in this room knew. I had buried her just the day before. They knew that. But they didn't know the worst part. Most people don't. Most people have no idea why it has become so

Important to me to reach out to so many others. Yes, the causes I support—Big Sisters of America, Save the Children, the United Negro College Fund, the American Cancer Society and the National Minority AIDS Council—are doing important work. Yes, my contribution to these and other groups has earned me civic awards which I treasure and hold dear—three NAACP Image Awards, a medal from the Congressional Black Caucus, even a cancer research laboratory dedicated in my honor. But what drives me to say "yes" to all these organizations is more, much more, than the joy of helping others. That's only part of it. The other part is something few people know about me, something that haunted me for years. I say "yes" every chance I get now because once, when it really, really counted, I said "no."

4    It was such a little thing that my sister had asked of me. I've done much bigger things for perfect strangers. And anyway, how long would it have taken me to do it—fifteen, twenty minutes, tops? But I said "no." I refused. There wasn't a good reason. Not really. It wasn't as if I was busy or had something pressing to do that couldn't wait. I just didn't want to do it. I had been going back and forth to the hospital for days and I finally had a quiet moment at home to relax. That's when the phone rang. It was my sister.

5    She wanted me to do her a favor. The chemotherapy treatments had made her so sick she didn't want to touch any of that hospital food.

6    "Please, Patsy," she said. "I'm hungry—hungry for one of your egg sandwiches. It's the only thing I have a taste for. Will you make it for me?"

7    "Now?" I asked. "Do you have to have it this minute? I don't feel like it right now. I'm tired. I'll make it later."

8    After that phone call, my sister got worse. Much worse. And later never came. She was on a respirator and in and out of consciousness. Days after that call, she died. The thought kept tormenting me—that I had refused to do the one thing she asked of me, the one thing that could have given my sister some small amount of pleasure as she was about to leave this world.

9    That's all I could think about as I gave the director the signal I was ready to begin. Maybe I was being punished. Maybe

I deserved to be. Maybe it was poetic justice that I would have
to sing this song, these words, this day:

*"If you asked me to,*
*I just might change my mind and let you in my life forever...*
*All you gotta do is ask me to;*
*I'll give you my world, I'll give you my heart,*
*I'll give you anything; just ask me, baby."*

10     I couldn't hold back the tears. The more I sang, the more I
thought—about what I had done, what I hadn't done, what I
could never be able to do again. The more I thought, the
harder I cried. Those tears you see on that video? There's nothing phony about them. They're real. The pain you couldn't possibly see was very real—almost unbearable. It got so bad that,
before the video could be released, most of the tears ended up
on the cutting room floor. That whole shoot was agonizing, but
I made it through. More than anybody, my sister would have
wanted me to. I know that sounds like a cliché, but it's true.
More than anybody, she wanted me to soar. In my heart I knew
that. In my head. I tried to convince myself that she had forgiven me. But still, every day for the next five years, I was tortured—by grief, by guilt, and most of all, by fear.

11     That probably sounds unbelievable, especially the fear part.
Most people who have seen me perform don't think I could be
afraid of anything. Not Patti LaBelle—that brazen, outrageous
diva who will do and say just about anything on stage. If
you've ever been to one of my shows you know they're part
concert, part revival, part confession, part church. Sometimes—
okay a lot of times—I even get to preaching. I know people
come to my shows to listen to me sing, but in between songs,
I make sure they listen to me talk. About faith in God and in
themselves. About hope—for today and tomorrow. About
love—in good times and bad. And while I believe every word
I say, Lord knows I do, here's the unadorned, barefaced, not-
so-pretty truth: I didn't always practice what I preach.

12     The truth is, I wasn't always the woman you see today, the
woman who tries to keep her feet on the ground and her priorities straight. That's only half the story—the cover. This book
is the other half—the uncover. The half that tells the whole

story. The half that took me most of a lifetime to face. The half I kept hidden from my fans as well as myself. Until now.

13    For years, people begged me to, but I'm ready now. Not just to talk about my life, but to talk about how precious life can be. If, that is, you know how to live it. If you don't block the blessings. I know this now the only way you can know it. By being on intimate terms with death. All my life, it's been in my face, taking what was mine, what I needed the most and loved the best. I lived in constant dread of death until finally, thankfully, I let go of that fear. And ever since then life has taken me on a magic carpet ride, a ride that started the night I once thought I would never live to see.

14    May 23, 1994. It was a night I'll never forget—the eve of my 50th birthday. I had always been convinced I'd die before I was 44 and even when I made it to my 45th birthday, I thought I had as much chance of living to see 50 as I had of living to see 150. I wasn't paranoid. Not at all. My belief was based on family history. On facts and figures, dates and data. On nature's arithmetic, not mine.

15    You see, not one of my three sisters lived to see her 44th birthday. Not Vivian, not Barbara, not Jackie. Neither did my best friend, Claudette. I watched all four of them die; every single one of them eaten alive by cancer in the prime of her life. One day they were beautiful and planning their futures. The next, it seemed, they were weak and weary and planning their funerals. In between, I stood by helplessly as diabetes and Alzheimer's claimed my mother and father before their time.

16    That's why, for so long, no matter how hard I tried, I couldn't shake my fear of dying. I thought about it day and night. When it would come. How it would take me. All I would leave behind. How can I explain how real death was to me? It was everywhere, not just taking my family, but even my fans—so many of them—who I've watched perish from this scourge called AIDS. My life had become a slow dance with death.

17    God, how do you live with so much heartache? I had no clue. To cope, I threw myself into my work. I toured the country like a mad woman. I gave concerts everywhere—in big cities and small towns, in huge outdoor stadiums and

small indoor clubs. Touring kept me moving. And, as long as I kept moving, I could run away from everything—from my guilt and my grief, from my feelings and my fears and, most of all, from that bottomless pit of pain in my heart. I wrapped my very soul in my song. I had to. For comfort, for consolation, for camouflage.

18    Within no time, I became a master at hiding my fears. It wasn't too hard. All it usually took was a smile and a song. But as hard as I tried, I could never hide it from myself. You push it down but it's always there. The hurt, the hate, the horror.

19    For the longest time, I refused to even hope that I would be the lucky one, the only one of my mother's four daughters to beat the family curse. Hope hurt too much—I learned that each time I put someone else I loved in the ground.

20    When I got too crazy, my husband tried to reason with me. Other than a slight heart murmur, I was as healthy as a horse. Hadn't all my doctors told me so? In my head, I knew he was right. But where it counted in my gut—I couldn't shake the feeling that death was just toying with me.

21    Of course, the crazy thing was I had so much to live for. Most people who have spent as much time as I have thinking about death feel as if they have nothing in life. As my husband always reminded me, I had plenty. Everything anyone could want and more. A wonderful marriage. Three beautiful sons. Money. Fame. A fantasy career that filled my life with so much joy. I had seen every dream I'd ever had come true. I had toured the world, sold out Broadway, starred in my own prime-time television special and series. It was wonderful beyond description. All of it. But it never seemed to help. At least not for long. If there was one thing I knew, it was how fast it all could be taken away. Everything could be planned but nothing was ever promised.

22    I suppose every time we lose someone we love we all ask questions. Questions that might help us—even in some small way—to face death. Theirs and ours. I asked God all the time. Every single day for five straight years. Why had He spared me and none of my sisters? Was there something I was supposed to do? If so, what? What was the purpose of my life? If there was some larger reason for me to be here, then why was I suffering so much trying to figure it all out?

23    The answers to my life-and-death questions didn't come in a way that I recognized then. And so I started the countdown. Since my youngest sister's death, I felt as though I was living on borrowed time. I knew what I had to do and I had no time to waste. Because I know what it's like to lose someone before you've had a chance to say your good-byes, I started saying mine. At every show I gave, I bid my fans—many of them friends—farewell. Not in so many words, but in my own special way. I did it by leaving what I hoped would be a lasting gift, a legacy of love to all those who had given so much love to me. That's when I started the talking between the singing. I didn't hold anything back, either. Nothing. I talked about everything my mistakes had cost me. I thought by holding a mirror up to each and every one of them, then maybe, just maybe, I could save somebody else from making the same ones. I was preparing myself by purging myself.

24    So imagine my surprise when I actually made it to 50. I'll never forget it—the night before my 50th birthday was one of the most vivid, most amazing experiences of my life. I remember everything about it. Lighting the candles in the bedroom of my L.A. condo to fill the room with a golden glow. Lying awake, watching the clock, staring out at the Hollywood Hills stretched out like a blanket below my window. I felt this incredible calm and peace. At last, it was complete, it was total, it was absolute. I felt like I had finally been released. After all those years of begging God for answers, I realized that He had been answering me all the time. In every song I sang. In every person I touched. In every spirit I lifted. At last, the messenger was getting the message: I hadn't been preparing to die at all— I was learning to live.

25    Sipping a glass of wine and staring out the window at a thousand lights dancing across the Hollywood Hills, I imagined all those people in all those houses, living their lives, thinking about tomorrow and the day after and next year as if they would live forever. I imagined how all those people out there were taking life for granted, as we all tend to do. I thought about how I had learned to take nothing—not one single blessed thing—for granted. How I wanted to live every moment as if there would not be another.

## Theme

1. LaBelle begins her story with the image of herself alone on a video set. In how many other, more important ways does she show herself to have felt alone in her life?

2. Explain how the lyrics of the song she sings in the video both inform and comment on the singer's own situation.

## Technique

1. LaBelle is very hard on herself in describing her reaction to her sister's last request. Imagine some of the things she might have said to soften the image she gives of her behavior to make it seem less selfish. Now point to some of the ways she avoids making any excuses for herself in her account.

2. Her family tries to convince her that her fears might be irrational, but their attempts do not succeed. Point to some of the ways LaBelle expresses the strength of her fears in spite of what might be said to diminish them or comfort her.

## Writing

LaBelle gives her essay the same title as the autobiography it introduces—"Don't Block the Blessings." Write an essay that explains as fully as you can what her own writing shows she means to express by her title.

# Dan Aykroyd

## Michael O'Donoghue                                     (1995)

> *Dan Aykroyd was born in Canada and majored in criminology*
> *at Carleton University in Ottawa before dropping out to join the*
> *Second City Troupe in Toronto. His appearances in the early*
> *days of* Saturday Night Live *led to his long friendship with fellow*
> *Blues Brother John Belushi, and to a long career as a writer and*
> *film actor.*

1    In the late summer of 1975, I received orders to report to the Rockefeller Center offices of NBC's new late-night gamble, *Saturday Night Live*. After two formal auditions there was one more *rite de passage* that would either certify or cancel my acceptance into the advanced guard of North American satirists: encountering a handler of the more finely hammered steel in the trade, Michael O'Donoghue.

2    My disadvantage was owning a Harley-Davidson. Not that Mike didn't like machines. He loved his BMW, and more than once I heard him say, "Boy, those Nazi bastards still build a great car." No, that day I wore vulnerability on my back. Having ridden down from Canada to Manhattan, I was wearing the garb of many bike riders in my part of the world—black leather jacket, black jeans, black T-shirt, black metal-toe-shank boots, leather peaked Harley-wings cap. From a rear pocket dangled a red cotton handkerchief. That it was an oil rag was of no consequence to M.O.D., who saw in my appearance a type of New Yorker as yet unknown to me: the Christopher Street Gay Bar Leather Boy.

3    So as I walked for the first time down the hallway at my new job, Mike stepped out from a doorway as if he'd been waiting.

---

SOURCE: By Dan Aykroyd from *Rolling Stone,* January 12, 1995. Copyright © Rolling Stone LLC 1995. All rights reserved. Reprinted by permission.

Like a hybrid of Nevada trapdoor spider and Indian cobra, he darted and injected: "Jesus, are you in the wrong part of town or what, pal? Aykroyd, you look like the biggest, ugliest leather queen I've seen since Rondo Hatton tried to fuck Montgomery Clift. Listen, they're having a great sale at the Anvil bar on anal drawstrings, and from the width of your ass, you'll be needing a yard of 100-pound Fiberglass test!"

4   Any reaction other than laughter might have barred me from further contact. Then I looked at him while attempting to summon a rejoinder from my reeling brain. Here was a sartorially impeccable, slender, red-haired, pink Irishman. In his hand he held a long black Egyptian cigarette, and although they were writer's hands, I saw a bony, clawlike strength, my first thought was, "This is someone I don't want to fuck with physically. The hands could snap your throat, and he'll bite, too." There was nothing one could really do at that point but go home and change or right there flat come out of the closet. I had been leveled, no comeback possible.

5   My future with O'Donoghue was one of immobilizing laugh sessions under the tutelage and encouragement of this Dean of Shock Value. The boiler of masterfully savage stews like the Claudine Longet Invitational Ski Shoot, Jamitol, Shimmer Floor Wax/Dessert Topping, the Temple of the Jack Lord, he wrote the best language the Not Ready for Prime Time Players ever spoke and also gave genuine support when others wrote something good. Real laughter from Mike was a silvery imprimatur. If we wrote something bad, however, there was no politesse in the inevitable scorching. Tom Davis and I received one the night we launched a sketch called Danger Probe. The second the scene was over, as we skittered away under the audience scaffold, Mike was there, cigarette and wineglass in hand, to declare: "Oh, we'll be seeing lots more of those, I hope. That one will be way bigger than the Conehead sketches."

6   Broadsword, rapier, scythe, buzz saw, Mr. Mike of Mondo Video was also a purveyor of the most generous form of Edwardian-influenced hospitality. The grand gatherings at his turn-of-the-century Village townhouse always attracted a great mix, and you dressed in church clothes. Those classic,

elegant parties are the sweet syrup beneath the crust of my New York memories.

7      The house was done in the taste of an impeccable old-school gentleman. One wall held a display case filled with various sizes of miniature rhinos. Monstrous cats patrolled the premises. Writers, wits, humorists and artists would attend, the fare being an elixir of continuous irreverence. The Age of Innocence with good boo.

8      His impact on *SNL* began with the show's very first sketch—his language-teacher piece. He provided the arming mechanism for a generation's comic blast. During the show's crucial early days his boldness and slash-and-burn style freed the other performers and writers to push the limits of comic convention. Yet his work exemplified the discipline necessary for us to pull off our own visions. We performed his scripts with zeal and passionate affection, learning well from them, and went forth from this master's chamber as his journeymen. Without him, our accomplishments—and the glorious fun we had—would have been much less.

## Theme

1. The moments of personal encounter that Aykroyd describes here often include aggressive speech on the part of the man he obviously admires. In your own words characterize what it is that Aykroyd likes and admires in Michael O'Donoghue and how that man's speech fits in with Aykroyd's admiration.

2. A phrase like "New York sophistication" may be said to characterize one of the themes of the piece. Point to some of the elements of the essay that contribute to this sense and explain how they do so.

## Technique

1. "Sartorially" in paragraph four means "with regard to tailoring." How does Aykroyd use sartorial details in creating a

sense of the man he memorializes? Point to some examples and analyze how they work.

2. In his sketch, Aykroyd always appears as the rookie and O'Donaghue, the veteran, though Aykroyd is much more famous as an actor, comedian, and writer. Point to some of the ways Aykroyd's writing creates this effect.

## Writing

Using Aykroyd's brief essay as a model, write a memorial sketch of a mentor who has made a lasting impression on you.

# LL Cool J

## Impotent Demon                                                    (1997)

> *The rapper LL Cool J was born James Todd Smith in Bay Shore,*
> *Long Island, near New York City. As a child of four he experi-*
> *enced severe trauma when his father shot both his mother and*
> *grandfather. His mother's recovery from her wounds with the help*
> *of a physical therapist led to the events described in the following*
> *excerpt from LL Cool J's autobiography,* I Make My Own Rules.

1    **M**y mother almost died. The shotgun pellets entered her
lower back and fanned out. Several grazed her spinal column,
and for a while she couldn't walk. She spent more than six
months in the hospital recovering. During the first month, my
grandmother took me to see her in the hospital every other
day. I could only wave and smile at her through a glass parti-
tion, because they didn't allow little kids in intensive care.

2    After three months she was able to go from a wheelchair to
a walker. From the walker she went to a cane, and then to a
leg brace. At each transition, Roscoe was there. She met him a
few months before the shooting at Northport VA Hospital,
where she worked in the pharmacy. Roscoe was an assistant
to a physical therapist. After the shooting he made it his mission in life to help my mother recover.

3    All the doctors told her she would never walk again, but
Roscoe made her believe she could. And she did, which is a
testament to her determination. Another trait I inherited from
her. But from that point on, he had her head. With her grati-
tude, he wormed his way into her life. And my mother, feeling
empty and vulnerable, just let him. She fell in love with the
man she thought gave her the ability to walk again. I ain't mad

at her, though, 'cause I know how that is. If you thought someone saved your life, you might fall for them too.

4    Roscoe was totally different from my father. He was always
joking and playing around and laughing with my mother.
Roscoe was one of those pretty boys. He had hazel eyes, a
curly Afro, and a thick mustache. My father was big and tall,
with big muscles and a thick waist. Roscoe was little, about five
seven, the same height as my mother, and he wore platform
shoes. I don't remember when I first laid eyes on him. It was
like he was always there after my mother got out of the hospital. But I knew from jump he didn't like me, and I was definitely not fooling him. I must have been a threat to him.

5    Maybe because I was even smaller, he thought he could take
out his frustrations on me. Maybe he just had a Napoleon complex because he was short. (All he ever talked about was this
cousin of his who was "six feet four and two seventy-five" as
if to show that somewhere in his genes was a big person. But
that gene definitely missed him.)

6    Maybe he was jealous of the relationship I had with my
mother and her family. Maybe I was an obstacle, getting in the
way of his freedom with my mother. Or maybe I was just
someone easy to take out his frustrations on. Easy target—little Napoleon's punching bag. Whatever the motivation, though,
there's no real explanation for how he treated me.

7    When my moms got completely healthy she started working two jobs—the Suffolk County Developmental Center in
Melville, Long Island, from 3:20 P.M. until 11 P.M., and the St.
Alban's VA Hospital from midnight to 8 A.M. She had an hour
to get from Suffolk County to Queens. Some nights she had to
depend on Roscoe to drop her off and pick her up because he
was using her car. Some nights he was late. Sometimes he
made her wait for hours. He was too busy getting high, cheat-
ing on her, and beating on me.

8    My mother had a small, brick-and-tan house built for us in
North Babylon. She had to work the two jobs just to pay the
mortgage, and was carrying most of the weight. That left him
at home with me the majority of the time and it was on—playtime for him. His idea of big fun was beating on me.

9    Roscoe beat me for just about anything. He would beat me for watching television, for lookin' at him funny, for looking out of the window watching other kids play. He didn't need a good reason. It was just a power trip. While my mother worked, Roscoe was home abusing her son. He was usually home when I came in from school, and it was like, "Let the games begin!"

10    He'd make me take off all my clothes and put my arms up on my bunk bed with the *Star Wars* sheets while he beat me. It was like the scene in *Glory* when Denzel Washington was getting beat down like a slave, except I was like eight years old. He'd even pull me out of the shower to get a beating. He didn't care how he beat me or with what.

11    He would rotate beating me with extension cords, vacuum cleaner attachments, and fists. He would punch me in the chest and knock the wind out of me—and then tell me to "raise up," get up for another punch. One time he threw me down a flight of stairs in our house. He even beat me for looking in the refrigerator. There's nothing worse than being hungry and staring into an empty refrigerator because your mother's man ate all the food after smoking a pound of weed—and then getting a beating for being hungry. Yo, it could freak you out.

12    It's around this time that I started wearing hats all the time.

## Theme

1. Explain what LL Cool J means when he speculates about Roscoe's "Napoleon complex."

2. Explain how the mother's working hours help to explain her lack of help in the author's time of trouble.

## Technique

1. There is no warning in the early account of Roscoe about the role he will play in the author's life, though LL Cool J might easily have warned his reader early on not to be overly impressed by the help that Roscoe gave to his

mother. What do you think of the way LL Cool J handles the two sides of Roscoe? Explain your answer.

2. The author's title for this reminiscence is "Impotent Demon." The "demon" part is clear enough. Do you find "impotent" also effective? Explain your answer.

### Writing

Write an essay describing ways in which the author achieves an emotional attitude toward his past. Begin by characterizing that attitude and go on to say what he does and does not do as a writer to create it.

# Marc Anthony

## Eulogy for Tito Puente                                              **(2002)**

*Born Marco Antonio Muniz, Marc Anthony became a leading
voice in Latin music. In the eulogy that follows, he describes how
the bandleader and singer Tito Puente inspired and aided him
in his career and in his young life.*

1    Tito Puente seemed superhuman to me. He was the founding father of Latin music as we know it, the master of masters.
He took all the hits in the beginning. Without Tito, who would
have carried it on this long? Who would have helped generations make Latin music their own? He and I came from the
same neighborhood in Spanish Harlem, and, knowing that, I
felt nothing was impossible. The day I met him, he said I
reminded him of his son, and thereafter he treated me as a son,
always telling me, "Keep it up. You're on the right track." He
had no idea how much those words meant to me. Tito's presence inspired us all. He was a man who was revered, honored,
and respected in his lifetime. I thank God for giving me the
opportunity to know and care for one of the most amazing
men ever to walk the earth, for his funny stories and infectious
laugh, for his honesty and generosity, but most of all for his
friendship. This year he honored me by playing with me at
Madison Square Garden. He knew I was nervous, so he hung
out with me in my dressing room before the show. That was
Tito for you. He was my friend, mentor, godfather, and inspiration, and it's painful knowing I'll never see him walk through
a door and fill up a room again.

SOURCE: By permission of the author.

## Theme

1. Examine the moments when Marc Anthony uses different
   senses of the metaphor of fatherhood in his characterization
   of and tribute to Tito Puente. How are the different senses
   of fatherhood differentiated? How are they connected? In
   what ways does the metaphor help to make the eulogy
   forceful and moving?

2. Note the different locations whereby Marc Anthony estab-
   lishes and expresses his relations with Tito Puente. How, for
   example, do different meanings of what is geographically the
   same "New York" create different senses of who the two men
   are, where they come from, and where they are headed? That
   is, Spanish Harlem has connotations different from Madison
   Square Garden, though both are located in New York. What
   are these connotations in each case and how do they contribute to what Tito Puente meant to Marc Anthony?

## Technique

1. The text of the eulogy is set all in one paragraph, though
   the author frequently seems to be starting off on new
   themes. How does the paragraph's organization or apparent
   lack of organization contribute to the expression of the
   author's emotions?

2. The last sentence lists some of the different relations
   between Marc Anthony and Tito Puente. In your view have
   each of these relations been addressed earlier in this brief
   eulogy? For example does the impression "filling a room"
   connect to anything earlier in the essay?

## Writing

Think of someone who has meant a great deal to you and imagine you have just received the news of his or her death. Using
Marc Anthony's essay as a model, write a brief eulogy.

# Alice Walker

## Do it for Someone You Love                        (2004)

*Alice Walker was born in Georgia as the eighth (and last) child
of sharecroppers. After attending Spelman, a college for African-
American women in Atlanta, she transferred to New York's Sarah
Lawrence College and spent her junior year in Africa as an
exchange student. After college she became a writer and received
the Pulitzer Prize for her novel,* The Color Purple.

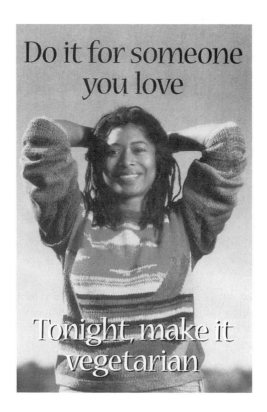

## Theme

1. What is it that the public service advertisement implies you are doing besides serving food when you serve vegetarian food?

2. How are you invited to feel about yourself if you go along with the advertisement's directive? Make a list and explain how you arrived at it. For example, are you invited to think of yourself as "compassionate?" By what implied reasoning?

## Technique

1. The word "it" makes a frequent appearance in the text of the ad. Is "it" always used in the same way? Find some more explicit words that might serve to replace each instance of "it." Don't be afraid to modify the sentences themselves somewhat in order to fit in your choices. Are there any apparent advantages in using the word "it" instead of more explicit words to achieve the advertisement's purpose?

2. What does Alice Walker's appearance and facial expression do to help achieve the purpose of the advertisement? For example, if she had appeared in a physician's white coat, the suggestion might have been humorously made that she was giving medical advice. What does she in fact contribute visually here?

## Writing

Write an essay analyzing the various ways, including the visual, by which valuable emotions such as compassion and love are linked to vegetarian food in this public service advertisement.

# Chaka Khan

## Personnel: Up Close and Personal     (2003)

*Born Yvette Marie Stevens, Chaka Khan was 18 when she joined Rufus, the band that made her famous. Since that time she has appeared mainly as a solo artist and is ranked number 17 in VH1's 100 Greatest Women of Rock & Roll.*

1    **W**hen I decided to start my own record label in 1998, I named the company Earth Song Entertainment. With Earth Song, I vowed to give the universe good, true, *honest* music. I also vowed never to exploit a fellow artist—never to do anything to anyone I wouldn't want done to me! (For one, I vowed that artists would own their own masters.)

2    During the last months of my crack relapse, my record label languished, of course. After I got clean, Earth Song became a top priority.

3    One of the best business decisions I made was to ask my mother to be my business manager/accountant. Over the years, I'd had my share of managers and accountants who were at times, shall we say, more generous to themselves than to me. But that was something I had to take responsibility for—you know, as in "Fool me once, shame on you. Fool me twice ..."

4    My finances were pretty much always a wreck. I'd work my butt off—recording, touring, doing club gigs and special events—and end up with very little to show for it. For one, I'd spend a lot of money on a whim. I was also careless in small ways, too (and the little things add up!).

5    "Yvette, you don't have to give the brother a fifty."

6    That was Mark one day back in the 1980s. We were in New York going I don't remember where when a homeless guy

---

SOURCE: From *Chaka!* by Chaka Khan. Reprinted by permission.

asked, "Can you spare a little something so I can get something to eat?" When I reached into my pocketbook, a Grant was the first thing that came to hand. Thanks to Mark, I switched up to a Lincoln. But there were times when neither Mark nor anyone else with good sense was with me when a panhandler made a plea.

7    When it came to getting ripped off by people who supposedly worked for me—yeah, I'd heard legions of stories about singers, musicians—all varieties of artists—getting taken by their "people"—managers, accountants, agents, lawyers. But I was too caught up with my drugging and drinking and dramas to put serious energy into scrutinizing my money matters and not getting flimflammed.

8    When young artists ask me about career do's and don'ts, "You might want to get a law degree," I sometimes advise. Well, perhaps that's a bit extreme. But they should at least take pains not to let anyone hurry them into signing a contract. I advise all young artists to develop the patience to read a contract—to make sure they understand what they're agreeing to before they lay down their John Hancocks. Above all, I tell them to be eagle-eyed when it comes to anyone handling their money and giving them financial advice. My mother has always been rock solid and above reproach.

9    Having Tammy as my personal manager revealed what a difference it makes when you have people who truly love you—and are honest!—at the top of your team. It wasn't just about having people who wouldn't steal from me; there was also the issue of having people who would not hustle me into decisions on gigs and other business matters out of their own self-interests.

10   As I worked on Earth Song's infrastructure, I also worked on product. I was working in the studio in late 2000 when I met Douglas Rasheed.

11   My engineer had suggested I take a listen to some of Doug's tracks. I didn't know anything about the guy other than that he was a cowriter of "Gangsta's Paradise." I liked that song the moment I heard it. And I liked the material Doug brought to Earth Song. And then, wouldn't you know it, I started really liking Doug.... The feeling was mutual.

12    *No, Chaka, a man is the last thing you need right now, Stay focused on your work!*

13    But there was something special about Doug.

14    *With every guy there's always been something special, and what has it gotten you?* But during our first conversation, we *talked*—Doug hadn't been flooding me with flattery or otherwise trying to soup me up. He had been himself, it seemed.

15    *But which self? People have many.*

16    Yes, I entered 2001 yet again in love—but determined to stay grounded and be as good to myself as I was to Doug—and I'd let time reveal if he was "Mr. Right."

17    In the meantime, we partnered up on a CD. Earth Song would have to do a lot of work to ensure that the CD was excellent and got out there—financial backers, a marketing plan, and so forth. I definitely understood by then that it would take a lot of capital and a fair amount of time for me to do this right.

## Theme

1. Chaka Khan tells us that late in her career she hired her mother as her business manager. What are the different benefits—business and personal—that she claims accrued to her as a result of that decision?

2. List the financial dangers to a performer that Chaka Khan claims to have herself experienced. In each case explain how the personal and the financial aspects of the situation interacted.

## Technique

1. Chaka Khan writes: "Over the years, I'd had my share of managers and accountants who were at times, shall we say, more generous to themselves than to me." Explain how the interjected phrase, "shall we say" changes the meaning of the words that follow it. Does the phrase, for example, make the words about generosity seem more harsh? Clearer? More emphatic? What does the phrase do?

2. Toward the end of the excerpt Chaka Khan sets some of her words in italics. What is the purpose and effect of this technique? For example, are the words in italics understood to be said more loudly or with more emphasis?

## Writing

Chaka Khan writes toward the end of her selection: *"But which self? People have so many."* Write an essay that analyzes the different "selves" you find Chaka Khan expressing in this short selection from her autobiography.

# EXERCISES

1. Mia Farrow and LL Cool J both experienced great difficulties with people who played important roles in their lives. Of course, clear differences exist between their accounts in terms of passive and active aggression. But what about the different way each writer responds to the difficulties he or she faced, now that the difficulties are over and may be calmly evaluated? Discuss the tones and manners by which these two writers try to come to terms in the present with things that deeply upset them in the past. What are some alternative approaches that they have *not* used?

2. Mick Jagger, Dan Aykroyd, and Marc Anthony all write in response to the recent deaths of significant others. Discuss the differences and similarities of those responses both as tributes to the figures they had lost and expressions of the impact those figures continued to make on the authors.

3. Though Chaka Khan writes a relatively short essay, she manages to give a sense of her past, present, and future, especially when we learn that she went on to marry the man she introduces at the end of her piece. How do other writers in the chapter manage the problem of time? That is, how do they convey the sense of the importance of their significant others throughout their lives rather than merely at important turning points in those lives? Discuss the ways time becomes an issue both for the writers' lives and for their writings.

4. In the only visual expression in the chapter, Alice Walker presents a simple message in complex and multifaceted ways. Discuss how the other writers in the chapter manage to give us a sense of how complex an apparently simple lesson can be. For example, Chaka Khan surely tells us more about what she has learned than that it is risky to trust strangers.

5. Most of the significant others written about in this chapter inhabit the same world of entertainment as the writers

themselves. Does this seem to make a difference in the kinds of tributes that are paid to them? That is, the figures are praised both as entertainers and as human beings. Discuss the ways the different authors manage to combine these categories in their writing.

## Suggestions for Writing

1. Dan Aykroyd and Mia Farrow both pay attention to questions of home decoration. Write an essay in which you analyze the ways each writer uses the physical details of an environment to convey a sense of the personality of the person inhabiting that environment.

2. Mick Jagger and Marc Anthony both pay tributes to fellow musicians. Write an essay that analyzes the ways in which they combine praise for artistry with praise for the human qualities of their significant other.

3. Several of the significant others described in the essays of this chapter behave very oddly. Write an essay in which you compare and contrast the way the writers involved manage to convey a sense of the oddity they observe, not so much by labeling its quality as by dramatizing how the trait played out in life.

4. As a child, LL Cool J could do little to help himself or combat the figure who oppressed him. Write an essay about a troublesome figure in your own past, paying special attention to the things you did or did not do in response.

5. Using any of the essays in the chapter as a stimulus, a model, or a point of departure, write an essay about a person who has made a significant, positive difference in your own life.

# PART II

# Constructing a Public Persona

# CHAPTER 4

# FINDING A LANGUAGE
# AND A STYLE

The chapters in this section shift the book's focus from issues involved in the discovery of your private identity to some of the ways that identity can be made available to others through public performance in life and in language. You have discovered well before college that the world does not automatically know who you are—it can know only the public persona that you create. You are like a book that others read, and therefore you need to make sure that you are a well-written book. However firmly you may know who you are and what you stand for, the world can understand you only through a public persona it can see and hear. That persona needs to be constructed in such a way that the identity you express through your language and style of living is being properly understood by the world in the ways you intend.

Because a sense of one's own identity can mean very little if it lacks a language for its verbal expression, the chapter that begins this section contains essays involving issues of language, beginning with basic matters of word choice and moving to larger questions of style. In the first selection Andy Rooney, the resident humorist on CBS's *60 Minutes,* responds to an invitation to be included in a textbook like the one you are reading—an anthology of essays, but one designed to serve a lower level of instruction. "Over-designed" may be said to sum up the objections Rooney raises to the editor's efforts to change his persona to fit her standards.

In the next essay, radio columnist Charles Osgood explores a different aspect of word choice—the current status of naughty words.

Osgood adopts a tone of mock bewilderment in responding to claims that the verbal environment is becoming less polluted. A very extensive collection of respectable euphemisms makes his satiric point.

A related aspect of language and style is the subject of an essay by Miss Manners, the woman who for decades has advised the readers of her lighthearted newspaper column on the ins and outs of etiquette. She argues through an exploration of a particularly modern form of ill-mannered talk that matters of etiquette are important—in fact they may be matters of life and death.

Next, Chris Rock looks at musical manners in a comic analysis of differing styles in contemporary genres and the different audiences that make them so popular. In "Rockology" he reveals that rap is rap and country is western and never the twain shall meet.

But before rap was ever heard of, James Brown, "The Godfather of Soul," had crafted a unique style of music based on influences that include some surprising, non-musical names—Marlon Brando for one. Brown tells us how he created the rhythm that made him famous in "On the *One.*"

"My Favorite Guys" explores style in some performative rather than verbal manifestations. As a highly successful professional football coach, John Madden has had to understand both the strengths and the weaknesses of players in all positions, but in the excerpt from his book reprinted here he focuses on the offensive line, the place where he himself started out in football.

Freddy Prinze, Jr. combines an individual visual presentation with a well known common advertising campaign that urges us to drink milk. The wholesome and the healthy are combined with familiar features of the star himself to make a point about "making it big."

The chapter ends by addressing the issue of writing itself in two different registers. First, Steve Martin makes some lighthearted jokes about how difficult it can be to write anything. His title says one thing, but his essay's style says another, and in "Writing is Easy!" you may be encouraged to learn that even a prolific and successful writer like Steve Martin knows just how you feel in your own lonely struggles with the art of composition.

Another even more prolific writer, Stephen King, ends the chapter with some serious advice. He finds reading to be the real key to writing and explains his point by combining personal anecdotes with general advice to help would-be writers find themselves in their craft.

# Andy Rooney

## A Text for Textbook Writers          (1989)

> *Andy Rooney is the resident comic curmudgeon on CBS's* 60
> Minutes, *the longest running news show in television history.*
> *He began his long writing career as a newspaper reporter and*
> *wrote for armed forces papers like* Stars and Stripes *during*
> *World War II.*

1   All I remember about the textbooks I had in school is that most of them weren't very good. We learned more from the teachers than from the books, and the teachers who relied most on textbooks were the weakest.

2   I have a letter written by Barbara Everett, "editor, Language Arts Department, Elementary-High Division" of the Merrill Publishing Company, one of the biggest in the textbook business.

3   You can bet that when anyone announces herself as editor of the Language Arts Department of anything, you're in for trouble.

4   It turns out that Barbara wants my permission to use an essay I wrote for inclusion in one of their seventh-grade textbooks, but she wants to make some changes in it.

5   "I have marked the changes we would like to make," the letter says. "I have made slight additions to paragraphs one and two so that the readability will be closer to seventh grade. In paragraph five I deleted references to cookies, which are junk food and therefore may not be mentioned in textbooks."

6   Well, Barbara, in answer to your question of whether Merrill may use my essay in its textbook, no.

7   I think seventh graders would probably understand the essay the way I wrote it but even if they could not, I have no inclination to try to make it any easier for them. No writer, except maybe Bill Buckley, likes to exclude anyone from

SOURCE: From *Not That You Asked* by Andrew A. Rooney. Copyright © 1989 by Essay Productions, Inc. Used by permission of Random House, Inc.

understanding what he's written but it is always wrong for a writer, or for that matter a parent or a teacher, to talk down or write down to anyone. If you write simply and directly, children will understand. Even if they are a little confused at first, they'll get the general idea. Then they'll associate the general idea with the words you've used and get to understand them. This is the learning process.

8    By the time children reach the seventh grade, teachers should be talking to them the way they talk to adults. For one thing, it is almost impossible for an adult to judge what changes should be made in a sentence to make it simpler for a child to understand, so the best course to follow is to say it or write it as well as you are able. Don't give them seventh-grade baby talk.

9    The trouble with most textbooks is they've turned into characterless pap. So many groups are applying so much pressure to teachers, boards of education, and textbook publishers that by the time everything anyone objects to has been deleted there's nothing of any substance left.

10    Children should be exposed to all the ideas there are so they can choose for themselves. One of the best teachers I ever had would have been thrown out of a lot of schools or colleges because he was left of liberal. As kids we talked and laughed about how favorably he looked on communism, but it didn't make any of us into communists. People underestimate the ability of young students to sort things out.

11    Now, Barbara, while I have your attention, let me talk to you about cookies. I don't know how to start but let me just say that the cookies Aunt Anna made were not junk food. There are a lot of commercial cookies that aren't junk food, either. Have you tried Pepperidge Farm's crisp molasses cookies recently, or their oatmeal raisin? On behalf of the cookie makers and cookie eaters of the world, amateur and professional, I resent your slurring reference to our product.

12    Have you never enjoyed an Oreo, a Hydrox, a Social Tea? Are you knocking Fig Newtons? There may not be a lot of wheat germ, fiber, or vitamin B in Animal Crackers but are they really bad for kids? Marijuana and cocaine I can understand not mentioning, but chocolate chip and macaroons? Does Merrill

really think that by never mentioning the word *cookie* in one of its textbooks, it will improve the health of the nation?

13    No, Barbara, I don't want anything I've written used in a junk textbook.

## Theme

1. In your own words explain Rooney's reasoning on changing the language of his essay "so that the readability will be closer to seventh grade."

2. In your own words explain Rooney's reasoning on the issues about cookies that were raised by the publisher.

## Technique

1. Explain the play on words that Rooney makes use of in his title. If you don't get the joke, look up the different meanings of "text" in a dictionary.

2. How does the list of names of cookies work to satirize the idea of omitting the mention of any cookies because they are "junk food?"

## Writing

Where do you stand on the issue of readability in textbooks? Are you with Rooney or the publisher? Write an essay in which you define, exemplify, and defend your position.

# Charles Osgood

**%@*&#**                                    **(1986)**

*Charles Osgood is a radio and television commentator. His daily radio program (sometimes including his own comic verse) has been broadcast for over thirty-five years and he entered the Radio Hall of Fame in 1990.*

1    Gosh! I just found out the doggondest thing! Did you realize that obscene language is on the way out? I sure as heck didn't. Golly Ned! I would not have guessed that on my own, to tell you the truth. Gee, the decline of obscenity sure hasn't turned up yet in the kind of conversation that I have occasion to hear every day. In fact I would have guessed that obscene language was replacing regular ordinary language as the standard means of communication. But an English professor at Cleveland State University, William Chisholm, is on record as saying that the doggone pendulum is now swinging away from dirty words and toward good old-fashioned respect and decency. Well, I'll be a son of a gun!

2    Shucks! To hear the professor tell it, foul and filthy language has become so prevalent and commonplace in our society that nobody is really shocked and disgusted any more. If you are not going to shock and disgust people, there is simply no point in talking like that.

3    I must admit that the logic of this sounds to me a lot like that of Yogi Berra when somebody asked him about a certain restaurant. "Nobody eats there any more," said Berra, "it's too crowded." Well, if the reason nobody is cussing any more is that cussing is too prevalent, then *somebody* must be using

the bad words. Maybe people are just hearing tape recordings of bad words actually spoken in the 1960s at the height of the so-called "free speech" movement. Or the famous White House tapes that President Nixon made during the Watergate days. I don't think so, though. If the professor means that the words are still being used but without the intended shock value, or without any value whatsoever, I would go along with him there.

4    Another scholar, Reinhold Ahman, who edits some darn publication called *Maledicta: The Journal of Verbal Aggression,* swears that there are no strong swear words left any more. You can go to your neighborhood theater or tune in on your neighborhood cable TV channel and hear Eddie Murphy or Richard Pryor say exactly the same words that got Lenny Bruce thrown into jail not that many years ago.

5    Now, nobody seems to give a hoot. We have heard all the four-letter words too much and in every conceivable variation. Some people who have no idea what a noun is, will insert a profanity before every noun, as in: "Pass the %@*&# salt, please."

6    Others display amazing ingenuity as to obscenity placement. Would you think it possible to insert a profanity in the very middle of an adverb? The answer is "abso%$#@&lutely."

## Theme

1. Explain the reasoning on the subject of obscene language that is attributed to Professor William Chisholm in the essay's first two paragraphs.

2. Explain the reasoning Osgood himself presents in the third paragraph.

## Technique

1. Suppose that instead of using euphemisms—words like "gosh" instead of "God," for example—Osgood had laced his essay with the obscene language that makes the essay's subject. Would that tactic have been effective? Explain your answer.

2. Osgood uses euphemisms for most of the essay, but then at its end he gives groups of typographical symbols like those that make up his title. Does that switch-in substitute for obscene language have any effect? Explain your answer.

## Writing

Where do you stand on the issue of obscene language? Do you think its use is waning? Do you think it should wane? Write an essay in which you explain and defend your position.

# Miss Manners

## Rudeness Can Be Lethal (1994)

*Miss Manners is the pen name of Judith Martin, who has been
writing about manners and points of etiquette in a syndicated
newspaper column for decades. Her essay here is on a serious
topic, but the following lines are perhaps more representative of
her own language and style.*
*"Dear Miss Manners:*
*What is the correct way to walk in high-heeled shoes?"*
*Gentle Reader:*
*Left, right, left, right, left right.*

1    Oｎe of the leading causes of modern crime, Miss Manners gathers from paying attention to the news reports, is senselessness.

2    "Another senseless shooting," they keep announcing.

3    "A senseless stabbing ... a senseless murder ..."

4    We used to have such sensible crime.

5    Miss Manners can't help wondering what went wrong.

6    Sensible crimes were ones committed for love or money. When neither revenue nor revenge is involved, the modern crime seems to strike people as unreasonable.

7    But Miss Manners has also been paying attention to what the criminals themselves give as their motives, and they make a certain deplorable sense to her. People are now killing over—you're going to have a hard time believing this one—etiquette.

8    One of our leading causes of murder is a perceived lack of respect. Respect is a basic concept of manners, which features such principles as dignity and compassion, rather than strict justice, which it leaves to the law. Being treated respectfully is not one of our rights, nor is treating others respectfully a legal obligation. Only manners require it.

9    Yet "dissin' "—showing real or apparent disrespect—is cited as the motive in an amazing number of murders.

---

Source: *Miss Manners* reprinted by permission of United Feature Syndicate, Inc.

10     As a Washington, D.C. high school football player said when discussing the shootings of members of his team—one dead, three wounded last summer alone—"The biggest thing everybody is looking for is respect in the streets. It isn't money. They are just trying to make sure you respect them. People are just pushing each other to the maximum to get respect. And the maximum is death."

11     Remember what all those 18th-century Frenchmen in lace cuffs did when they got fussed about people looking at them cross-eyed? The chief difference now is that the duel has lost some of its frills, such as gloves, seconds, and allowing both participants to shoot at the same time. In keeping with modern practicality, the idea caught on that it is more effective to shoot when your victim isn't looking.

12     Failure to provide road courtesies is given as the motivation for the new sport of car-to-car shootings. Law is supposed to regulate the highway, but traffic law does not cover such courtesies as letting others pass, not playing a car radio so loudly that it annoys people in other cars, and not going slowly in a fast lane. So highway murderers seem to think of themselves as encouraging drivers' etiquette.

13     Fairness is a concept that manners shares with law, but only etiquette requires it in such informal situations as waiting in line. Some months ago, there was a stabbing in a Bethesda, Maryland grocery store over the fact that someone had broken into the checkout line out of turn.

14     Does all this sound as if Miss Manners is on the side of the criminals? She is, after all, devoted to stamping out rudeness, just as these people have claimed to be.

15     But she has her limits about how it can be done. And she makes a strict division between the jurisdictions of the law and of manners. Crime is not merely lethal rudeness.

16     Without even squabbling, she and Miss Justice managed to divide the task of regulating social behavior so that the law, with its fierce sanctions, agreed to punish behavior that is seriously threatening to life, limb, or property, while gentle Miss Manners tries to persuade people to avoid the kind of behavior that leads to such unpleasantness.

17     But when poor old etiquette fails, the law must take over. It was a humiliating defeat for manners when both smokers and

nonsmokers refused to curb their rudeness toward one another, and the law had to take over what used to be in the jurisdiction of manners.

18    Miss Manners' point about the new etiquette-motivated crime is that when there is no recognition of the need to observe courtesies, everyone finds life unbearable. Asking the law to regulate petty conduct would trespass on our basic rights, but allowing individual impulses to go totally unrestrained leads to mayhem.

19    There is no use telling Miss Manners that no one cares about etiquette any more. Even outlaws are outraged when others do not follow its rules.

## Theme

1. Explain in your own words what Miss Manners takes to be the sense behind some "senseless" crimes.

2. Explain in your own words the rationale of respect in paragraphs nine and ten.

## Technique

1. Miss Manners always speaks of herself in the third person. What effect does this technique create with regard to the emotional range of feelings that her essay expresses? Is the range a constrained or narrow one? Explain your answer.

2. In the analysis in paragraph ten the football player twice uses the word "just." Read his sentences aloud with and without the word. What effect on the emotional content of his sentences does his use of "just" create?

## Writing

What do you think of the level of public manners today? Write an essay in which you explain and exemplify your position.

# Chris Rock

## Rockology                                    (1997)

*Chris Rock was born and raised in Brooklyn, New York. He started his career as a stand-up comic and spent three years on* Saturday Night Live. *His first big acting break came in* Beverly Hills Cop II *and in 2005 he hosted the Oscar Presentations.*

1   Popular culture is who we are. It reflects our values, morals, interests, obsessions, ethics, hopes, and dreams.

### Rap This!

2   White people don't understand rap.

3   That's good. It's not for white people.

4   Anyway, it's not that complicated. Rap is to black people what country music is to whites. Rap is not made for anyone but the people it's made for. When Garth Brooks makes an album, he doesn't stop and think, "Okay, we need something for the black audience." He just makes his records for the country fan. Travis Tritt doesn't think of yuppies, he thinks of cowboy hats.

5   Same thing with rappers.

6   White people: the music's not for you.

7   You can listen, but don't complain.

| Country Music | Rap |
|---|---|
| Don't care what people think. | Don't care what people think. |
| Only want to please themselves. | Only want to please themselves. |
| Wear jeans and big hats. | Wear jeans and big hats. |
| Poor: Come from trailer parks. | Poor: Come from the projects. |
| Talk funny, use slang. | Talk funny, use slang. |
| Personal, dysfunctional topics. | Personal, dysfunctional topics. |
| Cracker music. | Nigger music. |

## The Rap Gap

8    Every generation says the next generation's music is not as
good as theirs. That's wrong, except for my generation's music.

9    I hate R&B right now. It's not as good as it used to be. Why?
Because reading levels are down. You can't read … you can't
write. How are you going to write a good song if you can't
even do "The Alphabet Song" straight through, without mixing
up M and N, and forgetting Y?

10   R&B music these days is almost all about sex. Only Baby-
face is writing about romance.

11   And it's all too literal. In the old days, people had metaphors
for what they wanted to say. Even the nasty songs aspired to
a certain level of craftsmanship. Remember "Pull Up to the
Bumper?"

### Theme

1. Chris Rock says that country music is different from rap, but
   he "proves" it by making a two-column list where all the categories on each side seem the same until the end—and
   even there he makes the same assertion, though in less than
   genteel terms. Does this apparent contradiction really have a
   point and make sense? Explain your answer.

2. In your own words explain Chris Rock's complaints about
   contemporary R&B. Why does he say that the lack of
   metaphor is the key to understanding the decline? Do you
   agree? Explain your answer.

### Technique

1. What do you think of Rock's listing techniques? Do you find
   them effective? Ineffective? Amusing? Annoying? Could other
   parts of his essay be expressed just as well in lists? Explain
   your answer.

2. Whether written in the form of lists or not, the essay depends
   heavily on the techniques of contrast. Make a list of the things
   contrasted. Does he find any things that he sees as similar—
   that is, anything comparable? Explain your answer.

## Writing

Do you agree with Chris Rock when he says white people don't understand rap? Write an essay that explains and defends your views.

# James Brown

## On the *One*                                                    (2005)

*James Brown, "The Godfather of Soul," is also known as "The Hardest Working Man in Show Business." Born to poverty in the south and sent to jail as a young man for armed robbery, Brown first discovered his musical abilities in a gospel group and worked his way to fame from that base. How hard he works as a musician and a composer may be seen representatively in the following excerpt from his autobiography,* I Feel Good.

1    Marlon Brando was another early rock & roll hero of mine, although he never sang a rock, R&B, or soul song in his life. Nevertheless, he was a cultural icon for rebellion. In 1954, he made a movie that shook the youth of America down to its motorcycle boots. It was called *The Wild One.* The way he looked, the way he dressed all in black leather, the attitude, the youth, and the cultural scream he produced—all of it put him right up there with the Elvises and the Robert Johnsons of the world—forerunners to the seismic shift that American youth was about to effect.

2    In the movie, a pretty young white girl says to Brando's character, "Johnny, what are you rebelling against?" To which he replies with a sneer, "Whattaya got?" That moment of two-stroke fury and frustration fuel-injected a generation with high-octane angst. Everyone who came after Brando used a style he had created. He may never have sung a note, but he was rock & roll to his cut-time core. A generation later, the afterburn of Brando's image was strong enough to inspire the youth movement toward racial integration that was hung on the hopes and dreams of his generation.

3    Elvis and Brando were both what I call a man's man. They did what they did, they sang songs, they playacted and were

never girlish about any of it. Far from it! The ladies idolized them because they were pretty, but the guys admired their strength and manliness and looked to them for *direction*. Years later, their same kind of bravado was carried on in the movies by Sylvester Stallone, Charles Bronson, Peter Falk, and Robert Blake, all of whom were down with focusing the eyes and the ears of their fans toward something that went beyond the messages in their individual films.

4    And I did it, too. What's more, I can tell you the exact moment when I went from being a soul singer to a cultural icon. It happened with the "One."

5    Getting down with the "One" is the whole key to understanding my music, where it came from and where it went. I don't call it the Two because the "One" stands alone at the head of the beat, with force, leadership, and most important, self-pride. I don't know what the actual musical origins for the "One" are because I never heard it in Beethoven or Tchaikovsky or even Gershwin, or in any of the earlier songs I myself had written. But I do know this: Black musicians, historically, if instinctively, even if we didn't know what to call it, never hesitated to hit it on the "One." We were actually playing a variation of it all along and simply didn't know it, going back to early blues and gospel. The "One" was an extension of our life experiences, when we always began our music on the downbeat.

6    One day I might have been fooling around with the guitar and hit a riff I liked, or maybe I was noodling on the piano and suddenly discovered something that was there already in my head. I don't read music, so most of the time when I'm writing, the way I start off a new song is to find out how to make the melody work on the instrument I'm using at the moment. It really doesn't matter what I play it on, because God has already given me the master sheet. After He's done that, it's up to me to put it onto the James Brown music assembly line. I'm just the messenger, then, in this process, not the originator.

7    The "One" is derived from the Earth itself, the soil, the pine trees of my youth. And most important, it's on the upbeat— ONE two THREE four, not the downbeat, one TWO three FOUR—that most blues are written in. Hey, I know what I'm talking about! I was *born* to the downbeat, and I can tell you

without question there is no pride in it. The upbeat is rich. The downbeat is poor. Stepping up proud only happens on the aggressive "One," not the passive Two, and never on low-downbeat. In the end, it's not about music—it's about life.

8    The "One" was not just a new kind of beat; it was a statement of race, of force, of stature, of stride. It was the aural equivalent of standing tall and saying *Here I am,* of marching with strength rather than tiptoeing with timidity.

9    It was something that once I delivered it, everyone tried to copy, and I don't blame them. Everyone wants to copy from the best. The only thing I don't like is how today they have programmed machines to try to copy the human sound of the "One." Machines can't do what I did—they haven't got a chance. Why? Because there has to be an element of the human imperfection to the beat, of the chance emphasis, of the identification with the cultural origins of the beat. Otherwise, no matter how well programmed, or maybe because of it, the music always sounds to me like canned food. And that's okay. Plenty of people have to exist on that stuff when there's no real food around. But if there's only canned food in the world, people will quickly forget what the taste of the real thing is, and the canned food will replace the original and become the new standard measure. That, my friends, is not good. So you see, that is why the "One" is more than a new beat. The "One" is a way of life expressed through the music of James Brown.

10   Once I have the basic sound, then I work on it with the band members to try to come up with an arrangement that fits the mood and meaning of the song. And then, when it's ready, the "One" gets fits onto it, like a custom saddle, until it is the proper equivalent to the way I strut onto a stage at the start of my show, with my head held high, my feet taking wide strides, and a big smile on my face. Then I hear the audience cheering, and I know all over again that no matter what may be going on in my life, I am living on the "One." And because of it, for the next two hours everything is going to be all right.

11   "I Feel Good" is one of my early songs that contained conscious elements of the "One." I cut a version of that song in Chicago, but didn't release it because something was missing for me. The intro was a light keyboard thing that kind of

danced over the melody, then went into this jumpy, staccato, sharp 1-2-3-4 beat that I thought at the time was a little *too* sharp. *Deedle deedle deedle dee*. That didn't do it for me.

12    The next time I tried to record the song a couple of years later, I was in Jacksonville, Florida. I remember one day I woke up and heard the sound of the opening clearly in my head. It still had the *deedle deedle deedle dee,* but now I heard the bottom—*dum dum da dum*. Yes! I knew I had to contact Mr. Bobbit, my manager, right away.

13    While I was still with Mr. Nathan's label, I had replaced Mr. Nathan as my manager with Charles Bobbit. He was somebody I knew and trusted, and eventually came to love. Mr. Bobbit and I have been through a lifetime of adventures together—he has been my moral support and my creative sounding board. I know him, I love him, and I trust him. No more so than when I dialed his number that day.

14    I reached Mr. Bobbit in his room and told him to drop everything because we had to immediately leave for Miami. "For what?" he said with bleary eyes and a scratchy voice.

15    "I have to go to Criterion Studios and recut 'I Feel Good.' "

16    Twenty minutes later we were in a plane heading for Miami.

17    As we worked, I began to shift the rhythm, moving the second part—that *dum dum da dum*—*over* the first part, and I did it to a one-three rhythm: *DUM dum DA dum*. That was it! That was the sound I was looking for! The song now had the masculine heft of the bass that it needed. Even though it wasn't completed in the "One," it anticipated what was coming—a solid, important, even crucial step forward in the evolution of what would come to be known as the James Brown sound.

## Theme

1. James Brown says that he can tell us "the exact moment when I went from being a soul singer to a cultural icon," and he begins by mentioning some non-musical cultural icons. According to Brown, what do their styles illustrate about his own style?

2. According to James Brown, how does original music differ from its "canned" imitations?

## Technique

1. Brown uses the technique of comparison and contrast to explain the meaning of what he calls the "One." Explain in your own words some of the differences he finds between the blues beat and his own sound.

2. Brown makes some very large claims for himself and his own originality, yet throughout the essay he mentions with praise the names of many people he admires. How does this technique work to modify your sense of Brown's personality?

## Writing

Write an essay in which you compare an example of "downbeat" music to something by James Brown, explaining how you do or do not find Brown's analysis in his essay to be justified by your examples.

# John Madden

## My Favorite Guys                                      (1986)

> *John Madden was a football player himself before becoming one of the youngest and most successful coaches in professional football when he took over the Oakland Raiders. He is nowadays, of course, best known for his broadcasting of NFL games on television.*

1   In my years with the Raiders and, before that, as an assistant coach at San Diego State, every so often I would let my offensive linemen beat the stuffing out of a tackling dummy. One by one.

2   "Take it into the weight room," I'd tell them. "Punch it. Wrestle it. Kick it. Bite it. Do anything you want to it."

3   They loved it. There's nothing like fighting something that you know isn't going to fight back. I'd put a watch on 'em. I'd let 'em fight that big bag for three minutes, like it was a round of boxing. Some people thought I was crazy. But I've got a theory about offensive linemen, who happen to be my favorite guys on any football team, probably because I was an offensive lineman once myself. My theory is that most offensive linemen were big when they were kids, whereas most defensive players were tough little kids who became big when they grew up. That might not sound significant, but in football it is. Big kids have a hard time being aggressive. Wherever they go, they're told, "Hey, don't pick on that little kid." If a big kid does anything aggressive to a smaller kid his own age, then he's a bully. If he's a big brother, he's not allowed to pick on his little brother or, worse, his little sister. But if a tough little kid does something aggressive to a big guy, he's cute.

---

4    "Hey, look at that tough little kid," people will say. "What a cute little kid."

5    The big kid has to live with not being allowed to be aggressive. I know. I was a big kid. When the big kid starts playing football, usually as an offensive lineman, all he hears is his coach telling him about some tough little kid. The coach is saying, "If he was only as big as some of the other guys I've got here, he'd be All-Everything someday." Or the coach is saying, "If some of my big guys were as tough as that little kid over there, you couldn't stop 'em." You hear that in high school, in college, even in the NFL.

6    As a coach, I realized that you can't take the tough little kid and make him bigger, but you can take the big guy and make him aggressive. And that's why I had my offensive linemen beat the stuffing out of a tackling dummy: to teach them to be aggressive.

7    One of my pet peeves is hearing people say that offensive linemen should be passive, especially pass blockers trying to stop an opposing defensive lineman or linebacker. Those people don't understand what it is to be an offensive lineman. Yes, pass-blocking is passive in that you have to accept the other guy's charge and keep yourself between him and your quarterback. And an offensive lineman has to be thoughtful, whereas a defensive player is more animalistic. But that doesn't mean an offensive lineman can't be aggressive.

8    As a coach, I had always preached that philosophy to my offensive linemen. And when Bob Brown joined the Raiders in 1971, he proved it to them.

9    As an All-Pro tackle, Bob had a boxer's instincts. He believed in punching a defensive end in the solar plexus—*boom,* with both fists. That's not as bad as it sounds because it has to be a perfect punch, just under the shoulder pads and above the hip pads, and that's a pretty small area. But when a defensive end put his hands up to grab Bob's shoulders, sometimes he was vulnerable.

10    "Anytime I got a good one in there," Bob used to say, "it'd take a quarter out of the guy."

11    Bob didn't mean twenty-five cents, he meant the next fifteen minutes of the game. And when Bob got his shot in, his

man would be floating around for the next fifteen minutes like a boat with no wind in its sails. I never considered that dirty football; to me it was aggressive football, aggressive pass-blocking. Don't let that defensive guy knock you back. Instead, you knock him back. That's what run-blocking has to be— aggressive. Pass-blocking has to be the same way. But some passing teams practice their passing so much, their offensive linemen forget how to be aggressive. Those teams usually don't run the ball well, especially in short-yardage situations.

12    The 49ers were that way years ago. Their offensive linemen spent so much time going backward as pass blockers, they forgot how to fire out as run blockers.

13    By nature, some offensive linemen are more aggressive than others, but I love 'em all. They're my guys. Anytime I felt bad about something, like if I had just cut some players in training camp, I always went over to where they were warming up at practice. We would always warm up in groups—offensive linemen here, wide receivers there, running backs over here, defensive linemen over there, linebackers somewhere else, defensive backs over there. Somehow, just being with the offensive linemen always made me feel better. Maybe it was because they were such solid guys—solid as rocks.

## Theme

1. Explain in your own words the theory behind Madden's use of the tackling dummy described in paragraph one.

2. According to Madden why do offensive linemen have to be active and passive at the same time?

## Technique

1. Madden uses several quotations from conversations throughout his account. What do they contribute? What effects would be missing without this representative aspect of Madden's style? If you think the quotations don't matter much, explain why you think so.

2. This account was written some years ago. Do the dates date the meaning for you? In other words, does the content lose its present significance for you because some of the examples are old fashioned? Explain your answer.

## Writing

Today John Madden is better known as a football broadcast announcer than as the highly successful coach of the Oakland Raiders that he once was. Write an essay showing through examples how the analytical habits of mind he developed as a successful coach influence his essay.

# Freddie Prinze, Jr.

## Got Milk?                                                    **(2003)**

*Born March 8, 1976 in Los Angeles, Freddy Prinze, Jr. didn't have far to go geographically to get to Hollywood, but it took him until 1989 to get his first real break when he played a punk kid in an episode of* Family Matters. *In the early twenty-first century he has co-starred with actor Matthew Lillard five times, most recently in the* Scooby-Doo *series.*

## Theme

1. In the slogan, "Make it Big," what does the "it" refer to? Isn't it more than one thing? How does each referent define a separate but related theme within the visual presentation?

2. How would you characterize the style of Prinze's clothing—unbuttoned suede jacket, jeans, sneakers? How does the style of the clothing define visually some of the themes of the advertisement?

## Technique

1. How would you characterize Prinze's facial expression? Cute? Sneaky? Caught-in-the-act? How is the facial expression in keeping with the general spirit of the advertisement?

2. In what ways does the text interact with the visual presentation to express the message of the advertisement as a whole?

## Writing

Write an essay in which you describe how the playful features of this advertisement contribute to the meaning it is designed to convey.

# Steve Martin

## Writing Is Easy! (1998)

> *Steve Martin is multitalented to say the least. He has won an*
> *Emmy as a comedy writer, his albums of comic monologues sell*
> *in the millions, and his acting career has combined serious and*
> *comic roles. In the following essay, Martin pretends to let us in*
> *on some tricks of the writing trade, but in fact reminds us that it*
> *is often more fun to have written than to write.*

1   **W**riting is one of the most easy, pain-free, and happy ways
to pass the time in all the arts. For example, right now I am
sitting in my rose garden and typing on my new computer.
Each rose represents a story, so I'm never at a loss for *what*
to write. I just look deep into the heart of the rose and read
its story and write it down through *typing,* which I enjoy
anyway. I could be typing "kjfiu joewmv jiw" and would
enjoy it as much as typing words that actually make sense. I
simply relish the movement of my fingers on the keys. Sometimes, it is true, agony visits the head of a writer. At these
moments, I stop writing and relax with a coffee at my favorite
restaurant, knowing that words can be changed, rethought,
fiddled with, and, of course, ultimately denied. Painters don't
have that luxury. If they go to a coffee shop, their paint dries
into a hard mass.

### Location, Location, Location

2   I would recommend to writers that they live in California,
because here they can look up at the blue sky in between those
moments of looking into the heart of a rose. I feel sorry for writers—and there are some pretty famous ones—who live in places

like South America and Czechoslovakia, where I imagine it gets pretty dreary. These writers are easy to spot. Their books are often depressing and filled with disease and negativity. If you're going to write about disease, I would suggest that California is the place to do it. Dwarfism is never funny, but look at the result when it was dealt with out here in California. Seven happy dwarfs. Can you imagine seven dwarfs in Czechoslovakia? You would get seven melancholic dwarfs at best, seven melancholic dwarfs with no handicapped-parking spaces.

### *Love in the Time of Cholera:* why it's a bad title

3  I admit that "Love in the time of ..." is a great title, so far. You're reading along, you're happy, it's about love, I like the way the word *time* comes in there, something nice in the association of *love* and time, like a new word almost, *lovetime:* nice, nice feeling. Suddenly, the morbid *Cholera* appears. I was happy till then. "Love in the Time of the Oozing Sores and Pustules" is probably an earlier, rejected title of this book, written in a rat-infested tree house on an old Smith-Corona. This writer, whoever he is, could have used a couple of weeks in Pacific Daylight Time.

4      I did a little experiment. I decided to take the following disheartening passage, which was no doubt written in some depressing place, and attempt to rewrite it under the influence of California:

> Most people deceive themselves with a pair of faiths: they believe in *eternal memory* (of people, things, deeds, nations) and in *redressibility* (of deeds, mistakes, sins, wrongs). Both are false faiths. In reality the opposite is true: everything will be forgotten and nothing will be redressed. (Milan Kundera)

Sitting in my garden, as the bees glide from flower to flower, I let the above paragraph filter through my mind. The following new paragraph emerged:

> I feel pretty,
> Oh so pretty,
> I feel pretty and witty and bright.

Kundera was just too wordy. Sometimes the delete key is your greatest friend.

## Writer's Block: A Myth

5 Writer's block is a fancy term made up by whiners so they can have an excuse to drink alcohol. Sure a writer can get stuck for a while, but when that happens to real authors, they simply go out and get an "as told to." The alternative is to hire yourself out as an "as heard from," thus taking all the credit. It is also much easier to write when you have someone to "bounce" with. This is someone to sit in a room with and exchange ideas. It is good if the last name of the person you choose to bounce with is Salinger. I know a certain early-twentieth-century French writer, whose initials were M.P., who could have used a good bounce person. If he had, his title might have been the more correct "Remembering Past Things" instead of the clumsy one he used. The other trick I use when I have a momentary stoppage is virtually foolproof, and I'm happy to pass it along. Go to an already published novel and find a sentence you absolutely adore. Copy it down in your manuscript. Usually that sentence will lead you naturally to another sentence; pretty soon your own ideas will start to flow. If they don't, copy down the next sentence. You can safely use up to three sentences of someone else's work—unless they're friends; then you can use two. The odds of being found out are very slim, and even if you are, there's no jail time.

## Creating Memorable Characters

6 Nothing will make your writing soar more than a memorable character. If there is a memorable character, the reader will keep going back to the book, picking it up, turning it over in his hands, hefting it, and tossing it into the air. Here is an example of the jazzy uplift that vivid characters can offer:

> Some guys were standing around when in came this guy.

7 You are now on your way to creating a memorable character. You have set him up as being a guy, and with that come all the reader's ideas of what a guy is. Soon you will liven your character by using an adjective:

> But this guy was no ordinary guy, he was a red guy.

8 This character, the red guy, has now popped into the reader's imagination. He is a full-blown person, with hopes and

dreams, just like the reader. Especially if the reader is a red guy. Now you might want to give the character a trait. You can inform the reader of the character trait in one of two ways. First, simply say what that trait is—for example, "but this red guy was different from most red guys, this red guy liked frappés." The other is rooted in action—have the red guy walk up to a bar and order a frappé, as in:

"What'll you have, red guy?"

"I'll have a frappé."

9      Once you have mastered these two concepts, vivid character writing combined with adjectives, you are on your way to becoming the next Shakespeare's brother. And don't forget to copyright any ideas you have that might be original. You don't want to be caught standing by helplessly while your familiar "red guy" steps up to a bar in a frappé commercial.

## Writing Dialogue
10    Many very fine writers are intimidated when they have to write the way people really talk. Actually it's quite easy. Simply lower your IQ by fifty and start typing!

## Subject Matter
11    Because topics are in such short supply, I have provided a few for writers who may be suffering in the darker climes. File some of these away, and look through them during the suicidal winter months:

12    "Naked Belligerent Panties": This is a good sexy title with a lot of promise.

13    How about a diet book that suggests your free radicals *don't* enter ketosis unless your insulin levels have been carbo-charged!

14    Something about how waves at the beach just keep coming and coming and how amazing it is (I smell a best-seller here).

15    "Visions of Melancholy from a Fast-Moving Train": Some foreign writer is right now rushing to his keyboard, ready to pound on it like Horowitz. However, this title is a phony string of words with no meaning and would send your poor book to the "Artsy" section of Barnes and Noble, where—guess what—it would languish, be remaindered, and die.

## A Word to Avoid

16  "Dagnabbit" will never get you anywhere with the Booker Prize people. Lose it.

## Getting Published

17  I have two observations about publishers:

1. Nowadays, they can be either male or female.
2. They love to be referred to by the appropriate pronoun. If your publisher is male, refer to him as "he." If your publisher is female, "she" is considered more correct. Once you have established a rapport, "Babe" is also acceptable for either sex.

18       Once you have determined your pronoun usage, you are ready to "schmooze" your publisher. Let's say your favorite author is Dante. Call Dante's publisher and say you'd like to invite them both to lunch. If the assistant says something like "But Dante's dead," be sympathetic and say, "Please accept my condolences." Once at lunch, remember never to be moody. Publishers like up, happy writers, although it's impressive to suddenly sweep your arm slowly across the lunch table, dumping all the plates and food onto the floor, while shouting "Sic Semper Tyrannis!"

## A Demonstration of Actual Writing

19  It's easy to talk about writing and even easier to do it. Watch:

> Call me Ishmael. It was cold, very cold, here in the mountain town of Kilimanjaroville.© I could hear a bell. It was tolling. I knew exactly for who it was tolling, too. It was tolling for me, Ishmael Twist,© a red guy who likes frappé. [Author's note: I am now stuck. I walk over to a rose and look into its heart.] That's right, Ishmael Twist.©

20       Finally, I can't overstress the importance of having a powerful closing sentence.

## Theme

1. Steve Martin gives us a lot of advice in a mock-self-help style, but it often seems that the joke is based on suggesting

how he could use a little help himself. Explain how you know he seems to need help in his first paragraph. Then find and discuss some other places in the essay where the announced problem seems more enacted than solved.

2. At the end of the essay Martin gives us "A Demonstration of Actual Writing." Explain how the paragraph he offers sums up the ridiculous advice given earlier.

## Technique

1. Martin entertains us by pretending to sound like a clueless know-it-all. How does he achieve the tone of voice he uses? What writing techniques help create this tone? Try rewriting some sentences in another tone to better understand how he creates his comic style.

2. By embodying the dangers it warns us to avoid, Martin's last sentence is representative of many other jokes in the essay. Rewrite the last sentence or create several sentences to give the ending the kind of punch he claims to provide. Explain how and why your ending differs from his.

## Writing

As a very prolific comic writer, Steve Martin can afford to joke about things like writer's block, though at the same time it seems that he has really known the experience. In either a serious or a comic style, write an essay of your own that describes writing problems you have faced since you began the course.

# Stephen King

## On Writing
(2000)

*Stephen King is the acknowledged "King of Horror Fiction" and many of his novels have been made into successful movies beginning as far back as the 1970s with* Carrie *(1974) and* The Shining *(1977). The following excerpt is taken from King's non-fiction book,* On Writing *(2000), a combination memoir and guidebook for aspiring writers.*

1   If you want to be a writer, you must do two things above all others: read a lot and write a lot. There's no way around these two things that I'm aware of, no shortcut.

2   I'm a slow reader, but I usually get through seventy or eighty books a year, mostly fiction. I don't read in order to study the craft; I read because I like to read. It's what I do at night, kicked back in my blue chair. Similarly, I don't read fiction to study the art of fiction, but simply because I like stories. Yet there is a learning process going on. Every book you pick up has its own lesson or lessons, and quite often the bad books have more to teach than the good ones.

3   When I was in the eighth grade, I happened upon a paperback novel by Murray Leinster, a science fiction pulp writer who did most of his work during the forties and fifties, when magazines like *Amazing Stories* paid a penny a word. I had read other books by Mr. Leinster, enough to know that the quality of his writing was uneven. This particular tale, which was about mining in the asteroid belt, was one of his less successful efforts. Only that's too kind. It was terrible, actually, a story populated by paper-thin characters and driven by outlandish plot developments. Worst of all (or so it seemed to me at the time), Leinster had fallen in love with the word *zestful*.

4   Characters watched the approach of ore-bearing asteroids with *zestful smiles*. Characters sat down to supper aboard their

mining ship with *zestful anticipation.* Near the end of the book, the hero swept the large-breasted, blonde heroine into a *zestful embrace.* For me, it was the literary equivalent of a smallpox vaccination: I have never, so far as I know, used the word *zestful* in a novel or a story. God willing, I never will.

5     *Asteroid Miners* (which wasn't the title, but that's close enough) was an important book in my life as a reader. Almost everyone can remember losing his or her virginity, and most writers can remember the first book he/she put down thinking: *I can do better than this. Hell, I am doing better than this!* What could be more encouraging to the struggling writer than to realize his/her work is unquestionably better than that of someone who actually got paid for his/her stuff?

6     One learns most clearly what not to do by reading bad prose—one novel like *Asteroid Miners* (or *Valley of the Dolls, Flowers in the Attic,* and *The Bridges of Madison County,* to name just a few) is worth a semester at a good writing school, even with the superstar guest lecturers thrown in.

7     Good writing, on the other hand, teaches the learning writer about style, graceful narration, plot development, the creation of believable characters, and truth-telling. A novel like *The Grapes of Wrath* may fill a new writer with feelings of despair and good old-fashioned jealousy—"I'll never be able to write anything that good, not if I live to be a thousand"—but such feelings can also serve as a spur, goading the writer to work harder and aim higher. Being swept away by a combination of great story and great writing—of being flattened, in fact—is part of every writer's necessary formation. You cannot hope to sweep someone else away by the force of your writing until it has been done to you.

8     So we read to experience the mediocre and the outright rotten; such experience helps us to recognize those things when they begin to creep into our own work, and to steer clear of them. We also read in order to measure ourselves against the good and the great, to get a sense of all that can be done. And we read in order to experience different styles.

9     You may find yourself adopting a style you find particularly exciting, and there's nothing wrong with that. When I read Ray Bradbury as a kid, I wrote like Ray Bradbury—everything green

and wondrous and seen through a lens smeared with the grease of nostalgia. When I read James M. Cain, everything I wrote came out clipped and stripped and hard-boiled. When I read Lovecraft, my prose became luxurious and Byzantine. I wrote stories in my teenage years where all these styles merged, creating a kind of hilarious stew. This sort of stylistic blending is a necessary part of developing one's own style, but it doesn't occur in a vacuum. You have to read widely, constantly refining (and redefining) your own work as you do so. It's hard for me to believe that people who read very little (or not at all in some cases) should presume to write and expect people to like what they have written, but I know it's true. If I had a nickel for every person who ever told me he/she wanted to become a writer but "didn't have time to read," I could buy myself a pretty good steak dinner. Can I be blunt on this subject? If you don't have time to read, you don't have the time (or the tools) to write. Simple as that.

10      Reading is the creative center of a writer's life. I take a book with me everywhere I go, and find there are all sorts of opportunities to dip in. The trick is to teach yourself to read in small sips as well as in long swallows. Waiting rooms were made for books—of course! But so are theater lobbies before the show, long and boring checkout lines, and everyone's favorite, the john. You can even read while you're driving, thanks to the audiobook revolution. Of the books I read each year, anywhere from six to a dozen are on tape. As for all the wonderful radio you will be missing, come on—how many times can you listen to Deep Purple sing "Highway Star"?

11      Reading at meals is considered rude in polite society, but if you expect to succeed as a writer, rudeness should be the second-to-least of your concerns. The least of all should be polite society and what it expects. If you intend to write as truthfully as you can, your days as a member of polite society are numbered, anyway.

12      Where else can you read? There's always the treadmill, or whatever you use down at the local health club to get aerobic. I try to spend an hour doing that every day, and I think I'd go mad without a good novel to keep me company. Most exercise facilities (at home as well as outside it) are now equipped with TVs, but TV—while working out or anywhere else—really

is about the last thing an aspiring writer needs. If you feel you must have the news analyst blowhards on CNN while you exercise, or the stock market blowhards on MSNBC, or the sports blowhards on ESPN, it's time for you to question how serious you really are about becoming a writer. You must be prepared to do some serious turning inward toward the life of the imagination, and that means, I'm afraid, that Geraldo, Keith Obermann, and Jay Leno must go. Reading takes time, and the glass teat takes too much of it.

13   Once weaned from the ephemeral craving for TV, most people will find they enjoy the time they spend reading. I'd like to suggest that turning off that endlessly quacking box is apt to improve the quality of your life as well as the quality of your writing. And how much of a sacrifice are we talking about here? How many *Fraiser* and *ER* reruns does it take to make one American life complete? How many Richard Simmons infomercials? How many whiteboy/fatboy Beltway insiders on CNN? Oh man, don't get me started. Jerry-Springer-Dr.-Dre-Judge-Judy-Jerry-Falwell-Donny-and-Marie, I rest my case.

14   When my son Owen was seven or so, he fell in love with Bruce Springsteen's E Street Band, particularly with Clarence Clemons, the band's burly sax player. Owen decided he wanted to learn to play like Clarence. My wife and I were amused and delighted by this ambition. We were also hopeful, as any parent would be, that our kid would turn out to be talented, perhaps even some sort of prodigy. We got Owen a tenor saxophone for Christmas and lessons with Gordon Bowie, one of the local music men. Then we crossed our fingers and hoped for the best.

15   Seven months later I suggested to my wife that it was time to discontinue the sax lessons, if Owen concurred. Owen did, and with palpable relief—he hadn't wanted to say it himself, especially not after asking for the sax in the first place, but seven months had been long enough for him to realize that, while he might love Clarence Clemons's big sound, the saxophone was simply not for him—God had not given him that particular talent.

16   I knew, not because Owen stopped practicing, but because he was practicing only during the periods Mr. Bowie had set

for him: half an hour after school four days a week, plus an hour on the weekends. Owen mastered the scales and the notes—nothing wrong with his memory, his lungs, or his eye-hand coordination—but we never heard him taking off, surprising himself with something new, blissing himself out. And as soon as his practice time was over, it was back into the case with the horn, and there it stayed until the next lesson or practice-time. What this suggested to me was that when it came to the sax and my son, there was never going to be any real playtime; it was all going to be rehearsal. That's no good. If there's no joy in it, it's just no good. It's best to go on to some other area, where the deposits of talent may be richer and the fun quotient higher.

17    Talent renders the whole idea of rehearsal meaningless; when you find something at which you are talented, you do it (whatever *it* is) until your fingers bleed or your eyes are ready to fall out of your head. Even when no one is listening (or reading, or watching), every outing is a bravura performance, because you as the creator are happy. Perhaps even ecstatic. That goes for reading and writing as well as for playing a musical instrument, hitting a baseball, or running the four-forty. The sort of strenuous reading and writing program I advocate—four to six hours a day, every day—will not seem strenuous if you really enjoy doing these things and have an aptitude for them; in fact, you may be following such a program already. If you feel you need permission to do all the reading and writing your little heart desires, however, consider it hereby granted by yours truly.

18    The real importance of reading is that it creates an ease and intimacy with the process of writing; one comes to the country of the writer with one's papers and identification pretty much in order. Constant reading will pull you into a place (a mind-set, if you like the phrase) where you can write eagerly and without self-consciousness. It also offers you a constantly growing knowledge of what has been done and what hasn't, what is trite and what fresh, what works and what just lies there dying (or dead) on the page. The more you read, the less apt you are to make a fool of yourself with your pen or word processor.

## Theme

1. King talks at great length about what reading can do for the aspiring writer. Explain his reasoning on the value of reading even bad books.

2. Explain King's reasoning on the value of reading good books as an important element in the formula for becoming a good writer.

## Technique

1. King says that reading and writing are not like work for him because he loves to read and write. Pick an example of his writing from this essay that seems to demonstrate the truth of this claim and explain how it does so.

2. How does the anecdote concerning King's son serve to enforce one of his points? In your view, what difference does the personal connection make in the effectiveness of the example?

## Writing

Does one of King's points hit home for you in that you feel you can write better than some of the writers represented in this book? If so, pick one and rewrite his or her effort with a view to improving its quality, being prepared to defend your changes. If not, pick an essay you admire and explain what you applaud by pointing to and analyzing specific examples.

# EXERCISES

## Intertextual Questions

1. Both Charles Osgood and Miss Manners raise issues about language as a potentially powerful and disruptive force in social relations. Both writers are witty in their approach to topics that have often been treated in a very serious style. In what other ways are their treatments similar? How do they differ?

2. Chris Rock and John Madden both use techniques of comparison and contrast to illustrate and explain different aspects of performative style in music and football. Suppose each had adopted the other's method of presentation. Try making a list of Madden's points and write out Chris Rock's claims in the form of expository prose. Then discuss the advantages and disadvantages of the two methods.

3. Steve Martin makes his points about writing through satire. In your view, does the implication of that satire support what Andy Rooney says about writing in a witty but more straightforward manner? Discuss your answer using examples.

4. Freddy Prinze, Jr. contributes the only visual essay here, though it too makes use of words. How do those words represent his persona through their style? For example, what kind of persona do the double meanings of his words suggest? What kind of public persona does his visual support of healthy living though milk suggest? Discuss the aspects of personality expressed by a combination of visual and textual means.

5. All the authors in the chapter create lively public personas of their own through their styles. Who is the most effective in projecting a personality in your view? Explain your answer by analyzing the strengths of the presentation you have chosen.

## Suggestions for Writing

1. Andy Rooney receives and responds to a letter. Write a letter of your own to Chris Rock, giving him the stimulus to write his

essay. Make sure you give him a basis for making all the points he does make and be as assertive as he himself is.

2. What do you think about the issues of "reading levels" for textbooks and the presence of vulgar speech in the examples of public discourse that textbooks present? Write an essay defining and defending your views on the proper standards of style and diction for textbooks in secondary education.

3. Most people have experienced the kind of rudeness Miss Manners addresses in her essay and most colleges have some form of speech code. Write an essay in which you argue for your views on the proper standards of public discourse at colleges and universities.

4. All the writers speak about matters of performance and all their essays enact their own performances as writers. Whose performance do you admire the most? Write an essay explaining and defending your choice.

5. Using examples from any of the essays in this chapter, write an essay of your own entitled "Writing is Hard."

# CHAPTER 5

# SELF-PRESENTATION

Discovering one's personal language style starts the construction of a public persona through which one is made known to the world. But that persona, once constructed, must also then be effectively presented. The essays in this chapter contain always thoughtful and sometimes amusing reflections on self-presentation in a wide variety of public contexts. The arenas include a commencement address, a political challenge, a fashion statement, some thoughts on fashion and some psychological advice. The themes addressed range from serious matters of social conscience and moral standards to more lighthearted issues like where to find a muumuu.

The chapter begins with Jon Stewart's commencement address to the graduates of William and Mary, from which he himself had graduated. Stewart presents for the most part the same self he has created for Comedy Central, one under no illusions about the motives of publicity value behind the invitation to speak: "As a person, I am honored…as an alumnus, I have to say I believe we can do better."

The next essay is a visual public service advertisement sponsored by PETA: People for the Ethical Treatment of Animals. Furs are conventionally associated with wealth and feminine allure, but Pamela Anderson, who is famously associated with both those qualities, turns the issues inside out in "Give Fur the Cold Shoulder."

Mary-Louise Parker continues the theme of feminine attraction with an essay on the meaning of nudity in photographs. Her exchange with editors at *Esquire* ("The Magazine for Men") shows us that she has thought out all the implications of having been asked to pose, including the implied differences in meaning between the words "nude" and "naked." One of her editors makes a brief reply from his own point of view.

The Reverend Jesse Jackson addresses visibility in an entirely different sense. In "Rainbow Imperative" he argues against the underrepresentation of African Americans in the advertising industry, which provides the financial underpinnings for much of the media that make up American mass culture. Jackson's point about self-presentation is that minorities should be involved in advertising not only as the consumers of media images, but also as the producers of them.

Jenny McCarthy puts a comic spin on worries about self-presentation during pregnancy, and the note of exasperation in her title is representative of the essay's theme. In "Where in the Hell Can I Find a Muumuu?" McCarthy takes us on a nine month tour, making fashion statements in words and otherwise all along the way.

The dual dynamic involved in how we present ourselves to others and how others influence our self-presentations makes the common theme of the last two essays in the chapter. Russell Simmons runs a media empire within the world of rap and hip-hop, but he still has to deal with issues of racial stereotyping. In "White People," an excerpt from his autobiography, Simmons tells us how he deals with different aspects of the problem. In the final essay Dr. Phil draws on his experience in the field of psychological counseling to formulate laws by which people who follow them can free themselves from self-defeating personas. "We Teach People How to Treat Us" illustrates with case histories how anyone can get into trouble by poor self-presentation and how to mend matters when that happens.

# Jon Stewart

## Commencement Address
## at William and Mary                                            **(2004)**

*Born in New York City in 1962, Jon Stewart (Jonathan Stuart Lei-
bowitz) has been the host of Comedy Central's* The Daily Show
*since 1999. His famously flip and sarcastic take on events loses
none of its bite when he addresses graduating seniors at his alma
mater, William and Mary.*

1   Thank you Mr. President, I had forgotten how crushingly dull
these ceremonies are. Thank you.

2   My best to the choir. I have to say, that song never grows old
for me. Whenever I hear that song, it reminds me of nothing.

3   I am honored to be here, I do have a confession to make
before we get going that I should explain very quickly. When
I am not on television, this is actually how I dress. I apologize,
but there's something very freeing about it. I congratulate the
students for being able to walk even a half a mile in this non-
breathable fabric in the Williamsburg heat. I am sure the environment that now exists under your robes, are the same
conditions that primordial life began on this earth.

4   I know there were some parents that were concerned about
my speech here tonight, and I want to assure you that you will
not hear any language that is not common at, say, a dock
workers union meeting, or Tourette's convention, or profanity
seminar. Rest assured.

5   I am honored to be here and to receive this honorary doctorate. When I think back to the people that have been in this
position before me from Benjamin Franklin to Queen Noor of
Jordan, I can't help but wonder what has happened to this

---

SOURCE: By permission of the College of William and Mary.

place. Seriously, it saddens me. As a person, I am honored to get it; as an alumnus, I have to say I believe we can do better. And I believe we should. But it has always been a dream of mine to receive a doctorate and to know that today, without putting in any effort, I will. It's incredibly gratifying. Thank you. That's very nice of you, I appreciate it.

6     I'm sure my fellow doctoral graduates—who have spent so long toiling in academia, sinking into debt, sacrificing God knows how many years for what, in truth, is a piece of parchment that in truth has been so devalued by our instant gratification culture as to have been rendered meaningless—will join in congratulating me. Thank you.

7     But today isn't about how my presence here devalues this fine institution. It is about you, the graduates. I'm honored to be here to congratulate you today. Today is the day you enter into the real world, and I should give you a few pointers on what it is. It's actually not that different from the environment here. The biggest difference is you will now be paying for things, and the real world is not surrounded by three-foot brick wall. And the real world is not a restoration. If you see people in the real world making bricks out of straw and water, those people are not colonial re-enactors—they are poor. Help them. And in the real world, there is not as much candle lighting. I don't really know what it is about this campus and candle lighting, but I wish it would stop. We only have so much wax, people.

8     Let's talk about the real world for a moment. We had been discussing it earlier, and I...I wanted to bring this up to you earlier about the real world, and this is I guess as good a time as any. I don't really know to put this, so I'll be blunt. We broke it.

9     Please don't be mad. I know we were supposed to bequeath to the next generation a world better than the one we were handed. So, sorry.

10     I don't know if you've been following the news lately, but it just kinda got away from us. Somewhere between the gold rush of easy internet profits and an arrogant sense of endless empire, we heard kind of a pinging noise, and uh, then the damn thing just died on us. So I apologize.

11     But here's the good news. You fix this thing, you're the next greatest generation, people. You do this—and I believe you

can—you win this war on terror, and Tom Brokaw's kissing your ass from here to Tikrit, let me tell ya. And even if you don't, you're not gonna have much trouble surpassing my generation. If you end up getting your picture taken next to a naked guy pile of enemy prisoners and don't give the thumbs up you've outdid us.

12    We declared war on terror. We declared war on terror—it's not even a noun, so, good luck. After we defeat it, I'm sure we'll take on that bastard ennui.

13    But obviously that's the world. What about your lives? What piece of wisdom can I impart to you about my journey that will somehow ease your transition from college back to your parents' basement?

14    I know some of you are nostalgic today and filled with excitement and perhaps uncertainty at what the future holds. I know six of you are trying to figure out how to make a bong out of your caps. I believe you are members of Psi U. Hey that did work, thank you for the reference.

15    So I thought I'd talk a little bit about my experience here at William and Mary. It was very long ago, and if you had been to William and Mary while I was here and found out that I would be the commencement speaker 20 years later, you would be somewhat surprised, and probably somewhat angry. I came to William and Mary because as a Jewish person I wanted to explore the rich tapestry of Judaica that is Southern Virginia. Imagine my surprise when I realized "The Tribe" was not what I thought it meant.

16    In 1980 I was 17 years old. When I moved to Williamsburg, my hall was in the basement of Yates, which combined the cheerfulness of a bomb shelter with the prison-like comfort of the group shower. As a freshman I was quite a catch. Less than five feet tall, yet my head is the same size it is now. Didn't even really look like a head, it looked more like a container for a head. I looked like a Peanuts character. Peanuts characters had terrible acne. But what I lacked in looks I made up for with a repugnant personality.

17    In 1981 I lost my virginity, only to gain it back again on appeal in 1983. You could say that my one saving grace was academics where I excelled, but I did not.

18     And yet now I live in the rarified air of celebrity, of mega stardom. My life a series of Hollywood orgies and Kabala center brunches with the cast of *Friends*. At least that's what my handlers tell me. I'm actually too valuable to live my own life and spend most of my days in a vegetable crisper to remain fake news anchor fresh.

19     So I know that the decisions that I made after college worked out. But at the time I didn't know that they would. See, college is not necessarily predictive of your future success. And it's the kind of thing where the path that I chose obviously wouldn't work for you. For one, you're not very funny.

20     So how do you know what is the right path to choose to get the result that you desire? And the honest answer is this. You won't. And accepting that greatly eases the anxiety of your life experience.

21     I was not exceptional here, and am not now. I was mediocre here. And I'm not saying aim low. Not everybody can wander around in an alcoholic haze and then at 40 just, you know, decide to be president. You've got to really work hard to try to…I was actually referring to my father.

22     When I left William and Mary I was shell-shocked. Because when you're in college it's very clear what you have to do to succeed. And I imagine here everybody knows exactly the number of credits they needed to graduate, where they had to buckle down, which introductory psychology class would pad out the schedule. You knew what you had to do to get to this college and to graduate from it. But the unfortunate, yet truly exciting thing about your life, is that there is no core curriculum. The entire place is an elective. The paths are infinite and the results uncertain. And it can be maddening to those that go here, especially here, because your strength has always been achievement. So if there's any real advice I can give you it's this.

23     College is something you complete. Life is something you experience. So don't worry about your grade, or the results or success. Success is defined in myriad ways, and you will find it, and people will no longer be grading you, but it will come from your own internal sense of decency which I imagine, after

going through the program here, is quite strong...although I'm sure downloading illegal files...but, nah, that's a different story.

24    Love what you do. Get good at it. Competence is a rare commodity in this day and age. And let the chips fall where they may.

25    And the last thing I want to address is the idea that somehow this new generation is not as prepared for the sacrifice and the tenacity that will be needed in the difficult times ahead. I have not found this generation to be cynical or apathetic or selfish. They are as strong and as decent as any people that I have met. And I will say this, on my way down here I stopped at Bethesda Naval, and when you talk to the young kids that are there that have just been back from Iraq and Afghanistan, you don't have the worry about the future that you hear from so many that are not a part of this generation but judging it from above.

26    And the other thing...that I will say is, when I spoke earlier about the world being broke, I was somewhat being facetious, because every generation has their challenge. And things change rapidly, and life gets better in an instant.

27    I was in New York on 9-11 when the towers came down. I lived 14 blocks from the twin towers. And when they came down, I thought that the world had ended. And I remember walking around in a daze for weeks. And Mayor Giuliani had said to the city, "You've got to get back to normal. We've got to show that things can change and get back to what they were."

28    And one day I was coming out of my building, and on my stoop, was a man who was crouched over, and he appeared to be in deep thought. And as I got closer to him I realized, he was playing with himself. And that's when I thought, "You know what, we're gonna be OK."

29    Thank you. Congratulations. I honor you. Good Night.

## Theme

1. William and Mary was founded during the eighteenth century in what is now the restored Colonial town of Williams-

burg, VA. Knowing the college's location helps you to get some of the in-jokes Stewart makes to people who have all shared the same environment. Point to some examples of the in-jokes and give your impression of the rough proportion of these to the kind of joke that any graduating senior at any college would understand. Do you find that Stewart's address makes an effective combination of focus on a specialized and on a general audience in his address? Explain your answer.

2. In paragraph 23 Stewart says "College is something you complete. Life is something you experience." Does that epigram seem to you to sum up the "serious" part of the speech? Explain your answer.

## Technique

1. In speaking of the "real world" toward the end of the speech, Stewart uses an academic metaphor: "The entire place is an elective." In your own words paraphrase the meaning of this metaphor and explain what gives it expressive validity.

2. In paragraph 25 Stewart says: "And the last thing I want to address is…." In what sense is what follows the last thing addressed? In what sense is it not? Is it only a signal of nearing the end in a vocal address? In what sense could there be said to be two last things in his speech? Explain your answer.

## Writing

Write an essay that analyzes some ways Stewart combines the serious with the humorous in his address to the graduates.

# Pamela Anderson

## Give Fur the Cold Shoulder                    (2004)

> *Pamela Anderson was born in Canada and got her start in show business as "The Blue Girl" for Labatt's beer. A* Playboy *appearance led to small parts in television until she became famous playing a lifeguard in* Baywatch.

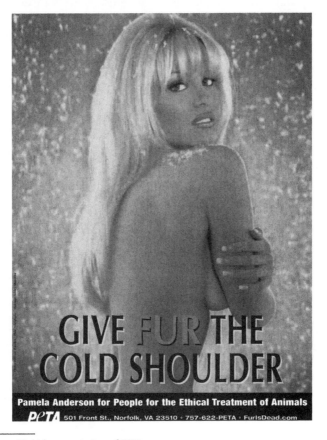

Source: Used by permission of PETA.

## Theme

1. In what different ways is the verbal statement enacted by the visual component of the public service advertisement? For example, Anderson looks confident and defiant at the same time, in keeping with the command she issues. How does her attitude in this and other regards contribute to the effectiveness of her expressed opinion about furs?

2. What meanings of "decency" and "indecency" are both visually and verbally at play in the advertisement? For example, what are some of the differences between the erotic meaning of indecency and its meaning with regard to our behavior toward animals? Which might be considered noble, which ignoble? Why so? In your opinion was the legendary Lady Godiva acting indecently? Explain your reasoning.

## Technique

1. To "turn a cold shoulder" toward someone is a metaphor. What does the metaphor mean? How is its meaning changed visually here?

2. Suppose that instead of Pamela Anderson, an unknown model had posed the same way with the same slogan. In your view, would anything be lost in the implications of verbal and visual expression? Explain your reasoning.

## Writing

Find a visual expression of another public cause not included in this book—one on the need for clean air, for example—and write an essay analyzing the visual techniques of argument it employs.

# Mary-Louise Parker

## On Nudity                                              (2002)

*Mary-Louise Parker was born in North Carolina and began her
acting career on the New York stage, winning a Theater Award
and a Tony nomination for her performance in* Prelude to a
Kiss. *Going on to movies, she has frequently been cast as "the
long-suffering girlfriend," appearing, for example, as John
Cusack's girlfriend in Woody Allen's* Bullets Over Broadway. *Her
latest TV series is* Weeds.

1   $\mathbf{A}$ few are sexy, but most are decidedly unglamorous, ones
in which I have sand on my feet, spaghetti on my face. Some
were taken while I slept. The truly awful ones, which wrecked
my day upon viewing, have doubtless by now been reincar-
nated as a paper towel or a Starbucks cup. It is difficult for anyone over the age of seven to see his or her body with any
sense of perspective, and I don't know at what point that
changes and being naked becomes naughty. My friend came
into her son's room one evening and found him sitting on his
bed very still and staring straight ahead with a small smile on
his face. "What are you so happy about, honey?" she asked
him. He looked at her, unblinking. "Because I am naked in my
mind," he said.

2      There can be a certain hopefulness that precedes seeing
your picture, naked or no. Maybe some small truth will be
revealed, maybe I will see myself how others see me, but,
more important, maybe I will look hot. Ultimately the pictures
I like are the ones in which I recognize myself, in which ego
doesn't figure into it. In one of my favorite pictures, conse-
quently, I am extremely naked, romping on a not-nude beach
on Plum Island, Massachusetts. I remember this sudden hap-

SOURCE: Reprinted by permission of *Esquire* magazine.

piness that I hadn't felt for a while. Tom Waits was blaring, the waves almost as loud, and there was rain starting, everything a beautiful blue, gray, and white, and it was freezing and perfect. Life felt so expansive and possible, and it all just made me want to, well, rip my clothes off and run wildly down the beach. So I did and encouraged my friend to do the same, and she promptly ripped off her clothes, too. We took photos, and when the cold became freezing cold, we put our clothes on and went home.

3    Your average photo tends to conceal rather than reveal. Only truly great art photos, by Robert Frank, for example, seem so true that you feel like a voyeur for just looking at them. They speak so much about their subjects in such an artful, deliberately nondeliberate way that they take my breath away. A naked photo is trickier; usually the intent is to get the viewer horny, or to fill out a subscription card. It's tough, too, because nudity is the greatest distraction. I didn't love the angle of my head in the naked photo I did for this magazine two years ago. The Polaroids I saw during the photo shoot showed this shiny naked chick kickin' it on a couch and feelin' it. But the one that was published made me look, I thought, sort of stiff or demure, like one of the somewhat hornier sisters on *The Waltons*. I sort of hated that about it, to which my niece responded: "Who you think is gonna be looking at your head with your crazy butt flyin' all up in the air like that?" (This theory of hers is proven whenever someone approaches me with ten copies of said photo; when I say, "I'll just sign right here on my naked ass," the picture holder counters with, "Oh, no, just below it, please.")

4    In the end, despite having my bottom dusted with gold powder while the photographer yelled out, "Work it, baby! Oh, yeah, work it, Mama!" I think the picture is very PG-13, nothing to blush about. The Catholic Church, though, might say otherwise. The *Catholic Digest* Web site and the U. S. Bishops' Office for Film and Broadcasting issue grave warnings about the dangers of nudity. The movie *The Full Monty* was recommended with reservations, based on its "brief rear nudity" and "fleeting homosexual innuendo." I confess I find *The Full Monty* about as racy as *The Parent Trap,* so perhaps we should

avoid all movies, not to mention the ground floor of the Louvre, due to the more-than-fleeting rear nudity in the Michelangelo gallery.

5      I wonder if it is even possible for a nude to avoid any controversy. It seems to come down to the compartmentalization of particular body parts into the proper and improper, which seems a bit random. I don't quite see how, if we have a shot of a woman fully clothed—more than fully, in a beekeeper's outfit, no less—and somehow a nipple is exposed by accident, like, "Tra la la, here I am just taking care of my bees, thinking pure and virtuous thoughts," and that scant bit of flesh just, like, busted out somehow, then is that porno? Is a nipple itself just inherently nasty? Is it possible to show a nipple somewhere, in a men's magazine, for example, and have the photo deemed artistic? Does a nipple, by its very appearance in *Esquire,* have to scream 'lick me'?

6      Now, despite my own apparent willingness to rip it all off now and then, I admit to a couple of reservations. On one hand, if the intent is to get you hot, then the subject is objectified to some degree. The issue is mostly gender specific, and if it reemphasizes a woman's worth being tied up in her looks and sexual appeal, if it feeds that concept in some way, then a nude photo isn't really innocuous, I guess. The second factor is what it represents for me as an actress. I don't want to encourage the perception of acting as mere posing, akin to modeling, or that physical beauty is a prerequisite for talent: The question posed to any model or pretty girl who has found success singing disco or figure skating is, inevitably, "Are you going to try acting?" Since more than one career was founded on a woman's ability to smile well or look good in shorts, it might perpetuate the idea that acting is something that you do when you are good-looking, and if you want to do it, you better "work it, baby, and oh, yeah, work it, Mama." You better bare your ass and hope you look good. Love me, lick me, hire me.

7      So there, for me, is the problem. The being naked part I kinda like. I wondered if there was a way to circumvent this inner conflict, to turn the naked-actress phenomenon around a bit. When I pitched half a dozen ideas for this piece, the "what if I write about being naked in *Esquire*" idea was mysteriously latched

onto, the first response being, "Would you consider posing naked again?" I received an e-mail from the editor the next morning in which the word nude appeared no less than five times in the course of one paragraph, and it ended with "We agreed that it would make sense if you posed nude again." So. Well, anyone who might suggest a very public display of nudity for me must be very open-minded, I thought. So I rang him up and said, "Well, yeah, I think it's an idea, and I was also thinking, actually, that as the editor of the piece, it would make sense for you to appear naked as well. And I thought maybe I should choose the photo of you that runs, so you can really experience that loss of control and possible objectification. Just as an idea. I mean, I thought it might make sense."

8      I was met with some sputtering and somewhat choked, mortified laughter, the way people laugh when they feel suddenly light-headed, or when they view something both compelling and grotesque, like, say, two cats having sex, or a child vomiting into his Easter basket. He said he would get back to me.

9      I didn't mean to be sinister or punishing, wouldn't dream of running an unflattering shot or making him show his willy if he didn't want to. We could just both do some fairly tame, PG-13 to R-rated photos, nothing much showing, if anything, just so he could get the feel of the experience. That way, whenever he suggests a photo or looks at one, he will have a whole other, more deeply informed point of view. And, champ that he is, he shocked me. God love him, he said yes. The whole thing ended up being wonderfully reciprocal. Egalitarian. I'll show you some of mine if you show me some of yours.

---

### Mary-Louise Parker Made Me Take My Clothes Off
### by A. J. Jacobs

I'd always dreamed of a movie star asking me to get naked, but this isn't exactly what I had in mind. Mary-Louise Parker was considering posing for *Esquire* but had an unusual—by which I mean deeply disturbing—request: that the editor of the piece pose naked as well. Huh. The editor. That would be me. That's problematic. I pointed out that my nipples weren't fit for mass consumption. I mentioned the possibility of subscription cancellations. "Well, think about it," she said.

I told my wife, counting on her to be equally disturbed. "Oh, you have to do it," she said. "It's only fair." (My wife later confessed that she thought a nude photo in a national magazine would finally force me to start doing ab crunches.) I told my boss, who was also unnervingly enthusiastic. "Maybe we could shoot you the way we did Monica Bellucci on our cover, with caviar on your chest." He wasn't kidding. This was not going well.

A few days later, I was in a cab on the way to the studio with *Esquire's* design director, who kept assuring me that there would be nothing edible on my solar plexus and no Mapplethorpian whips in my orifices. This would be very classy, an homage to a famous Yves Saint Laurent nude. Classy. An adjective I'm sure Linda Lovelace heard a few times.

In the dim, hangar-sized studio, they poured me chilled wine, put on a Norah Jones CD, handed me a white terry-cloth robe, and apologized for not having a fluffer. Everyone had a good laugh at that one. I took off my robe and sat cross-legged on this red cushion. The humiliation level? I'd say moderate to high—about the same as when I inadvertently drooled on my desk in sixth grade.

There was Nigel—the very nice British photographer—who kept telling me to "soook in yer goot!" which I eventually figured out was a reference to my problematic stomach. There was the look of horror when I lowered my leg too much and exposed what Nigel called my "chopper." There was the monumental indifference displayed by the cute young female assistants to my naked form, which apparently held as much allure as a wicker table. There was the evidence of my low position on the media chain: As I was leaving, they began setting up for Mary-Louise, bringing in the couscous and grilled chicken and champagne. But at least there were no problems with my chopper misbehaving. (I was genuinely worried about this; I had brought along a photo of my late grandma, just in case.)

So what did I learn from the exercise? Maybe more respect for the actresses I ask to pose naked. Certainly more respect for the transformative power of good lighting and goot-sucking. Certainly more sympathy for the parents involved. (When I told my mom, she looked at me in the way I imagine John

Walker Lindh's mom did when he told her he'd chosen a career in the Taliban military.) And I learned to never, ever scribble anonymous notes on nude photos around the office, like the one suggesting that I invest in several bottles of Nair. I saw that.

## Theme

1. Mary-Louise Parker expresses several points of view on the topic of nude photographs. Label and list them.

2. Her editor at *Esquire*, A. J. Jacobs, seems to have a more limited set of views about the experience of naked posing. Label and list his views.

## Technique

1. The words "naked" and "nude" are both used throughout Mary-Louise Parker's essay. Are they used interchangeably? If you think not, define the different implications and connotations of the two words.

2. The editors write to Mary-Louise Parker: "We agreed that it would make sense if you appeared nude again." She uses the same phrase about "sense" in her reply. But what does "making sense" mean in each side of this exchange? How is she making fun of the editor's language and what it expresses?

## Writing

Write an essay on the implications of the words "naked" and "nude" as applied to people in photographs.

# The Reverend Jesse Jackson

## Rainbow Imperative                                           (1999)

> *The Reverend Jesse Jackson was born in Greenville, South Carolina. He played quarterback on the Carolina A&T football team, before dropping out to become a civil rights activist associated with Dr. Martin Luther King, Jr. A one-time candidate for the Democratic presidential nomination, his Wall Street Project seeks a greater role for minorities within America's financial institutions. The following essay on the advertising industry is a part of that project.*

1   Three years ago, I started the Wall Street Project, on the anniversary of Dr. Martin Luther King's birthday. The mission of the Wall Street Project is to challenge corporate America to end the multibillion-dollar trade deficit with minority vendors and consumers. Dr. King understood then that beyond the struggle to end slavery, end legal segregation, and assure every American the right to vote is the struggle to promote equality in access to capital. It is my impression that the private sector must take the lead in making the marketplace more inclusive because expansion of the marketplace leads to sustainable economic growth.

2   We are, I believe, at the leading edge of the fourth stage of the civil rights movement: the battle for a broader sharing of wealth. This frontier demands that we move beyond the great political struggles of the past that led to the enactment of voting rights and public accommodation laws.

3   This frontier acknowledges that most of the decisions that affect our communities—for better or worse—are made far from the halls of government. They are instead made in corporate boardrooms, in the suites of investment bankers, in the offices of pension fund trustees, in radio and TV stations, and in advertising agencies.

SOURCE: Reprinted with permission from the September 20, 1999 issue of *Advertising Age*. Copyright © 1999 by Crain Communications, Inc.

4     We are no longer fighting for the right to spend our money. Today, we are the vital clients and shareholders whose presence is driving up the profits of corporations. What we are fighting for is our recognition as both consumers and trading partners. But we also want access to capital, opportunity, and the public airwaves. We want to own some of the cable and broadcasting entities that engage our communities.

5     Companies must begin to act as though our consumer dollars are not worth less then everyone else's. By purchasing stock in over 200 companies, we have changed the dynamics of protest. Corporate America must therefore work and spend to attract our consumer dollars. This is the new battleground of the future, as we continue fighting to make the American Dream an American reality for everyone.

6     Recently, the American economy has seen unprecedented growth. With this the reach of the minority consumer has also grown. Minority buying power is now a vital part of the American economic landscape. African-American and Hispanic consumers, for example, earned over $700 billion last year. Minority buying power is therefore pivotal to the success of any consumer product. As our country's demographics change, the importance of minorities as consumers will continue to increase.

7     Multicultural marketing therefore is not just another "cause," it is good for business. It is a sign of respect for the growing prominence of minority consumers. Multicultural advertising efforts should therefore be considered an intelligent response to the growing power of minority consumers and their spending habits.

8     Unfortunately, according to the American Association of Advertising Agencies, while consumer advertising spending last year rose to about $160 billion, only $1.1 billion of that amount was targeted to the African-American market. This is unequal treatment of a consumer market so fundamental to product success.

9     To maintain and increase a competitive market share in the future, companies must earn customer loyalty within communities of color. This can only be done by dramatically increasing the level of advertising expenditures that target ethnic consumers. While individual minority consumers have less dis-

posable income than their white counterparts, studies show
that they spend it at a faster rate.

10    Furthermore, minority consumers are both brand conscious
and loyal, thereby making targeted advertising efforts more
effective. Thus for many companies, multicultural advertising
must be more than a short-term scheme to avert some political crisis. Efforts to diversify all aspects of the advertising industry must be a fundamental part of a corporation's long-term
economic planning, because we all have a direct impact on the
bottom line.

11    Yet, while the reasons for multicultural advertising seem
endless, many continue to resist. Companies still have to be
convinced that targeted advertising campaigns work. They continue to take the purchasing power of their minority customers
for granted. Business leaders have cultural blinders, obstruct-
ing their ability to see nontraditional but lucrative markets.
They need to see that they are not their brother's keeper, they
are their brother's brothers. This new way of seeing combines
enlightened self-interest with a moral imperative.

12    For too long advertisers have had a distorted view of Hispanic, African-American, and other minority groups. As Pepe
Sutton, chairman of Inner City Broadcasting, said at the
Rainbow/PUSH Wall Street Project conference in January, "Ad
agencies are practicing covert racism based on stereotypes,
fueled by ignorance, and characterized by stubbornness and
entrenched structures."

13    While none of this is new, it was not until the infamous
internal memo from Katz Radio Corp. that the issue became
public. The memo, circulated by a Katz employee, instructed
sales representatives to steer companies away from purchasing
advertising on ethnic-oriented stations, noting that "advertisers
should want prospects, not suspects."

14    As the memo's author illustrates, minority consumers are
often misunderstood and disrespected. Such blatant disregard
assumes that the general market is the only factor in determining the success or failure of consumer goods and services.
Many in the advertising industry believe that minority consumers will not be moved by advertising, as majority consumers seem to be.

15    In other words, they believe that our markets are not viable. This is wrong. Minority consumers will identify with the products that best serve them and the companies that court them.

16    Advertisers should also support minority-owned and -operated media outlets. Many of these radio and TV stations produce compelling programming geared towards the growing minority communities. Yet while their programs are often well received and highly rated, they receive lower advertising rates than general program stations. As Federal Communications Commission Chairman William Kennard's report, "When No. 1 is Not Enough," indicates, advertisers are unwilling to pay the same advertising rates to media outlets with minority programming. The revenue gap between minority-owned and majority-owned media companies must end.

17    As our demographics change, advertisers that support diversity by reaching out to minority-owned media will be better positioned to reach America's most powerful consumers. The FCC study, by Kofi Ofori of the Telecommunications Civil Rights Forum, found that white-owned broadcasters get 30% more revenue than minority broadcasters with similar or stronger ratings. Companies will make a better case for their products if they make commitments to minority-owned stations.

18    It is not enough to court minority consumers. Advertisers should begin to cultivate minority-owned radio and TV by advertising with them and paying them fairly. Advertisers should form business partnerships with minority-owned media, as they are the future outlets for what will be the fastest growing consumer base of our nation. It is the responsibility of the companies that thrive on our consumer dollars to hire advertising agencies that will promote this concept. Companies must underscore to their agencies that the value of the minority consumer dollar is important.

19    Finally, the imbalance created when urban broadcasters receive less than their fair share of advertising means that minority-owned media have less capital to operate their businesses. Without this, minority-owned stations are unable to increase programming commitments. They are less able to present original programming. Neglected and overlooked

minority-owned stations don't have the capital necessary to acquire other stations and expand their business. In other words, discriminatory practices by advertising agencies prevent minority media outlets from effectively competing in a changing economy.

20    It is therefore the responsibility of all companies to fully engage minority consumers and minority-owned media. It is simply about expanding the marketplace for all people. This is the future of American business.

## Theme

1. "Equality in access to capital" is the goal announced by Jackson in paragraph one. Summarize in you own words his reasons for believing that the goal should be met.

2. Summarize in your own words Jackson's reasons for believing the goal of "equality in access to capital" has not been met in contemporary America.

## Technique

1. Jackson often presents a topic using comparison and contrast. Point to a particular example of his use of this technique and explain how it helps to support his general argument.

2. Jackson's paragraphs frequently begin with transitional words rather than the subject of his sentence. Point to some examples and explain how they help to organize his essay and to drive it forward.

## Writing

Jackson argues that the significance of minorities as consumers relates to their deserving a larger stake in the capital of industries that produce what minorities consume—the advertising industry, for example. Write an essay analyzing Jackson's arguments.

# Jenny McCarthy

## Where in the Hell Can I Find a Muumuu?    (2004)

*Jenny McCarthy dropped out of a nursing program and went on to become a devoted kick boxer, Playmate of the Year, an actress and a television host. In "Where in the Hell Can I Find a Muumuu," she shares her experiences with body changes during pregnancy while trying to maintain a media presence.*

1    Clothes shopping when you're feeling even a little bloated is tough on the self-esteem, if not on the wallet. Still, I've been pretty lucky, and with a stylist's help (just one of those celeb perks!), I've never had too much trouble finding clothes that make me look good. That all changed when I first started to show. Actually, and you probably know how this goes, I was likely the only one who thought I was showing. I was just growing what I now refer to as "a protective fat layer" around my belly. To me it was obvious I was pregnant but to the rest of the world Jenny McCarthy was simply eating too many Krispy Kremes.

2    One day I looked in my closet to put something on to start my day. I threw on a pair of pants only to realize that I couldn't quite button them. I got the zipper up but that damn button just wouldn't close. I thought to myself, well, this totally sucks. So I took them off and tried on all of my other pants until I found a pair that were always a little big on me. Except this time they just fit. I put on a nice fitted top only to look in the mirror and see that "protective fat layer" around my belly. So I proceeded to try on every other top I had until I found the loosest fitting one. I ended up with a massive pile of clothes on my closet floor and an outdated baggy look for the day. Ugh.

Source: From *Belly Laughs* by Jenny McCarthy. Copyright © 2004 by Jennifer McCarthy. Reprinted by permission of Da Capo, a member of Perseus Books, LLC.

3   Finding something to wear will only get worse before it gets better, so here's my advice to you: Stretch this part out as long as you can and cram yourself into your regular loose-fitting clothes. You're in that awful stage where you don't yet look pregnant, just fat. No stylist in the world can really help you hide this. All of the pregnancy books will tell you to throw on one of your husband's shirts. Not terrible advice, but at this "fat" stage, I don't know about you, but I don't look that cute in a flannel!

4   Don't go out and buy maternity clothes yet. With the exception of some basic black stretch pants, maternity clothes are made for women with bellies. Or for women who have told the world they are expecting to get one. Early on, you honestly won't fit in them, and you'll look like a jackass with all that extra floppy fabric.

5   Of course, I thought I had it worse than anybody. Because of my work, I had to hide my pregnancy. Squeezing into my clothes and hiding my fat was freakin' impossible. And okay, maybe this particular brand of impossible won't happen to you, but national TV spot aside, you're going to be able to relate to the theme of this next story.

6   Dick Clark asked me to host the American Music Awards, and by the time I would have to do the show, I would already be a few months pregnant. Terrified to have my cover blown but excited about the job, I agreed.

7   Poor little rich girl, I know, but my wardrobe stylist and I went through a horrific disaster in trying to help me dress cool but all the while hide my belly. Pre-pregnancy, I usually wore a size 4 or 6, but now I was only barely squeezing into a size 12. We had at least ten "try-on" sessions, which all ended in tears. I would seriously break down and bawl. All of my pre-interviews were about what I was going to wear (ah, Hollywood priorities!). For the first time I heard myself dissing style. "Who cares about clothes?" I said. "It's about being funny." Yeah, right, not to Dolce & Gabbana.

8   Fast-forward to show time and I was about to go out onstage. I was feeling confident because no one had said anything to me about my weight gain. I was uncomfortable as hell, though, because I was wearing a corset so tight I couldn't

breathe. (Of course, I asked my doctor about wearing one at least a million times: "Am I hurting the baby?" No, he told me. "Am I smashing the baby?" No, he said. "Am I killing the baby?" "NO! You're only hurting yourself. He's not going to be in pain. You are!" "Well, okay then, as long as I'm the only one suffering I'm happy.")

9       The moment of truth: "Ladies and Gentlemen, here are your hosts Sean 'P. Diddy' Combs and Jenny McCarthy." I walked out onstage feeling good, feeling fine, connected with my mojo. Some people made faces at my weird clothing choices (Did I mention the corset?), but I didn't care as long as the world didn't think I looked pregnant.

10      Several hours later (I know, these shows really do go on!) and, to my relief, the end of the show finally arrived. I plopped down on the couch in my dressing room and welcomed my family, who had been sitting in the audience. "How did I do?" They all smiled and clapped and said I did really well except … "Except what?" I asked. My sister began to tell me how the people all around them had been commenting on how pregnant I looked. I guess it's true: You just can't keep a secret in Hollywood.

11      Again, this might not happen to you, but national airwaves aside again, you may have had a nightmare experience along these lines. The next day Howard Stern went on the air and made comments about how pregnant I looked. He said I had pregnant boobs. Coming from him, I *think* that's a compliment, but it's not exactly what a girl wants to hear.

12      First-trimester flab behind me (and on my behind), my next month was fun. I was obviously pregnant, the world knew it, and I could finally shop for maternity clothes. What I didn't know was how awful some maternity clothes can be. They have gotten better, I think, but not good enough. First of all, they are so overpriced. But you're kind of screwed—What choice do you have?—so you have to buy some. You have nothing else. Here's what I know: The key to shopping at this point is comfort. I bought comfy tanks and drawstring pants and cozy turtlenecks. I wore them almost every day until my ninth month, when I porked out beyond belief. I refused to go buy still more and still larger and expensive maternity clothes

to wear for just a few more weeks, so I begged my husband to go to Sears and get me a damn muumuu! I'm not kidding. I would beg anyone that heard my cry to go get me a muumuu. Nothing fit me right, and if it did, I just looked so incredibly large or I was really uncomfortable. I wanted a muumuu, just like the ones Mrs. Roper wore on *Three's Company.*

13    Then it happened! One of my friends heard my call. Behold the muumuu. She held up a giant, blue-flowered muumuu, and it had my name written all over it. I put it on and danced all around the house. My glory ended as soon as my husband saw me in it and begged me to take it off (not to get some action, believe me. Even the friend who bought it for me said it was just "wrong.") I say, "Bite me!"

14    If you get to that point where you just can't take it, please go get one. MUUMUU'S really do rock!

## Theme

1. McCarthy's essay on clothes to wear while pregnant divides itself roughly into two parts—what to wear before you show, and what to wear after. What are the values and assumptions behind her sense of proper style in the "before" phase? For example, does she sound as if she is ashamed of being pregnant and trying to pretend it never happened? Surely not—but how would you define her rationale?

2. What is different about the values and assumptions of fashion in the second part of the essay, the "after" phase? Again, how does the author assume a pregnant woman should dress and why does she seem to think so? For example, what is so awful about a muumuu for her and, conversely, what is so great about it?

## Technique

1. One general stance taken by the author in the essay is that of an experienced giver of advice to people who have not

had to deal with the issue of clothes and pregnancy. Is there any other audience addressed in your view? Explain your answer by analyzing evidence.

2. At the end of paragraph eight, McCarthy expresses a paradox: "Well okay then, as long as I'm the only one suffering, I'm happy." Explain in your own words how this apparent contradiction in terms may be seen to make real sense.

## Writing

Using McCarthy's essay as a model, write a fashion advice piece of your own. For example, "What High School Clothes You Should Bring to College."

# Russell Simmons

## White People                                              (2001)

> *Russell Simmons is one of the architects of the rap and hip-hop
> music industry. Founder of Def Jam with Rick Rubin, he pack-
> aged hip-hop and sold it to major mainstream music companies.
> In "White People," he analyzes self-presentation from the point
> of view of a minority businessman.*

1    During the mid-'90s people started telling me that my company, Rush Communications, was the most powerful, if not the
most profitable, black-owned entertainment company in the
world. I made the cover of *Black Enterprise* magazine sitting in
a hoodie, jeans, and sneakers on the hood of a Rolls-Royce—
the first businessman in that conservative African-American
magazine to rock it like that. It was a sign that the gatekeep-
ers of black culture were beginning to treat me with respect—
finally. As defined by many whites and blacks, I'd "made it."

2    Well, that thought turns my stomach, because in comparison to my white counterparts, my company isn't even significant—at least financially. I'm not saying that to make myself
seem smaller. I know my role in influencing pop culture is bigger than that of most of the people I compete with.

3    From the early '90s till now, my enterprises have been about
pushing outside the box of "black business" and growing into
the mainstream alongside hip-hop. Most of that growth has
been phenomenal—Def Jam grossing $200 million in 1999,
Phat Farm licensing agreements worth $150 million, the open-
ing of the Rush advertising agency in 1999, and the launch of
my Internet company, 360 Hip Hop, in 2000. There have been
some disappointments—Hollywood has yet to be good to me

SOURCE: From *Life and Def* by Russell Simmons and Nelson George. Copyright ©
2001 by Rush Communications, LLC. Used with permission of Crown Publishers, a
division of Random House, Inc.

as a businessman, though my time in the city of Los Angeles has been crucial to my growth as a man. In the '80s I spent most of my time promoting hip-hop as music; in the '90s I used that success to expand the reach of hip-hop culture.

4    Still, to accept the "powerful black company" designation would be to accept living in a box. I'm not gonna do that. In selling to the black community, there's a certain twist you can put in your advertising and marketing to remind buyers it's for black people. But you also don't wanna limit your buyers to one race. The only thing a black businessman might sell that's only for black consumers is hair products. If you are selling Afro Sheen or hair straighteners, your market is defined for you.

5    But what if you're selling a purple suit? Black people may be the chief buyers of purple suits. You may sell most of your purple suits to black men in the South or Midwest. That doesn't mean, however, that you limit your sales of purple suits to black people. There may be a whole community of white buyers who'd love a purple suit, and you should go get that money, too.

6    Often black consumers don't like it when you limit your sales efforts to just them because it can feel patronizing. FUBU, for example, has been very effective in communicating with black buyers but not alienating other ethnic groups. FUBU means "for us by us," which is a code phrase for saying it's a black-owned business, which appeals to racial pride among blacks. That, however, does not preclude any hip Asian or Hispanic kid from buying their clothes. With the interest and heat on urban culture we've seen in the last few years, I'd be crazy not to go for the widest possible audience for what I sell.

### The *R* Word

7    One key example of how I view the world is my feeling about the word *racist*. I don't use the word *racist* much. It's not productive. It doesn't help me to say, "Oh, yes, white people are racist. That's why I can't get ahead." You see, I realized a while ago that I have the ability to stomach racist white people and accept the rest of them for what they are.

8    The supermodel Naomi Campbell and I were talking about race one night, and she told me about how she transcended the "black thing" in a hundred ways and does it all the time. "I could be bitter," she once told me, "but I'm not." She went to

a white school where some of the students would say shit that was racist to her. But Naomi also knew other white people at school who weren't racist. Those who were racist could be racist all day, but she'd still deal with them the same as she dealt with everyone else. That's why she doesn't mind living, through her work and celebrity, in a predominantly white world—she's accepted that some white people are the way they are. When a cab doesn't stop for her, she calls a Rolls-Royce to pick her up, which I've done, too.

9    I don't get as upset as my white liberal friends when a cab doesn't pick me up or some other minor racist shit happens. My friends have a fit about that kind of thing, but I take it in stride, since it is just one of those everyday slights black people expect. I was on a plane talking with one of my best friends, Bobby Shriver, and a flight attendant said something to me like "shush." Bobby said to the guy, "Wait a minute. You didn't shush him, did you?" I said, "It's all right, Bob. I haven't been insulted. Bobby, he didn't shush you—he shushed me." Bobby said, "He did it because you're black." Bobby got madder and madder.

10    He was shocked because he wasn't aware that I had to deal with that shit all day. He brought it up two weeks later. I said, "Bobby, I don't give a fuck about it. I don't have time to worry about it." Well, Bobby went and got the flight attendant fired— that's how upset he was.

11    Many white people are shocked by the racism that goes on. They don't see it. I try to get angry, but my anger makes no difference. There's nothing I can do with that anger. So when I say, "I can stomach racist white people," it's because their small-mindedness doesn't mean shit to me. I just go with my agenda and continue building relationships. Anger can side-track you. It takes a lot of energy to be mad all the time. Some people can do that and still get things done. I cannot. I have to be moving forward or I fall into the trap of letting the anger control me.

12    I deal with white people in many areas of my business— music, film, television, clothing, advertising—if they're inter-ested in what I'm interested in, even if they're racists and don't even know it. When they do the obvious racist shit, I just point it out to them. "Look how stupid you are," I'll say. They don't think they're racist even then. "You know what?" they say.

"You're right. I wonder if I would have done that if you weren't black." We have a discussion and we laugh about it and that's it. And at the end of the day we're still friends. I'm not saying I'm right to be this way. I'm saying it works for me. I've lived by this code in business all my life. Although I now spend more and more time pushing for change in this country, it's fueled not by anger at any individuals, but by my personal disappointment at America's slow rate of change.

13   Now, someone could read this and say, "Well, Russell's a millionaire, so he can afford to turn the other cheek." But as this book makes clear, I wasn't given money. I had to find ways to make it. And that means dealing with all kinds of people to advance my agenda. Finding ways to get along with people is crucial to anything you do. A lot of the young businesspeople I meet have a lot of anger toward everyone—not just white people—and go into every business dealing as if it's a battle. Yes, you always have to protect yourself. At the same time you also need to be open. You have to watch everything, be curious about everyone and be willing to be taught. Not everyone you learn from is gonna be nice. Some of them might even be evil. However, at the end of the day, it's what you learn from these interactions that determines your success or failure.

14   It's simply easier to be in business with people you spend time with. You can discuss ideas with them freely and you can get work done together. If you're in a creative business, you need to have a good working relationship with the people you work with. Real communication has to go on.

15   I know a lot of successful black people on Wall Street, people like the investment bankers Ray McGuire and Tracy Maitlan. They speak a different language than I do. Obviously we share a cultural connection as black people. But they also speak the language of bankers. Numbers people speak a whole different language when they talk about business. That always makes me reflect on the comment that black and white people speak different languages. I don't believe that's true. Depending on their areas of expertise—be it banking, babies, or baseball—they speak the same language on a number of levels except on certain cultural issues.

16   My point is that I'm more interested in listening to the guy who owns a television network than the guy who works at the

network and happens to be black. The guy who owns the network is talking about places and things that I want to know about. If people you meet, white or black, have access to information you want, then you should be talking to them. Race should not be a consideration when people are telling you things that excite you.

## Theme

1. In paragraph three Simmons writes: "Still, to accept the 'powerful black company' designation would be to accept being in a box." By pointing to evidence in the essay, explain how the author shows what he means by this remark.

2. In paragraph six Simmons says: "I don't use the word 'racist' much. It's not productive." Explain how the author shows what he means by this remark using evidence from the essay.

## Technique

1. In paragraph one the author describes himself in a cover photo for *Black Enterprise* magazine. Explain what the different elements (clothing, make of car, etc.) of that photograph seem to express.

2. In paragraph two the author says: "that thought turns my stomach." Later in paragraph six he says: "I have the ability to stomach racist white people." Explain in your own words what the word "stomach" seems to mean as it is used in this essay. For example "heart" in other essays refers not literally to an organic pump, but figuratively to the seat of tender emotions.

## Writing

Write an essay explaining the views Russell Simmons holds on race relations. Use evidence from the text.

# Phillip McGraw, Ph.D.

## We Teach People How to Treat Us    (1999)

*Dr. Phil got his start in mass culture as Oprah Winfrey's resident guest expert on psychological matters. On Oprah, he fielded questions on everything from weight loss problems to mock trials, before moving on to his own series where he spreads his net still wider. In "We Teach People How to Treat Us" Dr. Phil explores how other people influence and may be influenced by our own style of self-presentation.*

No one can make you feel inferior without your consent.

—Eleanor Roosevelt

1    **Life Law #8: We Teach People How to Treat Us**
*Your Strategy*: Own, rather than complain about, how people treat you. Learn to renegotiate your relationships to have what you want.

2    The life laws you have learned thus far have focused on how and why you get the results that you do as you go through your life. This law is no exception. It deals specifically with how you define your relationships and how you get results. But it has an important added dimension. This law takes into account the fact that in addition to getting results, you yourself are a result, and therefore you shape the behavior of those with whom you interact. Because people learn by results, whether or not you reward, accept, or validate their behavior impacts their conduct, and will influence their subsequent choices. How you interpret and react to their behavior determines whether or not they are likely to repeat it. You therefore actively participate in defining your relationships.

3    So if you ever wonder why people treat you the way they do, see Life Law #3: *People Do What Works.* They do what they do because you have taught them, based on results, which behavior gets a payoff and which ones don't. If they get what they want, they keep that behavior in their repertoire. If they do not get the desired result, they drop that behavior and acquire a new one. Understand that here, as in all areas of your life, results, not intentions, influence the people with whom you interact. You may complain or cry or threaten to give them negative results, but if the bottom line is that you reward the behavior by providing a response that the other person values, then that person decides, "Hey, this works. I now know how to get what I want."

4    If the people in your life treat you in an undesirable way, you're going to want to figure out what you are doing to reinforce, elicit, or allow that treatment. If you're involved in a relationship in which someone is consistently abusive, exploitive, or insensitive toward you, find out what you're doing to encourage that behavior, so that you can realign the relationship in a more healthy direction.

5    Relationships are mutually defined: each participant contributes importantly to its definition. From the very outset, it is a give-and-take negotiation between the participants. Together, you and your partner hammer out the terms, rules, and guidelines. Therefore, if you don't like the deal, don't blame just your partner. You have ownership of that relationship just as much as he or she does. Here's how it works:

6    Person A starts out engaging Person B in some manner that sets a tone for the relationship. Person B then reacts to that original defining message by sending back a response either accepting or rejecting A's definition. If it is rejected, B may either totally withdraw, or modify it in some way. If B's response changes the definition, then A will in turn either accept or reject that new definition, and respond to B. This continues until a relationship has been worked out and adopted. Thus, you have been an active participant in creating the terms and conditions of every one of your relationships.

7    I once counseled a middle-aged couple who had been married twenty-seven years. John was an electrical contractor and Kay was a highly experienced medical receptionist. Both came

from large families and had raised four children themselves, all grown and out on their own. While they professed to love each other very much, they acknowledged they had come to me because their communication was terrible.

8      They arrived at my office one day right after a holiday, saying that they had recently had their worst fight in all their years together. Kay fumed, but said nothing, as John described the events leading up to the fight. He said that he had developed an annual tradition of staying up all night on Thanksgiving Eve to cook the turkey for the large family gathering that was always held at their home. On this particular Thanksgiving, they were expecting twenty-six family members for dinner. While he only occasionally drank alcohol, John said that his traditional Thanksgiving ritual was as follows:

9      "Every Wednesday night before Thanksgiving, I get a jug of Jack Daniel's and wait until she and any of the company turn in, and then I start cooking.

10     "I like to cook it real slow. So usually about midnight, I stick the bird in the oven, knock the top off the jug of whiskey, and start an all-night ordeal. Usually after a quart of Jack Daniel's, me and the turkey get done about the same time."

11     Over the years, Kay had not seemed to mind this ritual. Unfortunately, however, this particular year John apparently got a little ahead of the turkey with regard to the whiskey drinking and forgot to light the oven. By the time he discovered the problem, it was six o'clock in the morning and he had a twenty-eight pound turkey still refrigerator-cold. With reasoning that could only spring from a mind pickled in Jack Daniel's, he made the only logical decision: fry the turkey, piece by piece. When Kay entered the kitchen and found grease stains decorating every wall, turkey parts being fried in eight or nine different skillets and pans, and John up to his eyebrows in flour, she was decidedly unhappy. And as the old saying goes, "When momma ain't happy, ain't nobody happy."

12     This crisis had strained John and Kay beyond all reason. For ten days, they had essentially not spoken. Each blamed the other for the disastrous state of their relationship. In John's view, the reason they didn't have much of a marriage was that Kay almost never spoke. Kay insisted that they had a poor relationship

because John was always "running off at the mouth" and would never listen. Like most couples, they had not really come to me for help, but instead to have a referee or a judge who could declare which of them was right and which was wrong.

13    Not surprisingly, I couldn't fulfill that request, because neither John nor Kay was right or wrong. They had mutually defined their relationship. John had taught Kay that it was acceptable to treat him passively, with little or no communication, because for years and years he had accepted that behavior. Kay had taught John that he could dominate the relationship and do all of the talking, because she had allowed him to do so for twenty-seven years. By letting each other get away with the problem behavior, each had taught the other that his or her behavior was acceptable.

14    When they finally reached the point in their lives when only the two of them were left at home, and there were no children to act as buffers, their problems came to the forefront. At last, in the face of what they considered to be a major crisis—the Thanksgiving debacle—the foundation of their mutually defined relationship began to crack. It was time for them to recognize that each had taught the other how to treat him or her, and that in neither case was that treatment healthy. Once John and Kay stopped reinforcing each other's unacceptable behavior, they began to develop better communication skills and a greater degree of intimacy and trust (although I don't believe John ever got solo turkey duty again).

15    As John and Kay's history demonstrates, even a pattern of relating that is almost thirty years old can be redefined. If you can teach people how to treat you in the first place, you can reteach them how to treat you after that. It is in the give-and-take of relating, and of results, that relationships are successfully negotiated. You may not have known that you were negotiating and creating, but you were. Now you know: Being in a meaningful negotiation and not knowing it can be very dangerous.

16    The good news is that, because you are accountable, you can declare the relationship "reopened for negotiation" at any time you choose, and for as long as you choose. John and Kay did exactly that after almost thirty years. In any case, new

relationships or old, you are responsible for whatever state your relationships are in. Please understand that I mean you are responsible in the most literal sense, and even in the most extreme, seemingly one-sided circumstances.

## Theme

1. How does Dr. Phil treat you, the reader, in the course of his essay? Pick a representative passage and analyze the sense of audience he seems to assume. In paragraph five, for example, do the first three sentences seem representative? How does an apparent need for repetition here implicitly define the relationship between the imagined "you" and Dr. Phil?

2. Describe some ways in which the Great Turkey Disaster does or does not illustrate Life Law # 8. Point to examples and explain your reasoning.

## Technique

1. The selection begins with an epigraph that quotes Eleanor Roosevelt—the wife of Franklin D. Roosevelt, four-time president of the United States. Do you think this epigraph is an effective technique of introduction? Explain the ways in which the epigraph relates to what follows it.

2. Explain in your own words the differences and similarities of Life Law #8 and Life Law #3 as illustrated in the material of the selection. What do you think of the announcement of such laws as a technique of exposition and organization? Explain your answer.

## Writing

"When Momma ain't happy, ain't nobody happy"—so reads the old saying quoted by Dr. Phil. Using his selection as a model, write an essay that treats the old saying as a Life Law illustrated by evidence from your own experience or imagination.

## EXERCISES

### Intertextual Questions

1. Jon Stewart seems flattered but also a little embarrassed to have been chosen as a commencement speaker by his alma mater. Mary-Louise Parker displays something of the same ambiguity in her response to *Esquire*. Discuss the ways each celebrity deals with the issues of self-presentation in his or her response to accepting an invitation.

2. The Reverend Jesse Jackson and Russell Simmons both discuss problems for African Americans in mass media. To what extent do they agree on the nature of the problems and their solutions? To what extent do they disagree? Discuss their views on the issues they raise.

3. Pamela Anderson and Jenny McCarthy both address issues of fashion, but do so from vastly differing perspectives. Still, each presents herself in a witty and self-assured manner. What other aspects do the personas presented by the two women display?

4. Dr. Phil argues that "We Teach People How to Treat Us." In your opinion, who among the other contributors to the chapter would most agree with his contention based on what they have written? Would anyone disagree? Explain your answers using evidence from the essays.

5. In your view, which celebrity in this chapter made the most effective self-presentation of a public persona through language? Explain the reasoning behind your choice.

### Suggestions for Writing

1. Several of the writers in this chapter are very witty in their self-presentations. Who seems the most so to you? Write an essay in which you defend your choice through the analysis of examples including at least one passage by an author other than the one you have selected.

2. The female authors here all address issues that in one way or another focus on the female body. Write an essay in which you analyze the ways each expresses her views on this topic.

3. Race is an issue both for the Reverend Jesse Jackson and for Russell Simmons. Write an essay in which you analyze the ways each expresses his views on the topic.

4. Have you or someone you know ever had an experience that has been illuminated by Dr. Phil's essay? If so, write an essay in which you illustrate with your experiences the points he makes about the response of others to one's self-presentation.

5. Besides Jon Stewart, which person in this chapter would make the best speaker at your own commencement ceremonies? Write an essay explaining and defending your choice.

# CHAPTER 6

# A BUSINESS-LIKE MANNER

The first two chapters in this section have been concerned with some of the many ways individuals construct and express a self through language to meet a public who "reads" their identities in their verbal performances. One aspect of the social self, however, is famous for being very quickly taken for granted with minimal verbal evidence and absolutely no creative effort on your part. Have you ever been invited to stand and deliver up the treasure cave of your soul by the question that passes as the academic 'open sesame'—"What's your major?" If so, you know that if your answer meets with your interrogator's approval, you may be let off the hook—"Oh." But for many undergraduates engaged in a traditional liberal arts curriculum, declaring your major in public will not let you pass the self-appointed sentries who guard real life without being asked to give not only the password but the countersign as well—"What are you going to do with *that*?"

Better practice an answer—say firmly, for example, "Internet-based biomedical nuclear economics!"—because at Thanksgiving or some other family gathering you will quickly learn—if you haven't already—that many people are interested in your academic identity only insofar as it can be translated into your economic identity. Put another way, "What's your major?" is only the junior version of the great American question "What does he/she *do?*" where who you are is *what you do* and what you do is *what you do for a living*. It may surprise you to learn that reading carefully and writing clearly are skills valued in every area of business as they are in other areas of life.

Still, making a living is something almost everyone must do—star or no star—and even if President Calvin Coolidge was not correct in saying "The business of America is business," everyone should know something about such a defining aspect of contemporary American mass culture. Even if you do not go into business yourself, you will inevitably have to do a great deal of business with people who have. Further, as the selections to follow will show, *fame and fortune* is (from the point of view of celebrities themselves) not so much about the easily imagined pleasures of consumption as the difficulties of producing wealth. Producing in every sense of the word is both a topic about which they have a great deal to teach and also (like almost all written expressions) a potentially useful source for learning more about composition.

To outsiders, money may seem merely to go automatically with the territory of being a celebrity, but Ben Stein quickly disabuses us of that notion in the first essay here, "Let's Talk About Dollars and Cents." He gives his content the form of a letter from a parent to a child—a serious letter on a serious subject. No, his subject is not the birds and bees, but rather how difficult it is to accumulate and maintain "capital"—not just financial capital, but the capital of a good education, which is so often the first step to financial success. Stein takes his son and his reader through some family history organized by the theme of dollars and cents.

More flamboyant in style but equally down to earth in his topic, Donald Trump next gives his take on a basic skill in business and in life—"The Art of Negotiation." In this essay, "The Donald" discusses not the hiring and firing that made his TV show such a success, but how to make all sides of an agreement happy—something necessary for the agreement to become a business reality at all. All sides being happy is the conceptual basis of legalized contractual relations in business as in other areas of public life. He takes us through a case history focused on the acquisition of a landmark Wall Street building.

Diane Von Furstenberg broke into the world of international fashion with a revolutionary dress in the 1960s called "the wrap." But the one sure thing about fashion is that it keeps changing as time goes by, and as a designer Von Furstenberg resolved not to be a one-trick pony. How she kept up with the times, not only as an artist but also as a businesswoman, is the subject of "Fashioning

Sales," an excerpt from her autobiography. She tells us how she came to discover and benefit from what was at that time the leading edge of media mass marketing—the QVC Shopping Network. Combining the traditional artistic skills of fashion design with up-to-date methods of electronic sales brought her a renewed success—not that her many international contacts didn't help.

Making contacts was never Michael Jordan's problem either. When it came time for him to decide which basketball shoe to endorse, all the major companies eagerly came to him of their own accord. Yet even though he went into negotiations firmly committed to Adidas, his title "The Nike Deal" tells you that he changed his mind—and his essay tells you how and why he did so.

Cokie and Steve Roberts were happily married for 30 years when they wrote the following excerpt from their joint autobiography, *From This Day Forward*. As star-level journalists in both TV and print media, their problem was finding the time and the method to do justice to their identities both as professional people and as family members—a problem they share with many couples today. Their writing employs an experimental dual narration, and the technique is symbolic of both the problem and the solution the Roberts found.

Family and career are not the only compromises necessary for people in the media or anywhere else. One thing Spike Lee learned when he first started making movies was that the often claimed conflict between "art" and "commercial success" in film has been oversimplified. The costs of modern film production are so enormous that no one can keep making movies of any sort unless the movies keep making money. What are the tradeoffs involved? How can you organize all aspects of your business—including publicity—to maximize your freedom of expression? Spike Lee takes us on a quick tour of these and other business issues in "Art and Money in Movies."

"It takes money to make money" says the old business proverb, but Chuck D has frequently turned proverbial wisdom upside down in more ways than one throughout his career. He first published "Free Music Can Free the Artist" as an Op-Ed piece in *The New York Times*. In this piece, the lead rapper for Public Enemy shows his other identity as public intellectual. Downloading music from the Internet has seemed to many industry insiders a threat to the traditional economic foundations of the entire music business. But one thing Chuck D. points out is that the traditional economic foundations of the entire music business were not always formed in the interests of its artists. He suggests that the latest developments in technology may in fact prove to liberate writers and performers both artistically and economically.

As the once and future richest man in the world, Bill Gates has long been liberated economically. That has not stopped the founder of Microsoft from continuing to think ahead innovatively and to try to share his thinking with others. In "Adopt the Web Lifestyle," he points out through historical analogy how a technological advance can cause all sorts of changes in many other areas of life. Those who cooperate with innovation are those who will benefit from it. Partial proof of the prophecies he makes in this excerpt from his book, *Business @ the Speed of Thought,* exists. Since the late 1990s, when the book was composed and published, some of his prophecies have already come true.

The chapter closes with Oprah Winfrey taking us through a case history that exemplifies many of the business themes presented earlier, from the importance of mutual negotiation to the importance of choosing proper personnel; from the importance of artistic freedom to the importance of when to say no to "innovation"; from the importance of artistic control to the importance of delegating authority. Oprah Winfrey shows her multifaceted talents both as media executive and media performer in telling her story of how a major novel became a major motion picture in "Bringing *Beloved* to the Screen."

# Ben Stein

## Let's Talk About Dollars and Cents    (2000)

*Ben Stein's part as the boring teacher in* Ferris Bueller's Day Off *has been rated one of the fifty most famous scenes in American film. But he has been more than an actor and the host of the Comedy Central quiz show* Win Ben Stein's Money. *He is a lawyer, an author (sixteen books, seven novels) and a one-time White House speech writer for President Richard Nixon. Stein majored at Columbia in economics, and in the essay that follows he gives his son (and his readers) some good economic advice about how to gain money and how to hold onto it.*

1    $D$ear Tommy,

2    I hope that you are well and especially that your football season is going well. It must be difficult to be injured so close to the beginning of the schedule. I hope you are studying. Eleventh grade is a terribly important year.

3    I think it may be time for me to send you a few thoughts about money and how to make sure that you continue to have the standard of living you have come to love so much. I'd like to try to explain how you have been able to live so large and what you will have to do to keep it going for the rest of your life and for your children's lives. It has to do with a very important word called "capital."

4    First of all, my grandfathers on both sides came to this country with virtually nothing. My grandfather on my father's side was an Army cavalry officer for a long time and then a skilled tool-and-die maker at Ford Motor and then at General Electric. He accumulated no capital to speak of, in terms of finance, and too little in terms of education to allow him to make a decent living. He was unemployed for a large part of the Great Depression, and Pop's family was supported largely by his mother's work at a department store. On my mother's father's

side, there was a small amount of real estate, but it was largely lost in the Great Depression.

5    My father was the first Stein in all history, as far as we know, to have accumulated any real capital. He did that by getting a fine education at Williams College and then at the University of Chicago. He was a stone genius, and among his many aspects of genius was that he knew that he must regularly convert his human capital—his intelligence and education and connections—into financial capital: namely, savings. He always lived well below his means and saved the difference. A result was that when he grew older, he could send my sister and me to good colleges; I went to Columbia and Yale Law School; she went to Wellesley. I acquired some skills—law, economics, writing, acting, speaking—that paid a good wage.

6    I have been very lucky and have worked like a maniac, and the results are that I have earned a decent living for many years. Taking a leaf from my father, I have saved some of it—although much less than my father did. I also took the trouble—starting at about the age of 12—to read about investing and had some extremely good luck in that field (although I have also made some disastrous mistakes, both on the buy and sell side). When my parents died, I inherited money. Although it was not a huge amount, it was enough to make a difference.

7    Your mother, whose father was a hero in World War II and Vietnam, inherited a modest sum after he died recently. But she worked very hard as a lawyer and made a superb living for many years. We managed to save some of the money she made, as well.

8    Notice a few threads here, my boy: your forebears first acquired human capital—education, work skills, discipline, connections. Then we converted that into financial capital and, with some notable exceptions, it grew and added to our income stream. At all times, we have had to be cautious to keep from being ripped off in our investments. (The possibilities for being defrauded are endless.) We have been able to do this more readily than some others because we have known a bit about the world of investments and when and where to walk away from the table.

9    Now, for the first time in the history of the Steins and the Denmans—your mother's family, of course—we have enough capital so that even at today's very low interest rates, we could

live without working. That is, we do not have to rely entirely upon selling our labor. Our savings can take care of us, albeit at a level far more modest than what you are used to.

10    But, Tommy, several elements went into this, and you have to continue them all to keep up this standard of living: acquiring good work habits (this does not include playing computer games); getting an education in a field that pays a living wage (not a field that's fun and trendy but offers no possibility for a job); learning at an early age to save; and, very important, living at a level that does not exhaust your savings. We hope to be able to leave you some money, but it would be possible for you to run through it in no time if you were careless. And, in any event, you don't get any of it until you are 40.

11    The common denominator of all of these bits of advice is the invaluable capital of self-discipline: the self-discipline to learn good work habits, the self-discipline to acquire education in a field where there is a market for your skills, the self-discipline to make connections and be a good friend, the self-discipline to do a good job at your work, the self-discipline to learn about investments, and the self-discipline to save.

12    When you have these, you gradually make yourself secure. You do not have to worry about tiny or even large sums of money. You are impervious to economic ups and downs, except for very large downs. You do not wake up at 3 a.m. worrying about money. Most of all, you have capital. That's the magic word. Capital—human and financial—lets you have an aura of safety around yourself and allows you to enjoy yourself and not live in a cage of fear and insecurity. And the first step and the last step toward capital is self-discipline.

13    My grandfathers did not even remotely have the opportunities you have—the chance to accumulate free education, have connections, have money waiting to be inherited. You are the first member of my family ever to grow up in luxury. But you can lose it all quickly if you don't remember where capital comes from and don't bear in mind that indiscipline with money can leave you back where my grandparents were. Shirtsleeves to shirtsleeves can be avoided only by rolling up your sleeves and going to work on yourself. Capital in this society comes from your own state of mind.

14    Love, Pop

## Theme

1. Stein speaks throughout his essay about different kinds of capital. For example, he mentions capital "in terms of finance" in paragraph three, "human capital" (four), and the "capital of self-discipline" (ten). In your own words, explain how (according to Ben Stein in the essay as a whole) one kind of capital is related to another.

2. Toward the end of his essay Stein relates capital to security. In your own words, explain what financial security means to Ben Stein and how it seems to differ from common terms heard elsewhere every day like "good job," "high income," or "rich."

## Technique

1. Stein's essay is written in the form of a letter, and this form seems to create some disadvantages for the writer. For example, the first paragraph has nothing to do with the main subject of the essay, and later Stein is seemingly forced by the letter format to explain to eleventh grade Tommy the last name of his maternal grandparents! Yet the essay seems in some other ways to benefit from its form. For example, the writing can more easily and naturally be informal, frank, straightforward, and down-to-earth in its style. In your view, does the letter format create other advantages for the essay? Explain your answer.

2. Stein builds his essay around the history of his family. In your view, what if anything would be gained by instead beginning with definitions of capital in its several aspects before proceeding to a family history? What if anything would be lost? Explain your reasoning in your answer.

## Writing

Using Stein's essay as a model, write the financial history of your own family and include the reasoning behind your own plans for your financial future.

# Donald Trump

## The Art of Negotiation                                    (2004)

> *"The Donald" is not only one of the world's richest men, but a television star. He boasts that he came from a privileged background, but inherited nothing while making his own fortune largely in real estate and casinos. Real estate, like any other business, requires negotiating skills and Trump displays some of his own in this excerpt from his autobiography.*

1   One of the best deals I ever made was the acquisition of the tallest building in lower Manhattan, a 1.3-million-square-foot landmark known as 40 Wall Street.

2   I got it for $1 million, and the negotiation was all about timing and intuition.

3   In the 1960s and 1970s, 40 Wall Street was truly a hot property—a fully occupied building. Then in the 1980s, it was bought by Ferdinand Marcos, who was busy dealing with a revolution in the Philippines. The skyscraper at 40 Wall Street fell into decline, proving once again that a business should never be run by a dictator, especially a real one about to be booted from power.

4   Then the Resnicks, a prominent real estate family, descended on 40 Wall Street, but after a long period of negotiation, it became clear that the Resnicks and Citibank weren't going to make a deal and that 40 Wall Street would be back on the block. I wanted very much at this time to make my move, but this was in the early 1990s and I was in no position to do so. The real estate market was terrible, and my own financial straits were woeful.

5   The next buyer was the Kinson Company, a group from Hong Kong. They made a great deal, and after the purchase

SOURCE: From *Trump: How to Get Rich* by Donald J. Trump and Meredith McIver. Copyright © 2004 by Donald J. Trump. Used by permission of Random House, Inc.

was complete, I requested a meeting with them to discuss a possible partnership. They weren't interested in a partnership, but they did want to make 40 Wall Street the downtown equivalent of Trump Tower, including a public atrium. It sounded like a beautiful idea. However, what they would do with the steel columns that supported a seventy-two-story building never seemed to enter their minds. I was dumbfounded.

6    As you can probably guess, the Kinson group proved to be relatively clueless about renovating, running, and leasing out a New York City skyscraper. They weren't in the real estate business to begin with—they were mostly in apparel—and they were in way over their heads. They poured tens of millions of dollars into the building but were getting nowhere. They had problems with tenants, contractors, suppliers, architects, even the owners of the land, a prominent family from Germany, the Hinnebergs. Eventually, Kinson wanted out, and they called me.

7    It was now 1995 and the market still wasn't so good. Kinson had every reason to want to get out, and they wanted to do it quickly and quietly. So the negotiations began, with me offering them $1 million in addition to assuming and negotiating their liens. I also made the deal subject to a restructured ground lease with the Hinneberg family.

8    They accepted my terms without question.

9    Why? Because they wanted out—and fast. They knew it and I knew it, and because I knew it, the negotiation was easy.

10   There was another crucial aspect to this deal, which proves the importance of knowing what the other side wants: All of the prior leaseholders had dealt with the agent of the Hinneberg family. The agent insisted on increasing the rent and raised other financial obstacles that he said the owner insisted upon. I had to see for myself what the Hinnebergs wanted— was it money, or something else? If you want the truth, go to the source and skip the translation by the intermediary.

11   I flew to Germany with Bernie Diamond, my general counsel, for a face-to-face meeting with the owner, who seemed impressed by the fact that I would travel across the Atlantic to see him. I learned that what he really wanted was peace of mind in connection with his ownership of the land, but all he

was getting was aggravation and litigation. I told him I would agree to turn the present disaster into a first-class office building if he would forgo all rent during the renovation period and revise the lease to permit rental to quality subtenants and bank financing for part of the building improvements. He agreed— and it was the first of many instances that confirmed my belief that Walter, Christian, and Walter Hinneberg Jr. are among the finest people with whom I've ever done business.

12      Very soon after acquiring 40 Wall Street, the markets turned for the better, and the downtown area experienced a renaissance in terms of both commercial and residential properties and developments.

13      I make a great deal of money from 40 Wall Street. Aside from owning the most beautiful building in lower Manhattan, I have the added attraction of owning a particularly lucrative one, all because I watched the property carefully for decades, waiting for my moment, and knew what the other side was thinking.

## Theme

1. In paragraph two Donald Trump says that the negotiation for 40 Wall Street "was all about timing and intuition." After reading about the course of the negotiations as a whole, do you find this an accurate summary? Explain your answer.

2. The negotiations for 40 Wall Street were multifaceted. Explain in your own words the different ways in which Trump was able to come to terms with not only the owners of the building, but also the owners of the land it was built on.

## Technique

1. Paragraph six begins with the words: "As you can probably guess," and Trump's addressing the reader directly here helps to create an informal, conversational style. Point to some other techniques by which the author maintains that style.

2. It might be said that the first sentence of the last paragraph does not add anything to the facts expressed in the rest of the paragraph. In your view, does the sentence add anything else? Explain your answer.

## Writing

Rewrite a portion of Trump's account using an outside narrative point of view, e.g., "One of the best deals Trump ever made was the acquisition of the tallest building in lower Manhattan...."

# Diane Von Furstenberg

## Fashioning Sales                                           (1998)

> *Cinderella figure (she married a prince), international designer,
> writer, socialite, and businesswoman, Diane Von Furstenberg
> first made her mark on the culture with her invention in the
> 1960s of the "wrap" dress, a design which saw something of a
> comeback in the new millennium. Design is only one aspect of
> fashion as she tells us in the following essay. Here she describes
> how she teamed up with the legendary (or notorious) Barry Diller
> (see Joan Rivers, "Responding to Suicide" in Chapter 1) to use the
> new telemarketing to make another comeback in her long career.*

1    I HAD BEEN on my way to Paris in the summer of 1991 when
I ran into Joe Spellman, the marketing genius for Elizabeth
Arden and Unilever, in the Concorde lounge at JFK. I was on
my way to Venice for the debutante ball of Elizabeth de
Balkany, the granddaughter of the former king of Italy, that
count Giovanni Volpi was giving for her in his palace. I was
very much looking forward to it, mostly because my twenty-
year-old daughter was going to be there. I had been only
slightly older than Tatiana when Egon and I had gone to
another Volpi ball two decades earlier.

2     I still carried the memories of the gondolas dropping off the
debutantes and titled young men at the torchlit palace on the
Grand Canal. The women all looked beautiful, helped by the
makeup artists and hairdressers who had been flown in from
Paris, including Alexandre de Paris, who took three suites at
the Bauer Grünwald hotel. Now it would be my daughter's turn
to experience her first Venetian ball and be a young beauty
herself in a gray lace dress made by her father, who had

become a couture designer in Rome. For me, however, the encounter with Joe Spellman at the airport had a special beauty of its own.

3    "Diane, if you wanted, you could have the biggest name in the new millennium," he told me as we waited for the plane. I was flattered, and since I respected his marketing intuition, I was intrigued. Gradually an interesting idea for a new partnership began to take shape.

4    Joe got in touch with Lester Gribbetz, a wizard in home furnishings and the former co-chairman of Bloomingdale's, who got in touch with Marvin Traub, a wizard in fashion and the flamboyant former chairman of Bloomingdale's. I would meet to explore rebuilding my brand as partners with these three wizards. They agreed that I had had an important name in fashion and offered to create a new venture that would build it into a new brand. My potential partners were experts in the three fields in which I had once excelled: fashion, beauty, and home. I was really excited at the prospect.

5    But there was a little part of me that kept asking: This is all well and good, but is the partnership right for me? The three men were all consultants, very involved with other businesses. We were talking about creating the new company as equal partners, which meant the profits would be split four ways while I would end up doing most of the work.

6    I went along with the discussions, however, because I felt it was the best option I had at the time and might lead somewhere. And it did. It was Joe Spellman who brought up the idea at one of our meetings in the winter of 1992. "How about selling on television?" he asked.

7    I knew the moment that I walked into the QVC studio in West Chester, Pennsylvania, that I had found an answer. It was February 29, leap year, and the four of us had taken the Metroliner down from New York to see the operation. QVC was popularly dismissed as tacky by the retail establishment in New York for selling "collectibles" such as faux vintage dolls and model cars, but my friend Kenny Lane and TV-star-turned-jewelry-designer Joan Rivers were supposedly reaping windfalls on television. True to form, Marvin joked as we toured the studio, but I saw a golden opportunity. As I followed the three

men down the corridor, I found myself thinking aloud, "I want to own this place."

8   Susan Lucci, the soap opera actress, happened to be on the air selling hair products when we arrived. To our amazement, we watched the sales mount on the computer to $600,000.

9   Susan was doing what I had been doing for years. Talking directly to women through a television camera was like making a personal appearance on a national level. The setting was more removed, but the format would allow me to reopen a dialogue with women. And the market was already in place.

10   With malls taking over America, home shopping essentially brought a television mall into everybody's home, store by store. And the audience seemed to take to it. In only five years of operation, this home shopping channel had amassed forty-two million viewers, three million of whom were regular shoppers. Teleshopping was a new and interesting way of selling, and I wanted to try it.

11   Unlike the discouraging manufacturers and retailers I'd talked to, Darlene Daggett, the force behind QVC's fashion merchandising department, was eager to talk to me. She wanted personal appearances by well-known fashion designers like me to attract a more sophisticated audience. I, in turn, needed an audience. All that remained was coming up with the concept and working out a contract.

12   Developing a line of clothes to sell on television was daunting at first. I had never designed clothes that women couldn't first try on. I decided to return to an idea that I had had before but never developed: a line of silk pieces called *Silk Assets*— dresses, pants, skirts, blazers, and tops—that were tied together by prints and coordinating colors. The tops would be big shirts, tank tops, and tunics, cut generously enough to be worn in different ways; the pants and skirts would have somewhat elasticized waists. But who would make them?

13   My partners, it was turning out, did not want to commit to buying inventory. The partnership, in fact, was beginning to come apart. Barry was acting as my business adviser, and at a meeting at his office at Fox in New York, my would-be partners announced they would not be involved in the apparel line at all. "That's okay," I said. "I'll do it myself."

14    I was relieved. I remember dancing out on the street after the meeting and feeling free. I already had an idea as to how I could have the clothes manufactured and not have any inventory responsibilities.

15    "This is what we could do," I told Darlene Daggett. "I will design the clothes. I will source them by finding and supervising the right manufacturer, make sure that you get the shipment on time and that the quality is right. But when the time comes to open the letter of credit to buy the merchandise from the factory and bring it in, you will do it. The factory in Hong Kong will ship directly to you, and you will own the inventory. That way, by going direct, you will be able to take a generous markup for yourselves and give the customer fantastic quality and a fabulous price." My compensation, I told her, would be 25 percent on top of cost. By Monday morning, we had a deal. And I went off to the Orient to have the clothes made.

16    Once again I was stepping off into the unknown, but, to my amazement, so was Barry. We were on our way to Cloudwalk from the airport after one of my first trips to the Far East to find a factory when he announced abruptly that he was thinking of leaving Fox. I was absolutely astounded. He had such an incredible success in his seven years at Fox since leaving Paramount. Though everyone had said it was impossible to create a fourth network, he had. But Barry, who was turning fifty and reevaluating his own life and career, had finally realized that Fox wasn't his and never would be. Fox was owned by Rupert Murdoch, who had his own dynastic family—and the company was theirs.

17    "What are you going to do?" I asked him. "I don't know," he said. He had just gotten a laptop computer, and he used it for the first time to draft the announcement of his resignation from Fox. The announcement would go through countless editing with my insistence that he keep it short and unsentimental. Then he took his laptop and set off to drive around America, where he started thinking about new ways to use digital communication. So Barry, too, was looking for a new opportunity at the same time I was about to realize one of my own.

18    I sold out the entire collection of *Silk Assets* in my debut on QVC in November 1992—$1.3 million dollars in just two hours.

There was enormous excitement on the set. Along with the cheering people there from my office was Kate Betts, a new, young, clever editor at *Vogue* who had come to observe the debut. Her article, "Show and Sell," would begin, "*Vogue* witnesses a fashion phenomenon in the making."

19      There was just as much excitement backstage in the greenroom, where Barry and all the top management of QVC had watched the galloping volume of sales on a computer and cheered as if they were at the races. What they didn't know was that while *Silk Assets* was being manufactured during the summer of 1992, Barry had begun negotiations with QVC's major stockholders—Comcast and Brian and Ralph Roberts. It would soon be announced that he had taken control of the home shopping network. I would be part of the business. Because I had introduced Barry to QVC, I got 10 percent of his share. Besides all the other things we were to each other, we were now business partners as well.

20      Together we launched the entire teleshopping industry into orbit. Between Barry's involvement and my success, the shopping network was all over the front pages. Suddenly I went from has-been to pioneer again.

21      For Barry, however, the transition from being the head of Fox to QVC was odd and somewhat unpredictable. I felt terribly guilty although amused on the first day he was in his new office at this new company that was selling fake diamond rings when he called me and asked, "Could you please tell me what I am doing here?" But there was a lot of excitement. Everyone who was anyone was coming to visit the operation in Pennsylvania and talking about electronic retailing.

22      They couldn't stock enough of my silk separates. On one show in 1993, I would sell 2,200 pairs of silk trousers in less than two minutes. On another night, at midnight, I sold $750,000 worth of merchandise in just fifteen minutes. In the four good years I would spend on that home shopping channel, *Silk Assets* would generate more than $40 million in sales.

23      As the apparel line did well on television, there were finally stirrings of interest at Revlon about an idea I'd come up with for a new environmental fragrance line. The basic concept of the line, which we would call *Surroundings,* was to bring the

beauty of the garden indoors in the form of a candle, an air spray, a soap, body lotion, and a hair and body shampoo.

24    Just as *Surroundings* was about to be launched, however, Revlon decided to unload everything that was not under the Revlon brand. *Surroundings* was doomed, but Revlon's decision to consolidate was an opportunity for me. Having sold the trademark for my fragrance and beauty business to Beecham in 1983 for $22 million, I would buy it back from Revlon a decade later for $250,000.

## Theme

1. There are many twists and turns in the story of this author's marketing success. Point to those you think are the most important and explain your choices.

2. Diane Von Furstenberg has been successful both as a designer and as a businesswoman. Point to some examples that exemplify her abilities and skills in each category.

## Technique

1. The art of name dropping in this excerpt moves from lists of European aristocrats to leading names in American business. What sense of the author's personality is created for you by this contrast of social categories? Explain your answer with examples.

2. Most people in the author's account are given two names, but her most important partner is called only "Barry." This man is in fact Barry Diller, one of the most successful movie and television executives of the twentieth century. What does the contrast in naming help to create in your sense of Diane Von Furstenberg?

## Writing

Write an essay that explains how Diane Von Furstenberg shows herself to be innovative both as a fashion designer and as a businesswoman.

# Michael Jordan

## The Nike Deal                                     (1998)

*Michael Jordan was once called the best-known athlete in the world and is still called the best basketball player in history. Born in Brooklyn, New York, and raised in North Carolina, he left the University of North Carolina (UNC) to begin a legendary career with the Chicago Bulls.*

1  I never wanted to sign with Nike. I had been an Adidas fanatic since high school. In fact, I didn't even want to meet with Nike. In the summer of 1984, I had been flying all over the country for various awards banquets, the Bulls, and the Olympics. I was tired of traveling. When it came to meet with Nike, I told everyone, my agent David Falk, Coach Smith, even my parents, that I wasn't going. I had no intention of signing with Nike and I had no desire to fly to Portland, Oregon.

2  My parents finally sat me down and said, "This is important. You need to listen to what those people have to say." I felt like I was dragged out to Oregon to listen to something I had no intention of acting upon. So I walk into the meeting and there's Rob Strasser, Phil Knight, Tinker Hatfield, Jack George, Peter Moore, and Howard White. Now I'm not pleased about being there and I'm barely listening. But Strasser got my attention. They were talking about giving me my own shoe and effectively redefining the entire athletic shoe industry. Strasser did most of the talking. He was a big guy, smooth, energetic, and motivating. Still, I was skeptical because I didn't even like Nike shoes. The money was substantial for that time, $250,000 a year for five years with an annuity, incentives, and royalties on all Nike basketball-related items. It was a great deal, but it was

SOURCE: From *For the Love of the Game* by Michael Jordan. Copyright © 1998 by Rare Air, Ltd. Used by permission of Crown Publishers, a division of Random House, Inc.

also risky because no one in the industry had done anything like that. Julius Erving became identified with a specific shoe, but he was never compensated the way I was going to be. Growing up, everyone would say, "I want a pair of Dr. J's." They were Converse shoes. In retrospect, they squeezed the equity out of Julius Erving without ever paying for it. The meeting was interesting, but when it ended I'm thinking, "Fine, now let's go see what Converse has in mind. Then I'm going to sign with Adidas."

3      Before I went to Converse I talked to Bill Sweek, a sales rep from Adidas I had met at North Carolina. I did this on my own. No one, including Falk, knew about my meeting with Bill. I told him what Nike was offering and said, "All you have to do is come close." In the meantime I had to see Converse, which was a very traditional, conservative company. Converse had Magic Johnson, Isiah Thomas, Larry Bird, Mark Aguirre, Dr. J, all the top players. I met with them at their corporate headquarters outside Boston. The place just looked traditional and I really didn't feel comfortable there. But I had some experience with Converse because we wore them for games at North Carolina and I felt obligated to listen. Their offer was pennies compared to the dimes Nike was offering. Their top guys were all making $100,000 a year and Dr. J wasn't even making royalties on his shoe. They were afraid of making an exception with me, which I understood. Besides, I wasn't comfortable with Converse. I remember having bad vibes.

4      My heart was still with Adidas, but they never made an offer. They didn't want to take a chance with the U.S. basketball market because they didn't want to jeopardize the international brand. The decision was a lot easier for Nike. The company's stock had dropped by more than half and was down around $6 a share in 1984. Strasser had to take a gamble. And he did. He wanted to change the entire market by betting on one person. Nike didn't have a second choice. He was a genius. It worked.

5      Nike had an advertising campaign in mind, but they were afraid to put it into motion until they saw me play. I started the 1984–85 season wearing the black and red shoes. Three games

into the season, the NBA did us a huge favor. The league banned the shoes because it didn't conform to the rest of the Bulls uniform. But I kept wearing them and David Stern started fining me. I think it started out at $1,000 a game, then went to $3,000, and eventually $5,000. Nike didn't even blink. Nike said they were willing to pay every penny and I totally agreed. It would have cost millions of dollars to come up with a promotion that produced as much publicity as the league's ban did. The whole thing worked perfectly. The first commercial showed my head, and the camera slowly moved down my body to my feet. When the camera hit the shoes a big "X" was stamped on the screen and the announcer said, "BANNED." Right after that, sales went crazy.

## Theme

1. At the end of paragraph two Jordan says: "Fine, now let's go see what Converse has in mind. Then I'm going to sign with Adidas." In your own words, explain what you understand to be all the motivations behind Jordan's statement. For example, if in fact he was a longtime "Adidas fanatic," why would he want to go to talk to Converse at all?

2. In your own words explain the reasoning behind Jordan's claim in paragraph five that "It would have cost millions of dollars to come up with a promotion that produced as much publicity as the league's ban did."

## Technique

1. The persona Jordan creates through his writing comes over as a mixture of modesty and assertive self-confidence. Point to some of the moments when he creates one or another of these impressions and explain how he achieves them.

2. Several people are merely listed in the meeting described in paragraph two. From the essay as a whole do you learn anything more about any of their identities other than that they

are all associated with Nike? Other people not at the meeting are named in the essay. Which are identified further? How are they identified?

## Writing

Write an essay in which you define and analyze Michael Jordan's skills as a negotiator. You may wish to compare him with Donald Trump in this regard.

# Cokie and Steve Roberts

## Problems of a Two-Career Family    (2000)

*Cokie Roberts has been a longtime co-anchor of the ABC news program* This Week *as well as a news analyst for National Public Radio. She writes a weekly column with her husband, Steve, a sometime bureau chief for* The New York Times *and a senior writer for* Newsweek *who appears on CNN and PBS. After thirty years of wedlock the couple shares some of their experience with the issues encouraged by all two-career families.*

1    In many ways, this was the married life we had always planned, back during that first spring in Boston when the possibility seemed so remote. Steve had his dream job, covering Congress for *The New York Times,* and Cokie had her dream house, the one she had grown up in. Our daughter slept in Cokie's girlhood room and Steve farmed her father's garden. As our circle of friends and relatives continued to expand, every passing year required new and creative ways to fit everybody in for Christmas and Passover, birthdays and book parties. What we didn't anticipate back in Boston—or in New York or Los Angeles or Athens for that matter—was that our jobs would be equal. In fact, that they would be the same. And that sameness had its drawbacks. If you're sitting up in bed at eleven o'clock discussing the intricacies of the federal budget, you're doing something wrong. But the pluses far outweighed the minuses. We walked in each other's shoes every day, faced the same problems, covered the same stories. One member of Congress even complained one day about "stereophonic

SOURCE: Pages 232–235, *From This Day Forward* by Cokie Roberts and Steve Roberts. Copyright © 2000 by Cokie Roberts and Steve Roberts. Reprinted by permission of HarperCollins Publishers, Inc. William Morrow.

Robertses" as we fired questions at him from different sides of the room. And there was one phrase neither one of us could ever say to the other, a phrase that has gnawed and nibbled away at the foundation of many good marriages—"you just don't understand, dear."

2    **SR:** This new equality in our work situations required me to take more responsibility at home, particularly when Cokie started hosting her show on public television, *The Lawmakers.* It was broadcast live, on Thursday nights. And it happened that the wife of the other *New York Times* reporter, covering the Hill, Martin Tolchin, taught at George Washington on Thursday nights. Marty and I had kids exactly the same ages and both of us were on duty the same time. I used to say, only half in jest, that you could pass by the *New York Times* booth on Capitol Hill and overhear the high-powered correspondents saying into the phone, "Now, dear, set the oven at three hundred and fifty degrees ..."

3    **CR:** Which of course happens with women correspondents constantly.

4    **SR:** That's true. We had one friend, a female reporter with two little boys at home, who was so tired all the time that she actually fell asleep one day in the front row of the press gallery, her arms draped over the balcony. The kids and I worked out a routine that we all looked forward to. Lee was already interested in the law, and a show called *The Paper Chase,* set at Harvard Law School, was on just after Cokie's show. So we'd have supper, and then watch our two favorite programs.

5    **CR:** Then I would get home and we'd watch *Hill Street Blues.* It's the only time we've ever organized a family night around television. But I took on that job without any idea of how much work it would be. I had the family, NPR, and then *The Lawmakers,* and the schools didn't help much. Even in a neighborhood like ours, I was surprised how few mothers worked and how the schools were completely geared to at-home moms. I think it's still true. The schools don't take responsibility for the fact that the world has changed. At the first hint of a snowflake, they close at one o'clock in the afternoon and send children home to empty houses and there's no way for parents to know unless they've listened to the radio all day in the office. And how was a mother on a factory line sup-

posed to get the information? For the few serious snowstorms we have in the Washington area, the schools could come up with a better system of communication. I had long conversations with the principal and teachers and tried to be infinitely reasonable, but I never felt the people on the other end were equally reasonable. The teachers would always try to schedule conferences at one o'clock in the afternoon. I'd say, "Could we possibly have it at eight o'clock in the morning?" Well, no.

6    **SR:** I think that's changing, now that so many mothers are working.

7    **CR:** Maybe, but I doubt it's changed enough. When summertime rolled around and the kids went to day camp, I'd have to try to figure out how to get them home in the afternoons. At the beginning of a session I'd get up all my nerve to ask the other mothers for help. I'm so bad at this, I can't even ask a good friend for a ride home, but I'd plead with these other mothers, "I'll drive your children every single solitary morning for the rest of their lives if you, you, you, you, and you will drive my children home in the afternoons." Living in the suburbs and working downtown, dealing with the logistics of getting children from school to camp to piano lessons to theater lessons is worthy of the most well-staged military campaigns. The ideal, of course, is having enough money to hire a nanny who drives, but we didn't have that. In fact, we gave our babysitter driving lessons and her first day out she wrecked a car.

8    **SR:** At one point you actually hired a cab.

9    **CR:** I hired a cab to take Rebecca and another little girl whose mother worked to piano lessons. We had the same driver every week. That worked out quite well. But with all the stress of balancing work and family, one incident made me feel better. I went to Becca's school one day to talk to the kids about the coming election. I tried to bring a few things along to make it more interesting, so I had my tape recorder with me and my press credentials, and I happened to be wearing a navy-blue suit. Halloween came soon after that visit, and I wanted to see this fabulous parade where the whole elementary school marched around the neighborhood in their costumes. I was at the Capitol and I went tearing out to Bethesda to see the parade in the middle of the day. Flabbergasted, Becca demanded, "What are you doing here? I don't care about

you coming to see the parade." And I said, "Well, I care." It was her last one, her last year in that school. Then, as I looked at the parade, there were all these sixth-grade girls in blue suits with tape recorders! They were dressing up as reporters!

## Theme

1. The Roberts say that having what they call "equal" jobs has its pluses and minuses. Briefly summarize both the positive and the negative aspects of their two-career marriage.

2. In paragraph five, Cokie Roberts writes: "The schools don't take responsibility for the fact that the world has changed." Though the word "responsibility" does not come up again, the concept it names is frequently a subject. Point to the places where responsibility becomes an issue in the essay. What seems to be the range of meaning of the word? What are the Roberts responsible for and what are the responsibilities of others?

## Technique

1. The closeness of the Roberts' marriage extends into its narration, with outside, collective, and individual points of view appearing as narrative techniques. Does this mixture succeed in your opinion? Explain your answer with examples.

2. The Roberts speak from the point of view of "high powered" reporters. In your opinion, how well do they also understand the point of view of the "mother on the factory line" mentioned in paragraph five? Explain your answer.

## Writing

Rewrite the first paragraph of the Roberts' narrative from one consistent point of view, and then, in a second version, write it from another but also consistent point of view. Start one version, for example, with "The Roberts" and the next with "We." Conclude by remarking on what you have learned about the narrative problems they face.

# Spike Lee

## Art and Money in Movies    (1992)

*Son of a jazz musician and a teacher, Spike Lee graduated from Morehouse College in Atlanta, Georgia, before attending the Tisch School of Arts graduate film program. His first big hit was the comedy* She's Gotta Have It *(1986), made for $175,000 but earning $7 million. After that, Spike Lee flourished, creating many other hits including* Do The Right Thing, Clockers, *and* Mo' Better Blues. *But as he shows here, talent needs money in the movie business, as in any other business, and how that problem may be solved is illustrated with some examples from his own career.*

1    While we were shooting *Jungle Fever* in late 1990, I made up an initial design for the "X" cap. I'd already decided I had to do *Malcolm X,* and marketing is an integral part of my filmmaking. So the X was planned all the way out. I came up with a simple design—silver X on black baseball cap. The colors could be changed later on as the campaign advanced. It looked good. I started wearing it, and we began selling it in our store, Spike's Joint, and in other places. I gave them away strategically. I asked Michael Jordan to wear it, and he has. Then I asked some other stars to wear it and, what can I say, it just caught on. Then the knock-offs started appearing. These X caps are coming from everywhere now. It's raining X caps, X this, X that, sometimes without the wearers knowing the story behind the X. The word of mouth is beginning to pick up on this already.

2    See, I realized that being a black filmmaker, I'm never going to have the same amount of money spent to market my films as I would if I was a white filmmaker with the same number of notches on his gun, the same amount of success. And I don't

want to duplicate what happened to a lot of the black filmmakers of previous generations in front of me—and some from today as well. They were artists and not businessmen, or at least more artist than businessman. I'd already been warned about that, not by a lecture but by life experience. When I was in film school, I would see these guys who had spent four or five years, and sometimes even longer, trying to raise money for their films. And these were often good films. But they were seen, if they were seen at all, as nothing but a blip on the screen before the public. If anything, we'd end up seeing them at a screening at a museum, or at a university, or during Black History Month, and that's all. But I knew I didn't want hundreds of people to see my films. I want millions of people to see my films.

3      I have to film and market and act accordingly. I want my films to be seen by as many people as possible, and I know a lot of that comes down to not only the quality of the product—which of course has to be good—but marketing. There are many good films that haven't been seen, or have been seen by fewer people than should have seen them. It comes down to marketing in the end, and my activity comes from knowing that nobody is going to spend $20 million advertising and promoting my films, at least not to date.

4      So I knew I had to get the necessary image out there, do the interviews, make the people know about this film. Then they would want to come see it, once I had. And marketing is something I'm very proud of—the only person who does marketing better than me, as far as artists go, is Madonna. She's the Champ.

5      I had hard experience from when *Do The Right Thing* came out in 1989, the same summer that *Batman* came out from Warner Brothers. We spent a lot of time figuring how we were going to combat that, to get our little share of the audience. *Do The Right Thing* did $28 million—pretty good for a film that cost $6.5 million. It didn't just happen like that. Today, Horatio Alger would have to book promotional dates and understand multilevel marketing. We had to plan how to get ink in the face of *Batman* and all that paid-for hype on television and radio and with toy companies and other promotions with retail-

ers. One thing we figured we could get for free—editorial space in the newspapers. That's why controversial or political subject matter can work well at the box office. I'm used to getting out there and pushing my films in any way I can. Film content is always in my plan. I try to show excellent taste in what I do, but I also do try to make thought-provoking films that are entertaining. It's a hard juggling act, balancing what is good business and good art, but it can be done.

## Theme

1. Spike Lee writes at the end of this selection: "It's a hard juggling act, balancing what is good business and good art, but it can be done." Point to some places in his account where you observe Spike Lee demonstrating his awareness of what "good business" means to him.

2. According to Spike Lee, what is the advantage of a politically controversial subject matter in a project? What are the disadvantages?

## Technique

1. In what ways do the author's allusions to older generations of black filmmakers support his points about marketing movies today?

2. Toward the end of the selection, Spike Lee mentions Horatio Alger, a famous old-time writer of rags-to-riches novels for young readers. What does Spike Lee's literary allusion contribute to his point and how does it do so?

## Writing

Write an essay in which you show how Spike Lee frequently uses a contrast between the past and the present, both in social history and in his own career, to organize his writing and emphasize its claims to authority on the subject it addresses.

# Chuck D

## "Free" Music Can Free the Artist        (2000)

> *As founder of Public Enemy, Chuck D became one of the most
> important figures in the history of hip-hop and its most respected
> intellectual. He helped to redefine the form as music with a mes-
> sage. His radicalizing of rap's content is still being felt. In the pas-
> sage that follows he explores some paradoxes of the music
> industry and presents (as usual) a radical explanation and a
> radical plan of action.*

1    Unlike many of my fellow artists, I support the sharing of
music files on the Internet. The Recording Industry Association
of America has sued Napster, an Internet application that helps
people find, copy, and share songs free of charge on the Web,
arguing that it encourages users to violate copyright laws. Some
artists have spoken out against Napster as a threat to their liveli-
hoods, and most recently Dr. Dre and the band Metallica have
become involved in lawsuits against the service.

2    But I believe that artists should welcome Napster. We should
think of it as a new kind of radio—a promotional tool that can
help artists who don't have the opportunity to get their music
played on mainstream radio or on MTV.

3    As someone who has been connected to hip-hop and rap
music for 22 years, I've seen how difficult it has become for
the majority of artists, songwriters, producers, and independent
labels to get their music to the fans directly, without signing
with a major label and subjecting themselves to rules that are
in the best interest of the label.

4    Beginning in the late 1980's when video hit the scene, record
companies upped the ante on what it took to promote and market a song, totally squeezing the small, independent entrepreneur

out of the distribution game. Now, with most radio stations playing popular favorites and with the high cost of making and distributing music videos, it is almost impossible for an independent record producer or an artist to get music to fans.

5    I believe this structure has hurt the artist more than someone passing a song around free of charge.

6    Not that most artists ever have much say about how their work is marketed and sold anyhow. Most contracts only guarantee artists a few cents in royalties from each record sold. And if a song doesn't become a hit, the label can cease selling it but still own rights to it forever.

7    The major labels have also benefited from being a step ahead on the technology that allows the listener to hear and keep music. As the technology progressed from phonograph to stereo hi-fis, eight-track, cassettes, and CD's, record companies have been the only ones able to repackage the music they own to fit the new format. And in fact, when companies like Sony bought record companies, they gained control of the music to add to their control of the device needed to hear it.

8    The last straw was the CD period, when labels increased their markup without raising artists' royalties in kind. At the same time, record companies created the concept of a disposable artist; with jacked-up marketing and promotional costs, record companies stopped nurturing career artists. They have been able to fatten profits by flipping small batches of artists in and out.

9    That is today's music industry.

10    Well, Napster has been a thorn in that bull's side. By exposing people to music, companies like Napster are creating new fan interest and establishing a new infrastructure for unknown artists to attract an audience—a new radio for the new millennium.

10    But the question remains: Will the corporations that dominate concede to sharing the musical marketplace? We'll see. Until then we will slowly see formations of new rules and regulations that will eventually support many more artists than the record companies of yesterday. The Internet has created a new planet for musicians to explore, and I'm with that.

## Theme

1. Why are many of Chuck D's fellow musical artists against file sharing programs like Napster?

2. Summarize Chuck D's arguments in support of Napster and similar ventures.

## Technique

1. In his argument, Chuck D walks a fine line between selflessness and selfishness. Point to some of the ways in which he tries to escape being crudely categorized in either way in order to speak in an enlightened way.

2. The essay ends with the phrase "I'm with that." In what ways does the style here differ from that in the rest of the piece? Do you think the change makes for an effective ending? Explain your answer.

## Writing

Where do you stand on the topic of "free" music? Write an essay that defends your views, being sure to respond to the views that oppose your own.

# Bill Gates

## Adopt the Web Lifestyle                                (1999)

*Would you take advice from the richest man in the world? Bill
Gates is the chairman and chief software architect of Microsoft
Corporation, a firm with sales in the dozens of billions of dollars,
year after year. Gates dropped out of Harvard to devote all his
energies to Microsoft, which he had begun as an undergraduate.
He does not advise dropping out of school, but he does give some
hints about his own style of thinking in this selection from*
Business @ the Speed of Thought.

Throughout the territories of every civilized nation, wherever
human language is known, or commerce has marts ... the
electric wires which web the world in a network of throbbing
life utter their voices in all their varied tongues.

—A writer in 1878 describing the effects of the telegraph
(from *The Victorian Internet*)

1    **I**f you asked your friends why they use the phone to communicate with their friends or why they turn to the television
for entertainment or breaking news, they'd look at you kind of
funny. If you asked your friends whether they'd adopted "the
electricity lifestyle," they'd think you were downright nuts. People in developed countries take their electrical devices for
granted; we just use them. But people who are now in their
fifties can remember when just a few families had TVs. Our
grandparents can remember when much of rural America was
without electricity. A few people alive today were born before
the widespread use of electricity in cities. The telegraph first
connected the far corners of the globe with fast communications a century ago. It's taken more than a hundred years for
the "electricity lifestyle" to reshape civilization.

2    When streets and houses were first wired, the only use for
electricity was for lighting. Electricity's potential to reshape

everyone's lifestyle was unforeseen. Electric light was safer, cleaner, brighter, and more flexible than natural gas, kerosene, or candles. Once the infrastructure was in place, though, innovative new products were created that took advantage of electricity. Electric refrigerators, phonographs, and air conditioners were applications of the new technology to existing needs. The most revolutionary applications of electricity were the phone, the radio, and the television. All of these new devices reshaped our economies and our lifestyles. People hadn't dreamed of these devices before the infrastructure was available.

3    Because the Internet is a worldwide communications infrastructure that depends on electricity, you could say that its popular acceptance is an extension of the "electricity lifestyle." But the Internet is enabling a new way of life that I call "the Web lifestyle." The Web lifestyle, like the electricity lifestyle, will be characterized by rapid innovations in applications. Because the infrastructure for high-speed connectivity has reached critical mass, it is giving rise to new software and hardware that will reshape people's lives. Intelligent devices such as the PC are becoming more powerful and less expensive. Since they are programmable they can be used for many different applications. Within a decade most Americans and many other people around the world will be living the Web lifestyle. It will be a reflex for these people to turn to the Web to get news, to learn, to be entertained, and to communicate. It will be just as natural as picking up the phone to talk to somebody or ordering something from a catalog is today. The Web will be used to pay your bills, manage your finances, communicate with your doctor, and conduct any business. Just as naturally, you'll carry one or more small devices using a wireless connection to stay constantly in touch and conduct electronic business wherever you are.

4    For a lot of people the Web lifestyle is well on its way today. By 1998 more than sixty million Americans were using the Web regularly, up from twenty-two million the year before. By 1998 the average user accessed the Web eight to nine separate days a month, spending a total of about 3.5 hours a month online.

5    It's exciting to see that people living the Web lifestyle are using the Internet to learn and buy in new ways. When the *Sojourner* landed on Mars in the summer of 1997, NASA's Web site drew forty-seven million hits in four days from people

seeking more detail than they could get from the traditional news media. Whatever you think of the Starr report on President Clinton, the Internet was the only feasible medium for disseminating the 445-page document quickly. Six to nine million people viewed it the first weekend after its release. Businesses are providing a wide variety of information and services, whether it's real-time stock quotes, sports scores, or city guides. You can buy almost anything on the Web, from Impressionist paintings to metal cartoon superhero school lunchboxes, which have become collectibles. The Web is an ideal vehicle for community building, too. There are sites for tracking missing children and helping people adopt pets and for every activity imaginable. Sites that involve citizens are getting excellent traffic flow. One Web site shows all the industrial polluters in the United States, offering maps and the ability to search by company name or locale. It drew 300,000 users in the first five hours it was up—almost all by word of mouth.

6      A cultural change as substantial as a move to the Web lifestyle will be generational to some degree. It's the kids growing up with the new technology and taking it as a given who will show us the full potential. On most U.S. college campuses, the critical mass for a Web-ready culture already exists. Personal computer use, high-speed networking, and online communication are widespread. Universities are dispensing with paper forms and registering students for classes over the Web. Students can look at their grades and even turn in their homework over the Web. Teachers hold online discussion groups. Students e-mail friends and family as naturally as they call them. Students are the ultimate knowledge workers. Their "job" is to learn and explore and find unexpected relationships between things. The specifics of the academic courses don't matter as much as learning to think and analyze. Students are developing Internet skills that will help them learn throughout their lives. For business, there is an opportunity to learn from the way students use the Internet today to organize and manage their lives. Their approach is a guide to how the general population will use the Internet ten years from now.

7      The adoption of technology for the Web lifestyle is happening faster than the adoption of electricity, cars, TV, and radio....

Usage spreads through the workplace exposure to PCs and through friends and relatives. Many people who use PCs at the office install them at home for work and then use them for far more. A lot of people over fifty-five years old, who wouldn't usually integrate new technology in their lifestyle, are motivated to use the Internet as a way to stay in touch with their friends and families. A friend of mine recently received e-mail from two distantly related women in their seventies—they were "into the Internet" to research genealogy. Radical new uses of the Internet that none of us can accurately predict today will reshape the world as fundamentally in the twenty-first century as the unexpected uses of electricity did in the twentieth—and faster.

## Theme

1. Bill Gates makes the Web lifestyle depend on an analogy with what he calls the "electricity lifestyle." Explain with examples what Gates means by the difference between the electric lifestyle in general and the Web lifestyle in particular.

2. This essay was written in 1999. How much of what it predicts has come true? Point to some examples. Has anything that Gates predicts here failed to materialize?

## Technique

1. Gates says that the Web lifestyle will be adopted at an even faster pace than the electricity lifestyle. Point to some examples by which he expresses his sense of rapid change and explain how they give a sense of pace within the process.

2. Gates makes an analogy between students' use of the Web and the uses made by business. Do you find it a generally accurate analogy? Explain your answer by evaluating the examples given.

## Writing

Write an essay analyzing the ways in which Gates uses analogy to organize his essay and to move it forward.

# Oprah Winfrey

## Bringing *Beloved* to the Screen    (1998)

*Starting as a reporter/anchor at the age of 17, Oprah created a broadcasting empire and has become one of America's leading businesswomen. She is an entertainment executive whose enterprises range from her world-famous talk show to book clubs and movies. As a performer, she has earned Oscar and Golden Globe nominations for her portrayal of Sofia in Steven Spielberg's adaptation of Alice Walker's novel,* The Color Purple. *In the piece that follows, Oprah discusses artistic and business decisions involved in her production of the filmed version of another bestselling novel,* Toni Morrison's Beloved.

1    This has been a truly amazing journey. If anyone had told me what it was going to require of me—of all of us—I wouldn't have believed it, but it probably wouldn't have made any difference if I had. I believe that intention becomes experience, and it was always my intention to bring *Beloved* to the screen from the first moment I read it in 1987. I called Toni Morrison immediately. I didn't even know her. I had to call up the fire department in her town to get her number, and when I got her on the phone, she just laughed. She didn't think a film could be done, but she was willing to let me have the rights—if I wanted to try. It was truly an honor to write that check as one Black woman to another. No agents. No lawyer. No negotiations. Just "This is what you asked and here it is."

2    I was so excited, it never even occurred to me how hard it was going to be. A novel is one thing, but the elements that make a successful film are so different that it's almost like starting from scratch. I didn't realize that when we first started, of course. But I felt so strongly that the world needed to experience this book, to feel this sense of connection to what happened to us. It explains so much about why we are who we are and how that came to be.

SOURCE: From "The Courage to Dream" by Oprah Winfrey and Pearl Cleadge. Used by permission from Harpo Productions.

3    If I had been thinking intellectually, instead of just going from my gut, I probably never would have attempted it, but I don't work on the corporate schedule with the corporate mind. I never have. Sometimes it causes a lot of anxiety with people around me because I don't operate that way, but I don't even know how to. If I had had to sit in a room 14 years ago and come up with the vision for what has now become *The Oprah Winfrey Show,* I couldn't have done it.

4    I just let myself move with the flow, and things evolved from year to year. I can't tell you what I'm going to be doing five years from now, because I really don't know. I give myself over to the universal process. I open myself up to that, and I know, whatever is to come will come.

5    To some people I know that sounds like real confidence, but it's not. It's true faith. It's knowing that the creation of my life is bigger than my individual personality—bigger than any one person, and it's going to be great. I did not design this. I have helped with my own thoughts and actions to cocreate it, but I did not design it. There is no way I could have. You know how there are times in your life when something truly extraordinary happens? Filming *Beloved* was an experience like that for me. It took me to places inside myself I had never had the ability, or maybe even the courage, to go before.

## Reaching into History

6    *Beloved,* set in post-Civil War Ohio, tells the story of Sethe, who years before risked death to escape from the horrors of slavery in Kentucky. She has lost her husband and buried a child—and is, by Morrison's description, a woman of "iron eyes and a backbone to match." Sethe lives with her daughter, Denver; her mother-in-law, Baby Suggs; and a ghostly presence whom she assures the rare visitor is "not evil, just sad." Struggling to keep the past from overwhelming her, Sethe finds herself unexpectedly welcoming Paul D, a man she knew from the plantation where they were enslaved and, soon after, a mysterious intruder who calls herself Beloved. It is Beloved's presence that tips the delicate balance of Sethe's world, releasing memories that threaten to engulf and destroy her unless she can come to

terms with the unspeakable legacy of slavery and embrace the love and peace her new life offers.

7    When we finally got a script we could all agree on—that took years—and Jonathan Demme signed on to direct, I became acutely aware of the huge responsibility we had taken on. I was determined to do my very best.

8    In preparing to play Sethe, I remembered talking to a very talented guy who did an exhibition about the Underground Railroad for the Smithsonian. As part of his preparation, he partially recreated the experience. He even had himself shipped part of the way in a box, as some slaves did trying to get to freedom.

9    Right before we were getting ready to start shooting, I called and asked if he could put together something similar for me. He agreed, and I was so excited until I realized that nobody connected with the film wanted me to do it. They were worried about insurance, starting on time, the possibility of accidents.

10    Part of it was that I wanted to have a better understanding of how it would feel to be running for your freedom and not have any idea which way to go to get there. I wanted to see if I could tap into the kind of panic the slaves must have felt, but also that determination, that spirit that says, "I don't know if my shoes can carry me, but I've got to go." I wanted to try to be in that space for myself. But the deeper reason—that was harder to talk about—was that I needed to really, truly understand the moment where Sethe decides to kill her baby girl, rather than let her be taken back into slavery. I knew that desperate enslaved mothers had sometimes done this, but I had to reconcile that moment for myself before I could truly say I understood Sethe well enough to let her character speak through me.

11    So they blindfolded me and said: "Now we're going to take you back to 1862. When the blindfold comes off, everybody around you will be representative of that period. Your name is Rebecca and you've been living free in Baltimore, but you've been kidnapped into slavery. You'll feel some disorientation, but just surrender yourself to the experience."

## Blindfolded and None

12    Then they took me way out in the woods and left me alone. After about an hour or so—which is a long time when you don't know where you are, and you're blindfolded—I could hear people coming toward me. I heard the voice of this White man on a horse. He gets down, comes up to me and says, "Hey, gal, you must be the nigger they brought in last night." He starts talking to me in a very demeaning way. I'm thinking. Okay, this is playacting. I can go there. No problem. Then he says this is his plantation and other people will be around to show me how things work here. And then he touches my face and says, "You're a nice-lookin' one, too." Now I'm thinking, Okay, we're going all the way there, huh? But I say, "I'm a freedwoman. I think there's been some mistake." And he says. "You don't think nothin', gal. You're mine now. You don't think nothin'." And he walked away. So I'm sitting there alone again, still blindfolded, and I keep hearing his voice in my head saying, You don't think nothin', because you're mine. You're mine.

13    A feeling of profound sadness came over me as I began to understand for the first time what it must have felt like not to be able to even claim your own thoughts. I believe we're born to cocreate with God, and if that is taken away from you, if you are denied that gift because someone has defined you as a slave, then who are you? They have taken away that precious thing that makes you a human being, so what's left?

14    The longer I sat there—and it seemed like hours!—the more it felt like death without the possibility of salvation, and all of a sudden I just started to cry. The pain was so raw—cellularly raw—that I was almost hysterical, and then suddenly, sitting there all by myself, I touched Sethe's terrible, unspeakable moment, and I understood it in my bones. That's when I knew I was ready to tell her story.

15    One of my biggest challenges was to find a director who shared my passion for the material. I talked to a lot of them—Black ones, White ones, female, foreign. Some didn't share the vision I had, some had other commitments, and some told me that they didn't feel they knew enough about the Black experience to take on the project. Then Jonathan Demme agreed to read the script last December. He called me on January 6 to

say he wanted to be a part of what we were doing. He is one of the great directors of our time, known for avant-garde films like *Stop Making Sense* and *Silence of the Lambs,* which won several Academy Awards, including Demme's award for best director, and I was ecstatic.

16    Now, it's no secret that Jonathan is a White male, and I know to some folks that raises a red flag, but let me just say that I believe it is nothing short of divine that he came to direct this picture. If you knew his heart, it wouldn't even be a question. Jonathan has a big Black heart. He was able to embrace the material in such a beautiful way without ever sentimentalizing it. He understood that the miracle of the collaboration between us was that I am the descendant of slaves and he is the descendant of slave owners, and we could now do this together. That's what makes it a great American story.

## Channeling Our Past

17    This role was different from anything I had ever done as an actress, because I had a different relationship to Sethe. When Jonathan and I first talked about how I would approach the role, I said, "I don't really think she can be acted, but I think she can be channeled. I think I can empty myself and give myself over to her, and that's how I intend to do it." So that's what we did.

18    The walls in my library at home are covered with my collection of slave memorabilia—papers, names of slaves from plantations, the actual plantation documents where they're listed by price along with the cattle. So I had some of those things with me in my trailer, and I would meditate every morning before we started shooting. I'd say the names of these slaves and ask for their help. Before doing every scene, I would go and call them up, literally. A couple of times during some really difficult moments, I'd say, "Where are y'all? I need you"— and I could feel their presence all around me.

19    We all felt that way. None of us really think we acted this movie. We were all channeling. Danny [Glover] and I had a very difficult scene about the failed escape attempt and the terrible aftermath of that to do over two days. It wasn't physically difficult, but it just wiped you out to have to call up all these terrible memories.

20    By the time I got home, my bones were aching. I took a pain reliever and went to bed, but it didn't work on that ache at all. The next day I saw Danny, and he was looking around for an acupuncturist because he was aching. I said, "I'm aching, too." And he said, "Baby, we took the journey. We went all the way there." And he was right, too. We did.

21    That's another reason this film is something brand-new. It allows us to show our hearts—not just our anger, but our hearts. And it's not about blaming. That's the beautiful thing. This movie isn't about blaming anybody. It just shows you this is how it happened. This is how it was. This is how it is.

22    One of the most important parts of the story for me is the tenderness that we see between Sethe and Paul D, the character Danny plays. Both these people were slaves. They have been through everything, and when they are reunited in this scene years later, they get to make love, to hold each other, as free people. How do you show everything they must be feeling, especially the tenderness? The absolute sweetness and vulnerability of that moment?

23    I remember years ago falling apart at the end of an episode of *The Cosby Show,* when Bill lays his head in Phylicia Rashad's lap. It was just the end of the show, just one small moment, but it made me cry because I realized watching it that I had never seen us on television like that before. We just don't get to express love and tenderness and affection in that way, so I wanted very much for that feeling to come through in what we were doing with *Beloved.*

24    There was only one small problem: I had never done a love scene before, and the very thought of doing it in front of this big crew and everybody was totally nerve-racking for me. Plus, I'm a 44-year-old woman, with a 44-year-old woman's breasts. When I looked at the storyboards where they had sketched out that first scene, Sethe had her top off. So I went to Jonathan and I said, "Listen. We have to talk about this." And I'm thinking, Whoever thought I'd be in this position to have to say what I'm getting ready to say? But I had to tell him, so I took a deep breath and I said, "You see this picture with her breasts up while she's lying down? When I lie down, my breasts do, too." And he totally got it. He just said, "Well, it's not about breasts," and that was that.

## Love Without Nudity

25   Once that was settled, we had to think about different ways to show them making love without the nudity. We tried a lot of different things. We even shot some scenes with just their toes intertwined. Then we tried some shots with him touching her hair really gently. After a few takes, Paul D started slowly unbraiding Sethe's hair, and that was it. It perfectly captured the tenderness we were looking for without my breasts' having to make their big-screen debut, so I was really glad about that.

26   Of course, I'm aware that people who have not read the book will have a very different experience from the people who have read it. I also realize it's a difficult marketing challenge, because nobody has ever seen a film like this before. We have never seen a film of ourselves during this period that explains our hearts, and it takes a minute to get ready for that.

27   I saw the film for the first time with an African-American audience in Cincinnati, and it took some of them a while to settle in because they weren't prepared for it. People get jittery when they see Black people in period costumes. They're not sure if somebody's going to pull out a banjo or dance a jig or start talking like Stepin Fetchit or whatever.

28   But once you see that isn't what we're doing, once you surrender yourself to the film we've made, you discover it's a love story and a ghost story, and mostly it's a story about healing and transformation.

29   You discover that it's uplifting. That's why it's already a success to me, because my whole life is about lifting myself up and bringing along everybody else I can. This isn't a big action blockbuster. This is not *Titanic,* although some people will try to get you to judge yourself against that standard. But I'm more interested in this work being received in the manner in which it's being offered—as a gift. That is my intention. I give it as a gift, and I know that every person who receives it and really gets it is transformed in some way. And for people who don't get it, it wasn't time. But you know how old people will say, "It's all right, baby. You gonna understand later"? That's the way I feel. It's all right, baby. When it's time, it'll come to you soft as cream. After that early screening in Cincinnati, a young woman saw me and came over to say hello. When I asked her

how she liked the movie, all she could say was, "It's deep, girl. It's deep." But I know exactly what she meant.

## Building on a Legacy

30  Although it's a new beginning, this movie, this process, is also a continuation of my work. I believe in evolvement. I am here because of everything that's happened in the past; we all are, and the key is to let that knowledge be part of your consciousness so you can use it in your life. That's why I hope part of what this movie will do is cause us as a nation to remember who we are and where we come from and what that means to us.

31    Many of us have forgotten that we have the courageous spirit of our ancestors to carry us. We have all those people looking out for us who want us to get to the other side, who want us to succeed. They are literally holding us up, pushing us forward, encouraging us to fly. Their legacy is the strength it took to say to a world determined to deny you, "I am a human being and I intend to be free. I have that right." They are truly the ground we stand on.

32    Years ago, when I was running myself crazy trying to please everybody, I told Sidney Poitier it didn't matter how hard I worked, I couldn't seem to do enough to live up to other people's expectations, and he said, "That's because you're carrying their dreams. What you have to do is find out what you expect of yourself and learn to live with that." That really helped me a lot. I had to let go of other people's expectations and learn to live from the purest part of myself. I had to learn to do only what I really felt a passion for doing. I'm not saying I've got it all figured out, but I can say that I try to live my life with absolutely pure intention. That is my guiding principle. The intention creates the experience. That's why you have to be really sure about the intention—not what you think or might like to have, but your purest intention—because that's the result you're going to get.

33    One of the things that's kind of funny as I look back on it now is that I shut down for *Beloved*. I put aside everything except the film. Once we went out to the set on Blue Stone Road and started shooting, that was it. That was the first time I ever did that, because I knew I could not do it any other way.

I shut down contact with the rest of the world. From June until September, whatever it was would just have to wait. I had a lot of pressure on me right at that moment about whether or not I would continue to do my show. People kept telling me I had to make a decision right away. They'd tell me I had syndicators who had to know, but I just said, "Well, this decision can't be made because right now I'm barefoot on Blue Stone Road."

34  I'm sure they thought I had lost my mind, but once we were finished shooting and I could really focus on the show, all the things I had learned, all the ways I had grown doing *Beloved* became a part of my decision to continue the show through the year 2002.

35  All those experiences, all the places I had to go inside myself to bring Sethe to life, made me see my role on *The Oprah Winfrey Show* so much more clearly. This is our thirteenth year—I'm calling it Lucky 13—and I've never been more certain of our direction. We're calling it 'Change Your Life TV' because that's what we're trying to do—help people make their lives better.

36  We will bring in more experts and emphasize the spirit. Every day we will have a segment called 'Remembering Your Spirit' to encourage viewers to go after their soul's desires. I want my work, all my work—movies, books, television—to be a light in people's lives.

37  The world seems like a crazy place sometimes, but I'm going to continue to do this work and to be focused and positive, because even though I don't know what the future holds for me, I know who holds the future, and as far as I'm concerned, we can't ask for more than that.

## Theme

1. Explain in your own words the ways in which the author tried "channeling" and why she did so.

2. Explain in your own words the various things that Oprah Winfrey wanted to express through the phrase "love without nudity." What techniques did she employ to achieve her goal in her film?

## Technique

1. Throughout the essay Oprah moves between "I" and "we." Explain her apparent motivation and the effect she achieves by her switching pronouns.

2. Oprah chose Jonathan Demme for her director and says: "Jonathan has a big Black heart." This statement is of course not literally true. Explain the truths Oprah wishes to express through figurative language. For example, by "heart" she does not mean to refer to an organic pump, nor by Black to refer to a particular color. What does she mean by these figures of speech? What other figures of speech does she employ in her writing?

## Writing

Oprah says of her director that "he was able to embrace the material in such a beautiful way without ever sentimentalizing it." In your view does Oprah's own writing deserve this praise? Write an essay explaining and defending your answer.

# EXERCISES

**Intertextual Questions**

1. Bill Gates urges you to adopt the Web lifestyle. Based on your reading, how would you characterize the lifestyles of the different writers in this chapter considered as businesspeople? For example, Donald Trump seems much more aggressive and hard hitting in his negotiating style than, say, Oprah Winfrey in hers. Pick some of the writers appearing here and discuss how they manifest their different attitudes by their actions in art, business, and in life.

2. Ben Stein and Diane Von Furstenberg emphasize the importance of contacts in their business lives, while other writers in the chapter focus on going it alone. Pick some examples and discuss the differing ways in which other people seem to matter to the economic identities and business lives of the celebrities appearing here.

3. Most of the figures in this chapter write from the point of view of producers of culture. Which of them best seems to understand the point of view of a consumer of mass culture like yourself? Analyze some evidence in explaining your answer.

4. Bill Gates made one of the largest fortunes in the history of the world. In her many cultural roles Oprah Winfrey is one of the most widely known figures in America. Any remarks by Bill Gates and Oprah Winfrey come backed by a great deal of authority. Yet their writing itself creates a sense of authority by its style—by the range of examples chosen, for instance. Pick another writer from this chapter and discuss how a sense of authority is established through style.

5. If you could pick a figure from the chapter that you would want to hear talk at greater length about the topic he or she discusses, who would it be? Discuss your reasoning with examples.

## Writing Exercises

1. Donald Trump became even more widely known when he made having the chance to work for him the basis of a TV show. Which of the people in this chapter would you like to work for in an *Apprentice* capacity? Write a letter of application that highlights your qualifications and alludes to what you have learned about business from your reading here.

2. Spike Lee emphasizes the importance of money to producing his art, but Chuck D talks in part about how even gaining nothing initially might in fact help the artist. Write an essay in which you analyze some of the different ways in which money matters in other essays within the chapter.

3. Bill Gates uses an extended analogy to make his point. What other techniques of writing exemplified in this chapter did you find effective? Pick some examples and write an essay that discusses the art of writing about economic issues to an unspecialized audience.

4. The importance of marketing is a topic discussed in more than one essay. Pick another economic function that appears in this chapter and write an essay that addresses its importance using evidence from your reading to support your contentions.

5. Ben Stein pretends his essay is an informal letter. Which writer seems to you to have the most formal writing style? Which writer seems to have the most effective writing style for his or her purposes? Pick an example and write an essay that analyzes how style contributes to the point of the essay as a whole.

# PART III

# Making a Lasting Contribution

# CHAPTER 7

# SERVING YOUR COUNTRY AND YOUR WORLD

The essays in this chapter focus on the public self in public service. The celebrity authors here represent a wide variety of views on the proper degree to which everyone should contribute to the common welfare of one's own country—and to that of the wider world as well. Of course the power of a nation is most evident in its armed forces, but frequently the writers of these essays seek to enlist other governmental powers to aid them in the peaceful public services whose importance they argue for. However, in at least two cases—those of Rush Limbaugh and Rudolph Giuliani—the limits of governmental action are also questioned. These men argue that the government does a disservice to its citizens by undertaking actions that may be either counterproductive or unaffordable. All in all, the issues focused on in this chapter—and the sides taken on those issues—are representative of the ways the public good and public service are prioritized through advocacy and debate in a modern democracy.

Since his retirement from professional basketball, Kareem Abdul-Jabbar has devoted himself to public service in the private sphere by becoming an author and by serving as a developmental coach for disadvantaged amateur teams and lower level professional ones. The selection of his writing reprinted here is taken from the book, *Brothers in Arms,* the story of African-American soldiers in American history. In it he describes the battle action of a tank battalion in World War II.

Serving your country may of course take place in peacetime as well as during a war. In the second essay Ralph Nader, perhaps the most famous consumer advocate in recent times, argues that citizens should not think that their public duties end with exercising their right to vote. He urges a much broader model of public responsibility, something he calls the "public citizen." As he sees it, the role of the public citizen is to mobilize the powers of government, not merely to vote for the politicians who ordinarily administer those powers.

Angelina Jolie might be described as a public citizen of the world. In a selection from her book about her public service activities, she describes a private mission she undertook to aid refugees in Ecuador who had been displaced from their homes by a combination of guerrilla warfare and governmental response. In "Mission to Ecuador" she gives a touching and highly individual account of how she worked with official international relief agencies to help people who had lost everything—sometimes even their entire families.

Rush Limbaugh's essay, "Conservatives Promote Independence," returns the focus of the chapter to domestic policies in peacetime. In particular, Limbaugh claims that the best way to help people in need of help is not by making them dependent on governmental programs, but by making them independent and self-sufficient through policies that focus on their strengths and not on their weaknesses. He criticizes his liberal opponents for trying to buy votes through short-sighted and short-term programs that act in ways counterproductive to their own announced goals.

In the next essay, "Use the Media For Public Health!" Jane Fonda focuses on the threat of diseases and conditions that do not confine themselves to political boundaries. She concludes that: "We need the media today (in rich countries as well as poor) to serve as a channel to inform a growing public about healthy practices, sensible lifestyles, as well as the importance of education and equality for girls." Suggesting that mass cultural media such as soap operas are in fact the best means of educating the masses about sensitive and sometime secretive health issues, Fonda argues that the dangers of some social taboos can only be met by social means.

Former New York City Mayor Rudolph Giuliani was almost universally applauded for his words and actions following the attacks on the World Trade Center on September 11, 2001. Before that time he was a very active mayor in all phases of city life, reducing street crime and fighting battles over budgets that surpass those of many sovereign nations in the rest of the world. Yet in this essay he argues that New York's assets are not unlimited and that the longstanding policy of open admissions is unhealthy both in educational as well as fiscal terms.

Rosie Perez makes a visual argument in a public service advertisement—"Why Does Rosie Perez Wear the Bracelet?" By contributing her image to a national campaign, Perez seeks to raise funds to combat HIV/AIDS. In this way she visually embodies the chapter's theme—the presentation of a public persona in the cause of a greater common good by serving her country and her world.

The chapter concludes with a famous essay by a winner of the Nobel Peace Prize. After Dr. Martin Luther King, Jr. was arrested during a civil rights protest, he made the classic defense of his movement in "Letter from a Birmingham Jail."

# Kareem Abdul-Jabbar

## Black Tankers of World War II    (1986)

> *Born Lew Alcindor in New York, Kareem Abdul-Jabbar became
> a Muslim at UCLA where he went to college after a nationally-
> noticed high school basketball career. On graduating he went on
> to a long and record-breaking career in professional basketball.
> After retiring, he became an author, actor, and a coach at the
> lower levels of basketball development in the belief that he needed
> to pay something back.*

1    Floyd Dade's tank rolled past the center of Guebling and
came under German fire. The Sherman took up position,
unable to move in any direction, behind a disabled tank of the
4th Armored Division. German soldiers, aware of their predica-
ment, continued directing fire at them but were unable to target them firmly because of the other tank. Dade and his crew,
assigned to guard a crossroads five hundred yards away, stayed
in position amid the barrage to keep it sighted.

2    Ruben Rivers, moving around the perimeter of Guebling
toward a low hill that gave him a line of fire on Bourgaltroff,
encountered two enemy tanks. Despite his life-threatening
injuries from two days before, Rivers calmly targeted the tanks
for gunner Everett Robinson, shooting an intense round of
armor-piercing and high-explosive shells until both German
tanks withdrew.

3    The 101st Infantry Regiment battled toward Bourgaltroff
against entrenched German forces. The tanks of Able Company
were ordered to stand by and hold their stations throughout
the night of the eighteenth. The sound of burp guns and M-1s
was constant, and the Germans sent up a series of flares. Ruben

SOURCE: From *Brothers in Arms* by William Broyles, Jr. Copyright © 1986 by
William Broyles, Jr. Used by permission of Alfred A. Knopf, a division of Random
House, Inc.

Rivers reported to Captain Williams a sound that was equally ominous. Throughout the night, the staff sergeant noted the distinctive rattle of large numbers of German tanks taking up position in the field.

4    Williams, coming by River's tank just before sunrise on the nineteenth, asked Rivers one last time to evacuate so that his injured leg could be saved. Rivers refused, telling him, "How in the hell can I go back and leave you all here?" The assault on Bourgaltroff was set to begin in earnest at dawn.

5    Lieutenant Colonel Lyons, commanding the 101st Regiment's 2nd Battalion, continued to believe that the direct attack on Bourgaltroff was a mistake. He felt that the 26th Division should instead encircle and close off the city, telling Captain Williams, "Division should pinch out this sector and be done with it." He would be proved correct; the attack would become a slaughter. Nonetheless, Lyons was again overruled by his superiors.

6    Lyons was concerned in particular with the German antitank guns, which were well-positioned throughout the vast meadow, as well as with the Panther and Tiger tanks. The enemy tanks could penetrate the sides of a Sherman from 1,200 meters; to penetrate the thicker German armor, American tanks had to close to a range of 400 meters, hardly an equal match. The turret on the Tiger was slow, not fully electric like the Sherman's. But the German crew could rapidly stop one track and essentially jump the entire tank around: The 761st called it pouncing "quick like a cat." One well-placed Tiger could cover a great deal of ground.

7    Able Company's plan of action was for Ruben Rivers and a companion tank, commanded by Sgt. Walter James, to cross the field toward Bourgaltroff and fire on the western edge of the city with high-explosive shells. Second Lt. Robert Hammond and an additional tank would move across the field more slowly, spreading out to destroy as many enemy infantry and machine-gun positions as possible. Captain Williams's tank, Floyd Dade's tank, and the rest of the company would in the meantime head down the road toward Bourgaltroff in column formation.

8    The assault was preceded by a heavy American artillery barrage. Dade's tank, commanded by Teddy Weston, rolled for-

ward just as dawn broke to lead the column on the road to Bourgaltroff. The 101st Infantry was already filtering past them into the meadow. As they did, they were mowed down by machine-gun fire. German antitank tracers started raining in. Rivers's tank advanced some distance across the field and was the first to spot and open fire on German positions.

9    Back along the road, Dade's tank took an artillery hit on its turret. Miraculously, none of the crew was injured and the tank was still mobile. But the tank's 76mm gun had been disabled. The Germans slowly zeroed in on the tank column. Artillery crashed in around the exposed vehicles, striking a second tank. Dade's tank backed up behind the shelter of a ruined house. Captain Williams, seeing that the situation was hopeless, ordered the others in the column to do the same.

10    Ruben Rivers sighted several Mark IV Panther tanks and enemy tank destroyers concealed behind a slope in the meadow. These vehicles had a wide field of fire and were devastating the American tanks and infantry. Rivers advanced, firing off tracers and armor-piercing shells. Captain Williams, from his position on the road, spotted enemy tracers flying in across the field toward where he knew Hammond's and Rivers's tanks were advancing. Williams, unable to keep the fear from his voice, radioed both tank commanders to pull back. Hammond attempted to fall back behind a clump of trees. Rivers, instead of retreating, pushed ahead to provide cover for the retreating infantry and other tanks in the field. He radioed Williams, "I see them. We'll fight them."

## Theme

1. Elsewhere in *Brothers in Arms*—the book from which this excerpt is taken—Kareem Abdul-Jabbar writes of George Patton, a famous general who revolutionized American tank warfare in World War II: "Patton had no great regard for African Americans; his letters and private journals abound with racist stereotypes and rhetoric. He was, however, perhaps above all a consummate pragmatist....when he needed all available skilled Sherman tank crews to spearhead his

assault on the Siegfried Line, he called for the 761$^{st}$." Point to some evidence Abdul-Jabbar gives to show just how skilled the African Americans of the 761$^{st}$ Tank Regiment were.

2. The description of battle shows not only the skill of the soldiers but their bravery. Point to some evidence that shows how the author creates a sense of courage in the people he describes.

## Technique

1. Elsewhere the author describes the sequence of commands needed for effective firing in a Sherman tank:

   **Commander to Driver:** "Driver... STOP"

   **Commander to Gunner:** "Gunner...TANK [thus naming the type of target]

   **Commander to Loader:** "AP" [calling for armor-piercing shells]

   **Commander to Gunner:** "Traverse left...Steady-on...One thousand."

   **Gunner to Commander:** "Ready!"

   **Commander to Gunner:** "FIRE!"

   This command sequence makes one example of the orderliness needed within the chaos of battle. Point to some other instances that show how the author maintains a sense of orderliness in his description of the chaotic battle.

2. In spite of the dramatizations of courage, discipline, and order maintained, the author creates an overwhelming sense of confusion. Point to some of the ways in which the writing dramatizes the chaos of war.

## Writing

Write an essay in which you analyze how the author creates a sense of military discipline and bravery on the part of the 761$^{st}$ Tank Regiment.

# Ralph Nader

## The Duties of Citizenship                                    (2000)

*Born in 1938, Ralph Nader went to law school after graduating from Princeton. The publication of his best-selling indictment of the auto industry,* Unsafe At Any Speed, *led to the establishment of the Center for Responsible Law. He has been a presidential candidate in every election since 1992.*

1    IN THE EARLY DAYS of the Republic, the federal government did little beyond run the post office, collect tariffs, and provide for the common defense. And the state governments did even less. Instead, the symbol of American democracy was the New England town meeting, where citizens would gather by the village green to discuss and decide public affairs for their local government. Town meeting self-government should not be overidealized. There were the power elites and the poor in each little town. Yet it did, in an age far simpler than today's, operate on a premise that regular participation in government, beyond merely voting at election time, was an obligation of every citizen. The very format of the town meeting helped assure that that obligation would be fulfilled. The voters were the local legislature.

2    A pundit of 150 years ago might have reasonably predicted that citizen-oriented governmental formats would continue and that citizen efforts would expand as the nation's economic, legal, and technological structures expanded, as growth made people interdependent with one another and with institutions near and far. Such a logical development did not occur; in fact, something closer to the opposite happened. City political

SOURCE: Introduction to "A Public Citizen's Action Manual" from the *Ralph Nader Reader.* Copyright © 2000 by Ralph Nader. Used by permission of Ralph Nader and Seven Stories Press.

machines and city councils replaced the town meetings. Institutions of government and business became bigger and more distant from the people they were supposed to assist or to serve. The power of citizens was delegated to secretive legislatures and executive bureaucracies surrounded and dominated by well-organized special-interest groups that in turn learned that their best investment was the financing or buying of elections. Although increasingly shielded by institutional corruption, complexity, and secrecy from being regularly accountable to the public, government institutions fed the propaganda that elections were enough of a mandate and that such elections were adequately democratic. Especially during the past thirty years, corporations and other special interests have become only bigger and more astute in using governmental power and tax revenues to support their goals and subsidize their treasuries. This interlock between government and business has further complicated the task of citizen effort. For no longer can citizens start with the assumption that government is uncommitted to a special-interest group.

3      The people's loss of the power to govern themselves has deepened as the need for such self-government has risen. Certainly, the costs of citizen powerlessness are accelerating, if only because more people are being affected more ways by more events beyond their control. The American Revolution rang with the declaration that "the price of liberty is eternal vigilance." That is also true for "justice" and "peace"—and for "clean water" and "clean air" and "safe cars" and "healthy work places." But these good things, the blessings of liberty, will not come to pass until we cease viewing citizen involvement as just a privilege and begin defining our daily work to include citizenship toward public problems as an obligation.

4      This process starts with the individual's use of his or her time and energy. Most people think they are good citizens if they obey the laws and vote at election time. First of all, this is not enough by its own measure because too many people and powerful groups do not obey the laws and almost half the people over eighteen do not vote. But by a broader measure, voting can never be enough simply because decisions affecting people are made by government between elections. It is what

citizens do *between* elections that decides whether elections are to be meaningful exercises of debate and decision or whether they are to remain expensive contests between tweedledees and tweedledums. It is not difficult to describe the citizenship gap. How many decisions in Washington, in the state capital, or in the city council involve even modest citizen participation? Why, at all levels of government, does the bureaucracy of executive branch agencies and departments decide matters without the legislature's knowledge or restraint?

5    The average worker spends about a quarter of his time on the job earning money to pay his taxes but spends virtually no time overseeing the spenders of those taxes. In the marketplace the same disparity between expenditure and involvement prevails. A consumer will spend thousands of hours driving a new automobile or eating food from a supermarket, but can find no way to spend any time to correct the overpricing, fraud, and hazards associated with these products. This is also the case with consumers taking out a loan or purchasing an insurance policy. It is no wonder that in the marketplace or in the halls of government, those who are organized and knowledgeable obtain their way. And those people who abdicate, delegate, or vegetate are taken.

6    Look at the United States today. Can anyone deny that this country has more problems than it deserves and more solutions than it uses? Its massive wealth, skills, and diversity should never have tolerated, much less endured, the problems and perils that seem to worsen despite a continuing aggregate economic growth. There seems to be less and less relationship between the country's total wealth and its willingness to solve the ills and injustices that beset it. The spirit of pioneering and problem-solving is weak. National, state, and local political leadership is vague at best, manipulative at worst. Facing the world, the United States stands as an uncertain giant with uncertain purposes toward a world in great need of its help and encouragement.

7    The reversal of these trends requires different leadership, to be sure, but it also requires a new kind of citizenship—public citizenship, part-time-on-the-job, and full-time—that engages in more exercise and less delegation of citizen power. The

impulse to become a public citizen can spring from many sources—for example, a fundamental compassion for people and a sense of how inextricably interdependent a society we have. But in a practical, animating way, the spark is learning by doing, developing the techniques and strategies for citizen organization and action. If it can be shown that civic action can solve problems, then more people will shuck their indifference or resignation and want to join the effort.

8    How much work there is to do can be gauged by how little has been done. Every week, thousands of government agencies are making decisions which will affect the environment, utility rates, food prices and quality, land use, taxes, transportation, health care, employment, job safety, rent, schools, crime, prisons, peace, civil liberties and rights, and many other conditions of social coexistence now and into the future. Surrounding these agencies are lobbyists and advocates for special economic interests, some of whom take jobs for a few years within these agencies to make themselves more useful to their private employers later. Using numerous combinations of the carrot and stick, these pressure groups more often than not get exactly what they want. On rare occasions, a few full-time public interest advocates are present at the scene of the action.

9    Greatly outnumbered and equipped with only the justice and knowledge of their cause, these full-time citizens have achieved remarkable successes in the courts and before regulatory agencies and legislatures. The national citizens' struggles against the Supersonic Transport (SST), cyclamates, and the laxness of the Atomic Energy Commission's neglect of adequate safety standards in nuclear power plants can be paralleled by hundreds of smaller victories at the state and local levels by an aroused citizenry. These Americans have learned that practice makes perfect and the more experience they accumulate, the more effective they become.

10    Given what a few citizens have done, it is a source of optimism to ask what many, many more like them could do in the future. A look at the past can make future projections of citizen impact more credible. Imagine that twenty-five years ago, citizens concerned about the future quality of life in America— say one out of ten adults—had gotten together to do something

about it. Our urban centers would not be choked with cars, or laced with concrete belts that strangle the polluted cities in ever-increasing slums, corruption, crime, noise, and public waste. Our rivers, lakes, and oceans would still be producing untainted fish and would be safe for swimming. Drinking water would not be increasingly imperiled by pollution. The air would not be as filled with vile and violent contaminants, and the land not ravaged by insensitive corporate and government forces wasting our resources faster than they are replenished. Consumers would not be exploited by shoddy goods and services, deceptive practices, and price-fixing that (according to Senator Philip Hart's studies) take at least 25 percent of every consumer dollar.

11    Thousands of American workers would not be dying or sickened each year because of the toxic chemicals, gases, and dust that pervade so many factories, foundries, and mines. Equal opportunity in education and employment and adequate medical care would have avoided the misery that cruelly affects many Americans. Nor would hunger and poverty have been belatedly "discovered" in the sixties to be affecting some thirty million Americans. Factory and office workers would not be federally taxed 20 percent of their wages while countless men of great wealth are assessed 4 percent or less and many corporations with enormous incomes pay nothing or next to nothing. Small businessmen and homeowners could not be squeezed by powerful corporations whose predatory practices, underpayment of property taxes, and other abuses serve to further concentrate their powers and plunders.

12    Our Congress and state legislatures would not have continued to be underequipped and indentured to pressure groups instead of monitoring the executive branches and responding to the real needs of all the people. The power and expenditures of the military establishment and their civilian superiors would have been scrutinized, and perhaps curtailed, many painful, costly years ago. Above all, our political system would have reverberated with higher quality and dedication as the momentum of expert citizen movements increased.

13    A small number of citizens throughout our country's history have kept the flame of citizenship burning brightly to the ben-

efit of millions of their less engaged neighbors. These true patriots have known that democracy comes hard and goes easy. To make democracy work, it takes work—citizen work. Many practical lessons can be learned from their experiences. Today, citizen groups are flowering all over the country, but they need to be better organized, better funded, and staffed with skilled, dedicated, full-time people. New citizen organizations such as Action for Children's Television in Boston (to stop television exploitation of children), Consumer Action Now in New York and Citizen's Action Program in Chicago (getting large industries to stop underpaying their property taxes), and GASP in Pittsburgh (fighting air pollution) are showing what can be done with minimum funds and maximum civic spirit. Courageous public citizens, such as education advocate Julius Hobson in Washington, D.C., are the true unsung heroes of American democracy. They have weathered community pressure to fight for a more just society in cities, towns, and villages around the country.

14    Many more citizens work to correct small abuses or deficiencies in the community once or twice and then retire to their former state of inaction. Such withdrawal does little to encourage others to engage in similar activities and does nothing to push initial drives beyond symptoms and tread mills to more fundamental reform that lasts. Easy disillusionment, the inability to rebound from difficulties, and lack of stamina must be candidly assessed and overcome through modest amounts of self-discipline. This is done in athletics and games all the time; it should also become the practice in the citizenship arena.

15    Citizen effort is everybody's business and everybody can engage in such effort. Who, for example, is better equipped to fight for women's rights or conduct consumer surveys than women, all too many of whom may be wasting much of their time daily watching soap operas, gossiping on the telephone, or "keeping in their place?" Who is better situated to further the job safety laws than workers exposed to occupational hazards and capable of organizing themselves or invigorating their unions to humanize the workplace? Who could be better motivated to reform the motor clubs than the disenfranchised members of these clubs—the millions of motorists? Who should be

more inclined to expose the gross underpayment of property taxes by large companies than homeowners, small businessmen, and taxpayers generally? These are not wholly rhetorical questions. There are people who have indeed done all these things with some success. Had they been joined by some of the 99 percent of their neighbors, co-workers, or co-members who were inactive, truly enduring progress would have taken place. Sometimes one or two individuals are enough; over two million Chevrolets were recalled for defects because of one inspector in a GM plant speaking out; cyclamates were taken off the market because of two outspoken scientists in the Food and Drug Administration. For the most part, however, there is need for organization around public issues particularly when the hurdles are high and the facts are not yet available to the public.

16    Citizenship is not an endeavor reserved only for the most talented; anybody can do it and everybody should do it.

17    The exercise by citizens of their rights and responsibilities is what makes a working democracy ever sensitive to the just needs of its people. Such citizen effort is a learning process which can be increasingly advanced with practice. For increasing numbers of Americans, citizenship should become a full-time career role, supported by other citizens, to work *on* major institutions of government and business for a better society. It is this fundamental role of the *public citizen* in a democracy that must attract more adherents and supporters from across America.

## Theme

1. According to your understanding of the essay as a whole, why does Ralph Nader say in paragraph four that he believes "voting can never be enough" to be "a public citizen?" Give examples of the activities he views as defining this term.

2. What evidence does Nader bring to substantiate his claim that the government and its regulatory agencies are not sufficient to protect citizens from "special interests"?

## Technique

1. What is the effect Nader achieves by putting quotes around the word "discovered" in paragraph 11 where he discusses several social problems?

2. In paragraph 15, Nader asks many questions and then says: "these are not wholly rhetorical questions." Explain the ways in which they do seem to be rhetorical questions for him, and then explain any ways in which the questions are not rhetorical ones.

## Writing

In paragraph three Nader writes: "The people's loss of the power to govern themselves has deepened as the need for such self-government has risen." Write an essay in which you show how Nader's essay does or does not support this statement and exemplify this claim.

# Angelina Jolie

## Mission to Ecuador                                   (2003)

> *Growing up in Los Angeles as the daughter of actor Jon Voight,
> Angelina Jolie was in effect born into the film industry. Like Sissy
> Spacek (Chapter 1) she trained and performed at the Lee Stras-
> berg Theater Institute. Jolie has also worked as an international
> fashion model and has starred in music videos. Her humanitar-
> ian interests are exemplified in the following description of a
> relief mission she voluntarily undertook.*

1   Colombia is by far the most serious humanitarian crisis in the
Western hemisphere and has one of the worst internal displacement problems in the world. Official government statistics put
the number of internally displaced persons (IDPs) since 1995 at
720,000, while nongovernmental organizations (NGOs) estimate
the figure to be closer to 2 million. According to the national
Association of Financial Institutions, 158,000 Colombians left the
country last year. Thousands of them have applied for refugee
status in other Latin American countries, North America, Europe,
and elsewhere. Although its mandate worldwide is the protection of refugees, UNHCR (United Nations Refugee Agency) has
been working with IDPs in Colombia since 1999 at the invitation of the Colombian government.

2       Since the collapse of the peace process in February 2002,
clashes between leftist guerrillas and right wing paramilitary
groups have intensified, causing more displacement and bringing untold suffering to the civilian population. On May 2, in an
incident that shocked the world, 119 people—including 48 children—died in the northwestern district of Bojaya, when a
homemade mortar hit a church crowded with civilians fleeing

SOURCE: From "Mission to Ecuador." Reprinted with permission of Pocket Books,
an imprint of Simon & Schuster Adult Publishing Group from *Notes On My Travels*
by Angelina Jolie. Copyright © 2003 by Angelina Jolie.

the fighting. On May 26, 53 percent of Colombian voters elected Alvaro Uribe Velez as their new president. Mr. Uribe, who will take office in August, has promised to take strong action against the FARC (Revolutionary Armed Forces of Colombia) and other irregular armed groups and bring the forty-year-old conflict to an end.

### Thursday, June 6—7 A.M.

3 Sitting in the L.A. airport, realizing it's been eight months since I've done a field visit. I've visited for individual days here and there when I've been able, but there's something selfishly I've been missing. To be gone away from this material world and completely surrounded by the urgent, focused life. Everyone focused on their own or someone else's survival. Basic survival and struggle to protect family, country, freedom.

4 This will be my first night away from my son Maddox. First time I am away since we came together three months ago. It was ridiculous how emotional I felt kissing him good-bye. Leaving him with my mom and brother. Realizing that family is so important.

5 And those friends, the ones who feel like family.

6 Then there is that rare occasion when strangers become family, like these aid workers I am about to meet. Everyone I am about to meet. They're not family. They have made strangers their priority. You can understand why fast friends are made.

7 Ecuador is one of the smallest countries in South America. It is slightly smaller than Nevada, with a land area of 276,840 square kilometers (106,476 square miles). Only two countries border it: Peru to the south and the southeast, and Colombia to the north. Chimborazo is the highest point at 6,267 meters (20,560 feet). Ecuador's mountain Cotopaxi in the Andes is the highest active volcano in the world. Ecuador has a population of 13,184,000, of which 65 percent are Mestizo (Indian and Spanish), a quarter Indian, 7 percent are Spanish, and 3 percent are black. Ecuador has 22 provinces, and gained its independence from Spain in 1822.

8 Warm greeting off the plane by ACNUR (Alto Comision ado de las Naciones Unidas para los refugiados: UNHCR in Spanish). It was true what the UNHCR staff told me, "You will feel

like you have family all around the world." Drawn to similar places, similar goals for the same people, for the same reasons. I believe if asked why, they would all say because refugees or displaced people are arguably the most vulnerable people in the world. And if you've met them, they are also some of the strongest, most beautiful, most capable people in the world. Amazing survivors.

9    The staff here mentioned how it is difficult to get the world's attention here. The fighting, the war in Colombia, going on for forty years now, seems only to be getting worse. The violence is on the news but not the victims. Not the people. Not the families.

10    There are no large camps. Everyone is spread out in shelters, etc.

11    I am also told it is hard to get refugees to be outspoken, allow media access, because they are in fear of combatants who also crossed over the border and want them to remain silent. I am told, "It's not paranoia—many have been killed."

12    Since we arrived at night, I am brought straight to my room in the guest house. I find extra blankets and a little heater. I'm glad it's colder than I had expected. I think they knew it would be. The ladies here had bought a poncho for me in case I didn't have enough warm clothes.

## Friday, June 7—7:15 A.M.

13    Breakfast, where we will start the briefing.

14    The first UNHCR office in South America was established in Buenos Aires, Argentina, to assist victims of the institutional breaches in the region. In the '70s, UNHCR opened a regional office in Lima, Peru. During the '90s, the new regional office was set up in Caracas, Venezuela, to cover northern South America and Panama for the victims of the internal conflict in Colombia. The situation became increasingly worse, leading to the opening of UNHCR offices in Bogotá and three other provinces in Colombia. In 2000, another UNHCR office was created in Quito, Ecuador.

15    I am told that every day people are displaced in Colombia. Then someone says. "And every day people are killed." I am told I will see a difference from the other countries I have vis-

ited. The refugees here are mostly urban. They are in small numbers. They are mostly professional people. They are not farmers. They are people who are used to living similarly to you, I would guess, the people reading this.

16     The U.N. is working together to have a "common house." U.N. specialized agencies are encouraged to have common premises wherever possible in the field. In Quito, UNHCR and other U.N. agencies have their offices in the same building. It would seem like an obvious thing for everyone to work hand in hand, but it is not always the case. I am told the Secretary General has been pushing the unity more and more. Here— WFP, UNDP, UNICEF, and UNHCR—all U.N. agencies work together.

17     Most democratic countries are not supposed to. It should be very unusual. Colombia is democratic, but agencies like UNHCR, Red Cross, etc., have to help protect the people.

18     *Protection* is a word repeated often in the conversations this morning. The protection of an estimated 20 million up-rooted people is the core mandate of UNHCR. The agency does this in several ways. Using the 1951 Geneva Refugee Convention as its major tool, UNHCR ensures the basic human rights of uprooted people and that refuges will not be returned involuntarily to a country where they face persecution. Longer term, UNHCR helps civilians repatriate to their homeland, integrate in countries of asylum, or resettle in third countries. Using a worldwide field network, UNHCR also seeks to provide at least a minimum of shelter, food, water, and medical care in the immediate aftermath of any refugee exodus.

19     After the briefing, I am overwhelmed by the complexity of the situation. I'm in a bit of a haze, but one thing I can already tell—there is much I feel I should have known. One would think with the humanitarian crisis as extreme as it obviously is in this part of the world, the human rights violations would have more media coverage. So I—we—all would know about it.

20     Seventy-four percent of the territory of Colombia is controlled by guerrilla or paramilitary groups. (The majority of the 40 million people live in the 25 percent of the main cities still controlled by a democratic state.) That is mostly border areas where they control resources—drugs, oil, coffee, emeralds. So

who is buying from these people? Who buys these exports? Who is supporting the rebels?

21   In this 74 percent of the country, the government is absent or very weak. There is no national protection in those areas. The Catholic Church is one of UNHCR's main partners here. That is true for all of South America.

22   My visit this time is only in Ecuador. I am reminded I am only seeing a small part of a very big operation. Venezuela and Ecuador bordering Colombia and Colombia itself have UNHCR offices. UNHCR is also covering Panama, but the border is a swamp jungle, one of the most inaccessible parts of the world. UNHCR is also covering Peru, but the border is jungle, same as the Colombia-Brazil border.

23   More briefings: massacres and kidnapping—3,000 per year. An average of nine or ten people a day.

24   Even though in the last three years more and more people are fleeing Colombia, the majority of people—civilian victims of conflict—remain in the country. A high amount of IDPs. It seems harder to get aid and awareness. Maybe harder for the international community to understand the severity of the situation. Recent figures now show between 500 and 900 people are displaced every day. I ask why do they stay. A UNHCR staff member told me that one reason is they have a better chance of getting a job inside Colombia.

25   The long-standing armed conflict in Colombia has left hundreds of thousands dead and displaced more than 1.5 million people. Thousands have fled to neighboring Venezuela, Panama, and Ecuador. In 2001, some 2,000 asylum applications by Colombians were registered in Ecuador, compared with only 30 in 2000. During the first half of 2002, there were 2,198 asylum applications. Also, Colombian refugees ranked seventh in the number of asylum applications submitted in the industrialized world between January and May 2002.

26   Four years ago the presidential campaign was won by talk for peace. Last February the peace process failed. This election was won by talk of war. To use force to deal with the situation—I can only imagine how this new way will affect the people. Humanitarian aid workers are preparing today for the conflict to get worse.

27    I visit an office inside a church to meet asylum seekers or those who have already been given refugee status—to hear their stories. Erta Lemos is the Office Director for the Committee for Refugees, one of the UNHCR's partners here in Quito. She says she is very happy to be the missionary for migrants. She has a nice smile and wears a crucifix made into a ring on her wedding finger. On the walls are all the UNHCR posters of children around the world. One looks just like Maddox.

28    Erta explains to us how this office works. It opens at 7 A.M. to accept people who are seeking asylum. Worst cases are people persecuted by paramilitaries. Most cases are single parents or children alone. Many cases are people who have been tortured.

29    "These cases also need emotional and spiritual support," she says.

30    First is a brief interview to see if they have a case for seeking asylum. If so, they start to fill out forms to document their case. Then a series of interviews. The office receives about twenty-five to thirty cases a day. Each case size is different. Some are one mother plus seven children, so that case is eight people. The office works closely with the Ecuadorian government on behalf of the people seeking asylum.

31    As we meet, I see people through the window begin their interview. Like other interviews where I have seen the person seeking protection, they seem broken, almost defeated. Their body language is the same—head slightly bowed, holding on tightly to any papers or packet they have.

32    As we enter, we walk through a hallway full of people. One man is walking his crying baby back and forth. A few children also sit along the wall. I can't tell but they seem alone.

33    I am told I am about to meet a man whose wife and children were killed in front of him. "Very traumatized but getting better." Erta just went out to get him. I'm nervous.

34    He is a little man, wearing a gray-and-black sweater and work shirt. You can see he has tried to dress well. With what little he has. There are so many holes in the sweater. His gray hair is combed back and his eyes are sad. I would guess he's in his late fifties. Kind face. Handsome man. Very gracious.

35   He explains he is from the same area where there was just another massacre three weeks ago. He keeps being reminded to please speak slowly so they can translate.

36   He had a small farm with corn. I think he's speaking fast because he is so uncomfortable with this memory. He seems to want to get through it as quickly as possible. "I even had a jeep," he says. Guerrillas started extorting money out of him.

37   He seems to get nervous. I wonder if it's because I'm writing. I ask them to tell him that I promise I will not use his name. That we just want people to understand the situation in his country.

38   He continues. The paramilitaries came to the village and started fighting the guerrillas. Guerrillas accused him of supporting the paramilitaries. There was a massacre. Seventy people in the village were killed. "We're not sure," he says. It was guerrillas. He's a little shaken when he talks and keeps rubbing his hands together.

39   He is asked a question in Spanish. Suddenly tears well up in his eyes and he can't speak. William says, "I asked him how his family was killed." I look at the man and he's looking at me as if he is saying, "Please don't make me talk about it."

40   I've stopped writing for the last few minutes. He was trying not to cry. William told him it was okay. He can talk only about what he wants. The man apologizes. Can you imagine? Someone apologizing because they can't tell you how their family was killed.

## Theme

1. Before she goes, what does Jolie imagine her purpose to be in going to Ecuador? Point to some of the remarks she makes that give meaning to her journey.

2. According to Jolie, what explains the rapidity of the deep friendships she formed with aid workers? Point to some of the evidence she uses to show these friendships at work.

## Technique

1. Jolie calls her trip both a "mission" and a "field visit." What are the differing implications of these names for the meaning of her trip? Point to moments in her narrative when it seems that each word is most applicable and explain why you think it is so.

2. Jolie's account of the situation moves back and forth from a large scale view to a highly personal and intimate one. Point to some moments when she shifts her point of view and analyze her apparent reasons for the shift.

## Writing

Write an essay in which you show how as a writer Angelina Jolie integrates the large overview of her subject with her intimate personal account of her experience.

# Rush Limbaugh

## Conservatives Promote Independence   (1994)

> *Rush Limbaugh became nationally famous in the 1990s as the outspoken, politically conservative host of a radio talk show. In July, 2001 he signed a long-term radio contract purported to be worth $285 million. In 2003 he admitted on air to an addiction to pain killers and came under criminal investigation.*

1   It must be stated that all too often conservatives are considered racists, or at least less sympathetic to minorities than are liberals. In my opinion, this phenomenon is purely related to the conservatives' strong commitment to free enterprise and their concern with the expansion of government and the welfare state. Liberals and the Democratic Party long have been perceived to be the political allies of blacks and other minorities because they advocate massive wealth-redistribution programs.

2   Conservatives have opposed affirmative action and quotas while liberals have generally supported them. Conservatives have been proponents, however, of civil rights (though they are often not given credit for this), but they draw the line with respect to affirmative action and quotas. For these reasons, not to mention their own racially charged propaganda, liberals have successfully convinced the overwhelming majority of blacks that they and the Democratic Party are their only homes.

3   Conservatives have always believed that blacks and other minorities would be better served in the long run by programs that foster independence, rather than those that foster dependency on government. As so many responsible black commentators have noted of late, "We are no longer living in the sixties. This is the nineties. We need to quit blaming other people and look to ourselves for self-improvement." That's right.

SOURCE: Reprinted by permission of *National Minority Politics*.

4    Though we have not eradicated racism in this country, conservatives believe that the blacks' best avenue to success is
through self-reliance. As long as the left and certain members
of the black leadership continue to exploit blacks by encouraging them to dwell on the past instead of looking forward, it
will be difficult for blacks to make significant further progress
in this society.

5    Somehow, the vision that Dr. Martin Luther King, Jr., had for
a color-blind society has been perverted by modern liberalism.
It is axiomatic for liberals today that blacks can be represented
only by black elected officials. This logic has so distorted the
original intent of laws such as the Civil Rights Act that we are
gerrymandering congressional districts to guarantee that blacks
are elected.

6    It has been my great pleasure to get to know Dr. Thomas
Sowell, the brilliant economist, author, and syndicated columnist. As a conservative black man, he says that the best thing that
ever happened to him was being born in the 1930s so that he
could become an adult before the unfolding of the civil rights
movement of the 1960s.

7    As a result he has focused on individual achievement rather
than becoming preoccupied and distracted by the defeatist vic-
timization game and the king of "Get-even-ism" the modern
civil rights movement so enjoys.

8    Another person from whom we can all learn, despite his
controversial nature, is Phoenix Suns star Charles Barkley.
There may be no harder-working man in all of professional
sports. Here's a guy who is not gifted with great height or
speed, but, because of his great work ethic, ebullient spirit, and
relentless pursuit of excellence, he has become one of the true
superstars of the National Basketball Association. He did it
without the help of the civil rights leadership. He didn't need
any affirmative action program. He was motivated by his sin-
gular drive to set himself apart and to excel.

9    Do you realize there are kids today who are ridiculed in
school for high achievement? In some quarters it is simply not
fashionable to succeed on your own merit and hard work.
Some black people are still called "Uncle Toms" today for trying to make it in the system.

10     Let me tell you, my friends: It's not conservatives who are afraid of what happens when blacks become entrepreneurs and successful businesspeople. It's not conservatives who label middle-class black achievers "Uncle Toms." We rejoice at every success of blacks, and there are far more than you might think.

11     Too many people who are living in desperate poverty today have been conditioned to depend on someone else for their prosperity. These people have not been trained to access the opportunities that still exist in America, but are instead depending on their leaders to do everything for them.

12     Conservatives believe that the great majority of people are capable. We have more faith in the individual human spirit than liberals do. Liberals provide excuses for people to fail, which is shameful, because America is not about failure and misery and mediocrity. There's room for everyone to make it here. One man's success is not another's failure. The American Dream still works.

13     I know, because I've lived it. I am not a theoretician. I use my own life as an example. I'm nothing special. I practiced certain kinds of values. I worked hard. The worst thing you can do is believe that the deck is stacked against you and that success based on your own efforts is impossible.

14     Unfortunately, I believe that is largely the message being sent out by the civil rights establishment. Too many young black people are getting the idea that they are going to get shafted, no matter what. The liberal establishment instills in blacks the idea that they are up against insurmountable odds.

16     I agree with Professor Walter Williams of George Mason University, who says: "We have things ass-backward in America. We lionize thieves and criminals as victims of society, while at the same time villifying productivity embodied in the likes of Bill Gates (Microsoft Corporation chairman) and Henry Ford as the rich! We constantly hear calls to those who've been most blessed to give something back'—that's nonsense! It is the thief who should be giving something back because he's produced nothing, whereas Bill Gates and his ilk have already served their fellowman by making life easier for us all and providing jobs in the process!"

16    Professor Williams has long understood this concept. Now, even some liberals seem to be catching on. For a long time now I have criticized the Rev. Jesse Jackson for celebrating victimhood rather than championing excellence and personal responsibility. But in 1993 a new Jackson emerged—or maybe it was the old Jackson whom many of us had forgotten.

17    During the 1960s and 1970s, Jackson had a great message for young people. He emphasized self-esteem, hard work, pride in oneself, and self-reliance. But something happened to that message in the 1980s. Jackson retreated from his "up with hope, down with dope" theme, as he became a predictable ultra-liberal who mortgaged his soul to the Democratic Party.

18    The onetime pro-life clergyman became an outspoken advocate of abortion on demand. The message of self-reliance was drowned out by demands for more welfare and other government-dependency programs. Preaching personal responsibility took a backseat to extortionist demands of government and corporations.

19    In 1992, however, presidential candidate Bill Clinton made a calculated decision that he didn't need or want Jackson on his side. This was best illustrated when Clinton publicly rebuked rapper Sister Souljah at a speech to members of the National Rainbow Coalition. Clinton abandoned Jackson in an attempt to woo Southern white conservatives who had long ago defected from the Democratic Party.

20    With Clinton in power, Jackson faded from view. He made some futile efforts to capitalize on issues like the HIV-infected Haitian immigrants and statehood for the District of Columbia. But it was more difficult than ever for Jackson to regain popularity. Jackson also saw others eclipsing him within the black movement.

21    In 1993, Jackson found it was getting difficult to compete in this unfamiliar environment. Thus, he is giving signs—fleeting though they may be—of returning to his roots. He not only sounds like the old Jesse Jackson, he sounds like me! He's talking about the same conservative principles and values that I am always discussing—personal responsibility, self-reliance, pride, and true self-esteem based on achievement.

22    Dr. Tom Sowell says much the same thing: "In many ways, blacks were more successful in overcoming the opposition of racists than in overcoming the effects of those who thought they were helping. Perhaps the most dangerous 'favor' done to blacks has been the making of excuses for all their problems. All human beings are so imperfect, no matter what color wrapping they come in, that to exempt any group from standards of performance and behavior is not a blessing but a curse." I can only add, Amen!

23    We all need to hear the message of personal responsibility, self-reliance, and honesty that you once preached, Reverend Jackson. This is a message for all Americans. Becoming the best we can be is the challenge. Let's stop exaggerating about the roadblocks to success in this country and start inculcating our citizens with confidence and the tools to succeed.

24    Liberals need to stop preaching class and racial hatred. They need to quit promoting the politics of hatred and alienation. We are all, first and foremost, Americans. We want to remove artificial barriers to anyone's improvement, many of which reside in the politics of class envy and government dependency. In this melting pot, all Americans can achieve if we can just overcome this nagging obsession with skin colors and religious denominations and be mindful of the truism that all human beings are equal in the eyes of God.

## Theme

1. Limbaugh argues against "dependency." In your own words summarize what he means by this key term, analyzing some of the examples he uses to illustrate the meaning of the word.

2. Limbaugh discusses the Reverend Jesse Jackson at some length. What does Jackson seem to exemplify for Limbaugh? Is it only one thing? Explain with examples.

## Technique

1. Limbaugh points to several African-American men as examples, and though he does not mention his race, Professor Walter Williams is one of them. Do you see Limbaugh's silence on this point as an advantage or a disadvantage to his argument? Explain your reasoning.

2. Limbaugh begins and ends his essay with the topic of racism. In your view, could his first and last paragraphs be justifiably switched without disadvantage, or does the present last paragraph make a better conclusion for the essay ? Explain your answer.

## Writing

Read in Chapter 5 the essay by the Reverend Jesse Jackson that begins on page 187. Now write an essay in which you explain whether Rush Limbaugh would approve or disapprove of the stances Jackson takes there, pointing to examples from both writers to justify your view.

# Jane Fonda

## Use the Media for Public Health!

*From a family of actors that includes her father Henry and her brother Peter, Jane Fonda combined her movie career in the 1970s with a famous (or notorious) opposition to the Vietnam War, making a highly publicized trip to Hanoi while the war was still going on. Though she retired from film and married media mogul Ted Turner, she continued her role in public advocacy. She has since divorced Turner, but her public service continues under the umbrella agency, Fonda, Inc.*

1     Public health will be a meaningless term unless it can truly be put across to the public. Over and above the doctor-patient relationship—of crucial importance itself, of course—a whole range of issues at present impinge on the health of people everywhere on our planet. Lifestyle decisions have to be made by individuals on such health-related issues as whether or not to smoke, whether or not to start a family, whether or not to practice safe sex.

2     Certainly, the first impact is on the individual, but these issues today are global in their consequences. The doctor in the surgery, the midwife in the maternity clinic, the nurse in the ward can do only so much to inform and educate the persons fleetingly in their charge. But to ensure that the vital health messages of our time reach people in urban slums or in remote villages calls for an effort beyond the capability of the hard-working health professionals. Yet the media—press, radio and television—are still rarely used by the health profession in general to transmit key messages—about the catastrophic effects of smoking, about the need for simple hygiene before and after childbirth, about the options available to both men and women to ensure that every child born is a wanted child.

SOURCE: By permission of Jane Fonda.

3    In many countries, family planning services are available. Yet many women do not turn to them, perhaps because local tradition urges them to have large families, or for status or cultural reasons, or because their partners forbid them to use contraception. All the medical services in the world will not overcome these barriers to improved health for women, children, and families as a whole.

4    But more than a decade of research has shown that the mass media, properly used, can indeed alter behaviour and cultural norms in ways that have an impact on health, gender bias, and literacy. In 1994, the International Conference on Population and Development, in Cairo, called upon countries to mobilize their mass media so as to educate their audiences about health matters, reproductive behaviour, and gender roles.

5    One significant example of what can be done occurred in Mexico in the 1970s when a "soap opera" which dealt boldly with such subjects as unwanted pregnancies became very popular among viewers, and was found to have contributed significantly to a 33% increase in new registrations at family planning clinics and a 23% increase in contraceptive sales over a 12-month period.

6    A similar radio and television series in Kenya, broadcast from 1987 to 1989, attracted the largest audience in that country's history and coincided with a 58% increase in contraceptive use and a decline in desired family size from 6.3 to 4.4 children per woman. When the broadcasts started, the programme could not talk directly about family planning because of local cultural constraints. Instead the producers focused on land issues and family health. The storyline showed an old man with four wives whose life was a mess; his land could not produce enough food for all his children and he could not afford to send them to school. But another family was shown—small, monogamous, and happy—which was much better able to offer the children a brighter future. The contrast was clear without the need even to mention family planning.

7    In 1984, Doordarshan Indian television screened a "soap opera" called Hum Log ("We people") whose attractive storyline promoted a higher status for women and popularized family planning. Research showed that, over a 17-month period,

70% of viewers had learnt that women ought to have the right to make personal decisions and that smaller families are happier ones. Although the show did not invite viewers to write in, no fewer than 400,000 letters flooded the studios.

8     Radio serials have also been used very effectively to convey health messages. In the remote villages of many countries, radio is still the only channel for mass communication. Moreover, in cultures where it is difficult to talk openly about sensitive issues such as birth control or sex education, radio call-in shows offer a way to have questions answered anonymously—but publicly. There is a knock-on effect too for such radio or TV shows: they frequently embolden newspaper editors to embark on hitherto taboo issues and to air them in public.

9     We need the media today (in rich countries as well as poor) to serve as a channel to inform a growing public about healthy practices and sensible lifestyles, as well as the importance of education and equality for girls.

## Theme

1. According to Fonda, why is it necessary for private individuals to be aware of and support public health?

2. Again according to Fonda, what part does the media need to play in the public/private dynamic of health care?

## Technique

1. In grammatical terms, Fonda's title employs the imperative mood of the verb "to use"—that is, the title makes a command. But what does the command command? In other words, what does the essay as a whole tell us we are to use the media for? Fill out Fonda's title with words of your own to express your idea of her overall theme. Surely such a title would not be, say: "Use the Media for Entertainment!" What would a fuller, yet still appropriate title be?

2. Are you familiar with the term "knock-on" that appears in paragraph eight? What meaning does her context suggest that the term has for her?

## Writing

Write an essay in which you extend Fonda's argument in favor of using popular culture for educational purposes. What media besides soap operas would you employ and what would be the goal of your campaign?

# Rudolph Giuliani

## The Big Apple's Big Blowup                    (1998)

*A lifetime New Yorker, Rudolph Giuliani was born in Brooklyn and majored in political science and philosophy at Manhattan College, where he graduated magna cum laude. After law school at NYU, he became first a United States District Attorney and later mayor of the city, serving at the time of the attacks on the World Trade Center. During his term in office he attempted several reforms and reorganizations in city government, and the following essay is representative of his willingness to undertake unpopular tasks.*

1   The City University of New York system is in need of even more reform than the (New York) public school system and has made no progress in establishing standards. In fact, CUNY's standards are declining.

2   Only 32 percent of incoming freshmen at CUNY senior colleges pass the basic CUNY skills test in math and writing and reading.

3   Sadly, only 14 percent of incoming freshmen at CUNY community colleges pass these three tests. These tests are geared to the 10th and 11th grade education standard.

4   That means almost 68 percent of incoming freshmen at CUNY senior colleges and 86 percent of incoming freshmen at CUNY community colleges can't read, write or do math at the 11th grade level.

5   And after what should be a higher education, these students show little progress. The overall graduation rate for the two-year community colleges is approximately 1 percent in two years. The overall graduation rate for the four-year colleges is now less than 9 percent in four years.

6   The trend is alarming. Since 1980, the graduation rate has declined steadily. Overall, it has plummeted. In the face of

SOURCE: Reprinted with permission from *Community College Week,* ccweek.com.

this continued and relentless decline, those who were running the system did nothing—not a single thing—to reverse the obliteration of standards not only of excellence, but of any standards at all.

7　Unless we act now, we must realize that this will have disastrous consequences for the future of the city.

8　Open enrollment is a mistake. It should be changed. Its consequences have been cruel. It has created in CUNY students false expectations, which the realities of life inevitably leave unfulfilled.

9　By eliminating any meaningful standards of admission and continually defining down standards for continuation, the entire meaning and value of a college education has been put in jeopardy for the many who are ready, willing, and able to meet and exceed higher standards.

10　For a college to have standards, it must first have an entrance examination that requires applicants to show that they have the basic skill and aptitude to earn a publicly subsidized higher education. And then to sustain the privilege of having others pay for substantial portions of their higher education, students must maintain good grades and meet strict attendance requirements.

11　Now, immediately, for the next entering class, the CUNY board should prescribe an entrance examination that demonstrates that applicants can meet and achieve passing grades in the basic subjects of learning. The exam should be competitive and only those with passing grades should be admitted to the limited positions available in the two-year and four-year programs. These students should be allowed to continue at these colleges only if they continue to pass examinations and meet attendance requirements.

12　The CUNY board also should now prescribe basic requirements for graduation from two- and four-year colleges. Obviously, these standards should include being able to read and write the English language. And each year for at least the next five years during this rebuilding period, the board should raise the standards for entrance and graduation.

13　In short, it should rebuild and restore the meaning of a college degree or certificate.

## Theme

1. List the principal reasons Mayor Giuliani gives in support of his contention that "open enrollment is a mistake."

2. What does Giuliani propose to do about the crisis he perceives? List the courses of action that he proposes and explain his reasoning in support of their effectiveness.

## Technique

1. Giuliani composed the text of "The Big Apple's Big Blowup" in 1998. A few years later he was highly praised by people of all political persuasions for his courage in response to the events in New York of September 11, 2001. Do you find courage to be one of the qualities expressed in his manner of writing? If so, show how it is exemplified. If not, explain your views.

2. The mayor often uses figures to bolster his point. Do you find that Giuliani uses numbers effectively in support of his argument? Explain your answer with examples.

## Writing

Where do you stand on the topic of open enrollment? Write an essay in which you attack or defend that educational policy.

# Rosie Perez

## Why Does Rosie Perez Wear the Bracelet?
### (2000)

*As an actress, Rosie Perez received an Academy Award nomination and a Golden Globe nomination for her work opposite Jeff Bridges in* Fearless. *She was discovered by Spike Lee (Chapter 6), who cast her in* Do the Right Thing. *She began a parallel career as a choreographer, working with (among others) Bobby Brown, LL Cool J (Chapter 3), and Diana Ross.*

SOURCE: By permission of Until There's a Cure Foundation.

## Theme

1. How would you describe the facial expression of Rosie Perez in the photograph? For example, she does not appear desperate, outraged, puzzled, amused—how does she seem to express herself visually? What does her expression contribute to the theme of the public service advertisement as a whole?

2. How does the text create a relation between Rosie Perez, the causes she promotes, and you yourself? How, for example, do the personal pronouns operate—"she," "you," "us?" Suppose "Rosie Perez" and "UNTIL" were substituted. What difference in tone would follow from the change?

## Technique

1. How would you describe Rosie Perez's costuming? Is it informal or casual in style? She is clearly not dressed as a dancer. She is not dressed in jeans. How is she dressed? What does the style of her outfit, jewelry, and hairstyle contribute to the visual appeal of the public service announcement?

2. The AIDS bracelet makes a major theme of the public service advertisement's verbal message. How is it featured visually? Look away from the photograph for an instant and then when you refocus on the picture, note the way your eyes move across the image. By what elements of composition are your eyes brought to focus on the bracelet?

## Writing

Write an essay that analyzes the ways the photograph of Rosie Perez contributes to the appeal made by the public service advertisement in support of UNTIL.

# Martin Luther King, Jr.

## Letter from Birmingham Jail                    (1963)

> *Martin Luther King, Jr. was born in Atlanta, Georgia, in 1929.*
> *He followed his father, Martin Luther King, Sr., into the ministry*
> *after a college education that began at the age of 15, having*
> *skipped part of high school—he was accepted at Morehouse Col-*
> *lege on the basis of his high college entrance examination scores.*
> *After college he graduated from a seminary and went on to take*
> *his doctorate at Boston University.*
>
> *As head of the Southern Christian Leadership Conference*
> *he was a pivotal figure in the civil rights movement. The essay*
> *that follows was to make him a world-famous figure, and in*
> *1964 he won the Nobel Peace Prize for his work. He died by*
> *assassination in 1968.*

*April 16, 1963*
*My Dear Fellow Clergymen:*

1    While confined here in the Birmingham city jail, I came across your recent statement calling my present activities "unwise and untimely." Seldom do I pause to answer criticism of my work and ideas. If I sought to answer all the criticisms that cross my desk, my secretaries would have little time for anything other than such correspondence in the course of the day, and I would have no time for constructive work. But since I feel that you are men of genuine good will and that your criticisms are sincerely set forth, I want to try to answer your statement in what I hope will be patient and reasonable terms.

2    I think I should indicate why I am here in Birmingham, since you have been influenced by the view which argues against "outsiders coming in." I have the honor of serving as president of the Southern Christian Leadership Conference, an organiza-

tion operating in every southern state, with headquarters in Atlanta, Georgia. We have some eighty-five affiliated organizations across the South, and one of them is the Alabama Christian Movement for Human Rights. Frequently we share staff, educational, and financial resources with our affiliates. Several months ago the affiliate here in Birmingham asked us to be on call to engage in a nonviolent direct-action program if such were deemed necessary. We readily consented, and when the hour came we lived up to our promise. So I, along with several members of my staff, am here because I was invited here. I am here because I have organizational ties here.

3      But more basically, I am in Birmingham because injustice is here. Just as the prophets of the eighth century B.C. left their villages and carried their "thus saith the Lord" far beyond the boundaries of their home towns, and just as the Apostle Paul left his village of Tarsus and carried the gospel of Jesus Christ to the far corners of the Greco-Roman world, so am I compelled to carry the gospel of freedom beyond my own home town. Like Paul, I must constantly respond to the Macedonian call for aid.

4      Moreover, I am cognizant of the interrelatedness of all communities and states. I cannot sit idly by in Atlanta and not be concerned about what happens in Birmingham. Injustice anywhere is a threat to justice everywhere. We are caught in an inescapable network of mutuality, tied in a single garment of destiny. Whatever affects one directly, affects all indirectly. Never again can we afford to live with the narrow, provincial "outside agitator" idea. Anyone who lives inside the United States can never be considered an outsider anywhere within its bounds.

5      You deplore the demonstrations taking place in Birmingham. But your statement, I am sorry to say, fails to express a similar concern for the conditions that brought about the demonstrations. I am sure that none of you would want to rest content with the superficial kind of social analysis that deals merely with effects and does not grapple with underlying causes. It is unfortunate that demonstrations are taking place in Birmingham, but it is even more unfortunate that the city's white power structure left the Negro community with no alternative.

6      In any nonviolent campaign there are four basic steps: collection of the facts to determine whether injustices exist; negotia-

tion; self-purification; and direct action. We have gone through all these steps in Birmingham. There can be no gainsaying the fact that racial injustice engulfs this community. Birmingham is probably the most thoroughly segregated city in the United States. Its ugly record of brutality is widely known. Negroes have experienced grossly unjust treatment in the courts. There have been more unsolved bombings of Negro homes and churches in Birmingham than in any other city in the nation. These are the hard, brutal facts of the case. On the basis of these conditions, Negro leaders sought to negotiate with the city fathers. But the latter consistently refused to engage in good-faith negotiation.

7      Then, last September, came the opportunity to talk with leaders of Birmingham's economic community. In the course of the negotiations, certain promises were made by the merchants—for example, to remove the stores' humiliating racial signs. On the basis of these promises, the Reverend Fred Shuttlesworth and the leaders of the Alabama Christian Movement for Human Rights agreed to a moratorium on all demonstrations. As the weeks and months went by, we realized that we were the victims of a broken promise. A few signs, briefly removed, returned; the others remained.

8      As in so many past experiences, our hopes had been blasted, and the shadow of deep disappointment settled upon us. We had no alternative except to prepare for direct action, whereby we would present our very bodies as a means of laying our case before the conscience of the local and the national community. Mindful of the difficulties involved, we decided to undertake a process of self-purification. We began a series of workshops on nonviolence, and we repeatedly asked ourselves: "Are you able to accept blows without retaliating?" "Are you able to endure the ordeal of jail?" We decided to schedule our direct-action program for the Easter season, realizing that except for Christmas, this is the main shopping period of the year. Knowing that a strong economic-withdrawal program would be the by-product of direct action, we felt that this would be the best time to bring pressure to bear on the merchants for the needed change.

9      Then it occurred to us that Birmingham's mayoralty election was coming up in March, and we speedily decided to postpone

action until after election day. When we discovered that the Commissioner of Public Safety, Eugene "Bull" Connor, had piled up enough votes to be in the run-off, we decided again to postpone action until the day after the run-off so that the demonstrations could not be used to cloud the issues. Like many others, we waited to see Mr. Connor defeated, and to this end we endured postponement after postponement. Having aided in this community need, we felt that our direct-action program could be delayed no longer.

10      You may well ask: "Why direct action? Why sit-ins, marches, and so forth? Isn't negotiation a better path?" You are quite right in calling for negotiation. Indeed, this is the very purpose of direct action. Nonviolent direct action seeks to create such a crisis and foster such a tension that a community which has constantly refused to negotiate is forced to confront the issue. It seeks so to dramatize the issue that it can no longer be ignored. My citing the creation of tension as part of the work of the nonviolent resister may sound rather shocking. But I must confess that I am not afraid of the word "tension." I have earnestly opposed violent tension, but there is a type of constructive, nonviolent tension which is necessary for growth. Just as Socrates felt that it was necessary to create a tension in the mind so that individuals could rise from the bondage of myths and half-truths to the unfettered realm of creative analysis and objective appraisal, so must we see the need for nonviolent gadflies to create the kind of tension in society that will help men rise from the dark depths of prejudice and racism to the majestic heights of understanding and brotherhood.

11      The purpose of our direct-action program is to create a situation so crisis-packed that it will inevitably open the door to negotiation. I therefore concur with you in your call for negotiation. Too long has our beloved Southland been bogged down in a tragic effort to live in monologue rather than dialogue.

12      One of the basic points in your statement is that the action that I and my associates have taken in Birmingham is untimely. Some have asked: "Why didn't you give the new city administration time to act?" The only answer that I can give to this query is that the new Birmingham administration must be prodded about as much as the outgoing one, before it will act. We are sadly mistaken if we feel that the election of Albert Boutwell as

mayor will bring the millennium to Birmingham. While Mr. Boutwell is a much more gentle person than Mr. Connor, they are both segregationists, dedicated to maintenance of the status quo. I have hope that Mr. Boutwell will be reasonable enough to see the futility of massive resistance to desegregation. But he will not see this without pressure from devotees of civil rights. My friends, I must say to you that we have not made a single gain in civil rights without determined legal and nonviolent pressure. Lamentably, it is an historical fact that privileged groups seldom give up their privileges voluntarily. Individuals may see the moral light and voluntarily give up their unjust posture; but, as Reinhold Niebuhr has reminded us, groups tend to be more immoral than individuals.

13    We know through painful experience that freedom is never voluntarily given by the oppressor; it must be demanded by the oppressed. Frankly, I have yet to engage in a direct-action campaign that was "well timed" in the view of those who have not suffered unduly from the disease of segregation. For years now I have heard the word "Wait!" It rings in the ear of every Negro with piercing familiarity. This "Wait" has almost always meant "Never." We must come to see, with one of our distinguished jurists, that "justice too long delayed is justice denied."

14    We have waited for more than 340 years for our constitutional and God-given rights. The nations of Asia and Africa are moving with jetlike speed toward gaining political independence, but we still creep at horse-and-buggy pace toward gaining a cup of coffee at a lunch counter. Perhaps it is easy for those who have never felt the stinging darts of segregation to say, "Wait." But when you have seen vicious mobs lynch your mothers and fathers at will and drown your sisters and brothers at whim; when you have seen hate-filled policemen curse, kick, and even kill your black brothers and sisters; when you see the vast majority of your twenty million Negro brothers smothering in an airtight cage of poverty in the midst of an affluent society; when you suddenly find your tongue twisted and your speech stammering as you seek to explain to your six-year-old daughter why she can't go to the public amusement park that has just been advertised on television, and see tears welling up in her eyes when she is told that Funtown is closed to colored children, and see ominous clouds of inferiority beginning to form in her little

mental sky, and see her beginning to distort her personality by developing an unconscious bitterness toward white people; when you have to concoct an answer for a five-year-old son who is asking: "Daddy, why do white people treat colored people so mean?"; when you take a cross-country drive and find it necessary to sleep night after night in the uncomfortable corners of your automobile because no motel will accept you; when you are humiliated day in and day out by nagging signs reading "white" and "colored"; when your first name becomes "nigger," your middle name becomes "boy" (however old you are) and your last name becomes "John," and your wife and mother are never given the respected title "Mrs."; when you are harried by day and haunted by night by the fact that you are a Negro, living constantly at tiptoe stance, never quite knowing what to expect next, and are plagued with inner fears and outer resentments; when you are forever fighting a degenerating sense of "nobodiness"—then you will understand why we find it difficult to wait. There comes a time when the cup of endurance runs over, and men are no longer willing to be plunged into the abyss of despair. I hope, sirs, you can understand our legitimate and unavoidable impatience.

15    You express a great deal of anxiety over our willingness to break laws. This is certainly a legitimate concern. Since we so diligently urge people to obey the Supreme Court's decision of 1954 outlawing segregation in the public schools, at first glance it may seem rather paradoxical for us consciously to break laws. One may well ask: "How can you advocate breaking some laws and obeying others?" The answer lies in the fact that there are two types of laws: just and unjust. I would be the first to advocate obeying just laws. One has not only a legal but a moral responsibility to obey just laws. Conversely, one has a moral responsibility to disobey unjust laws. I would agree with St. Augustine that "an unjust law is no law at all."

16    Now, what is the difference between the two? How does one determine whether a law is just or unjust? A just law is a man-made code that squares with the moral law or the law of God. An unjust law is a code that is out of harmony with the moral law. To put it in the terms of St. Thomas Aquinas: An unjust law is a human law that is not rooted in eternal law and natural law. Any law that uplifts human personality is just. Any

law that degrades human personality is unjust. All segregation statutes are unjust because segregation distorts the soul and damages the personality. It gives the segregator a false sense of superiority and the segregated a false sense of inferiority. Segregation, to use the terminology of the Jewish philosopher Martin Buber, substitutes an "I-it" relationship for an "I-thou" relationship and ends up relegating persons to the status of things. Hence segregation is not only politically, economically, and sociologically unsound, it is morally wrong and sinful. Paul Tillich has said that sin is separation. Is not segregation an existential expression of man's tragic separation, his awful estrangement, his terrible sinfulness? Thus it is that I can urge men to obey the 1954 decision of the Supreme Court, for it is morally right; and I can urge them to disobey segregation ordinances, for they are morally wrong.

17    Let us consider a more concrete example of just and unjust laws. An unjust law is a code that a numerical or power majority group compels a minority group to obey but does not make binding on itself. This is *difference* made legal. By the same token, a just law is a code that a majority compels a minority to follow and that it is willing to follow itself. This is *sameness* made legal.

18    Let me give another explanation. A law is unjust if it is inflicted on a minority that, as a result of being denied the right to vote, had no part in enacting or devising the law. Who can say that the legislature of Alabama which set up that state's segregation laws was democratically elected? Throughout Alabama all sorts of devious methods are used to prevent Negroes from becoming registered voters, and there are some counties in which, even though Negroes constitute a majority of the population, not a single Negro is registered. Can any law enacted under such circumstances be considered democratically structured?

19    Sometimes a law is just on its face and unjust in its application. For instance, I have been arrested on a charge of parading without a permit. Now, there is nothing wrong in having an ordinance which requires a permit for a parade. But such an ordinance becomes unjust when it is used to maintain segregation and to deny citizens the First-Amendment privilege of peaceful assembly and protest.

20    I hope you are able to see the distinction I am trying to point out. In no sense do I advocate evading or defying the law, as

would the rabid segregationist. That would lead to anarchy. One who breaks an unjust law must do so openly, lovingly, and with a willingness to accept the penalty. I submit that an individual who breaks a law that conscience tells him is unjust, and who willingly accepts the penalty of imprisonment in order to arouse the conscience of the community over its injustice, is in reality expressing the highest respect for law.

21     Of course, there is nothing new about this kind of civil disobedience. It was evidenced sublimely in the refusal of Shadrach, Meshach, and Abednego to obey the laws of Nebuchadnezzar, on the ground that a higher moral law was at stake. It was practiced superbly by the early Christians, who were willing to face hungry lions and the excruciating pain of chopping blocks rather than submit to certain unjust laws of the Roman Empire. To a degree, academic freedom is a reality today because Socrates practiced civil disobedience. In our own nation, the Boston Tea Party represented a massive act of civil disobedience.

22     We should never forget that everything Adolf Hitler did in Germany was "legal" and everything the Hungarian freedom fighters did in Hungary was "illegal." It was "illegal" to aid and comfort a Jew in Hitler's Germany. Even so, I am sure that, had I lived in Germany at the time, I would have aided and comforted my Jewish brothers. If today I lived in a Communist country where certain principles dear to the Christian faith are suppressed, I would openly advocate disobeying that country's antireligious laws.

23     I must make two honest confessions to you, my Christian and Jewish brothers. First, I must confess that over the past few years I have been gravely disappointed with the white moderate. I have almost reached the regrettable conclusion that the Negro's great stumbling block in his stride toward freedom is not the White Citizen's Counciler or the Ku Klux Klanner, but the white moderate, who is more devoted to "order" than to justice; who prefers a negative peace which is the absence of tension to a positive peace which is the presence of justice; who constantly says: "I agree with you in the goal you seek, but I cannot agree with your methods of direct action"; who paternalistically believes he can set the timetable for another man's freedom; who lives by a mythical concept of time and

who constantly advises the Negro to wait for a "more convenient season." Shallow understanding from people of good will is more frustrating than absolute misunderstanding from people of ill will. Lukewarm acceptance is much more bewildering than outright rejection.

24    I had hoped that the white moderate would understand that law and order exist for the purpose of establishing justice and that when they fail in this purpose they become the dangerously structured dams that block the flow of social progress. I had hoped that the white moderate would understand that the present tension in the South is a necessary phase of the transition from an obnoxious negative peace, in which the Negro passively accepted his unjust plight, to a substantive and positive peace, in which all men will respect the dignity and worth of human personality. Actually, we who engage in nonviolent direct action are not the creators of tension. We merely bring to the surface the hidden tension that is already alive. We bring it out in the open, where it can be seen and dealt with. Like a boil that can never be cured so long as it is covered up but must be opened with all its ugliness to the natural medicines of air and light, injustice must be exposed, with all the tension its exposure creates, to the light of human conscience and the air of national opinion before it can be cured.

25    In your statement you assert that our actions, even though peaceful, must be condemned because they precipitate violence. But is this a logical assertion? Isn't this like condemning a robbed man because his possession of money precipitated the evil act of robbery? Isn't this like condemning Socrates because his unswerving commitment to truth and his philosophical inquiries precipitated the act by the misguided populace in which they made him drink hemlock? Isn't this like condemning Jesus because his unique God-consciousness and never-ceasing devotion to God's will precipitated the evil act of crucifixion? We must come to see that, as the federal courts have consistently affirmed, it is wrong to urge an individual to cease his efforts to gain his basic constitutional rights because the quest may precipitate violence. Society must protect the robbed and punish the robber.

26    I had also hoped that the white moderate would reject the myth concerning time in relation to the struggle for freedom. I

have just received a letter from a white brother in Texas. He writes: "All Christians know that the colored people will receive equal rights eventually, but it is possible that you are in too great a religious hurry. It has taken Christianity almost two thousand years to accomplish what it has. The teachings of Christ take time to come to earth." Such an attitude stems from a tragic misconception of time, from the strangely irrational notion that there is something in the very flow of time that will inevitably cure all ills. Actually, time itself is neutral; it can be used either destructively or constructively. More and more I feel that the people of ill will have used time much more effectively than have the people of good will. We will have to repent in this generation not merely for the hateful words and actions of the bad people but for the appalling silence of the good people. Human progress never rolls in on wheels of inevitability; it comes through the tireless efforts of men willing to be coworkers with God, and without this hard work, time itself becomes an ally of the forces of social stagnation. We must use time creatively, in the knowledge that the time is always ripe to do right. Now is the time to make real the promise of democracy and transform our pending national elegy into a creative psalm of brotherhood. Now is the time to lift our national policy from the quicksand of racial injustice to the solid rock of human dignity.

27      You speak of our activity in Birmingham as extreme. At first I was rather disappointed that fellow clergymen would see my nonviolent efforts as those of an extremist. I began thinking about the fact that I stand in the middle of two opposing forces in the Negro community. One is a force of complacency, made up in part of Negroes who, as a result of long years of oppression, are so drained of self-respect and a sense of "somebodiness" that they have adjusted to segregation; and in part of a few middle-class Negroes who, because of a degree of academic and economic security and because in some ways they profit by segregation, have become insensitive to the problems of masses. The other force is one of bitterness and hatred, and it comes perilously close to advocating violence. It is expressed in the various black nationalist groups that are springing up across the nation, the largest and best-known being Elijah Muhammad's Muslim movement. Nourished by the Negro's frustration over the

continued existence of racial discrimination, this movement is made up of people who have lost faith in America, who have absolutely repudiated Christianity, and who have concluded that the white man is an incorrigible "devil."

28    I have tried to stand between these two forces, saying that we need emulate neither the "do-nothingism" of the complacent nor the hatred and despair of the black nationalist. For there is the more excellent way of love and nonviolent protest. I am grateful to God that, through the influence of the Negro church, the way of nonviolence became an integral part of our struggle.

29    If this philosophy had not emerged, by now many streets of the South would, I am convinced, be flowing with blood. And I am further convinced that if our white brothers dismiss as "rabble-rousers" and "outside agitators" those of us who employ nonviolent direct action, and if they refuse to support our nonviolent efforts, millions of Negroes will, out of frustration and despair, seek solace and security in black-nationalist ideologies—a development that would inevitably lead to a frightening racial nightmare.

30    Oppressed people cannot remain oppressed forever. The yearning for freedom eventually manifests itself, and that is what has happened to the American Negro. Something within has reminded him of his birthright of freedom, and something without has reminded him that it can be gained. Consciously or unconsciously, he has been caught up by the *Zeitgeist,* and with his black brothers of Africa and his brown and yellow brothers of Asia, South America and the Caribbean, the United States Negro is moving with a sense of great urgency toward the promised land of racial justice. If one recognizes this vital urge that has engulfed the Negro community, one should readily understand why public demonstrations are taking place. The Negro has many pent-up resentments and latent frustrations, and he must release them. So let him march; let him make prayer pilgrimages to the city hall; let him go on freedom rides—and try to understand why he must do so. If his repressed emotions are not released in nonviolent ways, they will seek expression through violence; this is not a threat but a fact of history. So I have not said to my people: "Get rid of your discontent." Rather, I have tried to say that this normal

and healthy discontent can be channeled into the creative out-
let of nonviolent direct action. And now this approach is being
termed extremist.

31    But though I was initially disappointed at being categorized
as an extremist, as I continued to think about the matter I gradually gained a measure of satisfaction from the label. Was not
Jesus an extremist for love: "Love your enemies, bless them that
curse you, do good to them that hate you, and pray for them
which despitefully use you, and persecute you." Was not Amos
an extremist for justice: "Let justice roll down like waters and
righteousness like an ever-flowing stream." Was not Paul an
extremist for the Christian gospel: "I bear in my body the marks
of the Lord Jesus." Was not Martin Luther an extremist: "Here I
stand; I cannot do otherwise, so help me God." And John Bun-
yan: "I will stay in jail to the end of my days before I make a
butchery of my conscience." And Abraham Lincoln: "This nation
cannot survive half slave and half free." And Thomas Jefferson:
"We hold these truths to be self-evident, that an men are created equal..." So the question is not whether we will be extremists, but what kind of extremists we will be. Will we be
extremists for hate or for love? Will we be extremist for the
preservation of injustice or for the extension of justice? In that
dramatic scene on Calvary's hill three men were crucified. We
must never forget that all three were crucified for the same
crime—the crime of extremism. Two were extremists for
immorality, and thus fell below their environment. The other,
Jeans Christ, was an extremist for love, truth and goodness, and
thereby rose above his environment. Perhaps the South, the
nation and the world are in dire need of creative extremists.

32    I had hoped that the white moderate would see this need.
Perhaps I was too optimistic; perhaps I expected too much. I
suppose I should have realized that few members of the
oppressor race can understand the deep groans and passionate yearnings of the oppressed race, and still fewer have the
vision to see that injustice must be rooted out by strong, per-
sistent and determined action. I am thankful, however, that
some of our white brothers in the South have grasped the
meaning of this social revolution and committed themselves to
it. They are still too few in quantity, but they are big in qual-

ity. Some—such as Ralph McGill, Lillian Smith, Harry Golden, James McBride Dabbs, Ann Braden and Sarah Patton Boyle—have written about our struggle in eloquent and prophetic terms. Others have marched with us down nameless streets of the South. They have languished in filthy, roach-infested jails, suffering the abuse and brutality of policemen who view them as "dirty nigger lovers." Unlike so many of their moderate brothers and sisters, they have recognized the urgency of the moment and sensed the need for powerful "action" antidotes to combat the disease of segregation.

33    Let me take note of my other major disappointment. I have been so greatly disappointed with the white church and its leadership. Of course, there are some notable exceptions. I am not unmindful of the fact that each of you has taken some significant stands on this issue. I commend you, Reverend Stallings, for your Christian stand on this past Sunday, in welcoming Negroes to your worship service on a non segregated basis. I commend the Catholic leaders of this state for integrating Spring Hill College several years ago.

34    But despite these notable exceptions, I must honestly reiterate that I have been disappointed with the church. I do not say this as one of those negative critics who can always find something wrong with the church. I say this as a minister of the gospel, who loves the church; who was nurtured in its bosom; who 'has been sustained by its spiritual blessings and who will remain true to it as long as the cord of Rio shall lengthen.

35    When I was suddenly catapulted into the leadership of the bus protest in Montgomery, Alabama, a few years ago, I felt we would be supported by the white church felt that the white ministers, priests and rabbis of the South would be among our strongest allies. Instead, some have been outright opponents, refusing to understand the freedom movement and misrepresenting its leader era; and too many others have been more cautious than courageous and have remained silent behind the anesthetizing security of stained-glass windows.

36    In spite of my shattered dreams, I came to Birmingham with the hope that the white religious leadership of this community would see the justice of our cause and, with deep moral concern, would serve as the channel through which our just grievances

could reach the power structure. I had hoped that each of you would understand. But again I have been disappointed.

37     I have heard numerous southern religious leaders admonish their worshipers to comply with a desegregation decision because it is the law, but I have longed to hear white ministers declare: "Follow this decree because integration is morally right and because the Negro is your brother." In the midst of blatant injustices inflicted upon the Negro, I have watched white churchmen stand on the sideline and mouth pious, irrelevancies and sanctimonious trivialities. In the midst of a mighty struggle to rid our nation of racial and economic injustice, I have heard many ministers say: "Those are social issues, with which the gospel has no real concern." And I have watched many churches commit themselves to a completely other worldly religion which makes a strange, on Biblical distinction between body and soul, between the sacred and the secular.

38     I have traveled the length and breadth of Alabama, Mississippi and all the other southern states. On sweltering summer days and crisp autumn mornings I have looked at the South's beautiful churches with their lofty spires pointing heavenward. I have beheld the impressive outlines of her massive religious-education buildings. Over and over I have found myself asking: "What kind of people worship here? Who is their God? Where were their voices when the lips of Governor Barnett dripped with words of interposition and nullification? Where were they when Governor Wallace gave a clarion call for defiance and hatred? Where were their voices of support when bruised and weary Negro men and women decided to rise from the dark dungeons of complacency to the bright hills of creative protest?"

39     Yes, these questions are still in my mind. In deep disappointment I have wept over the laxity of the church. But be assured that my tears have been tears of love. There can be no deep disappointment where there is not deep love. Yes, I love the church. How could I do otherwise? I am in the rather unique position of being the son, the grandson, and the great-grandson of preachers. Yes, I see the church as the body of Christ. But, oh! How we have blemished and scarred that body through social neglect and through fear of being nonconformists.

40    There was a time when the church was very powerful—in the time when the early Christians rejoiced at being deemed worthy to suffer for what they believed. In those days the church was not merely a thermometer that recorded the ideas and principles of popular opinion; it was a thermostat that transformed the mores of society. Whenever the early Christians entered a town, the people in power became disturbed and immediately sought to convict the Christians for being "disturbers of the peace" and "outside agitators." But the Christians pressed on, in the conviction that they were "a colony of heaven," called to obey God rather than man. Small in number, they were big in commitment. They were too God-intoxicated to be "astronomically intimidated." By their effort and example they brought an end to such ancient evils as infanticide and gladiatorial contests.

41    Things are different now. So often the contemporary church is a weak, ineffectual voice with an uncertain sound. So often it is an archdefender of the status quo. Far from being disturbed by the presence of the church, the power structure of the average community is consoled by the church's silent—and often even vocal—sanction of things as they are.

42    But the judgment of God is upon the church as never before. If today's church does not recapture the sacrificial spirit of the early church, it will lose its authenticity, forfeit the loyalty of millions, and be dismissed as an irrelevant social club with no meaning for the twentieth century. Every day I meet young people whose disappointment with the church has turned into outright disgust.

43    Perhaps I have once again been too optimistic. Is organized religion too inextricably bound to the status quo to save our nation and the world? Perhaps I must turn my faith to the inner spiritual church, the church within the church, as the true *ekklesia* and the hope of the world. But again I am thankful to God that some noble souls from the ranks of organized religion have broken loose from the paralyzing chains of conformity and joined us as active partners in the struggle for freedom. They have left their secure congregations and walked the streets of Albany, Georgia, with us. They have gone down the highways of the South on tortuous rides for freedom. Yes,

they have gone to jail with us. Some have been dismissed from their churches, have lost the support of their bishops and fellow ministers. But they have acted in the faith that right defeated is stronger than evil triumphant. Their witness has been the spiritual salt that has preserved the true meaning of the gospel in these troubled times. They have carved a tunnel of hope through the dark mountain of disappointment.

44     I hope the church as a whole will meet the challenge of this decisive hour. But even if the church does not come to the aid of justice, I have no despair about the future. I have no fear about the outcome of our struggle in Birmingham, even if our motives are at present misunderstood. We will reach the goal of freedom in Birmingham and all over the nation, because the goal of America is freedom. Abused and scorned though we may be, our destiny is tied up with America's destiny. Before the pilgrims landed at Plymouth, we were here. Before the pen of Jefferson etched the majestic words of the Declaration of Independence across the pages of history, we were here. For more than two centuries our forebears labored in this country without wages; they made cotton king; they built the homes of their masters while suffering gross injustice and shameful humiliation—and yet out of a bottomless vitality they continued to thrive and develop. If the inexpressible cruelties of slavery could not stop us, the opposition we now face will surely fail. We will win our freedom because the sacred heritage of our nation and the eternal will of God are embodied in our echoing demands.

45     Before closing I feel impelled to mention one other point in your statement that has troubled me profoundly. You warmly commended the Birmingham police force for keeping "order" and "preventing violence." I doubt that you would have so warmly commended the police force if you had seen its dogs sinking their teeth into unarmed, nonviolent Negroes. I doubt that you would so quickly commend the policemen if you were to observe their ugly and inhumane treatment of Negroes here in the city jail; if you were to watch them push and curse old Negro women and young Negro girls; if you were to see them slap and kick old Negro men and young boys; if you were to observe them, as they did on two occasions, refuse to give us

food because we wanted to sing our grace together. I cannot join you in your praise of the Birmingham police department.

46    It is true that the police have exercised a degree of discipline in handling the demonstrators. In this sense they have conducted themselves rather "nonviolently" in public. But for what purpose? To preserve the evil system of segregation. Over the past few years I have consistently preached that nonviolence demands that the means we use must be as pure as the ends we seek. I have tried to make clear that it is wrong to use immoral means to attain moral ends. But now I must affirm that it is just as wrong, or perhaps even more so, to use moral means to preserve immoral ends. Perhaps Mr. Connor and his policemen have been rather nonviolent in public, as was Chief Pritchett in Albany, Georgia, but they have used the moral means of nonviolence to maintain the immoral end of racial injustice. As T. S. Eliot has said: "The last temptation is the greatest treason: To do the right deed for the wrong reason."

47    I wish you had commended the Negro sit-inners and demonstrators of Birmingham for their sublime courage, their willingness to suffer, and their amazing discipline in the midst of great provocation. One day the South will recognize its real heroes. They will be the James Merediths, with the noble sense of purpose that enables them to face jeering and hostile mobs, and with the agonizing loneliness that characterizes the life of the pioneer. They will be old, oppressed, battered Negro women, symbolized in a seventy-two-year-old woman in Montgomery, Alabama, who rose up with a sense of dignity and with her people decided not to ride segregated buses, and who responded with ungrammatical profundity to one who inquired about her weariness: "My feets is tired, but my soul is at rest." They will be the young high school and college students, the young ministers of the gospel and a host of their elders, courageously and nonviolently sitting in at lunch counters and willingly going to jail for conscience sake. One day the South will know that when these disinherited children of God sat down at lunch counters, they were in reality standing up for what is best in the American dream and for the most sacred values in our Judaeo-Christian heritage, thereby bringing our nation back to those great wells of democracy which were dug deep by the

founding fathers in their formulation of the Constitution and the Declaration of Independence.

48    Never before have I written so long a letter. I'm afraid it is much too long to take your precious time. I can assure you that it would have been much shorter if I had been writing from a comfortable desk, but what else can one do when he is alone in a narrow jail cell, other than write long letters, think long thoughts, and pray long prayers?

49    If I have said anything in this letter that overstates the truth and indicates an unreasonable impatience, I beg you to forgive me. If I have said anything that understates the truth and indicates my having a patience that allows me to settle for anything less than brotherhood, I beg God to forgive me.

50    I hope this letter finds you strong in the faith. I also hope that circumstances will soon make it possible for me to meet each of you, not as an integrationist or a civil-rights leader but as a fellow clergyman and a Christian brother. Let us all hope that the dark clouds of racial prejudice will soon pass away and the deep fog of misunderstanding will be lifted from our fear-drenched communities, and in some not too distant tomorrow the radiant stars of love and brotherhood will shine over our great nation with all their scintillating beauty.

                    Yours for the cause of Peace and Brotherhood,
                                    Martin Luther King, Jr.

## Theme

1. In paragraph three King says that he is in Birmingham "because injustice is here." Make a list of the paragraphs that make the local injustices in Birmingham their subject. Pick one example and show how King moves from these particular issues to larger issues of more general injustice.

2. In paragraph fifteen King raises the issue of illegality and acknowledges it to be "a legitimate concern." Summarize his response to that concern in your own words.

## Technique

1. In paragraph one King announces his intention to frame his answer to his critics in "patient and reasonable terms." Pick a moment in the essay where it seems to you that more inflammatory and unreasonable terms might have been easily employed. Now show how King's writing keeps his promise.

2. The essay takes the form of a letter addressed to "fellow clergymen." Point to some moments where the argument seems most directed to that audience. Are these moments that you as a general reader are unable to understand? Explain your answer.

## Writing

Pick a moment in the essay where you think Martin Luther King, Jr. argues an aspect of his case very effectively. Write an essay that analyzes the effectiveness of the argument in terms of its appeal to emotions as well as to reason.

## EXERCISES

**Intertextual Questions**

1. Many of the writers in this chapter have strong convictions about public service. Pick three authors and discuss how they dramatize and illustrate the strength of their belief in the value of public service.

2. Rush Limbaugh and Ralph Nader both focus on the topic of governmental responsibility, but their views differ strongly, to say the least. Discuss the ways in which they differ and the reasoning each uses to make his own case about the proper relation between a government and its citizens.

3. Kareem Abdul-Jabbar writes of Amercian soldiers serving in the armed forces abroad and Angelina Jolie undertakes a peaceful mission to Ecuador, while neither Rosie Perez nor Jane Fonda limit their concerns for public health to their own country. In your view, are there or should there be any limits to public service? That is, should one's own country be taken care of first, or does that prioritization seem selfish or shortsighted to you? Discuss the issue using examples provided by the chapter.

4. What do you think of Ralph Nader's call for people to act as "public citizens"? Do you see yourself someday acting in public affairs as he urges you to do? Explain your position, being sure to take into account his argument as a whole.

5. Besides Ralph Nader, which author writes from a point of view most nearly resembling your own point of view on participation in public affairs? Discuss the reasoning behind your choice.

**Suggestions for Writing**

1. Selflessness is a theme that runs throughout the chapter in many ways. Write an essay that examines the ways some of the authors here both encourage and embody selfless qualities in their writings.

2. In his essay, Ralph Nader defines what he thinks constitutes a "public citizen"—someone who is more than a voter. Of the writers in this chapter, which do you think best fits Nader's definition? Write an essay in which you explain and support your answer.

3. Many of the authors in this chapter write from a point of view that is explicitly or implicitly founded on assumptions about the proper role and function of governmental power. To what extent do the writers share these assumptions? Pick two authors and write an essay that examines their positions on the proper role of government in a modern democracy.

4. Jane Fonda and Rosie Perez both address different aspects of health care though different modes of expression. Write an essay that examines the ways these authors create a sense of the importance of their causes for their readers and viewers.

5. Thomas Jefferson said that "the price of freedom is eternal vigilance." Yet freedom can mean many different things. For example, freedom from government dependency is not the same thing as "free and open admissions." Write an essay that examines some of the various meanings given to the concept of freedom by the authors in this chapter.

# CHAPTER **8**

# CLASSIC PERFORMERS

In this last chapter, celebrities for the most part write about the subjects they are celebrated for, rather than the subjects of earlier chapters that are relevant to all of us. Some classic performers in different fields talk about their own art or field of expertise. Those fields range from pageants to public service advertisements, from movies to Broadway, from rock and roll to American food, from baseball to Salsa. The authors represented have set many records and have won many awards; here they have a chance to show why.

Regis Philbin begins things with "True Tales of the Miss America Pageant." For decades he has been a professional host on talk shows and game shows, but in this essay he tells us what it is like to act as master of ceremonies in the oldest and largest show of its kind. This genre of mass culture has evolved from the beauty contests of simpler times, and Regis gives us a backstage insight into what it has become.

As a co-founder and long-time editor of *Ms.* magazine, Gloria Steinem is not one to favor "beauty contests," but her opposition to the advertisers of beauty products who demand editorial considerations is even stronger. Steinem takes us on a tour through some of the pressure points in magazine publishing, including the myth that "advertisers simply follow readers."

Roger Ebert is the first film critic ever to win the Pulitzer Prize. In "Steven Spielberg: The Moviemaker" Ebert reviews not a particular movie but a whole career of a man who has won many awards himself for the creative films he has made over the years. Ebert examines what filmic elements have remained stable within the wide range of Spielberg's films, what he owes to cinematic tradition, and how he has made his own innovations within that tradition.

Julia Child created the first nationally popular television cooking show with *The French Chef,* which she started for PBS. In her essay she looks back over a long lifetime and tells us about some of the changes that have taken place in American food and eating habits. Among other things, she recalls the days when an icebox was really an icebox and the melting water from the big blocks in the cooler would drain out on the back porch floorboards.

Beginning in England in the 1920s, Alfred Hitchcock made an international name for himself as "The Master of Suspense." Movies like *Psycho, Vertigo,* and *North By Northwest* are still rerun on television and studied in film courses at colleges and universities. Hitchcock loved to make movies, and the essay here—though written about one of his lesser known films, *Rope*—shows his enthusiasm for innovative techniques that he brought to the cameras over and over again.

Frank Zappa is equally enthusiastic about his own art form, rock and roll. Zappa started as a performer with the Mothers of Invention, but went on to become a rock intellectual as well, testifying before Congress on censorship issues and receiving the thanks of the president of Czechoslovakia for inspiring freedom through his music during the days of Soviet oppression. In his essay here, Zappa defends the freedom of rock and roll against the attack of the American philosopher and social critic Allan Bloom who called it a "junk food for the soul."

Celia Cruz became known as "The Queen of Salsa," and was the leading female figure in Latin music for many, many years. Her career began in Cuba, but after she fled that country's regime for the United States, she began to perform all over North and South America. Her performances extended from the days of live radio variety shows to the days of music videos, and in her autobiographical essay here, she recalls how shocked she could sometimes be by some of the changes in the music culture that she had seen.

Mel Brooks has seen many changes himself after more than half a century in comedy. Whether as a stand-up comic performing first in summer resorts and then on television, as a maker of comedy recordings, as an actor, writer, and director of movies, or now as the producer of *The Producers* on Broadway, Mel Brooks has amused America since the 1950s. Here he gives us a brief tour of his long career in mass culture by means of an essay originally published in the *New York Times,* "Springtime for the Music Man in Me."

Modern mass culture includes professional sports, and professional team sports started in the United States with baseball, the game that used to be called "the national pastime." Hank Aaron is one of the all-time greats of baseball, having broken Babe Ruth's career record for homeruns. But hitting homers was not all that was required along the way to his achievement. Racism and hate mail were unfortunately part of the story, too, as he tells us in a selection from his autobiography, *I Had a Hammer.*

The chapter closes with a visual argument by another great hitter for a cause that often includes another kind of discrimination than that suffered by Hank Aaron. Barry Bonds makes a public service advertisement in the fight against AIDS, showing another side to a famous figure.

# Regis Philbin

## True Tales of the Miss America Pageant   (1995)

*Regis Philbin was born in New York City to a father who named him after his own Catholic high school alma mater. Regis himself went on to Notre Dame before beginning his long reign as king of the "host chat show" in California. Moving east in the 1980s he came to national popularity when he was joined by co-host Kathie Lee Gifford. He has hosted everything from game shows to the Miss America Pageant, the subject of the following excerpt from his autobiography* I'm Only One Man!

1    How exactly does Miss America get crowned by a guy like me? Even I wonder sometimes. I mean, it makes sense for someone like Kathie Lee—the human sunbeam—to take part in a coronation. After all, to hear her tell it, she's coronated every night by Frank the Human Love Machine. Anyway, we have the job together—following in the footsteps of legendary emcee Bert Parks. We're now in our fourth year as co-hosts of the Miss America Pageant—the biggest, most famous contest of beauty, brains, talent, and poise anywhere. It's also one of the few annual televised events left that involves the modeling of swim suits.

2    This year's big news: For the first time in pageant history, the ladies will do the swimwear modeling in their *bare feet*! No more of those traditional high heels. And this has caused shock waves? Beautiful women without shoes? Who cares? The real shame here is that the hosts don't get to emcee shoeless. I don't want to brag, but it's no secret that I was blessed with beautiful feet. Feet are my strong suit! Kathie Lee has a halo; I have spectacular feet. Perfectly smooth. Not a bunion or a callous. I've compared them with the best and prevailed every time.

Julio Iglesias came on the show recently, wearing sandals and flaunting his handsome Latin feet. I had to remove my shoes and bring him back down to earth. Sorry, Julio. You're a nice guy and a great singer, but just keep your shoes on around me!

3      After today's show, we head for Atlantic City. I ride down there in a car alone. Kathie Lee gathers her entourage—Cassidy, the nanny, the live-in couple, the assistant—then commandeers a jet and they all fly down. That's how it goes with us: I'm the loner, out on the open road. She's flying high, with gang in tow. To prepare for the Saturday night show, we spend a good part of the day at the Convention Center, where rehearsals have been grinding on all week. Then, at dinner, we get to know the contestants, trying to put together the faces with the names with the states. As always, these girls are sweet and personable, but full of drive and huge career plans. They all desperately want to win the big scholarship prize money that comes with the crown. No timid little shrinking violets in this setting.

4      Later, we watch the final trials of the talent competition, along with Leonard Horn, the Atlantic City attorney who runs the pageant. Leanza Cornett, the incumbent Miss America, hosts these proceedings. At one point, I get up and go to the men's room. My first mistake of the weekend. Inside the bathroom, I suddenly hear Leanza's voice over the sound system: "Ladies and gentlemen, in our audience tonight are the stars of their own show and the hosts of our show for the last four years ... How about a rousing hand for REGIS AND KATHIE LEE!" At this precise moment, I'm in no position to take a bow. I'm facing a wall. I'm as indisposed as a man can be, having started something I can't stop. If you know what I mean. Meanwhile, all alone in her seat, Kathie Lee rises and drinks in all of the applause. I hear Leanza say, "Where's Regis? Where's Regis?" Then I hear Kathie Lee shout with relish: "He went to the men's room!" What a classy guy I am. This never happened to Bert Parks! I finish my business as quickly as my metabolism allows. Then I run back into the auditorium, where the show has resumed and, frankly, nobody cares whether or not I'm available to thank them for the nice hand.

5      Now for my early prediction: By now, I've gotten pretty accurate at picking winners. And tonight I immediately see

sparks coming from Miss Alabama, Heather Whitestone. She's the young woman who's been hearing-impaired since she was eighteen months old. She performs an interpretive ballet (without actually hearing the music) and the crowd reaction is wholehearted and supportive. She's clearly the favorite—all of the contestants seem very protective of her. We'll know for sure Saturday night, but I've got a feeling that she'd make a tremendous impact as Miss America.

6    Time to answer Bryant Gumbel's hard-hitting questions about the swimsuit competition. Because NBC broadcasts the pageant, we do a live on-location interview every year for the Friday morning *Today Show*. We get to do battle with Bryant, who can't wait to talk about the bare feet controversy. Please! When was the last time you saw high heels on a beach? What's the big deal? So, by eight-fifteen, Kathie Lee and I are in place at the Convention Center. We do a little tease shot at eight-thirty and then wait our turn. First, Katie Couric has to visit with a computer wizard, who never stops talking. And Katie keeps asking questions. She can't get enough of this guy. And we're still waiting. Finally, they throw it to us. We have exactly two and a half minutes! Then the Big Brush-Off! I complain: "Bryant, the computer guy was on forever! This is it for us? Come on!" And Bryant laughs and laughs and keeps saying, "Bare feet, huh?" Who cares?

7    All day, we rehearse and rehearse, working on intros and cues. I feel the anticipation heighten. Tonight, the ladies parade along the boardwalk and we sneak off to dinner. And what an unforgettable dinner it is. Gelman has finally arrived in Atlantic City. He comes down every year. Says he does it to give us support. But I know better. (It couldn't have anything to do with all of these attractive, single young women. Couldn't possibly!) Kathie Lee's parents have also come to town, as well as her secretary and Mary Kellogg, our liaison with Disney. Anyway, Kathie arranges for us to head over to a little restaurant a few blocks from Trump Plaza, where everyone is staying. "Meet us at seven-fifteen in front of the hotel," Kathie tells me. So I go down and wait. And wait.

8    People are yelling, "Hey, Regis! REGIS!" I wave back and continue to wait. Then a couple of guys come over to keep me

company. One of them wants to know if I think he looks like Dustin Hoffman. I tell him Miss New Hampshire looks more like Dustin Hoffman than he does. (And, believe me, Miss New Hampshire does *not* look like Dustin Hoffman!) Meanwhile, nobody has come down to meet me. And that's because Kathie Lee changed our plans without telling me. It turns out that they're all upstairs at the hotel in Ivana's restaurant. And there's a lovefest under way at the table that might change the course of talk-show history.

9      Maybe it's because of the wine. Maybe it's just fate. But by the time someone comes to fetch me, a miracle has occurred. The rift of the century has been defused. Kathie Lee and Gelman have officially made up—ending a long, uncomfortable war of silences and dirty looks that's become part of my daily world. For my part, I've always enjoyed the tension between them. I figure that if everybody always gets along, our audience might fall asleep. Because Gelman is the producer, he decides who is booked as a guest and who isn't. Sometimes, though, Kathie Lee has disagreed with Gelman's ideas and it eventually created an icy wall between them. The breaking point, I think, came when Gelman refused to book Art Buchwald, an old pal of the Giffords. She pushed and pushed and Gelman wouldn't cave and it seethed in her heart and just kept festering.

10      But now suddenly all is forgiven! As I sit watching this, I feel my fun ending. Gelman is actually saying, "Kathie Lee, I love you!" And she's stroking his hand and saying, "Michael, I love *you!*" It's a terrible sight. Life is about to get boring. No more arguments. No more looks. No more daggers. How dull things are going to be! Now Gelman has her enraptured with stories about his organic garden! And she's going on about the joys of having children—while Gelman smiles and nods! Is this some kind of bad dream? Can somebody just wake me up! But no. It's actually happening. I can't take any more! I don't want to be here. Finally, when I can stand no more, I call for the check, pay it, and quickly make my escape. Love is in the air and my stomach hurts.

## Saturday, September 17

11  The big day. A full day of rehearsing and nurturing my throat for the famous "There she is …" coronation song. Kenny

Rogers will also sing to the ladies tonight, performing the old hit, "You Are So Beautiful." So all day, I take every opportunity to run up behind him and impress him with my best gravelly Kenny Rogers impersonation. "You are soooo beeeyoooteeful-llll," I croon to him. At least he keeps smiling. Meanwhile, I spend as much time as I can in my dressing room, where I've got the Notre Dame game on. At halftime they're down, 20–7. But I go back to my hotel to see them win, 21–20, which gives me the strength to go on.

12    It's always interesting to experience the final moments before the show. The dancers are on the floor stretching. The judges are wide-eyed and slightly dazed. And the contestants are hopeful, pensive, and almost giddy. You get attached to these ladies. You'd like to see all of them win. Backstage, Kathie Lee and I watch the opening number. The crowd is all attention. Then, the announcer booms: "Ladies and gentlemen, your hosts for the Miss America Pageant—Regis Philbin and Kathie Lee Gifford!" I start to walk across the stage and she's heading toward me from the other side. I grab her hand and we walk together to centerstage. The contestants are flanking us, applauding—it's an exciting moment.

13    So I begin: "Hello, everybody. We're happy to be here!" And, at this exact moment, her earring slips off and falls to the floor. It's a whopper of an earring, too. Hits the stage like a boulder. She's panicked. She can't be here on live prime-time television—the most glamorous event of the season—with only one earring. Nothing else to do but get down on all fours and find it. Our big entrance—and I'm bent over on the floor like a dog! Would Bert Parks do this?

14    Anyway, I scoop it up, she clamps it back on her ear—and the pageant has officially begun! Just how difficult is it to do the Miss America show? Does the pressure get to us? Actually, after what we do day after day on our own show, the pageant is a comparative breeze. Our show is unscripted. But this night is timed to the letter. There's the teleprompter right in front of us with everything we have to say. It's quite a luxury. The competition winds down to the final ten. Then the final five. And then it's time to shut off the prompter and go to work.

15      This is my favorite part of the show—interviewing the five finalists. One question on any subject I choose and one focusing on their main interest or platform. Miss Alabama is among the finalists, of course, and I still think she'll win. But anything is possible. The ladies are visibly nervous. As it turns out, Miss Alabama is the first one I interview. I make it a point to look directly at her and not talk too fast. (At lunch yesterday, I was too fast for her. But no problem now.) She reacts beautifully and spontaneously— as do the other finalists—especially to my first question. The second question about their vital interests sometimes brings more of a rehearsed response. But you do root for them all.

16      And then that moment comes. The cards with the results are delivered to me. The first four runners-up (or is it runner-ups? We've never figured that out!), followed by the winner. There's a lot of lip-biting as they line up. And, one by one, I announce their names and states. Unfailingly they react joyfully, even as they lose. When I used to watch the show at home, I always wondered how they managed this. And standing two feet away from them, I wonder even more. Maybe it's just relief. Finally, the winner: Heather Whitestone. Miss Alabama. The crowd goes crazy. She'd been their favorite all through the preliminaries. Now it is official. A good choice, too. She's down the aisle, waving to the audience. Kathie Lee and I do our chorus of that song, and it's over for another year.

17      But the toughest part of the whole night comes after the show. How to get back to my room? The audience spills out of the Convention Center in massive herds. I'm still wearing my tux, toting a garment bag. I weave through my gauntlet of shortcuts and slip into a side door of the Trump Plaza. So far, so good. Except now Trump's elaborate system of escalators has broken down. There's a monumental crush of people at the bottom waiting for the thing to start. I'm being swarmed. There's no air. "Where's Trump?" I yell. "Get him out of bed! What good are all those millions if he can't get his damned escalators to run!" The crowd laughs. I'm getting worked up. Please! Can't a guy just get to his room and collapse! Trump must have heard me. Just when I'm sure I'll be spending the night in the lobby, the escalators start. And I go to bed.

## Theme

1. "How exactly does Miss America get crowned by a guy like me?"—so the selection begins. We see the crowning, but what kind of a guy *do* we meet? For example, he is always joking , but what kinds of jokes does he favor and what kind of a personality is thereby implied? Using evidence from the writing characterize as fully as you can the personality you find expressed here by Regis Philbin.

2. At the time of the events described in the selection, Kathie Lee Gifford was the cohost with Regis on his daily show. What kind of person does Regis describe her as being? Again using evidence from the writing, characterize as fully as you can the figure presented here.

## Technique

1. Throughout the entire period described, the events might easily be characterized as "hectic." What techniques of writing help to create this sense of things? Point to and analyze some examples.

2. Regis can't decide whether the finalists who don't win should be called "runners-up" or "runner-ups." Which do you think is the best expression? Explain your reasoning.

## Writing

When he wrote the selection you have read, Regis of course knew who had won the contest he narrates—Miss Alabama. Write an essay in which you analyze the ways he attempts to maintain the suspense of this aspect of his story without being coy about concealing his knowledge of how it turned out.

# Gloria Steinem

## Sex, Lies & Advertising                                        (1990)

> *One of the most famous of modern feminists, Gloria Steinem was born in Toledo, Ohio, in 1934. She graduated magna cum laude form Smith College in 1956 and after two years on a fellowship in India began her career in journalism in New York City. A co-founder of* New York *magazine in 1968, she helped to found* Ms. *in 1971. The following essay was published in that magazine and records some of its troubles over the years.*

1    Suppose archaeologists of the future dug up women's magazines and used them to judge American women. What would they think of us—and what can we do about it?

2    About three years ago, as glasnost was beginning and *Ms.* seemed to be ending, I was invited to a press lunch for a Soviet official. He entertained us with anecdotes about new problems of democracy in his country. Local Communist leaders were being criticized in their media for the first time, he explained, and they were angry. "So I'll have to ask my American friends," he finished pointedly, "how more subtly to control the press." In the silence that followed, I said, "Advertising."

3    The reporters laughed, but later, one of them took me aside: How dare I suggest that freedom of the press was limited? How dare I imply that his newsweekly could be influenced by ads? I explained that I was thinking of advertising's media-wide influence on most of what we read. Even newsmagazines use "soft" cover stories to sell ads, confuse readers with "advertorials," and occasionally self-censor on subjects known to be a problem with big advertisers. But, I also explained, I was thinking especially of women's magazines.

4    There, it isn't just a little content that's devoted to attracting ads; it's almost all of it. That's why advertisers—not readers—

---

SOURCE: Published In *Ms.* Magazine, July/August 1990. Reprinted by permission of the author.

have always been the problem for *Ms*. As the only women's magazine that didn't supply what the ad world euphemistically describes as "supportive editorial atmosphere" or "complementary copy" (for instance, articles that praise food/fashion/beauty subjects to "support" and "complement" food/fashion/beauty ads), *Ms*. could never attract enough advertising to break even. "Oh, women's magazines," the journalist said with contempt." Everybody knows they're catalogs—but who cares? They have nothing to do with journalism. I can't tell you how many times I've had this argument in 25 years of working for many kinds of publications.

5    Except as moneymaking machines—"cash cows" as they are so elegantly called in the trade—women's magazines are rarely taken seriously. Though changes being made by women have been called more far-reaching than the industrial revolution—and though many editors try hard to reflect some of them in the few pages left to them after all the ad-related subjects have been covered—the magazines serving the female half of this country are still far below the journalistic and ethical standards of news and general interest publications. Most depressing of all, this doesn't even rate an expose. If *Time* and *Newsweek* had to lavish praise on cars in general and credit General Motors in particular to get GM ads, there would be a scandal—maybe a criminal investigation. When women's magazines from *Seventeen* to *Lear's* praise beauty products in general and credit Revlon in particular to get ads, its just business as usual.

6    When *Ms*. began, we didn't consider not taking ads. The most important reason was keeping the price of a feminist magazine low enough for most women to afford. But the second and almost equal reason was providing a forum where women and advertisers could talk to each other and improve advertising itself. After all, it was (and still is) as potent a source of information in this country as news or TV and movie dramas.

7    We decided to proceed in two stages. First, we would convince makers of "people products" used by both men and women but advertised mostly to men—cars, credit cards, insurance, sound equipment, financial services, and the like—that their ads should be placed in a women's magazine. Since they were accustomed to the division between editorial and advertising in news and general interest magazines, this would allow

our editorial content to be free and diverse. Second, we would add the best ads for whatever traditional "women's products" (clothes, shampoo, fragrance, food, and so on) that surveys showed *Ms.* readers used. But we would ask them to come in without the usual quid pro quo of "complementary copy." We knew the second step might be harder. Food advertisers have always demanded that women's magazines publish recipes and articles on entertaining (preferably ones that name their products) in return for their ads; clothing advertisers expect to be surrounded by fashion spreads (especially ones that credit their designers); and shampoo, fragrance, and beauty products in general usually insist on positive editorial coverage of beauty subjects, plus photo credits besides. That's why women's magazines look the way they do. But if we could break this link between ads and editorial content, then we wanted good ads for "women's products," too.

8    By playing their part in this unprecedented mix of all the things our readers need and use, advertisers also would be rewarded: ads for products like cars and mutual funds would find a new growth market; the best ads for women's products would no longer be lost in oceans of ads for the same category; and both would have access to a laboratory of smart and caring readers whose response would help create effective ads for other media as well.

9    I thought then that our main problem would be the imagery in ads themselves. Carmakers were still draping blondes in evening gowns over the hoods like ornaments. Authority figures were almost always male, even in ads for products that only women used. Sadistic, he-man campaigns even won industry praise. (For instance, *Advertising Age* had hailed the infamous Silva Thin cigarette theme. "How to Get a Woman's Attention: Ignore Her," as "brilliant.") Even in medical journals, tranquilizer ads showed depressed housewives standing beside piles of dirty dishes and promised to get them back to work. Obviously, *Ms.* would have to avoid such ads and seek out the best ones—but this didn't seem impossible. The *New Yorker* had been selecting ads for aesthetic reasons for years, a practice that only seemed to make advertisers more eager to be in its pages. *Ebony* and *Essence* were asking for ads with positive black images, and though their struggle was hard, they weren't

being called unreasonable. Clearly, what *Ms.* needed was a very special publisher and ad sales staff.

10    I could think of only one woman with experience on the business side of magazines—Patricia Carbine, who recently had become a vice president of *McCall's* as well as its editor in chief—and the reason I know her name was a good omen. She had been managing editor at *Look* (really the editor, but its owner refused to put a female name at the top of his masthead) when I was writing a column there. After I did an early interview with Cesar Chavez, then just emerging as a leader of migrant labor, and the publisher turned it down because he was worried about ads from Sunkist, Pat was the one who intervened. As I learned later, she had told the publisher she would resign if the interview weren't published. Mainly because *Look* couldn't afford to lose Pat, it was published (and the ads from Sunkist never arrived). Though I barely knew this woman, she had done two things I always remembered: put her job on the line in a way that editors often talk about but rarely do, and been so loyal to her colleagues that she never told me or anyone outside *Look* that she had done so.

11    Fortunately, Pat did agree to leave *McCall's* and take a huge cut in salary to become publisher of *Ms.* She became responsible for training and inspiring generations of young women who joined the *Ms.* ad sales force, many of whom went on to become "firsts" at the top of publishing. When *Ms.* first started, however, there were so few women with experience selling space that Pat and I made the rounds of ad agencies ourselves. *Ms.* was asking companies to do business in a different way meant our saleswomen had to make many times the usual number of calls—first to convince agencies and then client companies besides—and to present endless amounts of research. I was often asked to do a final ad presentation, or see some higher decision-maker, or speak to women employees so executives could see the interest of women they worked with. That's why I spent more time persuading advertisers than editing or writing for *Ms.* and why I ended up with an unsentimental education in the seamy underside of publishing that few writers see (and even fewer magazines can publish).

12     Let me take you with us through some experiences, just as they happened:

13     Cheered on by early support from Volkswagen and one or two other car companies, we scrape together time and money to put on a major reception in Detroit. We know U.S. carmakers firmly believe that women choose the upholstery, not the car, but we are armed with statistics and reader mail to prove the contrary: a car is an important purchase for women, one that symbolizes mobility and freedom. But almost nobody comes. We are left with many pounds of shrimp on the table, and quite a lot of egg on our face. We blame ourselves for not guessing that there would be a baseball pennant play-off on the same day, but executives go out of their way to explain they wouldn't have come anyway. Thus begins ten years of knocking on hostile doors, presenting endless documentation, and hiring a full-time saleswoman in Detroit; all necessary before *Ms.* gets any real results. This long saga has a semi-happy ending: foreign and, later, domestic carmakers eventually provided Ms. with enough advertising to make cars one of our top sources of ad revenue. Slowly, Detroit began to take the women's market seriously enough to put car ads in other women's magazines, too, thus freeing a few pages from the hothouse of fashion-beauty-food ads. But long after figures showed a third, even a half, of many car models being bought by women, U.S. makers continued to be uncomfortable addressing women. Unlike foreign carmakers, Detroit never quite learned the secret of creating intelligent ads that exclude no one, and then placing them in women's magazines to overcome past exclusion. (*Ms.* readers were so grateful for a routine Honda ad featuring rack and pinion steering, for instance, that they sent fan mail.) Even now, Detroit continues to ask, "Should we make special ads for women?" Perhaps that's why some foreign cars still have a disproportionate share of the U.S. women's market.

14     In the *Ms.* Gazette, we do a brief report on a congressional hearing into chemicals used in hair dyes that are absorbed through the skin and may be carcinogenic. Newspapers report this too, but Clairol, a Bristol-Myers subsidiary that makes dozens

of products—a few of which have just begun to advertise in *Ms.*—is outraged. Not at newspapers or newsmagazines, just at us. It's bad enough that *Ms.* is the only women's magazine refusing to provide the usual "complementary" articles and beauty photos, but to criticize one of their categories—that is going too far. We offer to publish a letter from Clairol telling its side of the story. In an excess of solicitousness, we even put this letter in the Gazette, not in Letters to the Editors where it belongs. Nonetheless—and in spite of surveys that show *Ms.* readers are active women who use more of almost everything Clairol makes than do the readers of any other women's magazine—*Ms.* gets almost none of these ads for the rest of its natural life. Meanwhile, Clairol changes its hair coloring formula, apparently in response to the hearings we reported.

15      Our saleswomen set out early to attract ads for consumer electronics: sound equipment, calculators, computers, VCRs, and the like. We know that our readers are determined to be included in the technological revolution. We know from reader surveys that *Ms.* readers are buying this stuff in numbers as high as those of magazines like *Playboy;* or "men 18 to 34," the prime targets of the consumer electronics industry. Moreover, unlike traditional women's products that our readers buy but don't need to read articles about, these are subjects they want covered in our pages. There actually is a supportive editorial atmosphere. "But women don't understand technology," say executives at the end of ad presentations. "Maybe not," we respond, "but neither do men—and we all buy it. "If women do buy it," say the decision-makers, "they're asking their husbands and boyfriends what to buy first." We produce letters from *Ms.* readers saying how turned off they are when salesmen say things like "Let me know when your husband can come in." After several years of this, we get a few ads for compact sound systems. Some of them come from JVC, whose vice president, Harry Elias, is trying to convince his Japanese bosses that there is something called a women's market. At his invitation I find myself speaking at huge trade shows in Chicago and Las Vegas, trying to persuade JVC dealers that showrooms don't have to be locker rooms where women are made to feel unwelcome. But as it turns out, the shows themselves are part of the problem. In Las Vegas, the only women around the tech-

nology displays are seminude models serving champagne. In Chicago, the big attraction is Marilyn Chambers, who followed Linda Lovelace of *Deep Throat* fame as Chuck Traynor's captive and/or employee. VCRs are being demonstrated with her porn videos. In the end, we get ads for a car stereo now and then, but no VCRs and some IBM personal computers, but no Apple or Japanese ones.

16      We notice that office magazines like *Working Woman* and *Savvy* don't benefit as much as they should from office equipment ads either. In the electronics world, women and technology seem mutually exclusive. It remains a decade behind even Detroit. Because we get letters from little girls who love toy trains, and who ask our help in changing ads and box-top photos that feature little boys only, we try to get toy-train ads from Lionel. It turns out that Lionel executives have been concerned about little girls. They made a pink train, and were surprised when it didn't sell. Lionel bows to consumer pressure with a photograph of a boy and a girl—but only on some of their boxes. They fear that, if trains are associated with girls, they will be devalued in the minds of boys. Needless to say, *Ms.* gets no train ads, and little girls remain a mostly unexplored market. By 1986, Lionel is put up to sale. But for different reasons, we haven't had much luck with other kinds of toys either. In spite of many articles on child-rearing; an annual listing of nonsexist, multi-racial toys by Letty Cottin Pogrebin; Stories for Free Children, a regular feature also edited by Letty, and other prizewinning features for or about children, we get virtually no toy ads. Generations of *Ms.* saleswomen explain to toy manufacturers that a larger proportion of *Ms.* readers have preschool children than do the readers of other women's magazines, but this industry can't believe feminists have or care about children.

17      When *Ms.* begins, the staff decides not to accept ads for feminine hygiene sprays or cigarettes: they are damaging and carry no appropriate health warnings. Though we don't think we should tell our readers what to do, we do think we should provide facts so they can decide for themselves. Since the anti-smoking lobby has been pressing for health warnings on cigarette ads, we decided to take them only as they comply. Philip Morris is among the first to do so. One of its brands, Virginia Slims, is

also sponsoring women's tennis and the first national polls of women's opinions. On the other hand, the Virginia Slims theme, "You've come a long way, baby," has more than a "baby" problem. It makes smoking a symbol of progress for women. We explain to Philip Morris that this slogan won't do well in our pages, but they are convinced its success with some women means it will work with all women. Finally, we agree to publish an ad for a Virginia Slims calendar as a test. The letters from readers are critical—and smart. For instance: Would you show a black man picking cotton, the same man in a Cardin suit, and symbolize the antislavery and civil rights movements by smoking? Of course not. But instead of honoring the test results, the Philip Morris people seem angry to be proved wrong. They take away ads for all their many brands. This costs *Ms.* about $250,000 the first year. After five years, we can no longer keep track. Occasionally, a new set of executives listens to *Ms.* saleswomen, but because we won't take Virginia Slims, not one Philip Morris product returns to our pages for the next 16 years.

18    Gradually, we also realize our naiveté in thinking we could decide against taking cigarette ads. They became a disproportionate support of magazines the moment they were banned on television, and few magazines could compete and survive without them, certainly not *Ms.*, which lacks so many other categories. By the time statistics in the 1980s showed the women's rate of lung cancer was approaching men's, the necessity of taking cigarette ads has become a kind of prison.

19    General Mills, Pillsbury, Carnation, Del Monte, Dole, Kraft, Stouffer, Hormel, and Nabisco—you name the food giant, we try it. But no matter how desirable the *Ms.* readership, our lack of recipes is lethal. We explain to them that placing food ads only next to recipes associates food with work. For many women, it is a negative that works against the ads. Why not place food ads in diverse media without recipes (thus reaching more men, who are now a third of the shoppers in supermarkets anyway), and leave the recipes to specialty magazines like *Gourmet* (a third of whose readers are also men)? These arguments elicit interest, but except for an occasional ad for a convenience food, instant coffee, diet drinks, yogurt, or such extras as avocados and almonds, this mainstay of the publishing industry stays closed to us. Period.

20     Traditionally, wines and liquors didn't advertise to women: men were thought to make the brand decisions, even if women did the buying. But after endless presentations, we begin to make a dent in this category. Thanks to the unconventional Michel Roux of Carillon Importers (distributors of Grand Marnier, Absolut Vodka, and others), who assumes that food and drink have no gender, some ads are leaving their men's club. Beer makers are still selling masculinity. It takes *Ms.* fully eight years to get its first beer ad (Michelob). In general, however, liquor ads are less stereotyped in their imagery—and far less controlling of the editorial content around them—than are women's products. But given the under-representation of other categories, these very facts tend to create a disproportionate number of alcohol ads in the pages of *Ms.* This in turn dismays readers worried about women and alcoholism.

21     We hear in 1980 that women in the Soviet Union have been producing feminist *samizdat* (underground, self-published books) and circulating them throughout the country. As punishment, four of the leaders have been exiled. Though we are operating on our usual shoestring, we solicit individual contributions to send Robin Morgan to interview these women in Vienna. The result is an exclusive cover story that includes the first news of a populist peace movement against the Afghanistan occupation, a prediction of glasnost to come, and a grass roots, intimate view of Soviet women's lives. From the popular press to women's studies courses, the response is great. The story wins a Front Page award. Nonetheless, this journalistic coup undoes years of efforts to get an ad schedule from Revlon. Why? Because the Soviet women on our cover are not wearing makeup.

22     Four years of research and presentations go into convincing airlines that women now make travel choices and business trips. United, the first airline to advertise in *Ms.* is so impressed with the response from our readers that one of its executives appears in a film for our ad presentations. As usual, good ads get great results. But we have problems unrelated to such results. For instance: because American Airlines flight attendants include among their labor demands the stipulation that they could choose to have their last names preceded by "*Ms.*" on their name tags—in a long-delayed revolt against the standard, "I am your pilot, Captain Rothgart, and this is your flight

attendant, Cindy Sue"—American officials seem to hold the magazine responsible. We get no ads. There is still a different problem at Eastern. A vice president cancels subscriptions for thousands of copies on Eastern flights. Why? Because he is offended by ads for lesbian poetry journals in the *Ms.* Classified. A "family airline," as he explains to me coldly on the phone, has to "draw the line somewhere." It's obvious that *Ms.* can't exclude lesbians and serve women. We've been trying to make that point ever since our first issue included an article by and about lesbians, and both Suzanne Levine, our managing editor, and I were lectured by such heavy hitters as Ed Kosner, then editor of *Newsweek* (and now of *New York Magazine*), who insisted that *Ms.* should "position" itself against lesbians. But our advertisers have paid to reach a guaranteed number of readers, and soliciting new subscriptions to compensate for Eastern would cost $150,000 plus rebating money in the meantime. Like almost everything ad-related, this presents an elaborate organizing problem.

23   After days of searching for sympathetic members of the Eastern board, Frank Thomas, president of the Ford Foundation, kindly offers to call Roswell Gilpatrick, a director of Eastern. I talk with Mr. Gilpatrick, who calls Frank Borman, then the president of Eastern. Frank Borman calls me to say that his airline is not in the business of censoring magazines: *Ms.* will be returned to Eastern flights.

24   Women's access to insurance and credit is vital, but with the exception of Equitable and a few other ad pioneers, such financial services address men. For almost a decade after the Equal Credit Opportunity Act passes in 1974, we try to convince American Express that women are a growth market—but nothing works. Finally, a former professor of Russian named Jerry Welsh becomes head of marketing. He assumes that women should be cardholders, and persuades his colleagues to feature women in a campaign. Thanks to this 1980s series, the growth rate for female cardholders surpasses that for men. For this article, I asked Jerry Welsh if he would explain why American Express waited so long. "Sure," he said, "they were afraid of having a 'pink' card."

25   Women of color read *Ms.* in disproportionate numbers. This is a source of pride to *Ms.* staffers, who are also more racially

representative than the editors of other women's magazines. But this reality is obscured by ads filled with enough white women to make a reader snow blind. Pat Carbine remembers mostly "astonishment" when she requested African American, Hispanic, Asian, and other diverse images. Marcia Ann Gillespie, a *Ms.* editor who was previously the editor in chief of *Essence,* witnesses ad bias a second time: having tried for *Essence* to get white advertisers to use black images (Revlon did so eventually, but Loreal, Lauder, Chanel, and other companies never did), she sees similar problems getting integrated ads for an integrated magazine. Indeed, the ad world often creates black and Hispanic ads only for black and Hispanic media. In an exact parallel for the fear that marketing a product to women will endanger its appeal to men, the response is usually, "But your [white] readers won't identify. In fact, those we are able to get—for instance, a Max Factor ad made for *Essence* that Linda Wachner gives us after she becomes president—are praised by white readers, too. But there are pathetically few such images.

26    By the end of 1985, production and mailing costs have risen astronomically, ad income is flat, and competition for ads is stiffer than ever. The 60/40 preponderance of edit over ads that we promised to readers becomes 50/50; children's stories, most poetry, and some fiction are casualties of less space; in order to get variety into limited pages, the length (and sometimes the depth) of articles suffers; and, though we do refuse most of the ads that would look like a parody in our pages, we get so worn down that some slip through. Still, readers perform miracles. Though we haven't been able to afford a subscription mailing in two years, they maintain our guaranteed circulation of 450,000. Nonetheless, media reports on *Ms.* often insist that our unprofitability must be due to reader disinterest.

27    The myth that advertisers simply follow readers is very strong. Not one reporter notes that other comparable magazines our size (say, *Vanity Fair* or *The Atlantic*) have been losing more money in one year than *Ms.* has lost in 16 years. No matter how much never-to-be-recovered cash is poured into starting a magazine or keeping one going, appearances seem to be all that matter. (Which is why we haven't been able to explain our fragile state in public. Nothing causes ad-flight like the smell of nonsuccess.)

My healthy response is anger. My not-so-healthy response is constant worry. Also an obsession with finding one more rescue. There is hardly a night when I don't wake up with sweaty palms and pounding heart, scared that we won't be able to pay the printer or the post office; scared most of all that closing our doors will hurt the women's movement.

28    Out of chutzpah and desperation, I arrange a lunch with Leonard Lauder, president of Estée Lauder. With the exception of Clinique (the brainchild of Carol Phillips), none of Lauder's hundreds of products has been advertised in *Ms.* A year's schedule of ads for just three or four of them could save us. Indeed, as the scion of a family-owned company whose ad practices are followed by the beauty industry, he is one of the few men who could liberate many pages in all women's magazines just by changing his mind about "complementary copy."

29    Over a lunch that costs more than we can pay for some articles, I explain the need for his leadership. I also lay out the record of *Ms.*: more literary and journalistic prizes won, more new issues introduced into the mainstream, new writers discovered, and impact on society than any other magazine; more articles that became books, stories that became movies, ideas that became television series, and newly advertised products that became profitable, and, most important for him, a place for his ads to reach women who aren't reachable through any other women's magazine. Indeed, if there is one constant characteristic of the ever-changing *Ms.* readership, it is their impact as leaders. Whether it's waiting until later to have first babies, or pioneering PABA as sun protection in cosmetics, whatever they are doing today, a third to a half of American women will be doing three to five years from now. It's never failed. But, he says, *Ms.* readers are not our women. They're not interested in things like fragrance and blush-on. If they were, *Ms.* would write articles about them. On the contrary, I explain, surveys show they are more likely to buy such things than the readers of, say, *Cosmopolitan* or *Vogue*. They're good customers because they're out in the world enough to need several sets of everything: home, work, purse, travel, gym, and so on. They just don't need to read articles about these things. Would he ask a men's magazine to publish monthly columns on how to shave before he advertised Aramis products (his line for men)?

He concedes that beauty features are often concocted more for advertisers than readers. But *Ms.* isn't appropriate for his ads anyway, he explains. Why? Because Estée Lauder is selling "a kept-woman mentality." I can't quite believe this. Sixty percent of the users of his products are salaried, and generally resemble *Ms.* readers. Besides, his company has the appeal of having been started by a creative and hardworking woman, his mother, Estée Lauder. That doesn't matter, he says. He knows his customers, and they would like to be kept women. That's why he will never advertise in *Ms.*

30   In November 1987, by vote of the *Ms.* Foundation for Education and Communication (*Ms.*'s owner and publisher, the media subsidiary of the *Ms.* Foundation for Women). *Ms.* was sold to a company whose officers, Australian feminists Sandra Yates and Anne Summers, raised the investment money in their country that *Ms.* couldn't find in its own. They also started *Sassy* for teenage women. In their two-year tenure, circulation was raised to 550,000 by investment in circulation mailings, and, to the dismay of some readers, editorial features on clothes and new products made a more traditional bid for ads. Nonetheless, ad pages fell below previous levels. In addition, *Sassy,* whose fresh voice and sexual frankness were an unprecedented success with young readers, was targeted by two mothers from Indiana who began, as one of them put it, "calling every Christian organization I could thing of." In response to this controversy, several crucial advertisers pulled out. Such links between ads and editorial content was a problem in Australia, too, but to a lesser degree. "Our readers pay two times more for their magazines," Anne explained, "so advertisers have less power to threaten a magazine's viability." "I was shocked," said Sandra Yates with characteristic directness. "In Australia, we think you have freedom of the press—but you don't." Since Anne and Sandra had not met their budget's projections for ad revenue, their investors forced a sale.

31   In October 1989, *Ms.* and *Sassy* were bought by Dale Lang, owner of *Working Mother, Working Woman,* and one of the few independent publishing companies left among the conglomerates. In response to a request from the original *Ms.* staff—as well as to reader letters urging that *Ms.* continue, plus his own belief that *Ms.* would benefit his other magazines by blazing a trail—

he agreed to try the ad-free, reader-supported *Ms.* you hold now and to give us complete editorial control. Do you think, as I once did, that advertisers make decisions based on solid research? Well, think again. "Broadly speaking," says Joseph Smith of Oxtoby-Smith, Inc., a consumer research firm, "there is no persuasive evidence that the editorial context of an ad matters."

32     Advertisers, who demand such "complementary copy," even in the absence of respectable studies, clearly are operating under a double standard. The same food companies place ads in *People* with no recipes. Cosmetics companies support *The New Yorker* with no regular beauty columns. So where does this habit of controlling the content of women's magazines come from? Tradition. Ever since *Ladies Magazine* debuted in Boston in 1828, editorial copy directed to women has been informed by something other than its readers' wishes. There were no ads then, but in an age when married women were legal minors with no right to their own money, there was another revenue source to be kept in mind: husbands. "Husbands may rest assured," wrote editor Sarah Joseph Hale, "that nothing found in these pages shall cause her [his wife] to be less assiduous in preparing for his reception or encourage her to 'usurp station' or encroach upon prerogatives of men."

33     Hale went on to become the editor of *Godey's Lady's Book,* a magazine featuring "fashion plates": engravings of dresses for readers to take to their seamstresses or copy themselves. Hale added "how to" articles, which set the tone for women's service magazines for years to come: how to write politely, avoid sunburn, and—in no fewer than 1,200 words—how to maintain a goose quill pen. She advocated education for women but avoided controversy. Just as most women's magazines now avoid politics, poll their readers on issues like abortion but rarely take a stand, and praise socially approved lifestyles, Hale saw to it that *Godey's* avoided the hot topics of its day: slavery, abolition, and women's suffrage. What definitively turned women's magazines into catalogs, however, were two events: Ellen Butterick's invention of the clothing pattern in 1863 and the mass manufacture of patent medicines containing everything from colored water to cocaine. For the first time, readers could purchase what magazines encouraged them to want. As such magazines became more profitable, they also began to

attract men as editors. (Most women's magazines continued to have men as top editors until the feminist 1970s.) Edward Bok, who became editor of *The Ladies' Home Journal* in 1889, discovered the power of advertisers when he rejected ads for patent medicines and found that other advertisers canceled in retribution. In the early 20th century, *Good Housekeeping* started its Institute to "test and approve" products. Its Seal of Approval became the grandfather of current "value added" programs that offer advertisers such bonuses as product sampling and department store promotions.

34    By the time suffragists finally won the vote in 1920, women's magazines had become too entrenched as catalogs to help women learn how to use it. The main function was to create a desire for products, teach how to use products, and make products a crucial part of gaining social approval, pleasing a husband, and performing as a homemaker. Some unrelated articles and short stories were included to persuade women to pay for these catalogs. But articles were neither consumerist nor rebellious. Even fiction was usually subject to formula: If a woman had any sexual life outside marriage, she was supposed to come to a bad end.

35    In 1965, Helen Gurley Brown began to change part of that formula by bring "the sexual revolution" to women's magazines—but in an ad-oriented way. Attracting multiple men required even more consumerism, as the Cosmo Girl made clear, than finding one husband. In response to the workplace revolution of the 1970s, traditional women's magazines — that is, "trade books" for women working at home — were joined by *Savvy, Working Woman,* and others for women working in offices. But by keeping the fashion, beauty, and entertaining articles necessary to get traditional ads and then adding career articles besides, they inadvertently produced the antifeminist stereotype of Super Woman. The male-imitative, dress-for-success woman carrying a briefcase became the media image of a woman worker, even though a blue-collar woman's salary was often higher than her glorified secretarial sister's, and though women at a real briefcase level are statistically rare.

36    Needless to say, these dress-for-success women were also thin, white, and beautiful. In recent years, advertisers' control over the editorial content of women's magazines has become

so institutionalized that it is written into "insertion orders" or dictated to ad salespeople as official policy.

37    The following are recent typical orders to women's magazines:

- Dow's Cleaning Products stipulates that ads for its Vivid and Spray 'n Wash products should be adjacent to "children or fashion editorial"; ads for bathroom cleaner should be next to "home furnishing/family" features; and so on for other brands.
- "If a magazine fails for 1/2 the brands or more," the Dow order warns, "it will be omitted from further consideration."
- Bristol-Myers, the parent of Clairol, Windex, Drano, Bufferin, and much more, stipulates that ads be placed next to "a full page of compatible editorial."
- S.C. Johnson & Son, makers of Johnson Wax, lawn and laundry products, insect sprays, hair sprays, and so on orders that its ads "should not be opposite extremely controversial features or material antithetical to the nature/copy of the advertised product."
- Maidenform, manufacturer of bras and other apparel, leaves a blank for the particular product and states: "The creative concept of the _____ campaign, and the very nature of the product itself appeal to the positive emotions of the reader/consumer. Therefore, it is imperative that all editorial adjacencies reflect that same positive tone. The editorial must not be negative in content or lend itself contrary to the _____ product imagery/message (e.g. editorial relating to illness, disillusionment, large size fashion, etc.)."
- The De Beers diamond company, a big seller of engagement rings, prohibits magazines from placing its ads with "adjacencies to hard news or anti/love-romance themed editorial."

Procter & Gamble, one of this country's most powerful and diversified advertisers, stands out in the memory of Anne Summers and Sandra Yates (no mean feat in this context): its products were not to be placed in any issue that included any material on gun control, abortion, the occult, cults, or the disparagement of religion. Caution was also demanded in any issue covering sex or drugs, even for educational proposes.

39     Those are the most obvious chains around women's magazines. There are also rules so clear they needn't be written down: for instance, an overall "look" compatible with beauty and fashion ads. Even "real" non-model women photographed for a woman's magazine are usually made up, dressed in credited clothes, and retouched out of all reality. When editors do include articles on less-than-cheerful subjects (for instance, domestic violence), they tend to keep them short and unillustrated. The point is to be "upbeat." Just as women in the street are asked, "Why don't you smile, honey?" women's magazines acquire an institutional smile. Within the text itself, praise for advertisers' products has become so ritualized that fields like "beauty writing" have been invented. One of its frequent practitioners explained seriously that, "it's a difficult art. How many new adjectives can you find? How much greater can you make a lipstick sound? The FDA restricts what companies can say on labels, but we create illusion. And ad agencies are on the phone all the time pushing you to get their product in. A lot of them keep the business based on how many editorial clippings they produce every month. The worst are products like Lauder's, as the writer confirmed, "with their own name involved. It's all ego."

40     Often, editorial becomes one giant ad. Last November, for instance, *Lear's* featured an elegant woman executive on the cover. On the contents page, we learned she was wearing Guerlain makeup and Samsara, a new fragrance by Guerlain. Inside were full-page ads for Samsara and Guerlain antiwrinkle cream. In the cover profile, we learned that this executive was responsible for launching Samsara and is Guerlain's director of public relations. When the *Columbia Journalism Review* did one of the few articles to include women's magazines in coverage of the influence of ads, editor Frances Lear was quoted as defending her magazine because "this kind of thing is done all the time."

41     Often, advertisers also plunge odd-shaped ads into the text, no matter what the cost to the readers. At *Woman's Day,* a magazine originally founded by a supermarket chain, editor in chief Ellen Levine said. "The day the copy had to rag around a chicken leg was not a happy one." Advertisers are also adamant about where in a magazine their ads appear. When

Revlon was not placed as the first beauty ad in one Hearst magazine, for instance, Revlon pulled its ads from all Hearst magazines. Ruth Whitney, editor in chief of *Glamour,* attributes some of these demands to "ad agencies wanting to prove to a client that they've squeezed the last drop of blood out of a magazine." She also is, she says, "sick-and-tired of hearing that women's magazines are controlled by cigarette ads." Relatively speaking, she's right. To be as censoring as are many advertisers for women's products, tobacco companies would have to demand articles in praise of smoking and expect glamorous photos of beautiful women smoking their brands.

42    I don't mean to imply that the editors I quote here share my objections to ads: most assume that women's magazines have to be the way they are. But it's also true that only former editors can be completely honest. "Most of the pressure came in the form of direct project mentions," explains Sey Chassler, who was editor in chief of *Redbook* from the sixties to the eighties, "We got threats from the big guys, the Revlons, blackmail threats. They wouldn't run ads unless we credited them."

43    But it's not fair to single out the beauty advertisers because these pressures came from everybody. Advertisers want to know two things: What are you going to charge me? What else are you going to do for me? It's a holdup. For instance, management felt that fiction took up too much space. They couldn't put any advertising in that. For the last ten years, the number of fiction entries into the National Magazine Awards has declined. And pressures are getting worse. More magazines are more bottom-line oriented because they have been taken over by companies with no interest in publishing. "I also think advertisers do this to women's magazines especially," Chassler concluded, "because of the general disrespect they have for women."

44    Even media experts who don't give a damn about women's magazines are alarmed by the spread of this ad-edit linkage. In a climate the *Wall Street Journal* describes as an unacknowledged Depression for media, women's products are increasingly able to take their low standards wherever they go. For instance: newsweeklies publish uncritical stories on fashion and fitness. The *New York Times Magazine* recently ran an article on "firming creams," complete with mentions of advertisers. *Vanity Fair* published a profile of one major advertiser, Ralph Lauren, illus-

trated by the same photographer who does his ads, and turned the lifestyle of another, Calvin Klein, into a cover story. Even the outrageous *Spy* has toned down since it began to go after fashion ads. And just to make us really worry, films and books, the last media that go directly to the public without having to attract ads first, are in danger, too. Producers are beginning to depend on payments for displaying products in movies, and books are now being commissioned by companies like Federal Express.

45 But the truth is that women's products—like women's magazines—have never been the subjects of much serious reporting anyway. News and general interest publications, including the "style" or "living" sections of newspapers, write about food and clothing as cooking and fashion, and almost never evaluate such products by brand name. Though chemical additives, pesticides, and animal fats are major health risk in the United States, and clothes, shoddy or not, absorb more consumer dollars than cars, this lack of information is serious. So is ignoring the contents of beauty products that are absorbed into our bodies through our skins, and that have profit margins so big they would make a loan shark blush.

46 What could women's magazines be like if they were as ad-free as books? as realistic as newspapers? as creative as films? as diverse as women's lives? We don't know. But we'll only find out if we take women's magazines seriously. If readers were to act in a concerted way to change traditional practices of all women's magazines and the marketing of all women's products, we could do it. After all, they are operating on our consumer dollars: money that we now control.

47 You and I could:

- Write to editors and publishers (with copies to advertisers) that we're willing to pay more for magazines with editorial independence, but will not continue to pay for those that are just editorial extensions of ads;
- Write to advertisers (with copies to editors and publishers) that we want fiction, political reporting, consumer reporting—whatever is, or is not, supported by their ads;
- Put as much energy into breaking advertising's control over content as into changing the images in ads, or protesting ads for harmful products like cigarettes;

- Support only those women's magazines and products that take us seriously as readers and consumers.

Those of us in the magazine world can also use the carrot-and stick technique. For instance: pointing out that, if magazines were a regulated medium like television, the demands of advertisers would be against FCC rules. Payola and extortion could be punished. As it is, there are probably illegalities. A magazine's postal rates are determined by the ratio of ad to edit pages, and the former costs more than the latter. So much for the stick. The carrot means appealing to enlightened self-interest. For instance: there are many studies showing that the greatest factor in determining an ad's effectiveness is the credibility of its surroundings. The "higher the rating of editorial believability," concluded a 1987 survey by the *Journal of Advertising Research,* "the higher the rating of the advertising." Thus, an impenetrable wall between edit and ads would also be in the best interest of advertisers. Unfortunately, few agencies or clients hear such arguments. Editors often maintain the false purity of refusing to talk to them at all. Instead, they see ad salespeople who know little about editorial, are trained in business as usual, and are usually paid by commission.

48   Editors might also band together to take on controversy. That happened once when all the major women's magazines did articles in the same month of the Equal Rights Amendment. It could happen again.

49   It's been almost three years away from life between the grindstones of advertising pressures and readers' needs. I'm just beginning to realize how edges got smoothed down—in spite of all our resistance. I remember feeling put upon when I changed "Porsche" to "car" in a piece about Nazi imagery in German pornography by Andrea Dworkin—feeling sure Andrea would understand that Volkswagen, the distributor of Porsche and one of our few supportive advertisers, asked only to be far away from Nazi subjects. It's taken me all this time to realize the Andrea was the one with a right to feel put upon. Even as I write this, I get a call from a writer of *Elle,* who is doing a whole article on where women part their hair. Why, she wants to know, do I part mine in the middle? It's all so familiar. A writer trying to make something of a nothing

assignment; an editor laboring to think of new ways to attract ads, readers assuming that other women must want this ridiculous stuff; more women suffering from lack of information, insight, creativity, and laughter that could be on the these same pages.

50    I ask you: Can't we do better than this?

## Theme

1. According to Gloria Steinem, why *should* advertisers have been attracted to the magazine *Ms.* as a venue for the advertisement of their products?

2. Steinem says that "the myth that advertisers simply follow readers is very strong." List some of the reasons her essay gives as evidence to refute this "myth."

## Technique

1. As she does about all advertisements, Gloria Steinem seems to feel at least two ways about cigarette ads. Point to a moment when this conflict becomes evident and analyze how she handles the issue of her own ambivalence. Does she do so successfully in your view? Explain your reasoning.

2. On the last page Steinem shows herself to be part of the problem chronicled in the rest of the essay when she recalls her editorial change of "Porsche" to "car." Explain how the conflict dramatized here is representative of the issue explored by the essay as a whole.

## Writing

Gloria Steinem quotes the Australian feminist Sandra Yates as saying of publishing in the United States: "In Australia, we think you have freedom of the press—but you don't." Write an essay in which you show how Steinem explores in her essay several different senses of the word "freedom" in the phrase "freedom of the press."

# Roger Ebert

## Steven Spielberg: The Moviemaker          (1998)

> *Roger Ebert was the first film critic ever to win the Pulitzer Prize.
> He writes for the* Chicago Sun-Times *and co-hosts a nationally
> broadcast television show devoted to the current cinema. In the
> following essay he reviews not an individual movie but the entire
> career of Steven Spielberg.*

1    Steven Spielberg's first films were made at a time when directors were the most important people in Hollywood, and his
more recent ones at a time when marketing controls the industry. That he has remained the most powerful filmmaker in the
world during both periods says something for his talent and his
flexibility. No one else has put together a more popular body of
work, yet within the entertainer there is also an artist capable of
*The Color Purple* and *Schindler's List.* When entertainer and artist
came fully together, the result was *E.T., the Extra-Terrestrial,* a
remarkable fusion of mass appeal and stylistic mastery.

2    Spielberg's most important contribution to modern movies
is his insight that there was an enormous audience to be created if old-style B-movie stories were made with A-level craftsmanship and enhanced with the latest developments in special
effects. Consider such titles as *Raiders of the Lost Ark* and the
other Indiana Jones movies, *Close Encounters of the Third Kind,*
*E.T.* and *Jurassic Park.* Look also at the films he produced but
didn't direct, like the *Back to the Future* series, *Gremlins, Who
Framed Roger Rabbit,* and *Twister.* The story lines were the
stuff of Saturday serials, but the filmmaking was cutting edge
and delivered what films have always promised: they showed
us something amazing that we hadn't seen before.

3    Directors talk about their master images, the images that occur
in more than one film because they express something funda-

mental about the way the filmmakers see things. Spielberg once told me that his master image was the light flooding in through the doorway in *Close Encounters,* suggesting, simultaneously, a brightness and mystery outside. This strong backlighting turns up in many of his other films: the aliens walk out of light in *Close Encounters,* E.T.'s spaceship door is filled with light, and Indy Jones often uses strong beams from powerful flashlights.

4  In Spielberg, the light source conceals mystery, whereas for many other directors it is darkness that conceals mystery. The difference is that for Spielberg, mystery offers promise instead of threat. That orientation apparently developed when he was growing up in Phoenix, Ariz. One day we sat and talked about his childhood, and he told me of a formative experience.

5  "My dad took me out to see a meteor shower when I was a little kid," he said, "and it was scary for me because he woke me up in the middle of the night. My heart was beating; I didn't know what he wanted to do. He wouldn't tell me, and he put me in the car and we went off, and I saw all these people lying on blankets, looking up at the sky. And my dad spread out a blanket. We lay down and looked at the sky, and I saw for the first time all these meteors. What scared me was being awakened in the middle of the night and taken somewhere without being told where. But what didn't scare me, but was very soothing, was watching this cosmic meteor shower. And I think from that moment on, I never looked at the sky and thought it was a bad place."

6  There are two important elements there: the sense of wonder and hope, and the identification with a child's point of view. Spielberg's best characters are like elaborations of the heroes from old *Boy's Life* serials, plucky kids who aren't afraid to get in over their head. Even Oskar Schindler has something of that in his makeup—the boy's delight in pulling off a daring scheme and getting away with it.

7  Spielberg heroes don't often find themselves in complex emotional entanglements (Celie in *The Color Purple* is an exception). One of his rare failures was *Always,* with its story of a ghost watching his girl fall in love with another man. The typical Spielberg hero is drawn to discovery, and the key shot in many of his films is the revelation of the wonder he has discovered.

Remember the spellbinding first glimpse of the living dinosaurs in *Jurassic Park?*

8    Spielberg's first important theatrical film was *The Sugarland Express,* made in 1974, a time when gifted auteurs like Scorsese, Altman, Coppola, De Palma and Malick ruled Hollywood. Their god was Orson Welles, who made the masterpiece *Citizen Kane* entirely without studio interference, and they too wanted to make the Great American Movie. But a year later, with *Jaws,* Spielberg changed the course of modern Hollywood history. *Jaws* was a hit of vast proportions, inspiring executives to go for the home run instead of the base hit. And it came out in the summer, a season the major studios had generally ceded to cheaper exploitation films. Within a few years, the *Jaws* model would inspire an industry in which budgets ran wild because the rewards seemed limitless, in which summer action pictures dominated the industry, and in which the hottest young directors wanted to make the Great American Blockbuster.

9    Spielberg can't be blamed for that seismic shift in the industry. *Jaws* only happened to inaugurate it. If the shark had sunk for good (as it threatened to during the troubled filming), another picture would have ushered in the age of the movie best sellers—maybe *Star Wars,* in 1977. And no one is more aware than Spielberg of his own weaknesses. When I asked him once to make the case against his films, he grinned and started the list: "They say, 'Oh, he cuts too fast; his edits are too quick; he uses wide-angle lenses; he doesn't photograph women very well; he's tricky; he likes to dig a hole in the ground and put the camera in the hole and shoot up at people; he's too gimmicky; he's more in love with the camera than he is with the story."

10    All true. But you could make a longer list of his strengths, including his direct line to our subconscious. Spielberg has always maintained obsessive quality control, and when his films work, they work on every level that a film can reach. I remember seeing *E.T.* at the Cannes Film Festival, where it played before the most sophisticated filmgoers in the world and reduced them to tears and cheers.

11    In the history of the last third of 20th century cinema, Spielberg is the most influential figure, for better and worse. In his

lesser films he relied too much on shallow stories and special effects for their own sake. (Will anyone treasure *The Lost World: Jurassic Park* a century from now?) In his best films he tapped into dreams fashioned by our better natures.

## Theme

1. According to Roger Ebert, what is Steven Spielberg's "master image?" That concept seems made up of components used by other directors, but how (according to Ebert) does Spielberg handle them differently?

2. Again according to Ebert, what are the weaknesses of Spielberg as a director? How does Ebert feel about those weaknesses? Point to and explain the evidence behind your answers.

## Technique

1. How does Spielberg's anecdote about the meteor shower in paragraph five sum up the themes of light and darkness that Ebert has proposed earlier?

2. The movie *E.T.* appears as the most frequently mentioned film in the essay. What kind of a subplot for the essay does that fact create? How does Ebert feel about the movie and what is the effect of bringing it up each time he does so? How does the movie function in Ebert's critique of Spielberg's career?

## Writing

How do you feel about the films of Steven Spielberg? Write an appreciation of your own of the films you know, being sure to defend or disagree with Ebert's major points.

# Julia Child

## A Slice of History                                        (2003)

> *Julia Child was born in Pasadena, California, and went east to attend Smith College in 1934 in the depths of the Great Depression. After serving in Asia as a member of the Office of Strategic Services during World War II, she moved with her diplomat husband to Paris where she underwent formal training in French cuisine. Later after producing a highly successful cookbook, she returned to America to create the first nationally popular television cooking show,* The French Chef. *In the following essay she recalls the changes in American eating during her long lifetime.*

1    When I was young, we always had good food at home, but it was good, plain New England food, the kind my mother had back in Massachusetts when she was growing up. We always had a soup course, meat, and vegetables. Things like roast beef and leg of lamb, which was cooked till it was well-done in those days—it was still good, juicy, and nice—with roast potatoes and mint sauce. We certainly didn't have one-stop shopping; supermarkets hadn't been invented yet. We'd usually telephone orders to our neighborhood grocery. The milkman delivered milk—in bottles. The vegetable man didn't have a lot of fancy vegetables, but you got nice farm vegetables in season. We didn't have a lot of canned foods unless they had been preserved at home. Until I was about 15, we didn't have a refrigerator, just an icebox, so that dictated what we could buy and how long we could keep it. We put it on the porch so when the ice melted, the water ran out through the floorboards.

2    My mother didn't cook very much—only on Thursdays, when the maid was off. We ate together around 6:30 P.M., when

my father was home. And unless there was a party, there wasn't any drinking. We never had wine.

3    I certainly remember when this frenzy for frozen food came in after World War II. People were very excited about it because it was new. And then there was Duncan Hines and the cake mixes; people used them a lot. In the '40s and '50s, the home economists were never mentioning anything about taste or flavor. They considered a meal okay as long as it had the right amount of nutrients. That's all they cared about. They'd say frozen green beans were the same as fresh, which is ridiculous. They're not at all, not in terms of taste, anyway.

4    Then people got tired of eating that way—at least some did—and cooking was really very much "in" for a short period in the 1960s. That was before women started going to work in such large numbers. There were many educated women who were unemployed or underemployed, and cooking was something they could do and enjoy. I think many people stopped doing that kind of cooking in the '80s, when there was so much takeout going on. Now people seem to be doing more cooking again. Women cook as a hobby, and more men are starting to do it—I think men take pride in cooking well. TV food shows may have sparked some of the renaissance. Now we have cooks as personalities.

5    The invention of the electric mixer [popularized in the 1930s] was a milestone. When I think of all the hand-beating we did before that! It was good for your arms, though. The food processor is also extremely useful for making pie dough, kneading bread, all that slicing and dicing. It's the essential machine for really fine cooking. I remember I was one of the first people to have one in the '70s. I think the microwave [the compact was introduced for home use in 1967] is very useful. In the beginning, they were very expensive, but now most American kitchens have them.

6    When I was a child, we were encouraged to eat a lot. Dieting really got big in the '60s, when fashion models were very thin. They weren't always, you know! Now, we're eating all this fat-free, fake stuff, and we're getting fat anyway because we're not satisfied. If you asked me years ago what one of my favorite things to eat was, I'd have said a great loin strip steak, but it's really very

hard to get a great steak anymore. The marbling used to be marvelous. Now, there's no fat. People are afraid of sugars too. We're drinking more diet sodas than ever, and they're making our sweet tooth harder to satisfy, because they're overly sweet.

7    We didn't know many vegetarians years ago. Not eating meat became the thing to do some places in the '60s, but the movement is much bigger in the '90s. Personally, I don't think pure vegetarianism is a healthy lifestyle. It's more fear of food—that whole thing that red meat is bad for you. And then there are people who don't eat meat because it's against their morals. Well, there's nothing you can do with people like that. I've often wondered to myself: Does a vegetarian look forward to dinner, ever?

8    I don't think we were as afraid of food in the early days, except for pesticides. I do take some steps—I wash everything I eat in hot water, which will wash away anything clinging to it better than cold. But there's so much cultism clinging to the fear of pesticides. Now there's worry about irradiation and bio-engineering, but I think the critics are often short on facts.

9    When I was young, it was an occasion to eat out. There was a whole ceremony involved: The waiter explained the menu, there was wine. More casual restaurants and the chains and such started up in the mid-'60s, and entire families could go out to eat regularly—although the quality of what we were eating is another discussion. Too much fried food!

10    There are many more ethnic restaurants today, especially in big cities. Our palates are now wider, more sophisticated. Farmers' markets and organic markets have also spurred large stores to be better—my local Star Market in Cambridge has a wonderful produce section. Part of it is the ongoing need to excite our taste buds—Americans don't like to be bored. And part is the inevitable result of globalization. Our world is getting smaller, and we've become much more adventurous in our quest for good things to eat.

## Theme

1. Julia Child provides a brief, informal history of food in twentieth century America. In your reading of her essay, what are

the major differences between the America of her youth and the America at the end of the twentieth century when she wrote? Make a list of points and be sure to explain what "major" means to you in this case.

2. Julia Child expresses an enthusiastic and wide-ranging appreciation for food. But what doesn't she like? Does there seem to be any pattern to the things she is not enthusiastic about? Explain your answer.

## Technique

1. In paragraph three Julia Child writes about her ice box: "We put it on the porch so when the ice melted, the water ran out through the floorboards." Surely this single sentence creates an image of a kind of American life vanished long ago. How does it do so? What qualities does the image suggest? Explain how the image creates a sense of the past for you.

2. For years Julia Child hosted a pioneering and very popular TV show called *The French Chef.* However, she has written. Does her style in the essay support her distinction? How do you think a "chef" might sound on some of the same topics she covers? Rewrite a portion as if it were written by a chef. How is Child's writing expressive of a "cook?" Explain your analyses.

## Writing

In your opinion, has food changed much in your own lifetime? Or is it pretty much the same? Using Child's essay as a model, describe the food of your childhood and youth.

# Alfred Hitchcock

## My Most Exciting Picture                                    (1948)

*Alfred Hitchcock was born in London in 1899. "The Master of Suspense" became very successful in the young British film industry, but moved to Hollywood in the 1930s in search of a wider audience and broader film possibilities. In the following essay we see some of the enthusiasm he brought to the making of movies.*

1    Shooting *Rope* was a little like unpuzzling a Rube Goldberg drawing.

2    A long time ago I said that I would like to film in two hours a fictional story that actually happens in two hours. I wanted to do a picture with no time lapses—a picture in which the camera never stops.

3    In *Rope* I got my wish. It was a picture unlike any other I've ever directed. True, I had experimented with a roving camera in isolated sequences in such films as *Spellbound, Notorious,* and *The Paradine Case.* But until *Rope* came along, I had been unable to give full rein to my notion that a camera could photograph one complete reel at a time, gobbling up 11 pages of dialogue on each shot, devouring action like a giant steam shovel.

4    As I see it, there's nothing like continuous action to sustain the mood of actors, particularly in a suspense story. In *Rope* the entire action takes place between the setting of the sun and the hour of darkness. There are a murder, a party, mounting tension, detailed psychological characterizations, the gradual discovery of the crime, and the solution. Yet all this consumes less than two hours of real life as well as "reel" life. (Actually, it took us 35 days to wrap up the picture.)

5    The sight of a "take" under these conditions is something new under the Hollywood sun. It's like being backstage at one of

SOURCE: Reprinted by permission of the Trustees of the Alfred Hitchcock trust.

those madhouses that comedian Joe Cook used to devise when he was explaining why he couldn't imitate the four Hawaiians.

6     Here, for instance, is a brief glimpse of the action in Reel 2 of *Rope*.

7     For a full nine minutes the roving Technicolor camera poked its nose into every corner of the "collapsible" Sutton Place apartment. Prop men crouched on their knees beneath the camera boom moving furniture and putting it back. Lights dimmed down in one corner of the apartment, went up in another. "Wild" walls slid silently on vaseline-greased rollers. Script supervisors, prop men, electricians, and camera crew waggled their fingers and made faces at each other in a series of soundless, prearranged signals. And the camera, which had started facing south, was now facing north.

8     One complete reel, 950 feet of film, was in the can. There was a sudden silence. Then came a loud whisper from one of the harried, exhausted prop men.

9     "This," he announced, "is the damnedest picture I ever worked!"

10    All of us, including myself, agreed with him.

11    Yet *Rope* was probably the most exciting picture I've ever directed. Observers called it "the most revolutionary technique Hollywood had ever seen." Some of our problems seemed, at first, totally insurmountable. James Stewart, our star, couldn't sleep nights because of his role in the picture. It wasn't so much the suspenseful drama as it was the bewildering technique that made him worry. Head grip Morris Rosen still was operating the camera boom in his dreams at four o'clock in the morning and wound up at the finish of the picture 12 pounds thinner. Once, Joe Valentine, our cinematographer, had the 6,000-pound camera dolly roll on his foot when he didn't move fast enough. Still another time, the roving camera rolled too far and smashed one wall of the apartment.

12    To shoot *Rope* with stage technique under sound stage conditions but with continuous action called for months of preparation and days of exacting rehearsals. Every movement of the camera and the actors was worked out first in sessions with a blackboard like football skull practice. Even the door was marked and plotted with numbered circles for the 25 to 30

camera moves in each reel. Whole walls of the apartment had to slide away to allow the camera to follow the actors through narrow doors, then swing back noiselessly to show a solid room. Even the furniture was "wild." Tables and chairs had to be pulled away by prop men, then set in place again by the time the camera returned to its original position, since the camera was on a special crane, not on tracks, and designed to roll through everything like a juggernaut.

13    All this technique, of course, was merely a means to an end. The audience must never be conscious of it. If an audience becomes aware that the camera is performing miracles, the end itself will be defeated.

14    Yet in *Rope* the camera did perform miracles, all because of the superb teamwork of the technical crew and their collaborative genius.

15    Broadway playwright Arthur Laurents (*Home of the Brave* and *Heart Song*) wrote the screenplay, the first time a scenario was written without time lapses. Laurents' scenes were unnumbered and there was almost no camera direction, merely indications of the changing camera position at major points throughout the story. Joe Valentine and I decided that one lens—a 35 mm—would give us all the coverage we needed, since it would be impossible to change lenses because of the continuous camera movement. Paul Hill, our Technicolor consultant, solved the problem of parallax, successfully modifying the camera for close-ups so that we could move in close enough to shoot the inside of a man's hat and the label on a hatband. And instead of following the camera with a mike boom, which would have created an insurmountable problem, we decided that the simplest solution was not to follow it. Instead, we set up four separate booms and two additional microphones up high. Operated by six sound men, these mikes picked up dialogue anywhere the camera wandered within the three-room apartment.

16    But the most magical of all the devices was the cyclorama— an exact miniature reproduction of nearly 35 miles of New York skyline lighted by 8,000 incandescent bulbs and 200 neon signs requiring 150 transformers.

17    On film the miniature looks exactly like Manhattan at night as it would appear from the window of an apartment at 54th

Street and First Avenue, the locale of the play. And since all the major action of *Rope* takes place in the living room of this apartment, with the spectators constantly viewing the background, it was impossible to use process shots or a backdrop. Both would have been too flat. We had to remember the core of the arc of view. So we had to employ the scale cyclorama and devise a "light organ" that not only would light the miniature and its panorama of buildings, but also could give us changing sky and cloud effects varying from sunset to dark— all seen from the apartment—to denote the passing of time.

18    In the 12,000 square feet of the cyclorama, the largest backing ever used on a sound stage, the spectator sees the Empire State, the Chrysler, and the Woolworth buildings; St. Patrick's, Radio City, and hundreds of other landmarks of the fabulous New York skyline. Each miniature building was wired separately for globes ranging from 25 to 150 watts in the tiny windows. (The electrician's eye level was at the 22nd story.) Twenty-six thousand feet of wire carried 126,000 watts of power for the building and window illumination—all controlled by a twist of the electrician's wrist, via a bank of 47 switches, as he sat at the light organ high up and far behind the camera.

19    Because the roofs of the buildings closest to the apartment were three-dimensional and built to scale, there was still another problem to solve. For verisimilitude, smoke and steam trailed toward the sky from the tiny chimneys. Pipes under the rooftops supplied this steam, but we discovered that the vapor left the chimneys too fast and rose too high for accurate perspective. The normal speed of the jetting steam was completely out of synchronization with the miniature.

20    One of the prop men rose to the occasion, placing dry ice over the pipes to retard the steam's speed and volume. After that the smoke trailed lazily into the sky at a rate of speed that was wholly in proportion to the size of the buildings in the miniature.

21    That electrician who sat high on a parallel behind the camera manipulating the light organ controlled the lighting of the miniature like an artist at a console. He could illuminate an entire building or just one window at a time. He could, at the exact and rehearsed line of dialogue which gave him his cue,

flood the Manhattan skyline with light from 200 miniature neon signs. By the time the picture went from the setting of the sun in the first reel to the hour of total darkness in the final *denouement,* the man at the light organ had played a nocturnal Manhattan symphony in light.

22 And then there were the cloud effects. Searching for what I demanded in a natural-seeming sky, I rejected the two routine methods of getting clouds. We could have painted them on the cyclorama, or we could have projected the clouds on the backdrop by means of painted lantern slides. But we did neither. I wanted the clouds to look like clouds even from ten feet away.

23 It was Fred Ahern, our production manager, who found the solution to the puzzle. Ahern came up with the perfect light-reflecting substance—spun glass. (Cotton wouldn't do because it soaks up and deadens light.) Five hundred pounds of spun glass were woven by scenic artists into chicken wire molds. Then actual clouds were photographed in all kinds of weather. We discovered that clouds are never the same even when the weather is constant, and it makes no difference what shape they are. Finally we decided on the cumulus or storm cloud, because it is white and fleecy before it turns gray and formidable. Every possible shaped cloud was created out of spun glass: wispy and full, fragile and menacing, circular and long.

24 *Rope* shows eight complete cloud changes during its nine reels. (The spun glass clouds were hung on standards and on overhead wires behind the buildings in the cyclorama, then slightly varied after each reel.) As a final check on our meteorology, we asked Dr. Dinsmore Alter of the famed Griffith Observatory for his opinion.

25 The cumulus clouds were fine, Alter told us, because there are more cumulus in the New York sky than anywhere else in the country, except high in the mountains. "And of course," said Alter, "you won't want any cirrus or high ice clouds."

26 "Cirrusly, I think not," I said, waiting for a laugh which was a lot weaker than a director has a right to expect on his own set.

27 To get authentic reproductions of changing sun and cloud effects and the falling of dusk, we had still photographers shoot the sun in three different locales. Once from the top of a New York skyscraper, once from the roof of an unfinished

building on Wilshire Boulevard in Los Angeles, and once by a camera crew from the edge of the Santa Monica pier on the Pacific Ocean.

28    Famed John Miehle, our head still photographer, took over the cloud reproduction assignment, using an 8 X 10 and shooting straight into the sun. Miehle recorded the setting sun at five-minute intervals for an hour and 45 minutes to get a continuous effect. All these progressive variations in sun and clouds were charted on a detailed time schedule, then later cued to dialogue and action reel by reel. Miehle's developed films were studied by Technicolor experts who were able to match nature without a flaw.

29    Oddly enough, we discovered that there were virtually no major differences in cloud and sunset effects between the photographs shot in New York and those obtained on the West Coast.

30    Miehle knew that in photographing the sun head-on he might get double images, and he did. But he also obtained magnificent effects. These were the effects that were used in *Rope* to denote the passing of time—the yellow glare of the late afternoon sun fading to a soft gray, the light reflections on the fleecy white clouds dying softly—and finally dusk and darkness coming on as the lights of the city appeared.

31    *Rope* was a miracle of cueing. Everybody: actors, cameramen, the prop crew, the electricians, the script supervisors, spent two solid weeks of rehearsals before a camera turned. Even before the set was built I worked out each movement on a blackboard in my home. Then in the studio, the stage (actually a stage within a stage, made noiseless by constructing a special floor one and one-half inches above the regular one, soundproofed with layers of Celotex and carpet) was marked with numbered circles. These indicated where each specific camera stop had to be made, and when. Each camera movement—and there were as many as 30 separate ones—had its predetermined focus. Because of this the crew men operating the camera had to hit the floor markings exactly on cue and without deviations. The entire floor plan was laid out in foot squares so that in the event of retakes we could go back to the exact spot.

32     For the actual take the door markings were removed and plotted on a board. Holding the cue board the script supervisor signalled the camera crew on every movement during the 10-minute take. It was like one of those fabulous "Tinkers-to-Evers-to-Chance" triple plays. To cue each separate camera movement (and everything had to be done in utter silence) the script supervisor would check his cue board, then nod to a crew man on his left who held a long bamboo pointer. This crew man placed the end of the pointer on a predetermined spot on the floor. His action triggered Morris Rosen, the head grip, who dollied the camera to the new position, while the focus puller on the camera crane, watching his own cue sheet, simultaneously changed the focus on the camera lens.

33     But that wasn't all. Remember I told you that shooting *Rope* was very much like a Rube Goldberg drawing.

34     That wooden chest in which John Dall and Farley Granger, as the two young intellectual murderers, placed the body practically played second lead in the picture. This chest with the body inside of it was always in the center of the living room—so far as the audience is aware.

35     Yet, actually every time the camera crossed the room the chest had to be rolled off stage just in advance of the camera crane. (We couldn't stop to make new camera setups.) Moving the chest was the assignment of the four prop men crouched on their hands and knees beneath the camera. Not only did they have to move the chest aside on cue but they also had to get it back into the scene again as the camera returned.

36     And all the time the young actor who played the strangled youth had to remain inside the chest! Since there were no time lapses or camera cuts in the usual scene, he was inside the chest for a full ten minutes, the shooting of 950 feet of film. After the third take, this actor began to get, well, a little tired. "I hope to God they get it on this take," he said fervently. "Those ten minutes seem like ten hours."

37     Every piece of furniture on the stage—every table, chair, plate, dish, and drinking glass—had to be moved on cue just like the wooden chest. Once, while the characters in the play were eating a buffet supper, Joan Chandler, who played the feminine lead, had to put her wine glass down on a table. But

the table was gone. Joan merely put the glass down where the table should have been, one of the crouching prop men (unseen by the camera, of course) raised his hand and Joan's glass found a resting place in it. Another time an actor had to reach for a plate off the unseen table. Again a prop man moved in, handed the actor a plate, and the action went on.

38      It really was uncanny.

39      Naturally, in rolling a camera back and forth in a three-room apartment for 10 minutes without a halt (from living room to kitchen and back) we had to have a collapsible apartment. Actually, the basic element was the series of wild walls. ("Wild" is a term used to designate moveable or detachable flats.) In *Rope* the walls were quite literally wild. They rolled on over- head tracks heavily greased with vaseline to soundproof the skids. A separate crew stood by to roll each wall at a given cue, admitting the camera when the actors had gone through the door. When the players returned in the same shot, the wall closed and the Technicolor camera dollied back to pick up a new angle during the split second needed to make the room solid again.

40      That camera was gliding back and forth following actors all over the place. You'd see James Stewart coming suspiciously close to the chest in the living room that hid the body of the strangled youth. And in the next minute Stewart would be drinking champagne in the kitchen—all in the same 950 feet of film and without a halt in the movement of the camera.

41      There was one rather knotty problem that Jimmy Stewart, recalling his experiences in the Air Force, helped us solve. In the final moments of the story when the body is discovered and the killers are trapped, the apartment living room is flooded at intervals by great pulsations of light from a huge neon "Storage" sign just outside the window. I wanted the effect to add dramatic tension, much like the increasing crescendos of an orchestra at the climax of a symphony.

42      But for a while our electrical experts were stumped. They knew that in order to get enough light into the room during the sign's pulsations, huge arc lights would have to be hooked up on a special parallel with the actual sign, then synchronized. Then Stewart thought of the bomb release switch used in heavy

bombers during the war. This switch controlled electrically the split second intervals during which bombs were dropped over the target. So we bought a bomb release at a war surplus store, adjusted it to synchronize the alternate flashing of the neon "Storage" sign with the opening and closing of these shutters on the three huge floodlights, and got exactly the effect we wanted.

43  Those 200 miniature neon signs in the New York skyline cyclorama helped me solve a little problem of my own. It's traditional, with me at least, that I appear fleetingly in every one of my pictures. But *Rope,* with a cast of only nine people who never leave the apartment, looked like the end of the Hitchcock tradition. There was just no way that I could get into the act.

44  Then someone came up with a solution. The result? The Hitchcock countenance will appear in a neon "Reduco" sign on the side of a miniature building!

45  Because of the way the picture was shot, the actors' performance varied very little from day to day. Actually, they found it a very stimulating experience. Their cooperation during the intensive pre-shooting rehearsals was truly magnificent.

46  Instead of reading the script through once or twice, the cast spent two weeks walking through the action from the beginning to the end, much like a stage play. Remember we weren't shooting just a line at a time, nor shifting our camera setup after a one-minute take. There were ten to eleven pages of dialogue on each shot. Actually, for the camera rehearsals we used no stand-ins as such. The stars themselves acted as puppets for the camera. After the camera movement rehearsals there were intensive dress rehearsals, when everyone's job, from script supervisor to prop man, was coordinated. Following that we put Reel 1 and Reel 2 on film. The maximum number of takes on any single reel was six and the minimum was three.

47  Stewart, of course, claimed that *Rope* was the toughest job an actor ever had. And I agreed with him. He told me that he wasn't sleeping nights. "What this means," Jimmy said, "is that if the rest of the cast is perfect and I fluff a line at, say 895 feet, it becomes the colossal fluff in screen history. The only way it can be reshot is to do the whole scene over again."

48  "Well," I said, "that's exactly why I picked you for the lead."

49     As it was, Stewart had to hang around the set 18 days before making a *bona fide* entrance for the rolling camera. It was the final dress rehearsal for Reel 3 in which Jimmy makes an entrance while Farley Granger is playing the piano. The piano stopped and silence ensued, as all eyes went to Stewart. He just made it into the room and was ready to open his mouth. "Just a minute," I said. "I'd like you to make your entrance differently."

50     Jimmy punched the air in a defeated gesture. "Hey, look," he complained, "I've waited three weeks for this!"

51     What amused everyone was that I never once looked at the action after the camera got rolling. There was no point, because I couldn't do anything about it. Once the camera started it had to keep rolling until the completion of the take. My job was done the moment I called "Action!"

52     One of the vital cogs in our machinery of advance planning was Film Editor Bill Ziegler. For the first time in his or anyone else's career as a cutter, a full-length feature had to be edited before it got on film. There were no close-ups, medium, or long shots in the conventional sense, that Ziegler could insert for a change of pace. Every move, every jump from reel to reel had to be planned so that the action would not drag on the screen. All of Ziegler's work, which usually takes place after a film is shot, had to take place while the action was going on.

53     All told we had 10,000 feet of film, shot without cuts, and from beginning to end like a stage play. And I think that in editing *Rope* this way we achieved suspense and an air of mystery without transoms opening, creaky doors, clutching fingers, or a house filled with eerie shadows.

54     Technicolor helped but it wasn't the star of the picture. *Rope,* incidentally, is the first time I've ever directed a Technicolor picture. I never wanted to make a Technicolor picture merely for the sake of using color. I waited until I could find a story in which color could play a dramatic role, and still be muted to a low key. In *Rope,* sets and costumes are neutralized so that there are no glaring contrasts. The key role played by color in this film is in the background. I insisted that color be used purely as the eye received it. After all, technique is merely a means to an end and the audience must never be aware that

the camera, the director, or the photographer is performing miracles. Everything must flow smoothly and naturally.

55    *Rope* is a picture in which material has been created definitely for camera movements. Scenes were planned for visual strength, which in turn was blended with movement. The continuous flow of action meant that the eye was occupied constantly. And the elimination of the conventional shifting camera excites the audience by making the picture flow smoother and faster.

56    All of us had a lot of fun with *Rope,* particularly the publicity people. One press agent suggested that we have a world premiere in the Philippines because hemp comes from there. Another wanted us to hang it on New York's Strand Theatre.

57    I thought it best to let the boys have their fun. Their work was just beginning; mine was done. You see, I had come to the end of *my Rope.*

## Theme

1. *Rope* is the story of two thrill killers and the discovery of their crime by an amateur detective played by the actor James Stewart, who also played the lead in some now more famous Hitchcock films—*Rear Window* and *Vertigo,* for example. But Hitchcock barely mentions either the story of his movie or the character played by James Stewart. What then does make the movie his "most exciting" for him? Support your answer with evidence from the text.

2. The art of cinema is a collaborative art. List the people and their functions credited by Hitchcock as making his picture successful.

## Technique

1. Hitchcock begins with an analogy. At the time *Rope* was made in the late 1940s, Rube Goldberg was a cartoonist famous for drawing elaborate contraptions in which a bizarre chain of causes (say, toast popping up to tilt a chute, thus

allowing a marble to roll, and so on) finally produce a banal effect (say, an alarm clock being turned off.) With this information do you now find Hitchcock's analogy pertinent? Explain your answer by referring to evidence from the essay.

2. Hitchcock uses the term "wild" first in paragraph seven and again before finally defining it. Did you have any trouble understanding what he meant before you came upon the definition? If not, explain how you knew what he meant. If so, explain the possible meanings that were confusing you.

## Writing

Hitchcock is clearly excited about the techniques of his production and their invisible success. Write an essay that explains the ways he conveys his excitement through his writing.

# Frank Zappa

## In Defense of Rock and Roll                                    (1988)

*A pioneering rock artist with the Mothers of Invention, Frank
Zappa defends popular music against the attacks of philosopher
and social critic Allan Bloom. Has rock really killed American
music and perverted the tastes of its fans? Or are performers and
what they perform only comments on the rest of society?*

### The Nature of Music

Music is the soul's primitive and primary speech...without articulate speech or reason. It is not only not reasonable, it is hostile to
reason.... Civilization...is the taming or domestication of the soul's
raw passions.... Rock music has one appeal only, a barbaric
appeal, to sexual desire—not love, not eros, but sexual desire
undeveloped and untutored...

—*A. Bloom*

1     This is a puff pastry version of the belief that music is the work
of the Devil: that the nasty ol' Devil plays his fiddle and people
dance around and we don't want to see them twitching like that.
In fact, if one wants to be a real artist in the United States today
and comment on our culture, one would be very far off the track
if one did something delicate or sublime. This is not a noble, delicate, sublime country. This is a mess run by criminals. Performers who are doing the crude, vulgar, repulsive things Bloom
doesn't enjoy are only commenting on that fact.

2     In general, anti-rock propositions began when rock n' roll
began, and most of these were racially motivated. In the fifties,
petitions were circulated which said, "Don't allow your children
to buy Negro records." The petitions referred to the "raw unbri-

SOURCE: Frank Zappa's "In Defense of Rock and Roll," originally published in *New
Perspectives Quarterly* (1988), is reprinted courtesy of Blackwell Publishing.

dled passion" of screaming people with dark skin who were going to drive our children wild. Some things never go out of fashion in certain ideological camps. They are like tenets of the faith.

3    Music's real effect on people is a new field of science called psychoacoustics—the way an organism deals with wiggling air molecules. Our ears decode the wiggling air molecules, and that gives us the information of a particular musical sound. Our brain says, "This is music, this is a structure," and we deal with it based on certain tools we have acquired.

4    I personally make music because I want to ask a question, and I want to get an answer. If that question and answer amuse me, then statistically, there are a certain number of other people out there who have the same amusement factor. If I present my work to them, they will be amused by it, and we will all have a good time.

5    I need to be amused because I get bored easily and being amused entertains me. If I could be easily amused, like many people who like beer and football, I would never do anything because everything that would be beautiful for my life would already be provided by American television.

6    But beer and television bore me, so what am I going to do? I am going to be alive for X number of years. I have to do something with my time besides sleep and eat. So, I devise little things to amuse myself. If I can amuse somebody else, great. And if I can amuse somebody else and earn a living while doing it, that is a true miracle in the twentieth century!

## Music and the Dark Forces of the Soul

> To Plato and Nietzsche, the history of music is a series of attempts to give form and beauty to the dark, chaotic, premonitory forces in the soul—to make them serve a higher purpose, an ideal, to give man's duties a fullness.
>
> —*A. Bloom*

7    This is a man who has fallen for rock's fabricated image of itself. This is the worst kind of ivory tower intellectualism. Anybody who talks about dark forces is right on the fringe of mumbo jumbo. Dark forces? What is this, another product from Lucasfilm? The passions! When was the last time you saw an

American exhibit any form of passion other than the desire to shoot a guy on the freeway? Those are the forces of evil as far as I am concerned.

8      If there are dark forces hovering in the vicinity of the music business, they are mercantile forces. We meet the darkness when we meet the orchestra committees, when we get in touch with funding organizations, when we deal with people who give grants and when we get into the world of commerce that greets us when we arrive with our piece of art. Whether it's a rock n' roll record or a symphony, it's the same machinery lurking out there.

9      The reason a person writes a piece of music has got nothing to do with dark forces. I certainly don't have dark forces lurking around me when I'm writing. If someone is going to write a piece of music, in fact they are preoccupied with the boring labor and very hard work involved. That's what's really going on.

## What Makes Music Classical

Rock music...has risen to its current heights in the education of the young on the ashes of classical music, and in an atmosphere in which there is no intellectual resistance to attempts to tap the rawest passions.... Cultivation of the soul uses the passions and satisfies them while sublimating them and giving them an artistic unity.... Bach's religious intentions and Beethoven's revolutionary and humane ones are clear enough examples.

—*A. Bloom*

10     This is such nonsense. All the people recognized as great classical composers are recognized at this point for two reasons:

11     One, during the time these composers were alive and writing they had patrons who liked what they did and who therefore paid them money or gave them a place to live so that the composers could stay alive by writing dots on pieces of paper. If any of the compositions these men wrote had not been pleasing to a church, a duke, or a king, they would have been out of work and their music would not have survived.

12     There is a book called *Grove's Dictionary of Music and Musicians,* with thousands of names in it. You have never heard of most of the people in that book, nor have you heard

their music. That doesn't mean they wrote awful music, it means they didn't have hits.

13    So basically, the people who are recognized as the geniuses of classical music had hits. And the person who determined whether or not it was a hit was a king, a duke, or the church or whoever paid the bill. The desire to get a sandwich or something to drink had a lot to do with it. And the content of what they wrote was to a degree determined by the musical predilections of the guy who was paying the bill.

14    Today, we have a similar situation in rock n' roll. We have kings, dukes, and popes: the A&R guy who spots a group or screens the tape when it comes in; the business affairs guy who writes the contract; the radio station programmers who choose what records get air play.

15    The other reason the classical greats survived is their works are played over and over again by orchestras. The reasons they are played over and over again are: (1) all the musicians in the orchestra know how to play them because they learned them in the conservatory; (2) the orchestra management programs these pieces because the musicians already know them and therefore it costs less to rehearse them; (3) the composers are dead so the orchestras pay no royalties for the use of the music.

16    Today, survivability is based on the number of specimens in the market place—the sheer numbers of plastic objects. Many other compositions from this era will vanish, but Michael Jackson's *Thriller* album will survive because there are 30 million odd pieces of plastic out there. No matter what we may think of the content, a future generation may pick up that piece of plastic and say. "Oh, they were like this."

17    I suppose somewhere in the future there will be other men like Bloom certifying that the very narrow spectrum of rock n' roll which survives composes the great works of the later half of the twentieth century.

## The Difference Between Classical Music and Rock n' Roll

Rock music provides premature ecstasy and, in this respect, is like the drugs with which it is allied…. These are the three great

> lyrical themes: sex, hate and a smarmy, hypocritical version of brotherly love.... Nothing noble, sublime, profound, delicate, tasteful, or even decent can find a place in such tableaux.
>
> —*A. Bloom*

18    Again, Bloom is not looking at what is really going on here. The ugliness in this society is not a product of unrefined art, but of unrefined commerce, wild superstition, and religious fanaticism.

19    The real difference between the classics and rock n' roll is mostly a matter of form. In order to say we have written a symphony, the design we put on a piece of paper has to conform to certain specifications. We have an exposition that lasts a certain amount of time, then modulation, development, and recapitulation. It's like a box, like an egg carton. We must fill all the little spaces in the egg carton with the right forms. If we do, we can call it a symphony because it conforms to the spaces in that box.

20    Compare that creative process to rock n' roll. If we want to have an AM hit record, we have another egg carton to fill. We have an intro, a couple of verses, a bridge, another verse, and then a fade out. All of which requires a "hook." That's a very rigid form. If we wander away from that form, our song's not going to go on the radio because it doesn't sound like it fits into their format.

21    Now, whether the person writing the song graduated from a conservatory or whether they came out of a garage, they know that in order to finish a piece they have to do certain things to make it fit into a certain form. In the classical period the sonata or a concerto or symphony had to be that certain size and shape or else the king was not going to like it. One could die. These were literally matters of life and death, but not in the way Bloom defines them.

## The Rock Business

> The family spiritual void has left the field open to rock music.... The result is nothing less than parents' loss of control over their children's moral education at a time when no one else is seriously concerned with it. This has been achieved by an alliance between

> the strange young males who have the gift of divining the mob's
> emergent wishes—our versions of Thrasymachus, Socrates' rhetor-
> ical adversary—and the record-company executives, the new rob-
> ber barons, who mine gold out of rock.
>
> *—A. Bloom*

22    There is some truth to that, but how did we get to this point
and what do we do about it?

23    We got here because teenagers are the most sought-after
consumers. The whole idea of merchandising the prepubes-
cent masturbational fantasy is not necessarily the work of the
songwriter or the singer, but the work of the merchandiser who
has elevated rock n' roll to the commercial enterprise it is.

24    In the beginning, rock n' roll was young kids singing to
other kids about their girlfriends. That's all there was. The guys
who made those records came from Manual Arts High School.
They went into a recording studio, were given some wine,
$25, and a bunch of records when their song came out as a sin-
gle—which made them heroes at school. That was their career,
not, "Well, we're not going to sing until we get a $125 thou-
sand advance."

25    Today, rock n' roll is about getting a contract with a major
company, and pretty much doing what the company tells you
to do. The company promotes the image of rock n' roll as
being wild and fun when in fact it's just a dismal business.

26    Record companies have people who claim to be experts on
what the public really wants to hear. And they inflict their taste
on the people who actually make the music. To be a big success, you need a really big company behind you because really
big companies can make really big distribution deals.

27    Even people who are waiting to go into the business know
it's a business. They spend a great deal of time planning what
they will look like and getting a good publicity photo before
they walk in the door with their tape. And the record companies tend to take the attitude that it doesn't make too much difference what the tape sounds like as long as the artists look
right, because they can always hire a producer who will fix up
the sound and make it the way they want it—so long as the
people wear the right clothes and have the right hair.

## Retaining Classical Music

> Classical music is dead among the young.... Rock music is as unquestioned and unproblematic as the air the students breathe, and very few have any acquaintance at all with classical music.... Classical music is now a special taste, like Greek language or pre-Columbian archeology, not a common culture of reciprocal communication and psychological shorthand.
>
> —*A. Bloom*

28      On this point, Bloom and I can agree, but how can a child be blamed for consuming only that which is presented to him? Most kids have never been in contact with anything other than this highly merchandised stuff.

29      When I testified in front of the Senate, I pointed out that if they don't like the idea of young people buying certain kinds of music, why don't they stick a few dollars back into the school system to have music appreciation? There are kids today who have never heard a string quartet; they have never heard a symphony orchestra. I argued that the money for music appreciation courses, in terms of social good and other benefits such as improved behavior or uplifting the spirit, is far less than the cost of another set of uniforms for the football team. But I frankly don't see people waving banners in the streets saying more music appreciation in schools.

30      When I was in school, we could go into a room and they had records there. I could hear anything I wanted by going in there and putting on a record. I won't say I enjoyed everything that was played for me, but I was curious, and if I had never heard any of that music I wouldn't know about it.

31      Once we're out of school, the time we can spend doing that type of research is limited because most of us are out looking for a job flipping hamburgers in the great tradition of the Reagan economic miracle. When all is said and done, that's the real source of America's barren and arid lives.

## Theme

1. In his first paragraph Zappa defends music that contains "crude, vulgar, repulsive things" by calling it a "commentary"

on society. Explain with examples how throughout the essay he sees rock music as an art of "commentary."

2. Zappa says that the facts of social ugliness do not come from music, but rather from other social sources. Explain with examples what he claims these sources are.

## Technique

1. Zappa frequently uses the word "boring." Explain how and why the word plays such a large part in his critical vocabulary. What does it allow him to do? What does he use the word to fight? What are its advantages as a weapon?

2. He refers to him as "Bloom." Suppose he had said "Professor Bloom" or "Dr. Bloom." Explain how and why these different ways of naming the same person create different impressions of the author and his subject.

## Writing

Write an essay on Frank Zappa that uses the format of his essay on Allan Bloom. That is, pick a series of quotations from Zappa and comment on them from your own point of view.

# Celia Cruz

## Changing Times                                        (2004)

> *Celia Cruz was a ten-time Grammy nominee who sang only in Spanish. Fleeing her native Cuba for the United States after Castro came to power, "The Queen of Salsa" became a success in her adopted country and throughout Latin America. She received a Smithsonian Lifetime Achievement award, a National Medal of the Arts, and honorary doctorates from Yale and the University of Miami.*

1    I don't think I'm exaggerating when I say that we were all looking forward to the arrival of 2002, which in my family's case brought with it both good and difficult moments. For instance, our album *Siempre Viviré* was a sensation. The title, *I Will Survive,* is my reality, since although no one lives forever in the physical sense, I believe that God has blessed me with immortality through my music. My music has been my passport to the world, since music is the one truly universal language. When I arrive in countries whose language I don't understand, all I need to do is sing and I am received with opened arms. As I said earlier, I love all types of music, and as a matter of fact, in Cuba I even used to enjoy the music of the Chinese immigrants who lived on the island. That's why when the salsa rap piece "La Negra Tiene Tumbao" was brought to me, I thought it would be wonderful to record.

2    Although the video was a bit risqué, the song became a hit. When we started filming it with the director Ernesto Fundora, who also did my video, "Mi Vida es Cantar," I knew it would be wonderful, since I really do enjoy his work. Once we

SOURCE: Pages 211–212 from *Celia* by Celia Cruz and Ana Cristinea Reymundo. Copyright ©2004 by Sarao Entertainment. Reprinted by permission of HarperCollins Publishers Inc.

arrived in Mexico to start filming, Ernesto explained the whole process to Omer, and when Omer explained it to me, it sounded perfect. The casting began for the main role, and a stunning young Guatemalan woman named Deborah David was chosen. We were introduced, but Omer and Ernesto never told me that Deborah would appear nude, with only body paint covering her. Since I had only one day to film, because I was on my way to perform in Venezuela, we had to work a long, full day, so I was too concerned with my own role to ask what other people in the video were doing. Pupi Fernández, my hairdresser in Mexico, prepared my whole wardrobe for the shoot. The dress I was to wear was decorated with peacock feathers, so Pupi did my hair beautifully, complete with peacock feathers throughout my coif.

3      After we recorded my part in the video, so much time seemed to pass before I saw it that I forgot all about it. We went to Miami to record Cristina's show as part of the promotional tour for the album, and before leaving for the studio, Omer pulled Pedro and me aside and said, "Celia, you know that times have changed, and we are in a new millennium. We've just received a copy of the video, and it's very modern. You look very good, but the model is wearing very few clothes. I think it would be best if you record Cristina's show tonight first, and then we'll ask her and Marcos if we can watch it in their office."

4      When I heard Omer's words, I knew immediately that something strange was going on, but I tried to ignore it. Later, when Cristina, Marcos, Pedro, Omer, and I were watching the video in the office, I almost fainted. I said that it couldn't be shown to the public that way. I was afraid that people would start saying that I had lost my mind. But Cristina convinced me that it was fine and acceptable the way it was and that people would love it. And she was right. The video was a great help for the single and the album in general, and it became especially popular among men. But the best thing about it is what it did for Deborah's career. She became so popular that she's now a famous fashion model in Mexico. I am very happy for her, and most important, I am very proud of her.

## Theme

1. Celia Cruz clearly values music very highly. In your own words explain her rationale for believing that music can make someone "immortal."

2. The story of the song "La Negra Tiene Tumbao" makes a subplot throughout the selection. Explain in your own words how that subplot serves to illustrate Cruz's contention about the universality of music.

## Technique

1. How does the detail of the peacock feathers at the end of paragraph two help to dramatize and support Cruz's explanation for not knowing in advance about the controversial aspects of the video she was involved in making?

2. In paragraph four Cruz writes: "The video was a great help for the single and the album in general, and it became especially popular among men." Surely how you read these words affects your sense of the writer. Is Celia Cruz being ironic in the last clause of the sentence? Does she express, say, a naïveté about the video? Or is it a mock naïveté ? Is she being playful or self-absorbed? Explain your answer.

## Writing

Celia Cruz prepares us fully in advance for the nature of the video that she made, yet she was herself very much surprised at the time. Using as much of her language as possible, rewrite her account so that the reader learns what has happened only at the same moment in the story that Celia Cruz does. In a paragraph explain how and why one version—hers or yours—would be the best choice as a presentation of the material involved.

# Mel Brooks

## Springtime for the Music Man in Me    (2001)

*Born Melvin Kaminsky in Brooklyn, Mel Brooks has been a star comedy writer and performer since the 1950s. His production of* The Producers *on Broadway won 12 Tony awards—the most ever given to one show. He tells us about the career that led to that show in the following essay, originally printed in* The New York Times.

1   Long, long ago. The early summer of 1935. I was 9 years old, happy as a lark, and living with my widowed mother and three older brothers in an $18-a-month fifth-floor walkup in a tenement at 365 South Third Street in the Williamsburg section of Brooklyn.

2   We lived in the back. Though it was the depths of the Depression, there was music in the air. Music everywhere. Not Vivaldi or Verdi, but the popular music of the day—Bing Crosby singing "From Monday On" on the radio, the Millers in the next apartment playing Russ Columbo records on their wind-up Victrola, a wannabe Benny Goodman practicing "Don't Be That Way" on his squeaky clarinet in the apartment across the backyard, a piano player in the open window of Heller's Music Emporium down the street, knocking out Broadway tunes as a come-on to peddle sheet music.

3   There was music coming out of me, too. A kid who grew up with his ear glued to the radio, I knew the lyrics of all of 1935's biggest hits and loudly sang them all day long as I happily danced along the sidewalks. Actually, I was a pretty good singer, on pitch and usually able to hit all of the top notes, and I always got 'em at family parties with my imitations of Jolson singing "Toot, Toot, Tootsie" and Eddie Cantor doing "If You Knew Susie."

4    And then there was whistling, which I was also pretty good at. But the greatest whistler I ever knew was my mother's brother, my Uncle Joe, a taxi driver who seemed to know every song ever written. He was a happy-go-lucky little guy, Uncle Joe, and I mean little, barely five feet tall. When you saw a cab coming down the street without a driver, that was Uncle Joe. In fact, he'd had to put in specially built-up "Adler's Elevator" clutch and gas pedals in order for his feet to reach them, while to see over his steering wheel, he sat up on a stack of five or six telephone books. (In the Depression, when practically nobody could afford a phone, the books were a lot thinner than they are now.) And he always whistled while he worked, 12 hours a day driving his clunky Checker cab all over Brooklyn and the lesser boroughs, like Manhattan.

5    My father died when I was two years old, and Uncle Joe, keenly aware that I was missing a dad, always took a special interest in me—bounced me on his knee, pulled my sled through the snow, and bought me chocolate creams at Loft's.

6    And it was Uncle Joe, one famous Friday evening, who breezed into our apartment with the news that one of his fares, in exchange for a free ride out to Coney Island, had given him two tickets to what was then the biggest hit musical on Broadway—Cole Porter's *Anything Goes,* starring William Gaxton, Victor Moore, and none other than Miss Ethel Merman.

7    The tickets were for the next afternoon, Saturday matinee, and Uncle Joe announced that if I wanted to go along with him to the show, he'd take me.

8    Did I want to go? You never heard a louder or faster "Yessss!" in your life! I hadn't ever seen a musical, on Broadway or anywhere else, but in those days when most of America's most popular songs were from Broadway shows, I already knew the tunes and the lyrics to a whole bunch of the numbers from *Anything Goes.*

9    Even in 1935 it was illegal for a New York taxi driver to carry a passenger in his car when he had his off-duty flag up, and so whenever Uncle Joe took me anywhere in his cab I had to hide on the floor in the back. And that's how, on that long-ago Saturday afternoon in June of 1935, I went to my first Broadway show—scrunched down in the back of Uncle Joe's bumpy old taxi. I could tell by the hum of the tires on the steel grid

when we were crossing the Williamsburg Bridge, but the rest of the ride was pure guesswork as we journeyed from South Third Street to West 52nd Street in Manhattan and the Alvin Theater (now named after my longtime friend Neil Simon), where *Anything Goes* was playing. Uncle Joe sat up on his phone books as he drove, whistling one Cole Porter tune after another, while I sang along with him from the back floor.

10  So our seats weren't exactly two on the aisle in the fourth row of the orchestra. How about in the next to the last row at the top of the balcony? But I couldn't have been happier. I was actually listening to Ethel Merman herself singing "I Get a Kick Out of You" on a stage, live, with me there. There were no microphones in theaters back then and we were miles away, but Uncle Joe and I nonetheless agreed that Merman sang just a little too loud. But, wow, I still thought she was the greatest thing since chocolate milk. I had goose bumps. I almost fainted. And what a score by Cole Porter! Soaring melodies, astonishing lyrics, one great song after another—not only "I Get a Kick Out of You" but also "You're the Top," "It's Delovely," "All Through the Night" and, of course, the show's wonderful title song, "Anything Goes."

11  And, oh, the glory of the sound that came from that orchestra pit, led by the brass section, those blaring trumpets and thrilling trombones reaching for the moon. "Anything Goes" was funny too—falling-down funny. When the final curtain fell, I leaped to my feet and cheered my nine-year-old head off; way up there at the top of the balcony, I figured that I was as close to heaven as I'd ever get.

12  I fell in love forever with Broadway musical comedy that afternoon and also began a lifetime of admiration for the music and lyrics of Cole Porter, who is still my all-time No. 1 favorite songwriter. (Years later, when I discovered to my amazement that Cole Porter wasn't Jewish, I was taken aback for a moment but then quickly forgave him. I'd become a practicing Episcopalian, too, if I could write songs like his.) I remember thinking while lying awake in bed that night after seeing *Anything Goes* that when I grew up I wanted somehow to be involved in a musical comedy, maybe even as the writer of its songs. Being a Broadway songwriter, I decided, would be even better than playing shortstop for the Brooklyn Dodgers, which up until then had been my most fantastic dream.

13    Something happened. Life got in the way of my becoming the next Cole Porter. At the age of 14, I got a paying job in music, but as a drummer rather than a songwriter, playing in a band every summer at a place called the Butler Lodge in the Catskills, where one night when I was 16 the comic M.C. suddenly took sick and I jumped in to take his place.

14    I got big laughs with terrible jokes like, "The girl I went out with last night was so skinny that when I took her to a restaurant the headwaiter said, 'Check your umbrella?' "

15    I never went back to the drums again—I was now a $25-a-week comic, and on my dressing room they'd hung a six-pointed star. In those days, every Catskill comic had his own introductory song—"My name is Donny, they say I'm funny," etc. And so I did at last write my first song, which I'm proud and ashamed to say went like this:

> Here I am, I'm Melvin Brooks,
> I've come to stop the show,
> Just a ham who's minus looks,
> But in your hearts I'll grow.
> I'll tell ya gags, I'll sing you songs,
> Just happy little snappy tunes
> That roll along.
> I'm out of my mind, so won't you be kind,
> And please love … Melvin Brooks!

World War II. Out of the Catskills and into the Army, which amazingly enough first sent me to college: I became a cadet at the Virginia Military Institute. (Talk about a little Jewish fish out of water, although I loved V.M.I., and the gracious Virginians couldn't have been nicer to the brash kid from Brooklyn.) But then the Army got serious and I was next a combat engineer being shot at by Germans in Belgium and the Rhineland, after which, when the shooting stopped, I was transferred into Special Services and became a G.I. comedian entertaining the troops with song parodies like Cole Porter's "Begin the Beguine" morphed into "When we begin to clean the latrine."

16    Out of the Army, back in New York, and sticking with comedy rather than songwriting, on to a whole lot of frantically happy years spent turning out comic sketches for television's "Your Show of Shows." Fast forward to 1964, when I risked a

steady paycheck from television to quit my job in order to write my first movie, *The Producers,* a comedy that for plot purposes needed a couple of original songs.

17    I said to my then wife, the incredibly beautiful and incredibly talented Anne Bancroft, whom I'm happy to say is also still my now wife, that I needed to find someone to write the songs.

18    "I know who could write them," she said.

19    "Who?" I asked.

20    "You," she said. "You're musical, you're a good singer, and besides, you've been talking my head off ever since I met you about how much you want to be a songwriter. So take a pad, a pencil, go into the next room, and I bet within an hour you'll come out with a very nice song."

21    I did what she said. I took a pad, a pencil and went into the next room. And lo and behold, one hour and one month later came out with "Springtime for Hitler." I had come up with not only the lyrics but also the tune, which I'd heard in my head, picked out on a piano, and then hummed into a tape recorder—a full 32-bar song that a musicologist friend of mine then transcribed into actual notes on actual music paper, a method of composing I've since used for all of my songs. (I went to V.M.I., not Juilliard.) I also wrote a second song for *The Producers* entitled "Prisoners of Love." I can't tell you how thrilled I was to see the first copies of the sheet music of my songs and the credit in the upper-right-hand corner: "Words & Music by Mel Brooks."

22    When it was first released, sad to say, *The Producers* was neither a critical nor a commercial success. As a matter of fact, it was slammed by critics all over the place, including even by the critic who wrote for the very newspaper you're now reading. Scathing reviews and the initial failure of the picture at the box office everywhere but in New York, Chicago, and Los Angeles left me more discouraged than I can tell you. I nearly gave up show business and was seriously considering going back to college. I'd major in organic chemistry, I figured, become a pharmacist, and open a little drugstore back in Williamsburg, at the corner of South Third and Hooper.

23    Fast forward again, to three years ago, the spring of 1998, when I got a phone call in my office at the Culver Studios in Los Angeles. I hadn't become a pharmacist after all. I'd become a

moviemaker. The call was from a very important man who shall remain nameless, David Geffen. David, in case you haven't heard, is a slightly well-off record-industry legend who together with Steven Spielberg and Jeffrey Katzenberg founded and now runs Hollywood's newest movie studio, DreamWorks SKG.

24     I consider David to be one of the wisest men in all of show business, and so when he told me over the phone that he wanted me to turn *The Producers* into a Broadway musical comedy that he would personally produce, I didn't dismiss the notion out of hand but nonetheless ultimately gave him a polite no. (For years, a number of other producers had been after me to make a musical out of *The Producers* and I'd given each of them a polite no, too.) But David Geffen doesn't take no, polite or otherwise, for an answer. Every time I picked up the phone, he was at the other end. In fact, after the 16<sup>th</sup> increasingly persuasive call in eight days, my polite no all of a sudden turned into a resounding yes! Of course I'll do it! But when I suggested that I'd like to try to write the songs for the show, music as well as lyrics, he said he already had another songwriter in mind, none other than Jerry Herman.

25     I could scarcely quarrel with his choice—I'd been an admirer of Jerry Herman ever since his first Broadway show, *Milk and Honey,* and I'd been in the audience marveling at his words and music at other memorable shows of his—*Hello, Dolly!, Mame, Dear World, Mack and Mabel* and *La Cage aux Folles.* So even though I wanted more than anything else to at least have a shot at writing my own score, I agreed to meet with Jerry. I went to his home in the hills of Beverly, where he led me into his music room and immediately told me two things: 1) how much he loved *The Producers,* and 2) how sorry he was that he didn't think he was the right man to write the songs for it.

26     But, he went on, he knew of another songwriter who would be absolutely perfect.

27     "Who is he?" I asked.

28     "Let me play you some of his songs," said Jerry, sitting down at his grand piano and first playing "I'm Tired," a song that the unforgettable Madeline Kahn sang in *Blazing Saddles,* and then "Hope for the Best, Expect the Worst," from my second movie, *The Twelve Chairs.*

29 "Wait a moment, hold it," I said. "I wrote those songs."

30 "Of course you did," said Jerry with a grin, "and you also wrote 'High Anxiety'—you're a very good songwriter."

31 "I am?" I asked.

32 "You are," he said. "What's more, you'd be crazy to do a Broadway musical of *The Producers* without including 'Springtime for Hitler' and 'Prisoners of Love.' So you've already got two major songs written. All you have to do is write a dozen or so more and you've got yourself a Broadway score. Go, with my blessings, do it!"

33 And I did. In fact, I wrote 17 more songs. With a lot of help along the way from a lot of people, but especially three very special people. First, Thomas Meehan, an old friend and the Tony Award-winning writer of the book of *Annie,* who wrote the book of *The Producers* with me, and who, during two and a half years of working at my side, showed me where the musical should sing and where it shouldn't, helped me to figure out what sort of songs I should write and what they should be about, and sat in with me on countless lyric-writing idea sessions.

34 Second, Glen Kelly, a musical genius and brilliant arranger who took my rude, simple 32-bar songs and turned them into—I'm both hoping and nervously believe—glorious Broadway show tunes.

35 And finally, Susan Stroman, the show's incredible Tony Award-winning choreographer and director, whose innovative ideas for staging have made my score work in the theater in ways that I would never have imagined. My songs were, like Adam, crudely formed out of the clay of the earth, and just as God blew life into Adam, Stro, as she is known to one and all, breathed life into my score—made it sing, made it dance.

36 As things turned out, when we finished the first draft of the show, a year ago, and I was chomping at the bit to get it onstage, David Geffen found himself far too busy with various projects at DreamWorks to be able to spend a year in New York as a hands-on Broadway producer and so graciously stepped aside to let other producers take over the show. "All I want is a couple of tickets down front for opening night," said David, "so I can stand up in the crowd and cheer you on!"

37    So now the long-ago dream of the 9-year-old Brooklyn boy who was once me has at last come true. This Thursday evening, a brand-new Broadway musical comedy called *The Producers* will open at the St. James Theater with the credit line I'd imagined a mere 66 years ago: "Music and Lyrics by Mel Brooks."

38    And, uh-oh, I am once again facing the critics with something called *The Producers.* I hope for the best, expect the worst, and of course there is always, waiting for me in Williamsburg, that little drugstore at the corner of South Third and Hooper.

## Theme

1. List the stages of Mel Brooks's life as a "Music Man."

2. Mel Brooks tells us his theme song when he was a stand-up comic ended with the words: "And please love...Melvin Brooks." In your view, what's to love or not love in the Mel Brooks who appears in this essay? Characterize the personality you find expressed in his autobiographical sketch, and point to the evidence that created your feelings about his persona.

## Technique

1. Brooks claims he found musical comedy to be exciting from a very early age. Point to some of the ways he conveys his excitement.

2. In your opinion, do the scenes that Brooks gives us of his life before he attended his first musical comedy contribute anything to the story of his life in musical comedy? Explain your answer.

## Writing

"And please love...Melvin Brooks." What about it? Do you love the Mel Brooks who appears as a personality in this essay? Write an essay explaining and defending your answer.

# Hank Aaron

## Race and the Record                                            **(1991)**

*Hank Aaron was born in Alabama in the middle of the Great
Depression when there were no African Americans at all in
major league baseball. He hit 755 home runs in his career, passing Babe Ruth's record in 1974. The following account of
the pressures of that year is taken from his autobiography* I Had
a Hammer.

1      With all that had happened in the previous year, I was
probably never as eager and ready for a season to begin as I
was in 1973. Willie Mays was behind me, Mathews and Billye
were alongside, and Babe Ruth was straight ahead. A ballplayer
needs something extra to keep him going at the age of thirty-
nine, and no player ever had as much to play for as I had that
year. I was on the verge of doing something that would give
me a place in baseball history, and I couldn't wait to do it. I
had been waiting and waiting all my life for something or
other; now it was up to me. Unless you grew up black in the
South, I don't think you can imagine the surge of freedom and
power I felt just knowing that I controlled my own destiny.

2      My high lasted for about a month, maybe less. Ironically, the
thing that brought me down was hitting home runs. It wasn't
that I couldn't hit them; the problem was that I couldn't hit anything else. Seven of my first nine hits in 1973 were home runs,
and for several weeks my batting average was down around
.200. That was all the critics needed to see. It was plain to them
that I was no longer a complete hitter. I was concerned only
with the record, and I had lost all interest in the good of the
team. They made that clear in their letters to me.

SOURCE: Pages 229–232 from *I Had a Hammer* by Hank Aaron and Lonnie Wheeler.
Copyright ©1991 by Henry Aaron and Lonnie Wheeler. Reprinted by permission of
HarperCollins Publishers Inc.

Dear Henry:

First I would like to say you are regarded by many as a good baseball player and a good hitter. To even remotely suggest that you are a great player or hitter, a person would have to be judged insane.

3   I went into the season wanting to break the record that summer, but it wasn't long before I changed my goal. I still wanted the record, but I didn't want to do it batting .240. I wanted to hit .300, and if the record came along the way, great. If not, it would come the next year. There was no time pressure. Only two things could keep me from breaking the record—a serious injury or a terrible batting average. If I couldn't get my average up to a respectable level, there was a chance I would stop short, because I'd never been a one-dimensional hitter and I didn't want to be one at the moment history came knocking. So, as far as I was concerned, everything was fine and dandy as long as I stayed healthy and the base hits fell in.

4   Not everybody shared that opinion, however.

Dear Nigger,

Everybody loved Babe Ruth. You will be the most hated man in this country if you break his career home run record.

Dear Nigger,

In my humble way of thinking, you are doing more to hurt Baseball than any other that ever played the game. You may break the record and you may replace Babe Ruth in the hearts of the liberal sportswriters, the liberal newspapers, TV and radio, as well as in the hearts of the long-haired Hippies. But you will never replace the Babe in the hearts of clear-thinking members of our Society. So, roll on in your undeserved glory, Black Boy.

Friend Hank,

If you should "break" Babe Ruth's record of 714 home runs, remember the Babe averaged a home run for every eleven times at bat. For several years he was pitching. If the Babe had been playing every day possible, his home runs would be close to 900.

I believe you are a man of high morals and wouldn't want to be the holder of a title that could be later classified as being tainted. Think it over Hank.

Dear Black Boy,

Listen Black Boy, We don't want no nigger Babe Ruth.

Dear Super Spook,
First of all. I don't care for the color of shit. You are pretty damn repugnant trying to break the Babe's record. You boogies will think that you invented baseball or something.

Dear Mr. Nigger,
I hope you don't break the Babe's record. How do I tell my kids that a nigger did it?

5    In May, when our crowds were so pitiful that you could practically hear somebody crack open a peanut, there was a small group of rednecks who sat in the right-field stands and heckled me for three straight nights. At first, it was the same stuff I was used to hearing, mostly about all the money I was making for striking out and hitting into double plays, but as they became drunker and louder they became more obscene and personal, and I became angrier and angrier. They were using Sally League language, and I wasn't going to let anybody take me back to the Sally League. Finally, in the ninth inning of the third night, I walked over to the stands and told them I was going to come up there and kick their asses if they didn't shut up. But before I could do anything I would later regret, the security police arrived and escorted them out of the park. I really can't say what might have happened if security hadn't come. All I know is that I was fed up.

6    I didn't expect the fans to give me a standing ovation every time I stepped on the field, but I thought a few of them might come over to my side as I approached Ruth. At the very least, I felt I had earned the right not to be verbally abused and racially ravaged in my home ballpark. I felt I had earned the right to be treated like a human being in the city that was supposed to be too busy to hate. The way I saw it, the only thing Atlanta was too busy for was baseball. It didn't seem to give a damn about the Braves, and it seemed like the only thing that mattered about the home run record was that a nigger was about to step out of line and break it. I was angry enough that I made a public statement in which I charged that America was still a racist country and all that Atlanta had to offer was hatred and resentment. I knew, of course, that there were plenty of good people and at least a few good baseball fans in Atlanta, but I was mad at the whole South. Later, I backed off a little

and said that the only thing wrong with Atlanta was that it had Georgia sticking out of it. The fact is, I like and admire Atlanta now, and in many ways I'm proud to live there, but I sure didn't feel that way in 1973.

## Theme

1. Hank Aaron begins this excerpt by announcing at least two themes: his desire to break Babe Ruth's home run record and his desire not to be "a one-dimensional hitter." Does he give examples from the hate mail he received that concern themselves with both themes or only one? Explain your answer.

2. Explain the ways in which Hank Aaron's attitude toward the city of Atlanta changed over time. Say how he felt in the beginning, how he changed, and where he came out.

## Technique

1. Hank Aaron often displays some mixed emotions. Pick a paragraph that shows this complexity in his emotions, and analyze how his emotional struggle gets expressed.

2. Each example of hate mail begins with what in the conventions of correspondence is called a salutation, and each salutation begins with a term of affection or compliment. What do you make of this? Why do you think the letters began that way? Does their opening make them seem more conventional? Polite? Hateful? Silly? Dim-witted? Explain your reasoning.

## Writing

Write Hank Aaron a letter that expresses your views of his achievement as an athlete and as a man.

# Barry Bonds

(2001)

*A sure-fire first-ballot Hall of Famer, Barry Bonds's power and speed won him three MVP awards in the 1990s and recognition as the best all-around player of the decade. He became the second 40-40 player in 1996 and narrowly missed repeating the feat in 1997, falling three stolen bases short. In late April 1996, he became only the fourth member of the 300-homer, 300-stolen base club, in 1998 he became the first 400-400 player in history and, by the time his career is over, he could become the only player to achieve the never-imagined 500-500 level. His combination of power, average, and speed rivals that of his father Bobby Bonds or even that of his godfather, Willie Mays. By the way, he also holds the single-season home run record. On the other hand, his personality and behavior has been considered insufferably insolent by the vast majority of fans and teammates. Does he show another side in this public service advertisement?*

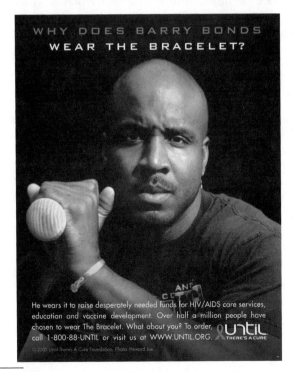

SOURCE: Used by permission of Until There's a Cure Foundation.

## Theme

1. How would you characterize the facial expression of Barry Bonds here? For example, does he look annoyed, defiant, bashful, cynical? How does the expression contribute to the theme of the public service advertisement, in your view?

2. How does the visual element that might be called "the bat theme" connect with "the bracelet theme," in your view? For example, does their dual display imply a dual degree of commitment? Explain the reasoning behind your answer.

## Technique

1. A famous athlete is used to advertise something—an old story. But what is new here?

2. Suppose the headline had read: "Barry Bonds Wears the Bracelet"? Compare this expression to what we really get and explain why you think one or the other makes the better choice for the purposes of the advertisement.

## Writing

Write an essay in which you explain what you think about the value contributed by celebrities who support public causes.

## EXERCISES

**Intertextual Questions**

1. Frank Zappa explains troubling content in rock as a commentary. Hank Aaron describes his experience with hate mail in sports, and some rappers—Eminem, for example—have been accused of homophobic songs. Do you think Frank Zappa would defend either the letter writers or the rappers or both on the same basis of cultural commentary? Explain your reasoning.

2. In different ways Julia Child, Celia Cruz, and Hank Aaron all describe changes in standards within modern mass culture— changes in domestic life, in the arts, and in professional sports. Have you noticed other changes in these or other fields during your own lifetime? Discuss any changes (or any continuities) that you have observed.

3. Do you think that movies like those of Alfred Hitchcock and Steven Spielberg make comments on modern mass culture as Frank Zappa says rock music does, or are they only entertainment? Discuss the issue using particular examples.

4. In your opinion, who is the most classic of the classic performers included in this chapter? Discuss your answer with the support of particular examples from the performer's career.

5. Though many forms of mass culture have been discussed in this chapter, surely not all of them have been. Make your own list of the fields that have been left out and include the classic performers that you think could best represent them.

**Suggestions for Writing**

1. Frank Zappa confines himself to defending some aspects of rock music as comments on larger aspects of modern life. For reasons other than those given by Allan Bloom, the Miss America Pageant has also been attacked as vulgar and insulting by some people. In your opinion, would Zappa be able to defend

the Miss America Pageant on the same basis that he defends rock? Write an essay that attacks or defends the Miss America Pageant, being sure to pay some attention to Zappa's ideas about art as commentary.

2. Steven Spielberg and Alfred Hitchcock are two of the most admired directors in movie history. Which director's work do you prefer? Write an essay explaining and defending your choice.

3. In Chapter 7 Jane Fonda urged her readers to "use the media for public health." Do you think Barry Bonds has done what Fonda urged? Write an essay in which you explore and explain some of the different ways in which Barry Bonds uses the media for public health.

4. Mel Brooks and Alfred Hitchcock clearly revel in the technical aspects of their respective arts. Write an essay that analyzes the ways each person enacts and expresses his excitement about the tricks of his trade.

5. Of the classic performers appearing in this chapter, whose work do you most enjoy? Write an essay explaining and defending your choice by analyzing particular examples of performance from the career as a whole.

# CELEBRITY WEB SITES

The following is a list of Web sites that you may want to visit to find more information about the celebrities whose selections are contained in this book.

## Part I: Constructing and Representing a Private Self

### Chapter One: Origins and Turning Points

1. Whoopie Goldberg, "Christmas in New York"
   www.achievement.org/autodoc/page/gol0pro-1
2. Sissy Spacek, "Homemade in Texas"
   www.famoustexans.com/spacek.htm
3. Joe Piscopo, "It's a Jersey Thing"
   www.joepiscopo.com
4. Margaret Cho, "Friendless in Frisco"
   www.margaretcho.com
5. Sammy Sosa, "Growing Up Poor in Consuelo"
   http://orioles.mlb.com
6. Tom Cruise, "My Struggle to Read"
   www.imdb.com/name/nm0000129
7. Joan Rivers, "Responding to Suicide"
   www.joanrivers.com
8. Sting, "The Mystery and Religion of Music"
   www.sting.com

### Chapter Two: Becoming and Overcoming

1. Queen Latifah, "Being a Queen"
   www.queenlatifah.com
2. Bill Murray, "Caddy Shot"
   www.imdb.com/name/nm0000195
3. Fran Drescher, "Now I'm Concerned"
   http://www.imdb.com/name/nm0000376/
4. Lance Armstrong, "Back in the Saddle"
   www.lancearmstrong.com

5. Toni Morrison, "Cinderella's Stepsisters"
   http://nobelprize.org/literature/laureates/1993/morrison-bio.html

6. Arnold Schwarzenegger, "Weight Training"
   www.schwarzenegger.com

7. P. J. O'Rourke, "On First Looking into Emily Post's Etiquette"
   http://www.buildfreedom.com/tribute/o'rourke/

8. Melissa Etheridge, "My First Album"
   www.melissaetheridge.com

9. Dr. Joyce Brothers, "Procrastination"
   www.stayhealthy.com/drjoyce

## Chapter Three: Significant Others

1. Mick Jagger, "George Harrison"
   www.mickjagger.com

2. Mia Farrow, "With Woody Allen, a House Is Not a Home"
   www.mia-farrow.com

3. Patti LaBelle, "Don't Block the Blessings"
   http://www.pattilabelle.com/

4. Dan Aykroyd, "Michael O'Donoghue"
   www.imdb.com/name/nm0000101

5. LL Cool J, "Impotent Demon"
   http://www.defjam.com/llcoolj/home.las

6. Marc Anthony, "Eulogy for Tito Puente"
   www.marcanthonyonline.com

7. Alice Walker, "Do it for Someone You Love"
   http://womenshistory.about.com/library/bio/blbio_walker_alice.htm

8. Chaka Khan, "Personnel: Up Close and Personal"
   www.chakakhan.com

# Part II: Constructing a Public Persona

## Chapter Four: Finding a Language and a Style

1. Andy Rooney, "A Text for Texbook Writers"
   www.cbsnews.com/stories/1998/07/08/60minutes/main13495.shtml

2. Charles Osgood, "%@*&# "
   www.cbsnews.com/stories/1998/07/09/sunday/main13584.shtml

3. Miss Manners, "Rudeness Can Be Lethal"
   www.unitedfeatures.com/ufsapp/viewFeature.do?id=21

4. Chris Rock, "Rockology"
   www.chrisrock.com

5. John Madden, "My Favorite Guys"
   www.biography.com/search/article.jsp?aid=9542594search=

6. James Brown, "On the *One*"
   http://www.funky-stuff.com/jamesbrown/

7. Freddie Prinze, Jr., "Got Milk?"
   www.imdb.com/name/nm0005327
8. Steve Martin, "Writing Is Easy!"
   www.stevemartin.com
9. Stephen King, "On Writing"
   www.stephenking.com

## Chapter Five: Self-Presentation

1. Jon Stewart, "Commencement Address at William and Mary"
   http://www.comedycentral.com/shows/the_daily_show/index.jhtml
2. Pamela Anderson, "Give Fur the Cold Shoulder"
   www.pamelaanderson.com
3. Mary Louise Parker, "On Nudity"
   http://www.imdb.com/name/nm0000571/
4. The Reverend Jesse Jackson, "Rainbow Imperative"
   www.rainbowpush.org
5. Jenny McCarthy, "Where in the Hell Can I Find a Muumuu?"
   http://www.imdb.com/name/nm0000189/
6. Russell Simmons, "White People"
   http://www6.defjam.com/site/aboutdefjam.php
7. Phillip McGraw, Ph.D., "We Teach People How to Treat Us"
   www.drphil.com

## Chapter Six: In a Business-like Manner

1. Ben Stein, "Let's Talk About Dollars and Cents"
   www.benstein.com
2. Donald Trump, "The Art of Negotiation"
   www.trump.com
3. Diane Von Furstenberg, "Fashioning Sales"
   www.dvf.com
4. Michael Jordan, "The Nike Deal"
   www.23jordan.com
5. Cokie and Steve Roberts, "Problems of a Two-Career Family"
   http://www.npr.org/templates/story/story.php?storyId=2101090
   http://www.harpercollins.com/global_scripts/product_catalog/
   author_xml.asp?authorid=19426
6. Spike Lee, "Art and Money in Movies"
   www.imdb.com/name/nm000490
7. Chuck D "'Free' Music Can Free the Artist"
   www.publicenemy.com
8. Bill Gates, "Adopt the Web Lifestyle"
   www.microsoft.com/billgates
9. Oprah Winfrey, "Bringing *Beloved* to the Screen"
   www.oprah.com

# Part III: Making A Lasting Contribution

## Chapter Seven: Serving Your Country and Your World

1. Kareem Abdul-Jabbar, "Black Tankers of World War II"
   www.sportsplacement.com/kareembio.htm

2. Ralph Nader, "The Duties of Citizenship"
   www.votenader.org

3. Angelina Jolie, "Mission to Ecuador"
   www.angelinajolie.com

4. Rush Limbaugh, "Conservatives Promote Independence"
   www.rushlimbaugh.com

5. Jane Fonda, "Use the Media for Public Health!"
   www.imdb.com/name/nm0000404

6. Rudolph Guiliani, "The Big Apple's Big Blowup"
   www.nyc.gov/html/rwg/html/bio.html

7. Rosie Perez, "Why Does Rosie Perez Wear the Bracelet?"
   www.imdb.com/name/nm0001609/

8. Martin Luther King, Jr., "Letter from Birmingham Jail"
   www.stanford.edu/group/King/

## Chapter Eight: Classic Performers

1. Regis Philbin, "True Tales of the Miss America Pageant "
   www.who2.com/regisphilbin.html

2. Gloria Steinem, "Sex, Lies, and Advertising"
   http://www.nwhp.org/tlp/biographies/steinem/
   steinem_bio.html

3. Roger Ebert, "Steven Spielberg: The Moviemaker"
   www.rogerebert.com

4. Julia Child, "A Slice of History"
   www.pbs.org/juliachild

5. Alfred Hitchcock, "My Most Exciting Movie"
   http://hitchcock.tv/

6. Frank Zappa, "In Defense of Rock and Roll"
   www.zappa.com

7. Celia Cruz, "Changing Times"
   www.celiacruzonline.com

8. Mel Brooks, "Springtime for the Music Man in Me"
   www.geocities.com/Hollywood/studio/1382/webring.html

9. Hank Aaron, "Race and the Record"
   www.sportingnews.com/archives/aaron

10. Barry Bonds, "Why Does Barry Bonds Wear the Bracelet?"
    www.barrybonds.com

# INDEX OF AUTHORS
# AND TITLES

**401**

**402**    Index